NUMBER SEVEN:
Texas A&M University Economics Series

Economics

Economics:

BETWEEN PREDICTIVE SCIENCE AND MORAL PHILOSOPHY

By James M. Buchanan

COMPILED AND WITH A PREFACE BY
ROBERT D. TOLLISON AND VIKTOR J. VANBERG

Texas A&M University Press
College Station

Copyright © 1987 by James M. Buchanan
All rights reserved
Manufactured in the United States of America
First edition

The paper used in this book meets the minimum requirements
of the American National Standard for Permanence
of Paper for Printed Library Materials, Z39.48–1984.
Binding materials have been chosen for durability.

Library of Congress Cataloging-in-Publication Data
Buchanan, James M.
  Economics: between predictive science and moral philosophy.
  (Texas A&M University economics series; no. 7)
  1. Economics.   2. Social choice.   3. Welfare
economics.   4. Economic policy.   I. Title.   II. Series.
  HB171.B855   1987   330   87-18096
  ISBN 0-89096-350-9 (alk. paper)

Contents

Preface   *page ix*

Part I. What Should Economists Do?
1. Positive Economics, Welfare Economics, and Political Economy   *3*
2. What Should Economists Do?   *21*
3. Is Economics the Science of Choice?   *35*
4. The Normative Purpose of Economic "Science":
   Rediscovery of an Eighteenth Century Method
   With Geoffrey Brennan   51
5. The Domain of Subjective Economics: Between
   Predictive Science and Moral Philosophy   *67*

Part II. Individual Choices and Social Outcomes
6. Politics, Policy, and the Pigovian Margins   *83*
7. Externality   *With William Craig Stubblebine   97*
8. Public and Private Interaction under Reciprocal Externality
   With Gordon Tullock   113
9. L.S.E. Cost Theory in Retrospect   *141*
10. Rights, Efficiency, and Exchange: The Irrelevance
    of Transactions Cost   *153*

Part III. Individual and Collective Choice
11. Social Choice, Democracy, and Free Markets   *171*
12. Individual Choice in Voting and the Market   *185*
13. Foreword to *The Politics of Bureaucracy*   *199*
14. An Economic Theory of Clubs   *207*
15. An Individualistic Theory of Political Process   *223*
16. Notes for an Economic Theory of Socialism   *237*

Part IV. The Economist as Contractarian
17. The Justice of Natural Liberty   *253*
18. Markets, States, and the Extent of Morals   *269*

19. Equal Treatment and Reverse Discrimination   *277*
20. Moral Community, Moral Order, or Moral Anarchy   *289*
21. The Constitution of Economic Policy   *303*

Part V. Fiscal Economics as Political Economy
22. "La Scienza delle Finanze": The Italian Tradition
    in Fiscal Theory   *317*
23. Fiscal Institutions and Efficiency in Collective Outlay   *357*
24. Towards a Tax Constitution for Leviathan
    With Geoffrey Brennan   *367*
25. The Political Biases of Keynesian Economics
    With Richard E. Wagner   *389*
26. Politics, Time, and the Laffer Curve   *With Dwight R. Lee*   *409*

Preface

Contemporary economics grew out of eighteenth century's "moral philosophy," a field that in modern terminology may be most adequately described as social science. Adam Smith, holding a chair in moral philosophy, lectured and published on a broad range of issues, many of which fell outside the scope of "economics proper" as defined by the majority of today's economics profession. Two centuries of disciplinary separation and specialization within the social sciences have resulted in an economics that has left more and more of the issues about which its founders were concerned for other social sciences — or nobody — to study. Part of this development is certainly a natural and unavoidable consequence of an academic discipline progressing and becoming mature. Over the past three or four decades, however, there has been a growing concern that the particular direction its specialization has taken has led economics to lose sight of issues that are central to its classical heritage, issues that cannot be pragmatically delegated to other social sciences but are essential to the very identity of the economic paradigm. In particular, the tendency to define and analyze economic processes and mechanisms as if they occur within an institutional vacuum has increasingly become a target of criticism. A number of new theoretical developments — among them "public choice," "the law and economics," "new political economy," and others — have been initiated with the aim of refocusing economists' attention to the institutional framework within which economic activities take place and to the kind of comparative institutional analysis which was at the core of Adam Smith's research program.

James M. Buchanan has played a most prominent role in shaping what has become known as "theoretical institutional economics," the converging set of those theoretical approaches in modern economics which all share a common interest in systematically integrating the institutional dimension into economic analysis. Buchanan's numerous publications, which span several decades and cover various subfields in economics, from public finance to methodology, exhibit a remarkable coherence in the sense of having a common underlying theoretical theme. All his contributions, from his earliest publications on public finance to his more recent essays on contractarian social philosophy, can be viewed as unfolding a general paradigm that they extend, modify, and apply to a variety of particular issues. "Constitutional economics" is the name that Buchanan prefers to use for this paradigm, a paradigm which he views essentially as a modern revival of classical political economy.

The 1986 Nobel Prize in economic science has been explicitly awarded to James Buchanan in recognition of his continuing and persistent contributions to a genuine constitutional political economy and in acknowledgement of his leadership role in the public choice movement. The award honors the body of his work rather than any single article or book. And it is this interpretation that informs the present collection of essays. Our purpose was to combine in one volume a selection of those contributions which we consider to be particularly significant for and informative of Buchanan's work from the early 1950s to the mid-1980s.

The selection and format of this book are ours, not Buchanan's; we should be held accountable for such matters. Yet we believe that our selection does not depart too much from what the author himself considers to be his major essays. In addition to his several well-known books, the articles combined here can be viewed to form the core of his contributions to economics, and they represent his unique and coherent explorations over time into the constitutional economics paradigm. Our design was to select representative papers from several areas that are central to Buchanan's work, from methodological concerns to basic economic theory to public finance and public choice. Our reason for compiling such a volume is simple. Buchanan now occupies a unique place in our profession. At such a time it seems appropriate and useful to issue a collection of his essays that, more than any previous single publication, provides a comprehensive overview over his entire work. Such a volume should be valuable to readers who want to get first access to Buchanan's work as well as to those who are already more familiar with his system of thought.

Certainly, all of the recipients of the Nobel Prize in economics have made their specific and often fundamental contributions to economic theory and are identified with these contributions. While Buchanan has made many such contributions, as illustrated in the papers of this volume, he is perhaps best thought of as a man who changed a generation of scholars' conception of the way the social and economic world works. He did not really work within a tradition; he created his own, a tradition which in recent years has come to be known as the Virginia school of political economy. It is a truly remarkable achievement to create a new paradigm and to populate it with students (in the broad sense of fellow travelers). It is also an achievement that may easily be overlooked because it is not strictly embedded in particular publications but is part and parcel of a man's intellectual influence on others over the years. This influence comes in many ways besides publishing articles and books: attending and participating in conferences, giving talks, writing comments on colleagues' papers, discussing, lecturing, grading papers, writing letters of recommendation, and so on. Such public goods make us better scholars, and it is to James Buchanan's dedication to such tasks that we dedicate this volume.

Several of the articles we have selected for inclusion here are from other books, and the original publishers have generously given their permission to reprint those chapters. "The Domain of Subjective Economics: Between Predictive Science and Moral Philosophy" is from *Method, Process, and Austrian Economics: Essays in Honor of Ludwig von Mises,* edited by Israel M. Kirzner (Lexington, Mass: Lexington Books, copyright 1982, D. C. Heath and Company). "Public and Private Interaction under Reciprocal Externality" (with Gordon Tullock) is from *The Public Economy of Urban Communities,* edited by Julius Margolis (Washington, D.C.: Resources for the Future, 1965). "L.S.E. Cost Theory in Retrospect" is the introduction to *L.S.E. Essays on Cost,* edited by J. M. Buchanan and G. F. Thirlby (London: Widenfeld and Nicholson, 1973); its copyright is held by, and permission is granted by, the London School of Economics and Political Science. "Rights, Efficiency and Exchange: The Irrelevance of Transactions Cost" is a chapter from *Ansprüche, Eigentums- und Verfügungsrechte* (Berlin: Duncker und Humblot, 1984), and "An Individualistic Theory of Political Process" is from *Varieties of Political Theory,* edited by D. Easton (Englewood Cliffs, N.J.: Prentice-Hall, 1966).

Kluwer-Nijhoff Publishing has given us permission to include "Equal Treatment and Reverse Discrimination," from *Social Justice,* edited by Randolph L. Braham (Boston: Martinus Nijhoff, 1981), and "The Political Biases of Keynesian Economics" (with Richard E. Wagner), from *Fiscal Responsibility in Constitutional Democracy,* edited by James M. Buchanan and Richard E. Wagner (Leiden and Boston: Martinus Nijhoff, 1978). The article " 'La Scienza delle Finanze': The Italian Tradition in Fiscal Economy" was originally published in Buchanan's *Fiscal Theory and Political Economy* (Chapel Hill: University of North Carolina Press, 1960).

Gordon Tullock has permitted us to reprint the Foreword to his book *The Politics of Bureaucracy* (Washington, D.C.: Public Affairs Press, 1965), and the Colorado College has allowed us to include *Moral Community, Moral Order, or Moral Anarchy,* the Abbott Memorial Lecture No. 17 presented at Colorado College on 6 May 1981 and originally published as one of the *Colorado College Studies.*

The editors of several journals have also allowed us to use their articles in this collection. From the *Journal of Political Economy* (with permission granted by the University of Chicago Press) come "Social Choice, Democracy, and Free Markets" (vol. 62, pp. 114–23); "Individual Choice in Voting and the Market" (vol. 62, pp. 334–43); and "Politics, Time, and the Laffer Curve" (with Dwight R. Lee; vol. 90, pp. 816–19). The University of Chicago Press also permitted us to include "Positive Economics, Welfare Economics, and Political Economy" from the *Journal of Law and Economics,* vol. 2, pp. 124–38.

Three articles – "Politics, Policy, and the Pigovian Margins," "Externality" (with William Craig Stubblebine), and "An Economic Theory of Clubs" – are from *Economica,* n.s., vol. 29, pp. 17–28; n.s., vol. 29, pp. 371–84; and n.s., vol. 32, pp. 1–14, respectively; permission for them is given by Tieto Ltd. "What Should Economists Do?" is reprinted from the *Southern Economic Journal,* vol. 30, pp. 213–22, and "The Normative Purpose of Economic 'Science': Rediscovery of an Eighteenth Century Method" is included from *International Review of Law and Economics,* vol. 1, pp. 155–66, with permission from the publisher, William Dawson & Sons, Ltd.

"Notes for an Economic Theory of Socialism" is from *Public Choice,* vol. 8, pp. 29–43, with permission from Kluwer-Nijhoff Publishing, and "Fiscal Institutions and Efficiency in Collective Outlay" and "Markets, States, and the Extent of Morals" are from *American Economic Review,* vol. 54, pp. 227–35, and vol. 68, pp. 364–68, respectively, with permission from the American Economic Association. "Towards a Tax Constitution for Leviathan" is from the *Journal of Public Economics,* vol. 8, pp. 255–73, with permission from Elsevier Science Publishers, and "The Justice of Natural Liberty" is from the *Journal of Legal Studies,* vol. 5, pp. 1–16, and permission to use it is given by the University of Chicago Law School.

As a final note, we would like to point out here that "The Constitution of Economic Policy" is James Buchanan's Nobel Lecture, presented in Stockholm on 8 December 1986.

ROBERT D. TOLLISON
VIKTOR J. VANBERG

Center for Study of Public Choice
George Mason University
Fairfax, Virginia

Part I.

WHAT SHOULD ECONOMISTS DO?

1.

Positive Economics, Welfare Economics, and Political Economy

Economic theory, as we know it, was developed largely by utilitarians. Admitting the measurability and interpersonal comparability of utility and accepting the maximization of utility as an ethically desirable social goal, neoclassical economists were able to combine an instinctively human zeal for social reform with subjectively satisfactory scientific integrity. The positivist revolution has sharply disturbed this scholarly equilibrium. If utility is neither cardinally measurable nor comparable among persons, the economist who seeks to remain "pure" must proceed with caution in discussing social policy. The "positive" economist becomes an inventor of testable hypotheses, and his professional place in policy formation becomes wholly indirect.

Milton Friedman has provided the clearest statement of the positivist position,[1] and he has called for a distinct separation between the scientific and the nonscientific behavior of individuals calling themselves economists. But economics, as a discipline, will probably continue to attract precisely those scholars who desire to assist in policy formation and to do so professionally. The social role of the economist remains that of securing more intelligent legislation, and the incremental additions to the state of knowledge which "positive" economics may make seems to shut off too large an area of discussion from his professional competence. Does there exist a role for the political economist as such? This essay will examine this question and suggest an approach.[2]

I. The New Welfare Economics

The "new" welfare economics was born in response to the challenge posed by the positivist revolution. The intellectual source of this subdiscipline is Pareto, whose earlier attempts to introduce scientific objectivity into the social studies led him to enunciate the now-famous definition of "optimality" or "efficiency." This definition states that any situation is "optimal" if all possible moves from it result in some individual being made worse off. The definition may be transformed into a rule which states that any social change is desirable which results in (1) everyone being better off or (2) someone being better off and no one being worse off than before the change. This Pareto rule is itself an ethical proposition, a value statement, but it is one which requires a minimum of premises and one which should command wide assent. The rule specifically eliminates the requirement that interpersonal comparisons of utility be made. As stated, however, a fundamental ambiguity remains in the rule. Some objective content must be given to the terms "better off" and "worse off." This is accomplished by equating "better off" with "in that position voluntarily chosen." Individual preferences are taken to indicate changes in individual wellbeing, and a man is said to be better off when he voluntarily changes his position from A to B when he could have remained in A.

The theoretical work completed during the last twenty years has consisted, first of all, in a refinement and development of the Paretian conditions for "optimality." Much attention has been given to a careful and precise definition of the necessary and sufficient attributes of a social situation to insure its qualification as a Paretian P-point, that is, a point on the "optimality surface." The application of this theoretical apparatus has taken two lines of development. The first, which is sometimes more specifically called the "new welfare economics," is an attempt to devise tests which will allow changes in social situations to be evaluated. This work, which has been associated with Kaldor, Hicks, and Scitovsky, includes the discussion of the "compensation principle" and the distinction between actual and potential increases in "welfare." The second line of development has been, in one sense, a critique of the Kaldor-Hicks approach. The ethical purity of the compensation tests proposed has been questioned, and additional ethical norms have been deliberately reintroduced through the device of a "social welfare function," which, conceptually, orders all possible states of society. With this, the problem of genuine choice among alternatives disappears, and the single "best" state of the world may be selected. This function may take any form, but its users have normally conceived the Paretian conditions to be relevant in defining a preliminary subset of social configurations. This approach, which is associated with Bergson, Samuelson, and Graaff, now appears to have more widespread support than the alternative one. Its supporters, notably Samuelson, argue that the Kaldor-Hicks efforts were "misguided" and erroneous[3] and that only the "social welfare function" construction offers real promise of further development. In the latter, allegedly, "the foundation is laid for the 'economics of the good society.' "[4]

II. Omniscience and Efficiency

Welfare economists, new and old, have generally assumed omniscience in the observer, although the assumption is rarely made explicit, and even more rarely are its implications examined.[5] The observing economist is considered able to "read" individual preference functions. Thus, even though an "increase in welfare" for an individual is defined as "movement to a preferred position," the economist can unambiguously distinguish an increase in welfare independent of individual behavior because he can accurately predict what the individual would, in fact, "choose" if confronted with the alternatives under consideration.

This omniscience assumption seems wholly unacceptable. Utility is measurable, ordinally or cardinally, only to the individual decision maker. It is a *subjectively* quantifiable magnitude. While the economist may be able to make certain presumptions about "utility" on the basis of observed facts about behavior, he must remain fundamentally ignorant concerning the actual ranking of alternatives until and unless that ranking is revealed by the overt action of the individual in choosing.

If a presumption of ignorance replaces that of omniscience, the way in which "efficiency" as a norm enters into the economist's schemata must be drastically modified. No "social" value scale can be constructed from individual preference patterns, since the latter are revealed only through behavior. Hence "efficiency" cannot be defined independently; it cannot be instrumentally employed as a criterion for social action. Discussions of "ideal output" and "maximization of real income" become meaningless when it is recognized that the economizing process includes as data *given ends* as conceived by individuals. Ends are not *given* for the social group in any sense appropriate to the solution of problems in political economy, and the normally accepted definition of the economizing problem is seriously incomplete in not having made this clear.

"Efficiency" in the sense of maximizing a payoff or outcome from the use of limited resources is meaningless without some common denominator, some value scale, against which various possible results can be measured. To the individual decision maker the concept of an "efficiency criterion" is a useful one, but to the independent observer the pitfalls of omniscience must be carefully avoided. The observer may introduce an efficiency criterion only through *his own estimate of his subjects' value scales.* Hence the maximization criterion which the economist may employ is wholly in terms of his own estimate of the value scales of individuals other than himself. *Presumptive efficiency* is, therefore, the appropriate conception for political economy.

The relationship of the *presumptive efficiency* criterion to the Paretian construction remains to be clarified. Given the assumption of ignorance,

Paretian "efficiency" cannot be employed in aiding a group in choosing from among a set of possible social policy changes. A specific change may be judged to be Pareto-optimal or "efficient" only after it has, in fact, been proposed and the individual preferences for or against the change revealed. Nevertheless, in discussing proposals before individual preferences are revealed, the economist may utilize a *presumed efficiency* notion which retains the Paretian features. In diagnosing a specific proposal, the economist makes a judgment as to its "efficiency" on the basis of *his own* estimate of individual preferences. The Paretian elements are retained in the sense that the observer makes no attempt to do other than to "translate" what he considers to be individual preferences. He accepts these preferences, or tastes, as *he thinks they exist*. He does not evaluate social alternatives on the basis of individual preferences as he thinks they should be.

This characteristic behavior of the political economist is, or should be, ethically neutral; the indicated results are influenced by his own value scale only insofar as this reflects his membership in the larger group. Conceptually, the economist may present a social policy change as "presumed Pareto-optimal," the results of which are wholly indifferent to him as an individual member of society. The propositions which the economist is able to develop through the procedure outlined are operational in the modern sense of this term. The presentation of a policy shift is a hypothesis concerning the structure of individual values and is subject to conceptual contradiction. The failure of recent methodological discussion to recognize this operational aspect of political economy appears to be based on an attempt to place the practitioner in a false position in the decision making complex. The political economist is often conceived as being able to *recommend* policy A over policy B. If, as we have argued above, no objective social criterion exists, the economist qua scientist is unable to recommend. Therefore, any policy discussion on his part appears to take on normative implications. But there does exist a positive role for the economist in the formation of policy. His task is that of diagnosing social situations and presenting to the choosing individuals a set of possible changes. He does not recommend policy A over policy B. He presents policy A as a hypothesis subject to testing. The hypothesis is that policy A will, in fact, prove to be Pareto-optimal. The conceptual test is *consensus* among members of the choosing group, not objective improvement in some measurable social aggregate.

Political economy is thus "positivistic" in a different sense from the more narrowly conceived positive economics. Both allow the expert to make certain predictions about the real world—predictions which are operationally meaningful. Propositions of positive economics find their empirical support or refutation in observable economic quantities or in observable market behavior of individuals. Propositions in political economy find empirical support or refutation in the observable behavior of individuals *in their capacities as collective decision makers* – in other words, in politics.

Propositions advanced by political economists must always be considered as tentative hypotheses offered as solutions to social problems. The subjective bases for these propositions should emphasize the necessity for their being considered as alternatives which may or may not be accepted. But this is not to suggest that one proposition is equally good with all others. Just as is the case with positive economics, the skill of the observer and his capacity in drawing upon the experience which has been accumulated will determine the relative success of his predictions. There are no fully appropriate analogies to this task of the political economist, but the role of the medical diagnostician perhaps comes closest. The patient is observed to be ill; a remedy is prescribed. This remedy is a hypothesis advanced by the diagnostician. If the illness persists, an alternative remedy is suggested and the first hypothesis discarded. The process continues until the patient is restored to health or the existence of no solution is accepted. While this analogy is helpful, it can also be misleading. In political economy the observer isolates an "illness" or rather what he believes to be an "illness" through his knowledge of the system. He presents a possible change. But this change is a "cure" only if *consensus* is attained in its support. The measure of "wellness" for the political economist is not improvement in an independently observable characteristic but rather agreement. If no agreement can be attained, the presumed "illness" persists, and the political economist must search for still other possible solutions. The political behavior of individuals, not market performance or results, provides the criteria for testing hypotheses of political economy.

III. Compensation and Externality

The "welfare economics" suggested here is simpler than that which assumes omniscience on the part of the observer. Much of the discussion in the subdiscipline has been devoted to two problems, both of which will be substantially eliminated in the approach suggested. First, the appropriateness or inappropriateness of compensation has been a central topic along with the discussion of the legitimacy or illegitimacy of certain tests. But, quite clearly, if the political economist is presumed to be ignorant of individual preference fields, his predictions (as embodied in suggested social policy changes) can only be supported or refuted if full compensation is, in fact, paid.[6] The potential compensation argument disappears, and the whole controversy over the appropriate tests becomes meaningless at this level of argument.

Many scholars have objected to the requirement that compensation be paid on the grounds that such requirement creates a serious bias toward the initial or status quo distribution of "welfare" among individuals of the group. This criticism seems misdirected and inapplicable if the purposes of compensation are conceived to be those outlined. Full compensation is essential, not in order to maintain any initial distribution on ethical grounds, but in order to decide which one from among the many possible social policy changes does, in fact, satisfy the genuine Pareto rule. Compensation is the only device available to the political economist for this purpose.

If the observing economist is assumed omniscient, the actual payment of compensation may seem unnecessary, and the requirement for payment may appear to introduce the bias mentioned. No additional information about individuals' preference fields is needed, and none can be revealed by behavior. A proposed change is no longer a hypothesis to be tested, and the relatively neutral ethics imposed by the Pareto rule may prove too restrictive. And, if the observer does not move in the direction of the Bergson-Samuelson welfare function, he may attempt to devise tests for potential compensation. In this way the whole debate about the Kaldor-Hicks-Scitovsky criteria for improvement has arisen. This approach constitutes a distortion of the Pareto rule. If ethical evaluations on the part of the observer are to be introduced, there is no place for the Pareto rule. This rule is designed for use in situations where individual values must count, not because they possess some inherent ethical superiority (which is quite a different point), but because individual action provides the only guide toward acceptable collective action.

The full-compensation requirement need not imply—indeed, it will not normally imply—the maintenance of the status quo in the distribution of either income or welfare. Presumably, if a given social change is approved by all parties, each must be better off in absolute terms. Therefore, at the simplest level of discussion, there is more "welfare" to go around than before the change. To be sure, the relative distribution of "welfare" may be modified significantly by a fully compensated change. This is true because the order of presentation will determine the final point chosen from among a whole subset of acceptable points. The political economist cannot, however, say anything concerning the relative merits of the separate points in this subset. This amounts to saying that the political economist's task is completed when he has shown the parties concerned that there exist mutual gains "from trade." He has no function in suggesting specific contract terms within the bargaining range itself.

An additional simple, but often overlooked, point on compensation needs to be made. The requirement of full compensation as here interpreted need not imply that the measured incomes of individuals or groups may not be reduced by acceptable social policy changes. "Welfare" is defined as that which is expressed by individual preference as revealed in behavior. And individual behavior may be fully consistent with a reduction in measured personal income or wealth. For example, a policy which combines progressive income taxation and public expenditure on the social services may command unanimous support even though the process involves a reduction in the measured real incomes of the rich. The existence of voluntary charity indicates that individuals are, in fact, willing to reduce their own incomes in order to increase those of others. And the peculiar nature of collective choice makes support for collective or governmental action perhaps even more likely. Many individuals may find themselves saying: "I should be willing to support this proposal provided that other equally situated individuals do likewise." Thus collective action may command relatively widespread support, whereas no purely voluntary action might be taken in its absence.[7]

A second major problem which has concerned theorists in welfare economics has been the possible existence of external effects in individual consumption and production decisions, sometimes called "spillover" or "neighborhood" effects. But this annoying complication also disappears in the approach to welfare economics suggested here. If, in fact, external effects are present, these will be fully reflected in the individual choices made for or against the collective action which may be proposed. External effects which are unaccounted for in the presumptive efficiency criterion of the economist and the proposal based upon this criterion will negate the prediction of consensus represented in the alternative suggested. The presence of such effects on a large scale will, of course, make the task of the political economist more difficult. His predictions must embody estimates of a wider range of individual preferences than would otherwise be the case. The compensations included in the suggested policy changes must be more carefully drawn and must be extended to include more individuals who might otherwise be neglected.[8]

Both the compensation and the externality problems may be illustrated by reference to the classical example of the smoking chimney. The economist observes what he considers to be smoke damage and discontent among families living adjacent to the smoke-creating plant. Using a presumptive efficiency criterion, he suggests a possible course of action which the group may take. This action must include, on the one hand, the payment of some tax by the previously damaged individuals who stand to gain by the change. On the other hand, the action must include some subsidization of the owners of the firm to compensate them for the capital

loss which is to be imposed by the rule of law which states that hencefor-
ward the full "social" costs of the operation must be shouldered. Some
such tax-compensation–smoke-abatement scheme will command unanimous consent from the group which includes both individuals living within
the damaged area and the owners of the firm. The problem for the political
economist is that of searching out and locating from among the whole set
of possible combinations one which will prove acceptable to all parties.
If the smoke nuisance is a real one, at least one such alternative must
exist. If no agreement of this sort is possible, the economist can only
conclude that the presumptive efficiency criterion was wrongly conceived
and the hypothesis based upon it falsified.

IV. The Scope for Political Economy

To this point, the behavior of the political economist has been the primary
topic of discussion. The argument has been that the political economist,
as such, has no contribution to make to the discussion of uncompensated
changes but that a "positive" political economy involving fully compensated changes can be defined. From this argument the inference may be
drawn that full compensation is desirable in all cases and the requirement
for compensation may appear to stultify much "desirable" social policy.

The appropriateness or inappropriateness of compensation must be
explicitly discussed quite apart from the methodology of political economy. The main point to be made is that the principle of compensation,
and, thus, the scope for political economy, is restricted to those social
changes that may legitimately be classified as "changes in law," that is,
changes in the structural rules under which individuals make choices.
Compensation is desirable here because only through the compensation
device can appropriate criteria for "improvement" be discovered. This is
merely to put in somewhat different language the classical liberal conception of democracy itself.

Within the structure of existing law, no grounds for the payment of
compensation exist. This point may be illustrated by reference to the theft
example used by Stigler in his critique of the new welfare economics.[10]
Could not the "real income" of society be increased by bribing potential
thieves instead of hiring policemen? This question is irrelevant. Presumably, those individuals who are thieves at any moment have supported
laws which are designed to prevent theft. Stealing is a recognized violation of existing law and, as such, deserves punishment without compensation. Quite clearly, no consensus could be expected on a proposed
change in the law that would involve bribing all future thieves. The suggestion that such a change might increase "real income" implies some

objective definition of real income which is independent of individuals' behavior.

A more practical example involves the government's prosecution of monopoly. The capital losses which are imposed upon firms successfully prosecuted should not, normally, be offset by compensation. This is because such action involves, in principle, no lawmaking. By contrast, the removal of a long-existing and specific exemption to the law should be accompanied by the appropriate compensating action.

There are, of course, difficult problems involved in distinguishing between changes in the law and the enforcement of existing law. But such problems are no different from those normally faced in the everyday definition of property rights, which are, of course, enormously difficult. The whole issue here may well be put in terms of property rights. The political economist in the specific role here discussed is concerned with social or collective action that modifies in some way the structure of legitimate property rights. Compensation is required for the reasons suggested above. On the other hand, law enforcement may modify the structure of actual property right, but, in principle, it does not disturb legitimate rights.

Political economy, therefore, applies to only one form of social change, namely, that which is deliberately chosen by the members of the social group acting in their collective capacities. Changes may occur for many reasons, and the set of possible changes that constitutes the domain for political economy is a relatively small subset of the total. Therefore, the requirement of compensation necessary to insure consensus or unanimity is not open to the commonly voiced objection that all progress involves social disturbance and that some individuals must be injured and some benefited by any significant social upheaval.

Changes may occur through shifts in tastes, introduction of new techniques, or growth in the supply of basic resources. These are normally considered to be the means through which an economy "progresses" or "grows." Changes of this nature are, however, different, philosophically, from those which are deliberately imposed through collective action. And this distinction is important. The free-market economic order is organized on the assumption that shifts may occur in the fundamentally exogenous variables. Imperfections of knowledge about the possible shifts in these underlying variables are incorporated with the appropriate offsetting entrepreneurial rewards and punishments. Any attempt to secure compensation for all losses would surely destroy the system. But changes imposed by collective action are different, and the uncertainty involved in attempts to predict such action cannot be discounted or offset in the ordinary market structure.[11]

V. The Social Welfare Function

The approach to political economy suggested in this essay may be compared with the Bergson-Samuelson approach which deliberately introduces ethical evaluations in the form of the "social welfare function." Both approaches aim at establishing a role for the economist qua scientist beyond positive economics narrowly defined. The differences between the two approaches lie in the treatment of individual values.

The "social welfare function" is an explicit expression of a value criterion. It incorporates fully the required information concerning the relative importance of conflicting aims, including the relative importance of separate individuals within the social group. The function orders all possible social situations and allows an external observer to select one as "best." Presumably, this "best" point will lie on a "welfare frontier" which contains a subinfinity of possible points. But the precise meaning of this "welfare frontier" is not entirely clear. If social situations are to be ordered *externally,* the "individual welfare scales" embodied must be those akin to those which enter into the presumptive efficiency criterion discussed above. Individual preferences, insofar as they enter the construction (and they need not do so) must be those which *appear to the observer* rather than those revealed by the behavior of the individuals themselves. In other words, even if the value judgments expressed in the function say that individual preferences are to count, these preferences must be those presumed by the observer rather than those revealed in behavior.

Several questions may be raised. Unless the relevant choices are to be made by some entity other than individuals themselves, why is there any need to construct a "social" value scale? There would seem to be no reason for making interpersonal comparisons of "welfare" based on hypothetical individual preferences except for the purpose of assisting in the attainment of *given ends* for the group or some subgroup. This central feature of the approach seems, therefore, to be contrary to one of the presuppositions of the free society. The function may be useful as a device in assisting the decision making of a despot, benevolent or otherwise, an organic state, or a single-minded ruling group. But, once this limitation is recognized, individual preferences, even as presumed by the observer, need not enter into the construction at all except insofar as it becomes necessary to consider predicted individual reaction to coercively imposed changes. The Pareto conception of "optimality" loses most of its significance.

The approach adopted here is based upon the idea that no "social" values exist apart from individual values. Therefore, the political economist, instead of choosing arbitrarily some limited set of ethical norms for incorporation into a "social welfare function," searches instead for "social compromises" on particular issues. His proposals are hypotheses about individual values, hypotheses which are subjected to testing in the collective choice processes. Actual values are revealed only through the political action of individuals, and consensus among individual members of the choosing group becomes the only possible affirmation of a "social" value. The order which is present among "social" decisions, if indeed there is one, is revealed in the decision process itself, not external to it. Whereas the "social welfare function" approach searches for a criterion independent of the choice process itself, presumably with a view toward influencing the choice, the alternative approach evaluates results only in terms of the choice process itself.

VI. Consensus among Reasonable Men

In developing the argument of this essay, I have assumed that the social group is composed of reasonable men, capable of recognizing what they want, of acting on this recognition, and of being convinced of their own advantage after reasonable discussion. Governmental action, at the important margins of decision, is assumed to arise when such individuals agree that certain tasks should be collectively performed. To this extent, my argument rests on some implicit acceptance of a contract theory of the state. Since it is carried out only after general agreement, collective action is essentially voluntary action. State or governmental coercion enters only insofar as individuals, through collectively imposed rules, prevent themselves from acting as they would act in the absence of such rules.

I am aware of the limitations of this conception of society, and I can appreciate the force of the objection that may be raised on these grounds. Societies in the real world are not made up exclusively of reasonable men, and this fact introduces disturbing complications in any attempt to discuss the formation of social policy.

In outlining the structure of a possible nonevaluative political economy, I am suggesting that we proceed on an *as if* assumption. Despite our knowledge that some men are wholly unreasonable, we assume this away just as we have done in the organization of our whole democratic decision making processes. Insofar as "antisocial" or unreasonable individuals are members of the group, consensus, even where genuine "mutual gains" might be present, may be impossible. Here the absolute unanimity rule must be broken; the political economist must try, as best he can, to judge the extent of unanimity required to verify (not refute) his hypothesis. Some less definitive rule of relative unanimity must be substituted for full agreement, as Wicksell recognized and suggested.

This necessary modification does not materially reduce the strength of the argument presented. But it does place an additional responsibility upon the political economist. He is forced to discriminate between reasonable and unreasonable men in his search for consensus. This choice need not reflect the introduction of personal evaluation. Relatively objective standards may be adduced to aid in the discrimination process. Reflection from everyday experience with groups which use unanimity as the customary, but not essential, means of reaching decisions should reveal that the genuinely unreasonable individual can be readily identified. This reduction of the unanimity requirement to some relative unanimity does not suggest that "unreasonable" as a characteristic behavior pattern can be determined on the basis of one issue alone. And it should be emphasized that in no way whatsoever does continuing disagreement with majority opinion suggest unreasonableness.

VII. Majority Rule, Consensus, and Discussion

The hypotheses which the political economist presents are tested by the measure of agreement reached, qualified only by the relative unanimity requirement introduced in the preceding section. But there remain two major practical difficulties to be confronted at this testing stage. These make the empirical testing difficult and, in some cases, impossible. First, collective decisions in democratically organized societies may be, and normally are, made on the basis of some variant of majority rule rather than consensus or unanimity, even if the latter is qualified to rule out limited "antisocial" dissent.

The economist, employing his presumptive efficiency criterion, presents for consideration a policy change which embodies the hypothesis that the adoption of this change will constitute "improvement" in the "welfare" of the group in accordance with the Pareto rule. This proposal is then voted upon, either by all individuals in a referendum or by their representatives in a legislative body. If a majority rejects the proposal, the economist's hypothesis is clearly refuted, and alternatives must be sought. The hypothesis is equally refuted if a minority dissents, but the proposal may be carried on the basis of majority decision. This adoption tends to preclude the presentation of alternative hypotheses more acceptable to the minority. Majority rule, considered as a final means of making decisions, has the effect of closing off discussion and of thereby limiting severely the efforts of the political economist.

This result of majority rule places before the political economist a great temptation and also places upon him significant responsibility. Knowing that collective decisions are made by majority rule, he will be tempted to present social alternatives which may command majority support rather than consensus. Adequate compensations for damaged minorities may be omitted in the proposals suggested with a view toward making the majority more receptive. Deliberate attempts in this direction would violate the neutral position outlined for the political economist here, but, given the inherently subjective basis for the presumptive efficiency criterion at best, the proposals presented may tend to reflect majority-oriented biases quite unintentionally. The danger that this bias will occur places upon the practitioner the responsibility of insuring that suggested proposals do, in fact, include compensations to damaged minorities estimated to be adequate and, contrariwise, do not include overcompensations to damaged majorities.

The probability that decisions will be made without consensus being attained adds responsibility to the economist's task. Much greater care must be taken with the construction and application of the presumptive efficiency criterion. Again the analogy with the medical diagnostician may be helpful. Majority rule tends to place the political economist in the position of the diagnostician who may propose a fatal dosage if his diagnosis should prove incorrect. Hence he must be more careful than otherwise in proposing alternative remedies.

The practical difficulties introduced by majority rule may not be great if there exists consensus that all collective decisions reached in this way are temporary or provisional and are subject to reversal and modification. If majority rule is understood to be, not a means of making final decisions, but rather as one of making provisional choices while discussion continues, the possibility remains that alternative hypotheses can be presented subsequent to a favorable majority vote. No barrier to discussion need be introduced by majority rule conceived in this way.

But if majority rule is conceived as merely a step in the discussion process leading toward final agreement, a second major problem of practical importance arises. The whole process of discussion which characterizes the democratic idea implies that, insofar as their behavior in making collective decisions is concerned, individuals do not have explicitly defined ends of an instrumental sort. If they do, discussion is bound to be fruitless, and an initial disagreement will persist. The purpose of political discussion is precisely that of changing "tastes" among social alternatives. The political economist, therefore, in constructing and applying his presumptive efficiency criterion, must try to incorporate the predicted preferences of individuals, not as they exist at a given moment, but as they will be modified after responsible discussion. In other words, he must try to predict "what reasonable individuals will reasonably want" after discussion, not what they "do want in a given moment" before discussion or what they "ought to want" if they agreed in all respects with the observer.

This recognition that individuals do not have *given ends* which can, at any moment, be taken as data by the observer appears to blur the sharp dividing line between "positive" political economy as here outlined and "normative" political economy which allows the observer to introduce his own ethical evaluations. This makes it more important that the attempt be made to test propositions in terms of expressed individual values instead of first attempting to estimate such values as a basis for decision.

VIII. Conclusion

Positive science is concerned with the discovery of "what is"; normative science, with "what ought to be." Positive economics, narrowly conceived, overly restricts the "what is" category. Political economy has a non-normative role in discovering "what is the structure of individual values." The political economist, in accomplishing this task, can remain as free of personal value judgment as the positive economist. To be sure, the objectivity of the political economist is more difficult to preserve, and his behavior in departing from it more difficult for observers to detect. His hypotheses must take the form of policy propositions, and these may tend to appear as recommendations rather than hypotheses. And, since such hypotheses must be based on some presumptive efficiency criterion, an element of subjectivity is necessarily introduced. But the presence of subjective evaluation of the outside world (which includes the preference fields of other individuals) does not imply the infusion of an individual value judgment concerning the "goodness" of the proposal presented.

In a sense, the political economist is concerned with discovering "what people want." The content of his efforts may be reduced to very simple terms. This may be summed up in the familiar statement: *There exist mutual gains from trade.* His task is that of locating possible flaws in the existing social structure and in presenting possible "improvements." His specific hypothesis is that *mutual* gains do, in fact, exist as a result of possible changes (trades). This hypothesis is tested by the behavior of private people in response to the suggested alternatives. Since "social" values do not exist apart from individual values in a free society, consensus or unanimity (mutuality of gain) is the only test which can insure that a change is beneficial.

In his diagnosis and prescription, the economist must call upon all the skills and resources which he possesses. These include the traditional "efficiency" tools, but, in utilizing these, he must beware of slipping into the easy assumption of omniscience. The individual preference patterns which he incorporates into his models must be conceived as presumed or predicted, and the changes which are based on these must always be considered tentative hypotheses to be subjected to testing in the polling places. The economist can never say that one social situation is more "efficient" than another. This judgment is beyond his range of competence. He presents a hypothesis that one situation is "presumed Pareto-Efficient," and he allows the unanimity test (appropriately modified) to decide whether his prediction is correct or incorrect. From this it follows that all his proposals must embody estimated full compensations.

The role of the political economist as outlined here may be quite limited. The applicability of political economy is inversely related to the rate at which majoritarian conceptions of the democratic process replace the classical liberal conceptions. Even in a world seemingly dominated by majoritarian views, however, the approach outlined here can be useful in establishing some norms for scientific objectivity. Beyond the area of "positive" political economy, there may be room for the individual to serve in a normative capacity as an especially well-informed citizen. Here his own ethical evaluations may be explicitly introduced, and he may choose to utilize certain welfare function constructions in this task. But this behavior must be sharply distinguished from his professional role, either as positive economist or as political economist.

Perhaps this essay may best be summarized by the consideration of a single example: the removal of a long-established tariff. The positive economist can predict that imports of the commodity will increase, that domestic prices of the commodity will fall, that exports will increase, that resources will be shifted from the domestic to the export industries, etc. The "positive" political economist, building on the fundamental theorems of positive economics, attempts to devise a proposal or proposals which will remove or reduce the tariff and be approved by an overwhelming majority of the whole social group. He advances a proposal which embodies a tariff reduction, along with estimated full compensation to the damaged industries financed out of a tax imposed on benefited groups. This proposal is advanced as a hypothesis. If the proposal is accepted by the whole group, the hypothesis is not refuted. If it is rejected, or approved by only a majority, the political economist should search for alternative schemes. In all this, as an observer, he is ethically neutral. His own evaluations of the alternatives considered do not, and should not, influence his behavior in any way other than that necessarily arising out of his membership in the group.

If complexities of the collective decision making process arise to prevent a genuine testing of the hypothesis, the economist may, if he desires, discard his "scientific" cloak. He may introduce his own ethical evaluations and state openly and frankly that he thinks tariff reductions would be "good" for the whole group.

It seems useful that these three types of behavior of individuals calling themselves economists be separated and classified, even if practical politics reduce the second type to relative insignificance.

Notes

1. M. Friedman, *Essays in Positive Economics* (1953) 3–43.
2. The approach which will be suggested here involves an extension of some of Wicksell's ideas on fiscal theory to modern welfare economics. For a recently published translation of Wicksell's fiscal theory, see "A New Principle of Just Taxation" in *Classics in the Theory of Public Finance*, eds. Musgrave and Peacock (1958)
3. Samuelson, Paul A., comment in *A Survey of Contemporary Economics*, ed. Haley (1952)
4. Samuelson, Paul A., "Social Indifference Curves," *Q.J. Econ. II, 37.* (1956), pp. 1, 22.
5. J. de V. Graaff in his book, *Theoretical Welfare Economics* (1957), p. 13, makes the assumption explicitly, but after one short paragraph proceeds with his argument.
6. There are two distinct meanings of the word "compensation." In ordinary discussion, compensation is conceived as an objectively measurable quantity; this conception has no relevance for welfare economics. Compensation must be defined in terms of the individual's choice process, and it becomes measurable only through an observation of choices made. Full or adequate compensation is defined as that set of payments required to secure the agreement of all parties to the proposed change.
7. This point has been stressed by W. J. Baumol in *Welfare Economics and the Theory of the State* (1952).
8. The discussion of this paragraph assumes that the membership in the group making the collective choice is at least as large as the "neighborhood" defined by the presence of external effects.
9. Objections will be raised to the procedure suggested here because its acceptance seems to leave the door open to exploitation of some parties to the contract by other unscrupulous parties. The owners of the smoke-creating firm may refuse to agree to any scheme except the one which grants them compensation equal to the full benefits of the proposed change. This possibility, or its converse, exists. But, in refusing to agree to any proffered compensation equal to or above the estimated value of the capital losses undergone, the owners must recognize that such opportunities might not recur.

As a second point, if the distributional results of a change are significantly important, this fact alone may reduce the extent of the bargaining range. Even though the objectively measured "income" of the previously damaged group were demonstrably increased by the adoption of the tax-compensation–smoke-abatement plan, this group might not agree if the owners secured the predominant share of the total benefits. They might veto the plan on distributional grounds, thereby preventing unanimity.

10. Stigler, "The New Welfare Economics," *Am. Econ. Rev.* 33 (1943), pp. 355, 356.
11. Some of the points made in this section may be clarified by the use of the game analogy, an approach to political economy that has been thoroughly developed by my colleague, Rutledge Vining. Political economy is concerned exclusively with the modifications of the rules of the game, and this branch of the discipline has no place in the discussion of strategic action taken by either side in

the game itself. The compensation requirement suggests only that all players agree on the rules before continuing the game. Changes made within existing law are analogous to the enforcement of agreed-on rules, and changes arising from the strategic contest itself are fully analogous to the changes taking place by a shift of the exogenous variables of the economic order.

2.

What Should Economists Do?

"But it is not the popular movement, but the travelling of the minds of men who sit in the seat of Adam Smith that is really serious and worthy of all attention."

Lord Acton, *Letters of Lord Acton to Mary Gladstone*, ed. Herbert Paul (London: George Allen, 1904), p. 212.

I propose to examine the "travelling of the minds of men who sit in the seat of Adam Smith," those who try to remain within the "strict domain of science," and to ask the following questions: What are economists doing? What "should" they be doing? In these efforts to heed the counsel of Lord Acton, I proceed squarely against the advice of a modern economist whose opinions I regard with respect, George Stigler. He tells us that it is folly to become concerned with methodology before the age of sixty-five. As a value statement, Stigler's admonition can hardly be discussed. But, as a hypothesis, it can be refuted, at least by analogy with an ordinary road map. I remain notorious for my failure to look quickly enough at highway route maps, hoping always that some intuitive directional instinct will keep me along the planned pattern of my journey. I learned many years ago that "optimal" behavior involves stopping soon after one gets "lost," after uncertainty beyond a certain limit is reached, and consulting a properly drawn map. The analogy with scientific methodology seems to be a close one. Unless we can, for some reason, accept the ever-changing activities of economists as being always a part of the necessary evolution of the discipline through time, as being "on the highway," it is essential that we look occasionally at the map or model for scientific progress that each of us surely carries around, consciously or unconsciously, in his head.

You will note that, by proposing to examine critically what economists do, I am also rejecting the familiar proposition advanced by Jacob Viner that "economics is what economists do," a proposition that Frank Knight converted into full circle when he added "and economists are those who do economics." This functional definition of our discipline begs the very question that I want to raise, if not to answer here. Economists should, I think, face up to their basic responsibility; they should at least try to know their subject matter.

Let me call your attention to a much-neglected principle enunciated by Adam Smith. In chapter 2 of *The Wealth of Nations* he states that the principle which gives rise to the division of labor, from which so many advantages are derived,

> is not originally the effects of any human wisdom, which foresees and intends that general opulence to which it gives occasion. It is the necessary, though very slow and gradual, consequence of a certain propensity in human nature which has in view no such extensive utility; the propensity to truck, barter, and exchange one thing for another.

Somewhat surprisingly, it seems to me, the relevance and the significance of this "propensity to truck, barter, and exchange" has been overlooked in most of the exegetical treatments of Smith's work. But surely here is his answer to what economics or political economy is all about.

Economists "should" concentrate their attention on a particular form of human activity, and upon the various institutional arrangements that arise as a result of this form of activity. Man's behavior in the market relationship, reflecting the propensity to truck and to barter, and the manifold variations in structure that this relationship can take; these are the proper subjects for the economist's study. In saying this, I am, of course, making a value statement that you may or may not support. Consider this paper, if you will, as an "essay in persuasion."

The elementary and basic approach that I suggest places "the theory of markets" and not the "theory of resource allocation" at center stage. My plea is really for the adoption of a sophisticated "catallactics," an approach to our discipline that has been advanced earlier, much earlier, by Archbishop Whately and the Dublin School, by H. D. Macleod, by the American, Arthur Latham Perry, by Alfred Ammon and still others.[1] It is not my purpose here, and it is not within my competence, to review the reasons for the failures of these men to convince their colleagues and their descendants. I note only that the view that they advanced, and one which has never been wholly absent from the mainstream of thinking,[2] is perhaps more in need of stress now than it was during the times in which they worked.

In a brief treatment it is helpful to make bold charges against ideas or positions taken by leading figures. In this respect I propose to take on Lord Robbins as an adversary and to state, categorically, that his all-too persuasive delineation of our subject field has served to retard, rather than to advance, scientific progress. You are, of course, all familiar with the

Robbins statement of the definition of the economic problem, the one that has found its way into almost all of our textbooks. The economic problem involves the allocation of scarce means among alternative or competing ends. The problem is one of *allocation,* made necessary by the fact of *scarcity,* the necessity to *choose.* Only since *The Nature and Significance of Economic Science*[3] have economists so exclusively devoted their energies to the problems raised by scarcity, broadly considered, and to the necessity for the making of allocative decisions.

In Robbins's vision, our subject field is a problem or set of problems, not a characteristic form of human activity. We were better off, methodologically speaking, in the less definitive Marshallian world when economists did, in fact, study man in his ordinary business of making a living. In his attempt to remain wholly neutral as to ends, Robbins left economics "open-ended," so to speak. Search him as you will, and you will not find an explicit statement as to *whose* ends are alternatives. His neutrality extends to the point of remaining wholly silent on the identity of the choosing agent, and few economists seem to have bothered with the difficult issue of identifying properly the entity for whom the defined economic problem exists. It is thus by quite natural or normal extension that the economic problem moves from that one which is confronted by the individual person to that facing the larger family group, the business firm, the trade union, the trade association, the church, the local community, the regional or state government, the national government, and, finally, the world.[4]

To illustrate the confusion that this lack of identification introduces, let me mention my most respected of all professors, Frank Knight, who has taught us all to think in terms of the five functions of "an economic system," presumably, "any economic system." In the Knightian introduction to our subject we talk about the "social organization" that performs these five familiar "social" functions. For whom? This is the question to which I return. Presumably, the answer is for the whole of the relevant collective group, for society. To be somewhat more explicit, let me cite Milton Friedman who says, if I remember his classroom introduction correctly, "economics is the study of how a particular society solves its economic problem."

Knight and Friedman are good examples for my purposes, since both of these men, despite their own differences on many particulars of economic policy, are men with whom, broadly and generally, I agree on principles of political-philosophical order. In their introductions to economics, both of these men seem to identify "society" as the entity that confronts the economic problem about which we, as professional economists, should be concerned, the entity, presumably, whose ends are to count in the appropriate calculus of margins. If they should be explicitly questioned, I am sure that both Knight and Friedman, and Robbins as well, would say that "society," as such, must always be conceived in terms of its individual members. Hence, when reference is made to a particular society solving its economic problem, this is really only shorthand for saying "a particular group of individuals who have organized themselves socially solving their economic problem."

The important point is, however, that we do, in ordinary and everyday usage, require a supplementary or an additional step in our basic definitional process before we break down the societal language into its meaningful individual components. This amounts to locking the barn door without being sure that we have ever had or will have a horse inside. Somewhat more technically, this procedure assumes that there is meaningful content in economics for "social welfare"; it prejudges the central issue that has been debated in theoretical welfare economics, and comes down squarely with the utilitarians. This seems to be a clear case where the basic conceptual apparatus has not yet been brought into line with modern developments. But this conceptual apparatus is extremely important, especially when most practitioners are too busy to bother with methodology. The definition of our subject makes it all too easy to slip across the bridge between personal or individual units of decision and "social" aggregates. In principle, this bridge is most difficult to cross, as most economists fully recognize when put to it. And, in one sense, my whole plea here is summarized by saying to economists, "get back or stay on the side of the bridge where you belong."

The utilitarians tried to cross the bridge by summing utilities. Robbins quite properly told them to cease and desist. But in remaining what I have called "open-ended," in emphasizing the universality of the allocation problem without at the same time defining the identity of the choosing agent, Robbins's contribution to method has tended to promote a proliferation of the very confusion that he had hoped to prevent. Economists, paying heed to Robbins, now know when they cross the bridge; they explicitly state their own value judgments in the form of "social welfare functions." Once having done this, they feel free to maximize to their own heart's content. And they do so within the bounds of methodological propriety, à la Robbins. They have, of course, abandoned his neutrality-of-ends position, but they have been straightforward about this. And, by the very fact of this neutrality, their explicitly stated personal version of "social" value is as acceptable as any other. They continue to work on an *economic* problem, as such, and this problem appears superficially to be the one that is generally referred to in the definitional introduction to our subject. These "social" economists are wholly concerned with the allocation of scarce resources among competing ends or uses.

I submit that theirs is not legitimate activity for practitioners in economics, as I want to define the discipline. In hastening to explain my heresy,

I should emphasize that my argument is not centered on whether or not economists explicitly introduce value judgments into their work. This important issue is a wholly different one from that which I am trying to advance here. I want economists to quit concerning themselves with allocation problems, per se, with *the problem*, as it has been traditionally defined. The vocabulary of science is important here, and as T. D. Weldon once suggested, the very word "problem" in and of itself implies the presence of "solution." Once the format has been established in allocation terms, some solution is more or less automatically suggested. Our whole study becomes one of applied maximization of a relatively simple computational sort. Once the ends to be maximized are provided by the social welfare function, everything becomes computational, as my colleague, Rutledge Vining, has properly noted. If there is really nothing more to economics than this, we had as well turn it all over to the applied mathematicians. This does, in fact, seem to be the direction in which we are moving, professionally, and developments of note, or notoriety, during the past two decades consist largely in improvements in what are essentially computing techniques, in the mathematics of social engineering. What I am saying is that we should keep these contributions in perspective; I am urging that they be recognized for what they are: contributions to applied mathematics, to managerial science if you will, but not to our chosen subject field which we, for better or for worse, call, "economics."

Let me illustrate with reference to the familiar distinction, or presumed distinction, between an economic and a technological problem. What is the sophomore, who has completed his "principles," expected to reply to the question: What is the difference between an economic and a technological problem? He might respond something like the following: "An economic problem arises when mutually conflicting ends are present, when choices must be made among them. A technological problem, by comparison, is characterized by the fact that there is only one end to be maximized. There is a single best or optimal solution." We conclude that the sophomore has read the standard textbooks. We then proceed to ask that he give us practical examples. He might then say: "The consumer finds that she has only $10 to spend in the supermarket; she confronts an economic problem in choosing among the many competing products that are available for meeting diverse ends and objectives. By contrast, the construction engineer has $1,000,000 allotted to build a dam to certain specifications. There is only one best way to do this; locating this way constitutes the technological problem." Most of us would, I suspect, be inclined to give this student good grades for such answers until another, erratic and eccentric, student on the back row says: "But there is really no difference."

I need not continue the illustration in detail. In the context of my earlier remarks, it seems clear that the second student has the proper answer, and that the orthodox textbook reply is wrong. Surely any difference between what we normally call the economic problem and what we call the technological problem is one of degree only, of the degree to which the function to be maximized is specified in advance of the choices to be made.

In one sense, the theory of choice presents a paradox. If the utility function of the choosing agent is fully defined in advance, choice becomes purely mechanical. No "decision," as such, is required; there is no weighing of alternatives. On the other hand, if the utility function is not wholly defined, choice becomes real, and decisions become unpredictable mental events. If I know what I want, a computer can make all of my choices for me. If I do not know what I want, no possible computer can derive my utility function since it does not really exist. But the distinction to be drawn here is surely that about the knowledge of the utility function. The difference is analogous to driving on a clear and a foggy highway. It is not that between economics and technology. Neither the consumer in the supermarket nor the construction engineer faces an economic problem; both face essentially technological problems.

The theory of choice must be removed from its position of eminence in the economist's thought processes. The theory of choice, of resource allocation, call it what you will, assumes no special role for the economist, as opposed to any other scientist who examines human behavior. Lest you get overly concerned, however, let me hasten to say that most, if not all, of what now passes muster in the theory of choice will remain even in my ideal manual of instructions. I should emphasize that what I am suggesting is not so much a change in the basic content of what we study, but rather a change in the way we approach our material. I want economists to modify their thought processes, to look at the same phenomena through "another window," to use Nietzsche's appropriate metaphor. I want them to concentrate on "exchange" rather than on "choice."

The very word "economics," in and of itself, is partially responsible for some of the intellectual confusion. The "economizing" process leads us to think directly in terms of the theory of choice. I think it was Irving Babbit who said that revolutions begin in dictionaries. Should I have my say, I should propose that we cease, forthwith, to talk about "economics" or "political economy," although the latter is the much superior term. Were it possible to wipe the slate clean, I should recommend that we take up a wholly different term such as "catallactics," or "symbiotics." The second of these would, on balance, be preferred. Symbiotics is defined as the study of the association between dissimilar organisms, and the connotation of the term is that the association is mutually beneficial to all parties. This conveys, more or less precisely, the idea that should be central to our discipline. It draws attention to a unique sort of relationship, that which involves the cooperative association of individuals, one with another, even when individual interests are different. It concentrates on Adam Smith's "invisible hand," which so few noneconomists properly understand. As suggested above, important elements of the theory of choice remain in symbiotics. On the other hand, certain choice situations that are confronted by human beings remain wholly outside the symbiotic frame of reference. Robinson Crusoe, on his island before Friday arrives, makes decisions; his is the economic problem in the sense traditionally defined. This choice situation is not, however, an appropriate starting point for our discipline, even at the broadest conceptual level, as Whately correctly noted more than a century ago.[5] Crusoe's problem is, as I have said, essentially a computational one, and all that he need do to solve it is to program the built-in computer that he has in his mind. The uniquely symbiotic aspects of behavior, of human choice, arise only when Friday steps on the island, and Crusoe is forced into *association* with another human being. The fact of association requires that a wholly different, and wholly new, sort of behavior take place, that of "exchange," "trade," or "agreement." Crusoe may, of course, fail to recognize this new fact. He may treat Friday simply as a means to his own ends, as a part of "nature," so to speak. If he does so, a "fight" ensues, and to the victor go the spoils. Symbiotics does not include the strategic choices that are present in such situations of pure conflict. On the other extreme, it does not include the choices that are involved in purely "integrative" systems, where the separate individual participants desire identical results.[6]

Crusoe, if he chooses to avoid pure conflict, and if he realizes that Friday's interests are likely to be different from his own, will recognize that mutual gains can be secured through cooperative endeavor, that is, through exchange or trade. This mutuality of advantage that may be secured by different organisms as a result of cooperative arrangements, be these simple or complex, is the one important truth in our discipline. There is no comparable principle, and the important place that has been traditionally assigned to the maximization norm that is called the "economic principle" reflects misguided emphasis.

Almost at the other extreme from the Crusoe models, the refinements in the theoretical model of perfectly competitive general equilibrium have been equally, if not more, productive of intellectual muddle. By imposing the condition that no participant in the economic process can independently influence the outcome of this process, all "social" content is squeezed out of individual behavior in market organization. The individual responds to a set of externally determined, exogenous variables, and his choice problem again becomes purely mechanical. The basic flaw in this model of perfect competition is not its lack of correspondence with observed reality; no model of predictive value exhibits this. Its flaw lies in its conversion of individual choice behavior from a social-institutional context to a physical-computational one. Given the "rules of the market," the perfectly competitive model yields a unique "optimum" or "equilibrium," a single point on the Paretian welfare surface. But surely this is nonsensical social science, and the institutionalist critics have been broadly on target in some of their attacks. Frank Knight has consistently stressed that, in perfect competition, there is no competition. He is, of course, correct, but, and for the same reason, there is no "trade," as such.

A market is not competitive by assumption or by construction. A market *becomes* competitive, and competitive rules *come to be* established as institutions emerge to place limits on individual behavior patterns. It is this *becoming* process, brought about by the continuous pressure of human behavior in exchange, that is the central part of our discipline, if we have one, not the dry-rot of postulated perfection. A solution to a general-equilibrium set of equations is not predetermined by exogenously determined rules. A general solution, if there is one, *emerges* as a result of a whole network of evolving exchanges, bargains, trades, side payments, agreements, and contracts, which, finally at some point, ceases to renew itself. At each stage in this evolution toward solution, there are *gains* to be made, exchanges are possible, and this being true, the direction of movement is modified.

It is for these reasons that the model of perfect competition is of such limited explanatory value except when changes in variables exogenous to the system are introduced. There is no place in the structure of the model for internal change, change that is brought about by the men who continue to be haunted by the Smithean propensity. But surely the dynamic element in the economic system is precisely this continual evolution of the exchange process, as Schumpeter recognized in his treatment of entrepreneurial function.

How should the economist conceive the market organization? This is a central question, and the relevance of the difference in approach that I am emphasizing is directly shown by the two sharply conflicting answers. If the classical and currently renewed emphasis on the "wealth of nations" remains paramount, and if the logic of choice or allocation constitutes the "problem" element, the economist will look on market order as a *means* of accomplishing the basic economic functions that must be carried out in any society. The "market" becomes an engineered construction, a "mechanism," an "analogue calculating machine,"[7] a "computational device,"[8] one that processes information, accepts inputs, and transforms these into outputs which it then distributes. In this conception, the "market," as a mechanism, is appropriately compared with "government," as an alternative mechanism for accomplishing similar tasks. The second answer to the question is wholly different, although subtly so, and it is this second conception that I am trying to stress. The "market" or market organization is not a *means* toward the accomplishment of anything. It is, instead, the institutional embodiment of the voluntary exchange processes that are entered into by individuals in their several capacities. This is all that there is to it. Individuals are observed to cooperate with one another, to reach agreements, to trade. The network of relationships that emerges or evolves out of this trading process, the institutional framework, is called "the market." It is a setting, an arena, in which we, as economists, as theorists (as "onlookers"), observe men attempting to accomplish their own purposes, whatever these may be. And it is about these attempts that our basic theory is exclusively concerned if we would only recognize it as such. The boundaries are set by the limits of such cooperative endeavor; unilateral action is not part of the behavior pattern within our purview. In this conception, there is no explicit meaning of the term "efficiency" as applied to aggregative or composite results. It is contradictory to talk of the market as achieving "national goals," efficiently or inefficiently.

This does not imply that efficiency considerations are wholly eliminated in the conception that I am proposing. In fact, the opposite is true. The motivation for individuals to engage in trade, the source of the propensity, is surely that of "efficiency," defined in the personal sense of moving from less preferred to more preferred positions, and doing so under mutually acceptable terms. An "inefficient" institution, one that produces largely "inefficient" results, cannot, by the nature of man, survive until and unless coercion is introduced to prevent the emergence of alternative arrangements.

Let me illustrate this point and, at the same time, indicate the extension of the approach I am suggesting by referring to a familiar and simple example. Suppose that the local swamp requires draining to eliminate or reduce mosquito breeding. Let us postulate that no single citizen in the community has sufficient incentive to finance the full costs of this essentially indivisible operation. Defined in the orthodox, narrow way, the "market" fails; bilateral behavior of buyers and sellers does not remove the nuisance. "Inefficiency" presumably results. This is, however, surely an overly restricted conception of market behavior. If the market institutions, defined so narrowly, will not work, they will not meet individual objectives. Individual citizens will be led, because of the same propensity, to search voluntarily for more inclusive trading or exchange arrangements. A more complex institution may emerge to drain the swamp. The task of the economist includes the study of all such cooperative trading arrangements which become merely extensions of markets as more restrictively defined.

I have not got out of all the difficulties yet, however. You may ask: Will it really be to the interest of any single citizen to contribute to the voluntary program of mosquito control? How is the "free rider" problem to be handled? This specter of the "free rider," found in many shapes and forms in the literature of modern public finance theory, must be carefully examined. In the first place, there has been some confusion between total and marginal effects here. If a pretty woman strolls through the hotel lobby many tired convention delegates may get some external benefits, but, presumably, she finds it to her own advantage to stroll, and few delegates would pay her to stroll more than she already does. Nevertheless, to return to the swamp, there may be cases where the expected benefits from draining are not sufficiently high to warrant the emergence of some voluntary cooperative arrangement. And, in addition, the known or predicted presence of free riders may inhibit the cooperation of individuals who would otherwise contribute. In such situations, voluntary cooperation may never produce an "efficient" outcome, for the individual members of the group. Hence, the "market," even in its most extended sense, may be said to "fail." What recourse is left to the individual in this case? It is surely that of transferring, again voluntarily, at least at some ultimate constitutional level, activities of the swamp-clearing sort to the community as a collective unit, with decisions delegated to specifically designated rules for making choices, and these decisions coercively enforced once they are made. Therefore, in the most general sense (perhaps too general for most of you to accept), the approach to economics that I am advancing extends to cover the emergence of a political constitution. At the conceptual level, this can be brought under the framework of a voluntaristic exchange process. The contract theory of the state, and most of the writing in that tradition, represents the sort of approach to human activity that I think modern economics should be taking.[9]

I propose to extend the system of human relationships brought within the economist's scope widely enough to include collective as well as private organization. This being so, you may ask, how are "politics" and "economics" to be distinguished? This is a proper question, and it helps me to illustrate the central point of the paper in yet another way. The distinction to be drawn between economics and politics, as disciplines, lies in the nature of the social relationships among individuals that is examined in each. Insofar as individuals exchange or trade, as freely contracting units, the predominant characteristic of their behavior is "economic." And this, of course, extends our range far beyond the ordinary price-money nexus. In so far as individuals meet one another in a relationship of superior to inferior, leader to follower, principal to agent, the predominant characteristic in their behavior is "political,"[10] stemming, of course, from our everyday usage of the word "politician." Economics is the study of the whole system of exchange relationships. Politics is the study of the whole system of coercive or potentially coercive relationships. In almost any particular social institution, there are elements of both types of behavior, and it is appropriate that both the economist and the political scientist study such institutions. What I should stress is the potentiality of exchange in those sociopolitical institutions that we normally consider to embody primarily coercive or quasi-coercive elements. To the extent that man has available to him alternatives of action, he meets his associates as, in some sense, an "equal," in other words, in a trading relationship. Only in those situations where pure rent is the sole element in return is the economic relationship wholly replaced by the political.

As I have noted, almost all of the institutions and relationships that economists currently study will remain subject to examination in the disciplinary frame that I propose to draw around "economics." The same basic data are central to the allocation approach and the exchange approach. But the interpretation of these data, and even the very questions that we ask of them, will depend critically on the reference system within which we operate. What will the shift in reference system produce? The most important single result will be the making of a sharp and categorical distinction between the discipline to which our theory of markets applies and that which we may call "social engineering," for want of any better term. Note that I am not here saying that social engineering is not legitimate endeavor. I am suggesting only that the implications concerning the uses of individuals as means to nonindividual ends be explicitly recognized. My criticism of the orthodox approach to economics is based, at least in part, on its failure to allow such implications to be appropriately made. If the economic problem is viewed as the general means-ends problem, the social engineer is a working economist in the full sense of the term. Thus it is that we now observe him developing more and more complicated schemata designed to maximize more and more complex functions, under more and more specifically defined constraints. We applaud all of this as "scientific" advance, and consider the aids that we may provide to the practicing social engineer in these respects as our "social" purpose. There is, I submit, something wholly confused about all of this. I, too, applaud and admire the ingenuity of the applied mathematicians who have helped, and are helping, choosers to solve more complex computational problems. But I shall continue to insist that our "purpose," if you will, is no more that of providing the social engineer with these tools than it is of providing the monopolist with tools to make more profits, or Wicksteed's housewife with instructions how better to divide out the mashed potatoes among her children. The proper role of the economist is not providing the means of making "better" choices, and to imply this, as the resource allocation-choice approach does, tends to confuse most of us at the very outset of our training.

I want to note especially here that I am not, through rejecting the allocation approach, decrying the desirability, indeed the necessity, for mathematical competence. In fact, advances in our understanding of symbiotic relationships may well require considerably more sophisticated mathematical tools than those required in what I have called social engineering. For example, we need to learn much more about the theory of n-person cooperative games. It seems but natural that the mathematics finally required to systematize a set of relationships involving voluntary behavior on the part of many persons will be more complicated than that required to solve even the most complex computational problem where the ends are ordered in a single function.

Although this will, of course, be challenged, the position that I advance is neutral with respect to ideological or normative content. I am simply proposing, in various ways, that economists concentrate attention on the institutions, the relationships, among individuals as they participate in voluntarily organized activity, in trade or exchange, broadly considered. People may, as in my swamp-clearing example, decide to do things collectively. Or they may not. The analysis, as such, is neutral in respect to the proper private sector-public sector mix. I am stating that economists should be "market economists," but only because I think they should concentrate on market or exchange institutions, again recalling that these are to be conceived in the widest possible sense. This need not bias or prejudice them for or against any particular form of social order. Learning more about how markets work means learning more about how markets work. They may work better or worse, in terms of whatever criteria might be imposed, than uninformed opinion leads one to expect.

To an extent, of course, we must all follow along the road that is functionally determined by the behavior of our disciplinary colleagues. The growth and development of a discipline is somewhat like language and, despite the fact that we may think that the current direction of change is misleading and productive of intellectual confusions, we must try to continue communicating one with another. It would be naive in the extreme for me to think that I could, through individual persuasion such as this, or in concert with a few others who might agree broadly with me on such matters, change the drift of a whole social science. Economics, as a well-defined subject of scholarship, seems to be disintegrating, for the reasons I have outlined, and realistic appraisal suggests that this inexorable process will not be stopped. Nevertheless, it is useful, or so it seems to me, to stop occasionally and look at the road map.

I may conclude by recalling a little adage that Frank Ward of the University of Tennessee had clipped on his office door when I first met him in 1940, when I was a very green, beginning graduate student. The adage said: "The study of economics won't keep you out of the breadline; but at least you'll know why you're there." I can paraphrase this to apply to methodology: "Concentration on methodology won't solve any of the problems for you, but at least you should know what the problems are."

Notes

1. For a review of this approach in terms of the doctrinal history, see Israel Kirzner, *The Economic Point of View* (New York: D. V. Nostrand, 1960), ch. 4. This book provides a good summary of the various approaches to the "economic point of view."

2. For a recent paper in which the exchange basis for economic analysis is plainly accepted, see Kenneth E. Boulding, "Towards a Pure Theory of Threat Systems," *American Economic Review* (May 1963), pp. 424–34, especially pp. 424–26.

3. (London: Macmillan, 1932).

4. In his presidential address to the American Economic Association delivered in 1949, Howard S. Ellis criticized the arbitrariness with which ends may be selected under the Robbins definition. Ellis's whole approach has much in common with that taken in this paper. In my view, however, Ellis, through his overemphasis on the "choice" aspects of economics, failed to make his critique of Robbins as effective as it might have been. See Howard S. Ellis, "The Economic Way of Thinking," *American Economic Review* (March 1950), pp. 1–12.

5. Richard Whately, *Introductory Lectures on Political Economy* (London: B. Fellowes, 1831), p. 7; the same point is made in Arthur Latham Perry, *Elements of Political Economy* (New York: Charles Scribner & Company, 1868), p. 27.

6. Boulding distinguishes threat systems, exchange systems, and integrative systems of social order. Cf. Kenneth E. Boulding, "Towards a Pure Theory of Threat Systems," *American Economic Review* (May 1963), pp. 424–34.

7. Paul A. Samuelson, "The Pure Theory of Public Expenditure," *Review of Economics and Statistics* (November 1954), p. 388.

8. Takashi Negishi, "The Stability of a Competitive Economy: A Survey Article," *Econometrica* (October 1962), p. 639.

9. In our book, *The Calculus of Consent* (Ann Arbor: University of Michigan Press, 1962), Gordon Tullock and I develop the theory of the political constitution in the manner sketched here.

10. This distinction has been developed at some length by Gordon Tullock in *Politics in Bureaucracy: A General Theory of Administrative Hierarchies* (Washington, D.C.: Public Affairs Press, 1965).

3.
Is Economics the Science of Choice?

"...from time to time it is probably necessary to detach one's self from the technicalities of the argument and to ask quite naively what it is all about."

F. A. Hayek, *Economics and Knowledge*

Robert Mundell commences his preface to *Man and Economics* with the assertion: "Economics is the science of choice."[1] Most professional scholars who check off the box marked "economist" on the Register of Scientific Personnel find no quarrel with Mundell's statement. Despite some danger of once again being called iconoclastic, I propose to examine this assertion seriously and critically. In the process, I shall not discuss what economics is or is not, should or should not be, at least in any direct sense. My question is more elementary and its answer is obvious once it is asked. I want to ask whether a *science* of *choice* is possible at all. Are we not involved in a contradiction in terms?

There is no need to go beyond the everyday usage of the two words. I am neither competent nor interested in detailed etymological inquiry. "To choose" means "to take by preference out of all that are available . . . to select."[2] Choice is the "act of choosing," or "selecting." In particular, "choosing" should be distinguished from "behaving." The latter implies acting but there is no reference to conscious selection from among alternatives. Behavior can be predetermined and, hence, predictable. Choice, by its nature, cannot be predetermined and remain choice. If we then define science in the modern sense of embodying conceptually refutable predictions, a "science of choice" becomes self-contradictory.[3]

This elementary proposition is recognized by those who accept the Mundell position. If this is the case, what are the reasons for adherence to what, at first glance, seems glaring methodological inconsistency? To the economist, choice seems to be imposed by the fact of scarcity. Given an acknowledged multiplicity of ends and a limitation on means, it becomes necessary that some selection among alternatives be made. It is in such a very general setting that economics has been classified as the study of such selection, or choice. Once this is done, replacing the word "study" with the word "science" becomes a natural extension of language. Is the science so defined devoid of predictive content? Some scholars might answer affirmatively, but surely there are many others who, at the same time that they acquiesce in Mundell's statement, busy themselves with the empirical testing of hypotheses. Are such professionals unaware of their methodological contradictions? It seems useful to try to answer these questions in some detail.

I. The Categories of Economic Theory

1. The Logic of Economic Choice

The legitimacy of a "science of choice" may be questioned, but there should be no doubts about the usefulness of a "logic of choice." Much of orthodox economic theory is precisely this, and is, therefore, concerned with choice, as such. This logical theory provides students with the "economic point of view" and it can be posed in either a normative or a positive setting. In the former, the logic reduces to the economic principle, the simple requirement that returns to like units of outlay or input must be equalized at the margins in order to secure a maximum of output. In this most general sense, the principle is empirically empty. It instructs the chooser, the decision maker, on the procedures for making selections without requiring that he define either his own preference ordering of output combinations or the resource constraints within which he must operate. Empirical emptiness should not, however, be equated with uselessness. If a potential chooser is made aware of the principle in its full import, he will weigh alternatives more carefully, he will think in marginal terms, he will make evaluations of opportunity costs, and, finally, he will search more diligently for genuine alternatives. The norms for choice can be meaningfully discussed, even if the specific implementation takes place only in the internal calculus of the decision maker. Instructing the decision maker as to how he should choose may produce "better" choices as evaluated by his own standards.

There is a positive counterpart to the logic of choice, and this extends theory to the interaction among separate decision makers. Commencing with the fact that choosers choose and that they do so under constraints which include the behavior of others, the economist can begin to make meaningful statements about the results that emerge from the interaction among several choosers. Certain "laws" can be deduced, even if conceptually refutable hypotheses cannot be derived. Analysis makes no attempt to specify preference orderings for particular choosers. The "law" of choice states only that the individual decision maker will select that alternative that stands highest on his preference ordering. Defined in purely logical terms, this produces the "law of demand." In this way, trade or exchange can be explained, even in some of its most complex varieties. Characteristics of equilibrium positions can be derived, these being defined in terms of the coordination between expected and realized plans of the separate decision takers.

In the strictest sense, the chooser is not specified in the pure logic of choice. Under the standard assumptions, the analysis applies to the individual. But the logic requires no such limitation; it applies universally. The norms for efficient choice can be treated independently of the processes through which decisions are actually made. It is not, therefore, explicitly in error to present decision making norms for nonexistent collective entities who do not, in fact, choose. Under some conditions, it may be helpful to discuss the economizing process "as if" such entities existed, although, as we shall note in Section II, this is the source of much confusion.

In its normative variant, the logical theory of choice involves the simple principle of economizing, nothing more. This is the mathematics of "maxima" and "minima." Much of modern economic theory is limited to various elaborations on this mathematics. By modifying the formal properties of the objective function and the constraints, interesting exercises in locating and in stating the required conditions for insuring satisfaction of the norms can be produced. Whether or not such exercises command too much of the professional investment of modern economists remains an open question.

The logical theory of interaction among many choosers may also be classified as pure mathematics. But this mathematics is not that which has attracted major interest of the professionals in that discipline, and there is some legitimacy in the economists' preemptive claim. Game theory, as one part of a general theory of interaction, owes its origin to a mathematician, but the elegant theory of competitive equilibrium was developed by economists. Major strides are being made in this purely logical theory of interaction among many choosers, some of which are aimed at relating game theory, more generally the theory of coalition formation, to the theory of competitive equilibrium. The marginal productivity of mathematically inclined economists in this area of research appears much higher than that which is aimed at working out complex variations of the simple maximization problem.

2. The Abstract Science of Economic Behavior

In the logical theory summarized, no objectives are specified. Choice remains free, and because of this, it remains choice. As we move beyond this pure logic, however, and into economic theory as more generally, if ambiguously, conceived, choice becomes circumscribed. Specific motivation is imputed to the decision maker, and it is seldom recognized that, to the extent that this takes place, genuine "choice" is removed from the theory. What we now confront is *behavior,* not choice, behavior that is subject to conceptually predictable laws. The entity that acts, that behaves, does so in accordance with the patterns imposed by the postulates of the theoretical science. The actor is, so to speak, programmed to behave in direct response to stimuli. The abstract science of economic behavior, as I have here classified this, has empirical content that is wholly missing in the pure logic of economic choice. This content is provided by restricting the utility function. Several degrees of restrictiveness may be imposed. Minimally, nothing more than a specification of "goods" may be introduced. From this alone, conceptually refutable hypotheses emerge. The acting-behaving unit *must* choose more of any "good" when its "price" relative to other "goods" declines.[4] Additional restrictiveness takes the form of specifying something about the internal trade-offs among "goods" in the utility function of the behaving unit. This step produces the *homo economicus* of classical theory who must, when confronted with alternatives, select that which stands highest on his preference ranking, as evaluated in terms of a *numéraire.* The pure economic man must behave so as to take more rather than less when confronted with simple monetary alternatives. He must maximize income-wealth and minimize outlays. He must maximize profits if he plays the role of entrepreneur.

Confusion has arisen between this abstract science of economic behavior and the pure logic of choice because of ambiguities that are involved in the several means of bounding the utility functions of the acting units. In the pure logic of choice, the arguments in the utility function are not identified; "goods" and "bads" are unknown to the external observer. In any science of economic behavior, the "goods" must be classified as such. But under minimally restricted utility functions, specific trade-offs among these may remain internal to the acting units. The individual "chooses" in the sense that his selection from among several desirable alternatives remains unpredictable to the observer. What we have here is an extremely limited "science" of behavior combined with an extensive "logic" of genuine choice. We move beyond this essentially mixed framework when the trade-offs are more fully specified. Additional "laws of behavior" can then be derived; and, more importantly, predictions can be made about the results of the interaction processes. These predictions can be conceptually refuted by empirical evidence. If internal trade-offs among "goods" in utility functions are fully specified, behavior becomes completely predictable in the abstract. Normal procedure does not, however, involve the extension to such limits.

As noted earlier, the pure logic of choice may be interpreted in either a normative or a positive sense. If choice is real, it is meaningful to refer to "better" and "worse" choices, and the simple maximizing principle can be of some assistance to the decision taker. By relatively sharp contrast, there is no normative content in the abstract science of economic behavior. The reason is obvious. The acting unit responds to environmental stimuli in predictably unique fashion; there is no question as to the "should" of behavior. The unit responds and that is that. Failure to note this basic difference between the pure logic of choice and the pure science of behavior provides, I think, an explanation of the claim, advanced especially by Mises, that economic theory is a general theory of human action.[5] The logical theory is indeed general but empty; the scientific theory is nongeneral but operational.

At this point, it seems useful to refer to the distinction between the "subjectivist economics" espoused by both Mises and Hayek, and the "objectivist economics" which is more widely accepted, even if its limitations are seldom explicitly recognized. In the logic of choice, choosing becomes a subjective experience. The alternatives for choice as well as the evaluations placed upon these exist only in the mind of the decision maker. Cost, which is the obstacle to choice, is purely subjective and this consists in the chooser's evaluation of the alternative that must be sacrificed in order to attain that which is selected. This genuine opportunity cost vanishes once a decision is taken. By relatively sharp contrast with this, in the pure science of economic behavior choice itself is illusory. In the abstract model, the behavior of the actor is predictable by an external observer. This requires that some criteria for behavior be objectively measurable, and this objectivity is supplied when the motivational postulate is plugged into the model. An actor behaves so as to maximize utility, defined in a nonempty sense. It becomes impossible, in the formal model, for an actor to "choose" less rather than more of the common denominator units, money or some *numéraire* good, when he is faced with such alternatives. Cost, in this objectivist theory, the pure science of economics, is measurable by the observer. This cost is unrelated to choice, as such, since the latter really does not exist. The opportunity cost of using a resource unit in one way rather than another consists in the *money* earnings of that unit in its most productive alternative use. These earnings may be objectively estimated and quantified. In this setting, the cost of a beaver is two deer, and there is no relationship between cost and sacrifice.[6] To say here that nonpecuniary elements may affect choice is to confuse the model of pure economic behavior with the model of the logic of choice. Insofar as nonpecuniary noneconomic elements actually enter the resource owner's calculus, the behavioral model is falsified.[7]

The motivational postulate, the behavior of *homo economicus*, effectively converts the purely logical theory of choice into an abstract science of behavior. It accomplishes this by replacing the subjectivity of the logical theory by objective payoffs. Generality in explanation is and must be sacrificed in crossing this bridge. But this is replaced by predictability. The abstract science of economic behavior is the familiar world of *ceteris paribus*. This science provides the analyst with tools for discussing the complex interaction of market processes to the extent that individual participants behave economically. Equilibrium characteristics can be objectively described in terms of quantifiable, measurable relationships among variables, among prices and costs. It is this abstract theory upon which most economists rely in making rudimentary predictions about reality. When asked: "What will happen when an excise tax is placed on Product X?", the professional responds: "The price of X to consumers will rise, and less will be demanded, provided that other things remain unchanged, and provided that men behave economically." The last qualifying phrase "provided that men behave economically" shifts the analysis into the science of behavior and enables conceptually refutable predictions to be advanced. By this qualifier, the economist states that he is preventing actors from behaving other than economically in the theoretical model that he is constructing. As we all recognize, many professionals do not go further than this; they do not consider it a part of their task either to examine the psychology of behavior more fully or to test empirically the predictions that the abstract science enables them to make.

Such methodological aloofness is acceptable only so long as the severe limitations of the scientist's role are appreciated. Failure to recognize these limitations leads naive professionals to claim far too much for the science and with such claims they infuriate those critics who concentrate attention on the noneconomic content in human choice patterns.

3. The Predictive Science of Economic Behavior

The abstract science is restricted to the derivation of propositions or hypotheses that are conceptually refutable. The realm of predictive science is entered only when these hypotheses are subjected to empirical testing against real-world observations. One of the features of modern economic research has been its shift toward the rigorous testing of hypotheses. The pound of *ceteris paribus* no longer protects the scientist; he must, through imaginative construction of hypotheses and through exhaustive search for appropriate data, try to corroborate the predictions that the theory allows him to make. Because of empirical constraints, the range of his efforts must be more limited than that allowed to the free-floating abstract theorist. Data are difficult to come by, and even when these can be assembled, the hypotheses tester must be prepared for frustration and failure. Data can, at best, reflect the results of genuine choices made by participants in a very complicated interaction sequence. The economic behavior implicit in these choices may be nonexistent in some cases, and swamped in effect by noneconomic considerations in many others. The predictive hypotheses may be refuted at the initial levels of testing. But the scientist cannot readily use such refutation for overthrowing the general laws of behavior derived from the central structure of his theory. He must normally acknowledge his probable failure to isolate the economic from the noneconomic elements of choice, and, accordingly, he must acknowledge the continuing challenge of empirical testability for his theoretically based hypotheses.

This amounts to saying that, despite his efforts, the predictive scientist remains chained to the vision of the economic universe produced in the abstract theory of economic behavior. He can, when successful, show that indeed "water runs down hill," but, with contrary results, he can rarely, if ever, refute the economic analogue to the law of gravity. At best, the predictive science is an extension of the abstract science. It must incorporate the basic motivational postulate of *homo economicus*; indeed this provides the source for deriving the hypotheses to be tested. The paradigms are unchanged over the two subdisciplines.

There are, however, significant differences. In some strict sense, the abstract science treats only of pure economic man, unalloyed by noneconomic behavioral traits. Accordingly, the theorems are simple, elegant and aesthetically satisfying. But the real world is a grubby place, and it is this world that must be the raw source for any science that aims at operational validity. In the face of the apparent divergence of the real world from the paradigms of the abstract science, the empirical corroboration of many predictive hypotheses is perhaps surprising.

The fact that his hypotheses refer to the behavior of *many* actors greatly facilitates the predictive scientist's efforts. He need only make predictions about the behavior of average or representative participants in the processes that he observes; he need not hypothesize about the behavior of any single actor. Hence even if noneconomic elements dominate the behavior of some participants, and even if these enter to some degree in the choices of all participants, given certain symmetry in the distributions of preferences, the hypotheses derived from the abstract theory may still be corroborated. For example, given comparable institutional constraints, the wage levels for plumbers and carpenters may tend toward equality even if a substantial proportion of plumbers exhibit strong noneconomic preferences for their chosen occupation and even if a substantial proportion of carpenters exhibit similar preferences for their own occupation.

So long as some sufficient number of persons indicates some willingness to make the occupational shift on purely economic grounds, the hypothesis about wage level equality is supported. The multiplicity of participants generates results that are identical to those predicted in the model that embodies the strict assumption that all actors behave economically.

4. The "Behavioristic" Science of the Economy

Unless he is able to call upon the motivational postulate of the abstract science, the predictive scientist can scarcely derive the hypotheses that he seeks to test. It is folly for him to abandon this postulate deliberately in some misguided attempt at imitating the methods of the natural scientists who find it impossible to introduce comparable behavioral postulates. "Scientism" of this sort has been effectively criticized by Hayek[8] and others, and this approach need not be examined in detail here. It seems clear that with no behavioral basis from which to begin his search for uniformities and regularities in the data that he observes, the pure "behaviorist" is reduced to massive efforts at observation with very limited prospects of successful results. He confronts a universe of prices, quantities, employment levels, measures for national aggregates. He presumably remains aloof from the behavior that generates these data as results, whether this behavior be economic or not. This is not to suggest that such efforts should be wholly abandoned. It seems clear, however, that the deliberate sacrifice of the directional hypotheses provided by the paradigms of economic science should be made with great caution.

A somewhat different behaviorist approach (and one that fits the terminology considerably better) involves an attempt to specify noneconomic elements that enter into the individual's choice calculus. This approach, which we may associate with the work of Herbert A. Simon and his colleagues,[9] calls upon psychological insight to assist in the development of motivational patterns that may be considerably more complex than the simple postulates of standard economic theory. Ultimately, the objective parallels those of orthodox economic science, the ability to make predictions about human behavior in the social interaction process. And, to the extent that the hypotheses of standard theory are refuted, such an approach as this offers the only avenue of advance for social science. This approach may proceed by relaxing or modifying the restrictions placed on individual utility functions, or, alternatively, the procedure may involve dropping the utilitarian framework.[10]

II. The Confusions of Economic Theory

Economics, as this discipline is currently interpreted, embodies elements of each of the four categories listed. The confusions arise from the failure

Player B

50, 50	20, 60
60, 20	30, 30

Player

A

Figure 3-1

of economists to understand the categorical distinctions. Many of the continuing and unresolved arguments over particular methodological issues can be traced more or less directly to this source.

1. The Derivation of Policy Norms

One of these arguments concerns the relevance of theory for deriving policy conclusions. I shall illustrate some of the confusion here through the familiar prisoner's dilemma of game theory, interpreted variously in terms of the categories described in Section I. The pedagogic advantages of this construction are immense; when properly employed the dilemma allows us to introduce in a two-person interaction model many of the relevant issues of economic policy in the large.

Fig. 3-1 presents the dilemma in a form slightly modified from its classic setting. The game depicted is positive-sum. The first term in each cell indicates the payoff to A, the player who chooses between rows. The second term shows the payoff to B, the player who chooses between columns. Each player's result depends on the behavior of the other, but, for each player, there is a dominating strategy shown by the second row and second column. The independent-behavior solution, shown in the southeast cell of the matrix, depicts the dilemma; the combined payoffs are larger in the northwest cell.

With nothing more than the payoff matrix of Fig. 3-1, something has been said about the interaction of the two players. Their choice behavior has been related to the structure of the game itself, and the possible conflict between the independent-adjustment solution and the combined-payoff potential outcome has been shown. Nonetheless, it should be noted that, to this point, nothing has been said about the nature of the payoffs. These have been treated strictly as numerical indicators of that which motivates choice behavior. In some respects, these payoffs may be thought of as being defined in utility units, so long as the purely subjective nature of utility in this context is kept in mind. In this setting, we have remained strictly in the pure logic of choice. There is absolutely no predictive content in the analysis.[11]

We move from this pure logic of choice into the abstract science of economic behavior when we define the payoffs objectively. To do this, we need only to put dollar signs in front of the numbers in the matrix illustration of Fig. 3-1. The solution seems to remain as before, but it is now limited to those situations where players do, in fact, behave economically. There will be no convergence to the southeast cell if players in the real world should choose to behave cooperatively rather than independently. The abstract theory of economics says that they will behave economically, that the southeast cell is the "solution" to the game. This prediction may be falsified, at least conceptually.

At this level, it becomes legitimate to derive limited policy implications from the analysis. As they behave in the real world, individuals are observed to adopt the dominating strategies, as these are identified in the eyes of the observer. In the objectified payoff structure imputed to the participants, there appears to exist a conflict between the independent-adjustment outcome and the jointly desired optimal outcome. Given nothing more than the potentiality of this conflict, it becomes plausible for the political economist to consider modifications in the choice structure that would enable individual participants to eliminate such a conflict, if indeed it should exist. If ways and means can be found to remove the restrictions of the potential dilemma, if institutional rearrangements can be made which will allow independent behavior of the participants to produce results that may be mutually more beneficial than those observed under present environmental conditions, these should, of course, be suggested. (In the strict prisoner's dilemma example, and limiting attention to the world of the two prisoners only, the introduction of communication between the two persons represents such an institutional change.) This point was recognized and well expressed by Sir Dennis Robertson when he called upon the economist to suggest ways to minimize the use of "that scarce resource Love."[12] Since Adam Smith, economists have been within the bounds of methodological propriety when they have proposed organizational-institutional arrangements that channel behavior that may be, but need not be, economically motivated in the direction of promoting what may be, but need not be, mutually desired economic objectives.

This very general policy position, which I shall call Smithean, requires minimal empirical backing along with minimal ethical content. All that is required is the conceptual possibility that payoffs relevant for individual behavior should be directionally linked with those emerging from the postulate of economic science. So long as a person may, other things equal, respond to the change in stimuli, as objectified, in the direction suggested by the central postulate of the theory, the economist is justified in his search for institutional arrangements that will remove the restrictiveness of the dilemma, should it exist. In a very general sense, this amounts to little more than opening up avenues for potential trades which participants may or may not find it advantageous to exploit. The policy prescription is, in effect, limited to suggestions for widening the range for potential choice.[13]

To the extent that the empirical testing of hypotheses supports the central behavioral postulate of the abstract theory, the productivity of Smithean institutional reforms is enhanced. But the corroboration of the behavioral postulate by empirical evidence implies much more than the *ceteris paribus* limits of the abstract theory. Such corroboration indicates that economic behavior dominates all noneconomic elements of choice in the specific context examined. This offers a temptation to go much beyond the general institutional reforms implied by the Smithean position. If man can be shown to behave in some more direct relationship to an objectified payoff structure than the *ceteris paribus* potentiality implied by the abstract theory, direct manipulation of his behavior seems to become possible through the appropriate modification in the conditions for choice. It is one thing to say that, when given the opportunity, an individual will choose more rather than less provided other elements affecting his choice remain unchanged. It becomes quite a different thing to say that the representative individual will choose more rather than less in terms of objectified units in the *numéraire* without regard to noneconomic influences on his choice situation. Rarely will the multidimensional complexity of real-world choice allow results of such simplicity to be adduced. But, if it should do so, specific control of individual behavior through imposed changes in the payoff structures might be possible.

It is precisely at this point that a pervasive and fundamental error emerges. The false step is taken when the explicitly objectified payoff structure that is postulated for use in the abstract theory of economic behavior is translated into direct guide lines for the explicit manipulation of choice alternatives. This procedure must assume that the actual *choice maker* in the real world *behaves* strictly as the pure economic man of the theorist's model. Markets are held to "fail" because of the dilemma-type situations that are confronted by the idealized man of the theorist's analytical model. As a follow-up to this, policy suggestions are made which incorporate this rarified behavioral postulate as reality. In a genuine sense, this whole procedure is absurd.

The point can be illustrated with the matrix of Fig. 3-1. The abstract theory bases its elaboration of the interaction processes on the postulate that individuals behave economically in the sense that they respond to objectified and externally measurable payoffs. In this context, it is meaningful to say that, in the model, Player A selects Row 2 rather than Row 1 because of the $10 difference in payoff, regardless of what he predicts about B's behavior. It is meaningful to say that, in this model, the opportunity cost to Player A, "that which could be avoided by his not taking Row 2," is $10 in foregone payoffs. But this opportunity cost, embodied in the theoretical model for behavior, cannot then be taken as the specific basis for policy prescription aimed at manipulating A's actual choice behavior. This violates the purpose and meaning of the abstract theory and, as suggested, has little or no empirical base. Despite this, such procedure is manifest in a substantial part of modern economic policy discussion.

It is not caricature to say that modern policy discussion, which I shall call Pigovian, proceeds as follows, still within the matrix illustration of Fig. 3-1. The economist proposes a "corrective" tax on Player A, a tax designed to make the costs that he privately confronts equivalent to those that are confronted by the collectivity in the two alternatives that are faced. The general welfare criterion becomes equality between *private* and *social* cost. To implement this result, private costs must be modified; but in order to know by how much, some assumption must be made about private payoff structures. The orthodoxy proceeds as if the purely economic man exists. The criterion calls for a tax of $10 + to be imposed on A's returns in Row 2 (or a subsidy of $10 + on his returns in Row 1). Given this change in his alternatives, Player A (similarly for Player B) will be motivated to "choose" that alternative that is jointly desired. The efficient collective outcome will be generated. The emphasis has been subtly shifted from the exploitation of potential gains-from-trade to the attaining of specifically defined results.

As the construction shows, if either A or B should behave noneconomically the suggested modification of the payoff matrix may not produce the desired results. Suppose, for example, that both players value independent action highly and are willing to sacrifice economic gain to secure this objective. In this instance, the independent-adjustment solution in the southeast cell remains dominant, regardless of the imposition of the suggested corrective tax or subsidy. Some tax (or subsidy) will, of course, result in behavioral change, but the outcome may be less rather than more desirable in some "social" sense. The dilemma indicated to be present in objectified payoff structure may not exist when payoffs relevant to genuine choices are incorporated in the matrix. The artificiality of any objectified payoff structure, as conceived by the external observer, tends to be overlooked with the consequence that "dilemmas" which exist only in the mind of the observer may be imputed to actual participants in an interaction process.

The point of emphasis is clear. The costs that influence "choice" are purely subjective and these exist only within the mind of the decision maker. The economist may, within limits, discuss this "choice" provided that he remains within what we have called the "logic of choice." He cannot, however, plug in the *homo economicus* introduced in his abstract models of economic behavior and then use this as the basis for constructing specific choice-influencing constraints aimed at welfare improvements. Individuals choose on the basis of their own preference orderings; they may, within limits, behave as the abstract theory of economics postulates. But rarely do they behave strictly as the automatons of the analytical models. Yet this is precisely the unrecognized assumption that is implicit in most modern policy discussion.

The critical distinction to be made is that between what I have called the Smithean policy position and what I have called the Pigovian policy norms. In the former, organizational-institutional changes, modifications in the structure of property rights, require only that possible conflicts between individually adjusted behavior and mutually desired collective outcomes be recognized. Specific definition of "efficient" or "optimal" results is not needed. Such results are allowed to emerge from the choice process itself. In the Pigovian framework, by contrast, property rights are normally assumed to be fixed exogenously. Corrective measures take the form of specific modifications in the choice conditions that are confronted by individual participants. Clearly, this approach to policy requires much more knowledge about the actual preference orderings of individuals. Efficiency in outcomes is no longer defined by the observed absence of further gains from trade as revealed by the behavior of traders. This Smithean definition is replaced by the objectively defined set of equalities central to theoretical welfare economics.

The error extends through much of modern economics. This was at the base of the debate over the possibility of socialist calculation that took place in the 1930s. Mises and Hayek were, I think, indirectly making essentially the same point that I have tried to make here. Their arguments failed to convince their fellow economists; most economists continue to think that efficiency, at least ideally, can be produced by the enforcement of output and pricing *rules,* that these can effectively substitute for the modification in *property rights* dictated by the particular economic setting.

2. "Scientific" Decision-Making for the Collectivity:
    Systems Analysis, Operations Research, Cost-Benefit Analysis

The confusions embodied in the Pigovian norms are complemented by an even more elementary set of confusions when the economist extends his range to the "choices" of the collectivity. He tends to be trapped in the scarcity-choice maximization nexus, and it is not at all easy for him to accept the fact that a collective "decision maker" or "chooser" is non-existent. Failing this, he tends to conceptualize some supraindividual entity which makes effective "choices," which maximizes some objective function subject to appropriately defined constraints. This procedure allows the analyst to produce interesting and self-satisfying results. But error arises when either the analyst or his interpreters consider such results applicable to real-world issues.

Analysis of this sort is two dimensions away from real-world relevance. In the first place, the "logic of choice" for the single decision maker is applied to a situation where no such person or entity exists. Since there is no maximizer, analysis is of questionable value when it is based on the assumption that one exists.[14] In the second place, the costs and benefits of alternative courses of action must be objectified if the analyst is to do more than present his own value orderings. This objectification runs into the same difficulty as that noted in connection with the Pigovian approach. There may be little or no relationship between the objectively defined costs and benefits and the evaluations that individuals place on alternatives in actual choice situations.

In this latter respect, the analyst has even less to fall back on than the Pigovian welfare economist. The abstract science of economic behavior with its embodiment of economic man does provide some basis for considering modifications in the conditions of choice, as faced by acting persons. For the cost-benefit analyst, however, there is no prospect of modifying the alternatives facing individual choosers. He must advance norms for choice itself. He is advising the collectivity quite specifically concerning how it "should" choose. Even if the complexities of group decision making are ignored, the subjective evaluations of individuals are of a different dimension from the objectively quantifiable measurements placed on alternatives by the analyst. And it should be emphasized here that this difficulty is not removed by allowing the careful analyst to introduce "nonquantifiable" elements into his calculus. In point of fact, the more subjective that his own calculus becomes, the *less* relevant become his efforts. At best, he may be able to place values on cost and benefit streams that would characterize the world in which all men behave economically. This calculus would be of limited, but perhaps of positive value. Once this standard drawn from the behavioral postulate of the abstract science is left behind, however, there is nothing that the analyst can provide that assists in the understanding of actual collective decision processes.

III. Conclusions

Modern economics, as practiced by professional scholars, embodies confusions that are fundamentally methodological. These have their historical foundations in the failure of economists to establish an effective synthesis between the objective and the subjective theories of value. The issues did not emerge with clarity, however, until efforts were made to extend the applicability of economic theory beyond its traditional limits. So long as the task of theory remained that of "explaining" the functioning of a market system, objective and subjective elements could exist side by side without open contradiction. During the past half century, however, theory has been called upon to do much more than this. It has been employed to derive norms for policy aimed at making allocation more "efficient." Economists have, in other words, proceeded as if theirs were a "science of choice."

It is in such extensions that the confusions that I have stressed in this paper have emerged. The critical methodological oversight was that which Hayek emphasized, with clarity but to little avail, in several of his fundamental papers in the late 1930s and early 1940s. The failure of economists to recognize that the sense data upon which individuals actually choose in either market or political choice structures are dimensionally distinct from any data that can be objectively called upon by external observers led directly to the methodological chaos that currently exists. Economics seems unlikely to escape from this chaos for many years, if indeed it survives at all as an independent discipline. Few economists are wholly free of the confusions that I have discussed. For myself, I advance no claim that my own thinking has yet fully rid itself of the paradigms of neoclassical orthodoxy.

Notes

I am indebted to David B. Johnson, Roland N. McKean, Gordon Tullock, and Richard E. Wagner for helpful comments.
    1. New York (1968).
    2. *Oxford Universal Dictionary* (1955).
    3. In a wholly determinist universe, choice is purely illusory, as is discussion about choice. I do not treat this age-old issue, and I prefer to think that the subject discussed as well as the discussion itself is not illusory.
    4. This approach may be associated with the work of A. A. Alchian and his colleagues. Cf. A. A. Alchian and W. R. Allen, *University Economics*, 2nd ed. (Belmont, Calif.: 1967).
    5. Cf. Ludwig von Mises, *Human Action* (New Haven: 1949).

6. For an extended discussion of the concept of cost in contrasting methodological settings, see my *Cost and Choice: An Inquiry in Economic Theory* (Chicago: Rand McNally, 1969).

7. To avoid ambiguity here, I should note that nonpecuniary "goods" can be introduced in individual utility functions in the minimally restricted limits that were discussed above. Given the specification of such "goods," conceptually refutable hypotheses about individual behavior can be derived. Nonpecuniary "goods" tend to be different for different individuals, however, and the limits of any predictive science are reached when those "goods" which are common to all persons are exhausted. This provides the basis for reliance on the strictly pecuniary motivation in the general model of the economic interaction process.

8. Cf. A. Hayek, *The Counter-Revolution of Science* (Glencoe, Ill.: 1955).

9. Cf. H. A. Simon, *Models of Man* (New York: 1957).

10. This summary review does not do justice to the approach under discussion. For the most part, the contributions here have been made by social scientists in disciplines other than economics. Indeed, to the extent that social "science" other than economics exists at all, it must be produced by those who adopt the approach summarized here.

11. Cf. John C. Harsanyi, "A General Theory of Rational Behavior in Game Situations," *Econometrica*, 34 (1966): 613 ff.

12. D. H. Robertson, "What Does the Economist Economize?" *Economic Commentaries* (London: 1956).

13. For an earlier and somewhat different statement of this position see my "Positive Economics, Welfare Economics, and Political Economy," *Journal of Law and Economics*, 2 (October 1959): 124–38. Reprinted in *Fiscal Theory and Political Economy* (Chapel Hill: 1960).

14. These comments apply only to the orthodox analyses under discussion here. It is possible to advance understanding of actual processes of group decision making through an extension of the pure logic of choice applied to individual participants in these processes. In this approach, there need be no presumption that the collectivity, as such, maximizes anything, or indeed itself exists.

4.

The Normative Purpose of Economic "Science": Rediscovery of an Eighteenth Century Method

WITH GEOFFREY BRENNAN

"...for governments may be so formed, or laws so framed, as will necessarily produce virtue and make good ministers even of bad men."

Viscount Bolingbroke

I. Introduction

The necessity of abstraction is self-evident. By its very nature, intellectual activity involves coming to terms with a chaos of observations through the imposition of an order which is itself an artifact of the mental process. In this activity, a selective strategy must be used. Irrelevances must be blotted out, where these consist of observations that tend to disprove, qualify, or overly complicate the sought-for mental picture. Any theory is abstracted from the reality perceived by the senses, and theory derives its potential value precisely because it *is* so abstracted. From this perspective, it follows that any theory, any model, can, and indeed must, be able to tolerate a certain amount of dissonance with perception before it loses its relative superiority over potential alternatives.

This perspective suggests that there may well be many possible mental orders or constructs that can "explain" a particular set of "facts" within the tolerated range of "error." Which particular order is chosen depends on many elements, including the tastes of the analyst, intellectual habits and fashions of the times, and the extent of congruence with the reality that is perceived (congruence that embodies predictive power as an important part). We leave as basically "mysterious" the causal linkage between changes in these elements and a switching of mental orders (paradigms).

In this paper, we are interested in one particular abstraction, one that is familiar to all economists. We are concerned with the model of man that is used in economic theory—the model of man that actually takes its name from the discipline, *homo economicus*. Our purpose is to develop a specific justification for that abstraction that has not been sufficiently recognized by our fellow practitioners. In the exposition that follows we shall argue three propositions:

1. The purpose for which a theory is to be used is itself an important consideration in choosing how it should be formulated (that is, what abstractions are acceptable);

2. The purpose for which *homo economicus* was used in classical political economy was largely that of comparing the properties of alternative socioeconomic arrangements (constitutions) and not that of explaining "scientifically" (making predictions about) the behavior of economizing actors;

3. There are important differences between choices that are made among alternative institutions and choices made within the structure of given institutions, differences that are relevant to the nature of the assumptions about human motivation that might be viewed as appropriate.

Our objective is to spell out these propositions in such a way as to demonstrate that, appropriately understood, they provide a justification for the usage of *homo economicus* for comparative institutional analysis, even if the *homo economicus* behavioral postulate may be somewhat less satisfactory than possible alternatives in some predictive sense. In the discussion, we shall necessarily emphasize the differences between "constitutional choice" (the choice among institutions) and "postconstitutional or in-period choice" (the choice among alternative options within given institutions).

II. *Homo Economicus* Defined in Empirical "Economic Science"

There is a necessary distinction to be drawn between the formal, but empty, economic theory that incorporates a pure "logic of choice" on the part of the actors, and the allegedly operationally scientific theory or "economic science" that embodies empirically refutable hypotheses.[1] There is a corresponding distinction between the motivational postulates attributed to the human agents in the two constructions, between man as a rational utility maximizer, with the arguments in the utility functions remaining unspecified, and man as a net wealth maximizer, which requires explicit specification of the arguments in utility functions, and the assignment of predominant weights to those arguments that may readily be transformed into monetary wealth.[2]

If we define *homo economicus* in the second of these two senses we have a basis for empirical scientific explanation. Man, as modeled, acts so as to maximize his own interests (or the interests of those for whom he acts) objectively defined, in his economic relationships with other persons. He need not be inherently self-interested in some personalized sense. As Wicksteed noted, *"non-tuism"* is all that is required here.[3] In the interaction behavior that is to be modeled, man is postulated to further that interest which he represents. His behavior in the economic relationship is not influenced by ethical or moral considerations that serve to constrain his pursuit of his objectively defined interest. *Homo economicus,* by construction, is not predicted to act other than in furtherance of his interest, vis-à-vis that of his trading cohorts, as he evaluates such interest at the moment of choice. He must act so as to advance his own net wealth (or that of the party or parties that he represents in the economic interaction).

Armed with this behavioral postulate, we can test "economic theory" against real world observations, and, as the record shows, we can explain much of what we see. There are not clearly defined limits on this model of "economic man"; there is no delineation between "economic" behavior on the one hand and "noneconomic" behavior on the other. *Homo economicus* remains *homo economicus.*

It may be useful to list some extreme examples in which the basic economic or economizing model of interaction is extended to behavioral settings that may not normally be classified as "economic" in nature. For example, if a judge's behavior in his assigned occupational role is modeled strictly in *homo economicus* terms, his decisions on the bench must be explained somehow as falling within a wealth-maximizing calculus; similarly, for elected politicians and for bureaucrats. Parents' behavior toward their own children may be "explained" as down payments on reciprocal care in their dotage. Conscientiousness on the job may be interpreted in terms of the quest for promotion in a hierarchy. Honesty in business dealing is interpreted as the best policy to increase sales over the long term.

III. *Homo Economicus* as Abstraction

The first point to be made is to reemphasize that the *homo economicus* construction *is* an abstraction from reality. Its purpose is that of allowing economists to impose intellectual order on the observed chaos of human interaction, without excessive distracting detail in dimensions of the analysis that are not centrally relevant. Critics of economics may, with some legitimacy, think that economists do not recognize their own construction. There seems little doubt that there are economists, some of them influential within the profession, who do act and talk as if they think of *homo economicus* in much more descriptive ways. There are many economists who appear to think that the rarified *homo economicus* construction is, if not a perfect image of real man, at least sufficiently close so that no great violence is done by assuming that real man is actually *homo economicus*. And, these economists would argue, *homo economicus* is surely the "best" model of man that is available. In short, these economists defend the use of *homo economicus* on empirical, "scientific" grounds.

The methodological position alluded to here has been articulated by George Stigler in his 1980 Tanner lectures at Harvard University:

> Do people possess ethical beliefs which influence their behavior in ways not dictated by, and hence in conflict with, their own long-run utility-maximizing behavior? . . . This question of the existence of effective ethical value is, of course, an empirical question and in principle should be directly testable . . . . Let me predict the outcome of the systematic and comprehensive testing of behavior in situations where self-interest and ethical values with wide verbal allegiance are in conflict. Much of the time, most of the time in fact, the self-interest theory . . . will win. . . . I predict this result because it is the prevalent result found by economists not only within a wide range of economic phenomena, but in the investigations of marital, child-bearing, criminal, religious and other social behavior. We believe that man is a utility-maximizing animal . . . and to date we have not found it informative to carve out a section of his life in which he invokes a different goal of behavior.[4]

Or, as Stigler closes the lectures, he remarks:

> . . . I arrive at . . . the thesis that flows naturally and irresistibly from the theory of economics. Man is eternally a utility-maximizer—in his home, in his office (be it public or private), in his church, in his scientific work—in short, everywhere. He can and often does err: perhaps the calculation is too difficult, but more often his information is incomplete. He learns to correct these errors, although sometimes at heavy cost.
>
> What we call ethics, on this approach, is a set of rules with respect to dealings with other persons, rules which in general prohibit behavior which is only myopically self-serving, or which imposes large costs on others with small gains to oneself. General observance of these rules makes not only for long term gains to the actor but also yields some outside benefits, and the social approval of the ethics is a mild form of enforcement of the rules to achieve this general benefit.[5]

In Stigler's conception, *homo economicus* literally does become a man for all seasons, and wealth maximization becomes the only game in town. Yet there is surely much behavior that cannot be explained, or explained without resort to fantastic mental contortions,[6] if we adhere strictly to the assumptions of the severe economic-man construction.

As many persons have noted, and as Douglass North has emphasized, the scope for "free-riding" in human interaction is so ubiquitous that if men genuinely were as economic theory depicts them, no sort of ordered society, whether market-dominated or not, would be possible. In this basic sense, the very existence of an ordered society casts doubt on the *homo economicus* model of behavior, if used as some all-inclusive explanatory hypothesis. For example, people vote, yet a proper income or wealth maximizing calculus would necessarily classify the voting act as irrational in large number electorates. Economic theory cannot "explain" voting except in the tautological terms that the act of voting is a consumption activity, and must be so because people do it. Likewise, individuals exercise courtesy and compassion in circumstances where these traits yield no apparent benefits save those inherent in the acts themselves. People volunteer to fight for their tribe, community, or country and, in so doing, take on risks of death, when it would be conspicuously more self-serving to allow others to take on defensive roles. And, more importantly for North's ultimate purposes, no satisfactory account of history — and particularly judicial history — can ignore the influence of changing views about the world and what constitutes moral behavior in it, on the actual behavior of those who seem to have made the decisions that influenced the course of events.

We are not, of course, calling upon our fellow economists to drop *homo economicus* and assume, *volte face,* that persons are saints — that ethical, or generally, noneconomic, considerations dominate human motivations in behavioral settings that may or may not be narrowly "economic." Nor do we want to suggest that a mere demonstration that some course of action is "best" on moral grounds will be sufficient to convince persons to act in accordance with such a norm. Our plea is the more modest one that calls upon our fellow economists to recognize that *homo economicus* has its own limits as a useful abstraction. We can only load the construction with so much, and we stand in danger of having our whole "science" collapse in an absurd heap if we push beyond the useful limits. The fact that the whole set of "noneconomic" motivations are more difficult to model than the "economic" should not lead us to deny their existence.

We are not even suggesting that more effective predictions about behavior may be made by refining and tempering the abstraction of economic man. The loss of elegance and simplicity that would necessarily be involved in any such attempts might not be offset by marginal extensions in the accuracy of the "scientific" predictions. Our implied criticism of the over-extended usage of the *homo economicus* abstraction in trying to explain human behavior "scientifically" lies in our conviction that "scientific prediction," in the sense normally indicated, is *not* what our whole exercise is about and that this application is not the usage for which the abstraction was intended.

We suggest here an alternative usage of the *homo economicus* abstraction that seems more acceptable in all respects. In one sense, we offer a *methodological*, rather than a predictive ("scientific"), defense of the whole construction. Simply put, our claim is that *homo economicus* rightly belongs in the analytical derivation of normative propositions about appropriate institutional design. In other words, the model of human behavior that we might properly use in choosing among alternative institutions may be different from the model that would be more appropriate in making predictions about behavior within existing institutional structures.

At one level of analysis our claim is very simple: at another level, however, it requires a rather subtle understanding of the difference between constitutional and post-constitutional choice. Our argument is that the *homo economicus* construction supplies a postulate about human behavior that is in many ways uniquely suited for the comparative institutional analysis that underlies genuine constitutional choice.

IV. *Homo Economicus* and Constitutional Choice

As a point of departure, let us agree that whatever model of man is to be used in evaluating alternative social orders—alternative rules of the economic/political/social game—it must be applied *uniformly* over all the possibilities to be compared. Simple requirements of methodological consistency require this. If we are to employ one set of behavioral postulates for one institution, and another set for another institution, no legitimate comparison of the two institutions can be made. The ultimate purpose of the exercise is to choose among alternative sets of rules—not among alternative "models of man." We must therefore make a prior selection of a single model of man. Otherwise it becomes analytically impossible to isolate the effects of the institutions as such; the whole analysis is muddied by the arbitrary change in behavioral assumptions midstream.[7]

This is a simple point, and stated in this manner seems totally unexceptionable. Yet we know that it has proved in economics to be a curiously elusive one. The model of political process implicitly assumed in most orthodox discussion of economic policy has made profoundly different assumptions about individual behavior from the corresponding assumptions made in market settings. It has only been in the last twenty years with the burgeoning of public choice that this grotesque asymmetry has been exposed, and the "benevolent despot" model of politics been seriously queried.

But what is more important, because it may be less obvious, is that the methodological requirement of uniformity in the behavioral postulate *remains* even if there is good empirical evidence and analytical presumption that behavior may be different between different institutions. This is so because those differences in behavior have to be *shown* to be attributable to differences in institutions; and if a different model of human behavior is adopted for each institution at the outset, the relevant results will be simply assumed, not analytically *derived*.

A simple example may illustrate here. Suppose it is widely recognized by individual participants that the invisible hand operates in market processes to transform purely self-interested behavior into behavior in the interests of others. Suppose it is also recognized that no corresponding process operates in majoritarian political institutions. Then individuals may well behave in a totally self-interested manner in the market, precisely because the consequences of such behavior are desirable, yet at the same time operate in an ostensibly more altruistic manner in the political mechanism because the consequences of contrary behavior are much more disastrous. A rational actor who is only mildly altruistic might be predicted to behave more altruistically in the political setting than in the market: he "conserves" his altruism in the setting where it is least productive, and "spends" it in the political mechanism where it is more productive. This is the essence of the "economizing" on the scarce resource, love—which economizing, Sir Dennis Robertson reminds us, is the prime virtue of the freely operating market order.

Suppose for the purposes of argument that this behavioral asymmetry is observed. Then it may be tempting for the "scientific observer" simply to note the fact that political agents seem more altruistic than market agents, and model behavior in the two institutions accordingly. But this procedure precludes any proper *explanation* of why behavior may differ —an explanation which is possible only if we maintain the methodological assumption that human motivations are the same across institutions. Moreover, the "empirical" procedure may well lead to the conclusion that people would be more altruistic if we relied more heavily on political rather than market institutions to coordinate individual actions, whereas, of course, no such conclusion can be drawn from the model of behavioral choice as given in the preceding paragraph. On the contrary, heavier reliance on political institutions may simply destroy the incentives to behave altruistically at all.

To recapitulate, then, the requirement of a uniform model of human motivations is fundamental to proper institutional analysis, and remains so even in the face of empirical evidence that might suggest behavioral asymmetry. This requirement establishes a need for a *uniform* model of man—but not necessarily for *homo economicus* as such. What additional arguments can we bring to bear to support the use of this *particular* model of human behavior?

Our central argument here is simple. The question we are interested in posing about any particular social order is whether the rules by which individual actions are coordinated are such as to transform actions undertaken by participants in their own *private* interests into outcomes that are in the interests of others. We know that this curious alchemy is in fact worked by the *market* – that the invisible hand operates, under certain more or less well-defined conditions, to convert private interest into public interest. The prime task of comparative institutional analysis is to inquire whether other institutions do the same, and, if so, whether those institutions do so under more or less restrictive conditions. The only assumption required to make this task an interesting one is the assumption that some individuals behave in their narrowly defined private interest at least some of the time. Clearly, if we lived in a world in which all individuals were motivated solely by a concern for the public interest – for example, a world of pure Kantians or Benthamite utilitarians, for whom each individual's own utility counts in determining his behavior no more and no less than anyone else's – then we should hardly be interested in whether the institutional structure served to transfer private interest into public interest or not: no distinction between private and public interest would make sense.[8] In this sense, the minimal agreement that the "invisible hand" mechanism is, *ceteris paribus,* a *virtue* in any social order is tantamount to setting aside as remote the possibility that *all* people are motivated by the public interest *all* the time. Further and more importantly for our purposes, in establishing whether any particular social order has this particular virtue, we can usefully abstract from public motivations entirely. In order to show that private interest is transformed into collective interest, we begin naturally by assuming agents to be privately motivated. If they happen to be publicly motivated *in part,* results may or may not be better: but it simply does not bear on the analysis whether they are so motivated. What is crucial is that *such privately motivated behavior as exists* is converted into public interest outcomes. To assume that private interest is all that makes men tick is simply to focus on what is relevant for the exercise in hand.

In short, then, the question of whether *homo economicus* is a good approximation to empirical reality determines the *significance* of the exercise of institutional comparison, but not the appropriate *method.* The invisible hand is doubtless a more spectacular virtue in a world where self-seeking behavior is more, rather than less, prevalent. But whether institutions other than the market may exhibit an invisible hand mechanism and under what circumstances, are matters that can only be established by examining the implications of self-seeking behavior within those institutions: to examine the implications of non-self-seeking behavior for such a purpose is manifestly absurd.

A simple example may help to elucidate here. Suppose you are hiring a builder to build you a house. In selecting from among available builders, you will take a number of things into account—his general competence, his conscientiousness, his honesty. The latter characteristic is important because you will not normally want to deal with a builder who you seriously believe is likely to fleece you. For empirical purposes, therefore, the assumption you will make about the said builder is that he is honest: you would not deal with him if you genuinely believed otherwise. But now you proceed to your lawyer's office to draw up a contract. And in this setting, the working hypothesis you make about the builder is quite different. For the contract-drawing exercise, you make the assumption that the builder *is* going to fleece you, not because you believe this necessarily is his objective but because this is the contingency against which you wish to guard. The nature of the exercise leads you, in other words, to make an assumption about human motivations that you believe may be (and certainly hope will be) a poor reflection of empirical reality.[9]

In constitutional design, and in comparative institutional analysis more generally, one's particular beliefs about what model of man is empirically most descriptive are less relevant in precisely the same way and for much the same reason. One calls forth the *homo economicus* assumption, not because it is necessarily the most accurate model of human behavior but because it is the appropriate model for testing whether institutions serve to transform private interest into public. It is as simple as that.

To avoid some possible misunderstanding, we should perhaps emphasize that, in the content of constitutional design, the notion of *homo economicus* can be broadened somewhat beyond the confines of the definition used widely in "economic science" (as described in Section II). For the purposes of predictive science, the elements in individual utility functions must be specified in clear, recognizable, and measurable terms. Application of the *homo economicus* construction for empirical or predictive purposes requires something like the assumption of net wealth maximization as a surrogate for maximization of consumption more broadly conceived. For the purposes of constitutional design, however, *homo economicus* can be seen to maximize almost anything at all, providing each individual conceives of others as operating without his interest in mind. That is, all that we require is that each individual, in choosing a set of rules, models the motivations of others vis-à-vis himself in such a way that *excludes* their inclusion of his own interests or well-being in their utility functions. *This* version of the *homo economicus* model in no sense rules out the possibility that each individual may be motivated by certain ethical or moral concerns, as long as we can take it that such ethical conduct on the part of anyone cannot be presumed to benefit everyone else. Burning people at the stake in order to secure for them better claims on eternal life is, for example, perfectly consistent with *homo economicus* assumptions at the constitutional level.

For the purposes of constitutional design, then, no specification of arguments in *homo economicus* utility function is required: the narrowly defined *homo economicus* of predictive science and the more open-ended construction in which the utility function includes any arguments other than the well-being of the chooser, become *methodologically equivalent.*

An example may be helpful here. Suppose that a person is considered to be examining the working properties of an institution that would grant some other persons (say, an appointed "governor") the power to tax, with accompanying coercive enforcement. So long as the potential chooser models the behavior of the "governor" so as to exclude his own (the chooser's) interests, the constitutional calculus remains the same whether the "governor" is modeled as using tax revenues for financing a private harem or for providing transfers to other persons in the community, or for any other purpose in which the chooser expects to have no interest.

It may be useful to summarize the argument to this point. We have insisted that the model of man to be used in comparative institutional analysis, whatever its precise characteristics, must for analytic reasons be uniform across institutions. And we have insisted that such uniformity must be maintained even in the face of empirical evidence to the contrary. We have argued further that the specific model of human motivations to be used in comparative institutional analysis must emphasize private interest as the prime motivating force, because the specific issue we are interested in examining at this level is whether alternative institutional rules are such as to convert *private motivations* into publicly desired actions. To the extent that the assumption of public motivation is included in the behavioral model, we come close to simply assuming what we wish to prove. We have termed this model of man, *homo economicus,* consistent with classical usage: it is, however, somewhat less restrictive a model of man than the net wealth-maximizing model used extensively in economic science.

This argument is, as we see it, complete. There is, however, a complementary line of reasoning that is worth mention here. It runs as follows. For the purposes of economic science, the model of man to be used is the one that gives the best "fit," the most reliable set of predictions about the effects of particular changes in parameters. What is required for such purposes is a model of the "average" or "representative" man. In constitutional choice analysis, however, we seek a model of man which is a "*weighted* average man," where the weights at stake involve the costs that various types impose on the social fabric.

Consider a simple example. Suppose we postulate a world in which half the individuals are Kantians and half are *homines economici*. Suppose that the citizenry in this world is examining the costs and benefits of alternative restrictions on the behavior of a dictator whose identity, and hence personality type, is presumed unknown. Clearly, a truly Kantian dictator will impose relatively little in costs upon those who are subject to his rule. A purely self-interested dictator on the other hand can be expected to impose enormously high costs on his subjects. For this reason, in any rational constitutional calculus, the model of man presumed will be much closer to the self-interest model than mere empirics might indicate. And this does not presuppose any particular risk-aversion on the part of the individual choosing constitutional restrictions. Clearly a risk-*neutral* individual will take into account the expected costs associated with dictators of different personality type; and the whole calculus will naturally be weighted towards a consideration of those cases in which most is at stake. The self-interest postulate takes on a significance in the constitutional setting, therefore, that it essentially lacks in its "scientific" or strictly predictive setting. *Homo economicus* is alive and well, and living in the analytical foundations of constitutional choice—his natural homeland.

V. *Homo Economicus* in Classical Political Economy

We consider our argument in this paper to be directly within the tradition of classical political economy. Modern economists can still learn much from the methods of the eighteenth-century philosophers, such as Mandeville, Hume, and, particularly, Adam Smith. Their reflections led them to the recognition that the peculiar alchemy of the market order allows the transformation of private interest into "public interest." Individuals with no concerns beyond their own net wealth could, by virtue of the invisible hand of the market, be induced to act as if they were furthering the interests of others than themselves. Adam Smith's butcher could be recognized to be acting in the interests of his customers without one whit of concern for their welfare. It is not required of Smith's butcher that he have no direct concern for his customers; he may well have had such concern. The significant thing is that we do *not* require him to have such a concern in his utility function; and we do not model him as having such a concern when we compare the market with alternative institutional arrangements.

It is in this cradle that *homo economicus* was nurtured. He was a creation for a purpose—this being the demonstration of the virtues of the free market as an institutional order. Smith makes it clear that *homo economicus* is not to be conceived as a generalized *description* of human nature. "Humanity does not desire to be great" (or, we may add, to be rich) "but to be loved".[10] And no one who has looked at the first pages of *The Theory of Moral Sentiments* can deny Smith's belief in the ubiquity of sympathy. Nonetheless, if one wishes to examine the extent to which a particular institutional order transforms private interest into public interest, it becomes entirely appropriate to focus on a model of man in which private interest predominates. To model man as publicly motivated in making such a comparison would be to assume away the problem that institutional design involves — the problem that was central to Smith's purpose.

In comparative institutional analysis, and ultimately in constitutional design, one calls forth *homo economicus,* not for its accuracy in prediction, but for its assistance in helping to identify and to classify patterns of outcomes attributable directly to institutional differences. The central contribution of the eighteenth-century philosophers lay in their demonstration that, even under strictly *homo economicus* assumptions about behavior, public interest is served by the market order. No such demonstration can be made with respect to alternative arrangements.

The imputation of *homo economicus* motivation to actors in political roles may seem to violate ordinary notions about descriptive reality more than the comparable imputation to actors in the marketplace. But this difference need not provide any justification for replacing the model used for institutional comparison. It may be that judges seek to "uphold the law" most of the time, that most government employees try to further their own conceptions of "public interest" most of the time, and that elected politicians are genuinely concerned about promoting the "good society." But, even if this were admitted, institutional arrangements would surely be preferred which made these congruent with narrow self-interest on the part of the relevant actors. A model of human behavior in which the natural impulse toward self-interest, narrowly defined, predominates is a highly useful artifact in helping us to identify that set of arrangements that "economize on love."

John Stuart Mill stated the point well:

> The very principle of constitutional government requires it to be assumed that political power will be abused to promote the particular purposes of the holder; not because it is always so, but because such is the natural tendency of things to guard against which is the special use of free institutions.[11]

We might add that what goes for political power goes for market power also, but this point hardly seems necessary. The *market* aspects of this truth have long since been widely recognized and accepted, which makes the continuing neglect (perhaps even denial) of the political aspects even more surprising.

VI. *Homo Economicus* and Public Choice

In our book, *The Power to Tax*,[12] we incorporated a theory of political process in which the *homo economicus* construction was allowed full play. Many of the modern developments in public choice theory can also be interpreted as variations on what might be called the *homo economicus* model of politics.

In developing our approach to taxation, and particularly in attacking the benevolent despot model of politics that has for so long monopolized orthodox economic policy debates, we have been subjected to understandable criticism. The argument has been consistently made that politics is simply not like our models of it, that the application of the *homo economicus* model to political processes does little more than expose our own disciplinary hubris. At the same time, some critics who are generally sympathetic to our approach have sought to defend our position on the grounds that politics is indeed "like that," like our models of it, and so, indeed, is every aspect of human behavior. Our growing reluctance to support this latter ("Stiglerian") defense of our position has been met with some shock and sometimes resentment from some of our colleagues. But the battle over the empirical status of *homo economicus* is *not,* in our view, the crucial issue at all. On empirical grounds, we are surely closer to Adam Smith than to our modern critics, whichever side those critics come from. We admit freely the possibility and indeed the likelihood of non-self-seeking behavior by human agents in all institutional settings. But like Adam Smith, we believe that *homo economicus* remains the appropriate model of behavior in the derivation of normative propositions about the institutions themselves.

There is no inconsistency here. Nor is there any retreat from positions we have taken earlier. The appropriate use of the narrowly "economic" model depends on a prior understanding of what the model is to be used for. And although *homo economicus* may be a useful tool in providing a superior set of hypotheses about political behavior—behavior within well-defined rules—than much of traditional political science has appeared to offer, this is not to argue that it is *the* most useful model of man for such explanatory or predictive purposes, or that there is not much that such a model fails to explain. The level of discourse at which the *homo economicus* construction seems uniquely appropriate is the constitutional level, and this may remain true even if the construction does not give precisely the "best" empirical fit.

Notes

This paper was originally prepared for a Liberty Fund Conference on "Science and Freedom" held in San Antonio, Texas in March, 1981. We are grateful to participants in that conference—particularly David Levy, Brian Loasby, Richard McKenzie, and Karen Vaughn—and to our colleague Bob Tollison for useful comments. Several improvements were also suggested by helpful referees. Remaining errors are our own responsibility. The epigraph is from the *Craftsman* (February 28, 1730), as cited by Duncan Forbes in *Hume's Philosophical Politics* (Cambridge: Cambridge University Press, 1975), p. 199.

1. J. M. Buchanan, "Is Economics the Science of Choice?", *Roads to Freedom,* ed. E. Streissler (Routledge and Kegan Paul, 1969), pp. 47–64.

2. In making this two-part distinction, we are "passing over" the in-between postulate, one that involves specification of the arguments in the utility function of persons, but which does not assign weights. In this in-between setting, there remains scope for positive prediction; for example, if we know that some argument, X, is valued positively in the utility function, we can predict that more X will be chosen as the relative cost of X falls. However, note that X may be "giving to others" or anything else. In other words, we do not require net wealth maximization as a behavioral postulate in order to have a "scientific" economics. For further discussion, see J. M. Buchanan, "Professor Alchian on Economic Method," *Freedom in Constitutional Contract* (College Station: Texas A&M University Press, 1978).

3. P. H. Wicksteed, *The Commonsense of Political Economy* (London: Macmillan, 1910).

4. By "utility-maximizing" behavior, Stigler means self-serving behavior, with some allowance for altruism within the family and among close friends. He is careful to distinguish this usage from the purely tautological use of utility maximization as in a pure logic of choice. G. Stigler, "The Economist as Preacher," Tanner Lecture II delivered at Harvard University, April 1980, pp. 23–24.

5. G. Stigler, "The Economist as Preacher," three Tanner Lectures delivered at Harvard University, April 1980.

6. Our colleague, David Friedman, one time in conversation explained the fact that individuals marry those who love them, on the grounds that this procedure reduces monitoring costs in household production processes. This sort of explanation makes creative use of the *homo economicus* model, but its empirical accuracy may seem questionable and it also tends to shift the model toward a pure logic of choice, albeit in a novel manner.

7. We need not argue here that institutions do not affect tastes—although such an argument is implicit in much of the neoclassical tradition. Even where preferences can be shown to be endogenous (i.e., influenced by the institutional environment), the model of man upon which the institutions exercise their influences must be the same *at the outset.* In what follows, however, we ignore the question of the influence institutions may have on tastes per se and focus on the effects of rules on the costs and benefits to the individual of alternative courses of action.

8. Of course, institutions may still be compared, but by reference to other criteria. For example, even in this world of publicly motivated individuals there is the question of how those individuals obtain the *information* necessary to enable them to act in accordance with their assumed norms. Interestingly enough, the market has virtues in this area as well, a point emphasized strongly by Hayek. See F. A. Hayek, "The Use of Knowledge in Society," *American Economic Review* 35 (1945), pp. 519–30. With imperfect information, it is reasonable to expect that perceptions of the "public interest" will differ. Then one can and must distinguish between the explicit private pursuit of public interest, and the emergence of "optimal" outcomes as an "unintended consequence" of the interactions within the institutional structure.

9. It could of course be argued (as a referee has done) that the contract-drawing exercise is based on uncertainty about the morality of alternative builders and that contract drawing is a *cheaper* way of saving on transactions costs than acquiring additional information.

Analogously, choosing the institutional structure to guard against the abuse of power may be looked on as a cheaper way of ensuring tolerable outcomes than acquiring information about which individuals are sufficiently benevolent to be entrusted with political power.

10. A. Smith, *The Theory of Moral Sentiments* (Liberty Classics, Liberty Press, 1976), p. 30.

11. John Stuart Mill, on "Representative Government" in *Essays on Politics and Society*, vol. 19, *Collected Works*, p. 505.

12. G. Brennan and J. Buchanan, *The Power to Tax: Analytic Foundations of a Fiscal Constitution* (Cambridge University Press, 1980).

5.

The Domain of Subjective Economics: Between Predictive Science and Moral Philosophy

> "We . . . are in part living in a world the constituents of which we can discover, classify and act upon by rational, scientific . . . methods; but in part . . . we are immersed in a medium that . . . we do not and cannot observe as if from the outside; cannot identify, measure, and seek to manipulate; cannot even be wholly aware of, inasmuch as it . . . is itself too closely interwoven with all that we are and do to be lifted out . . . and observed with scientific detachment, as an object."
>
> Isaiah Berlin

I. Introduction

Any discussion of the methodology of subjective economics must at once confront an elementary fact along with a necessary hypothesis. That fact is that, in any science of human behavior, the observer is himself among the observed. The hypothesis is that human beings *choose*. Without this hypothesis the activity of the observer becomes meaningless exercise. The fact and the accompanying hypothesis impose constraints or limits on any "positive economics," if the model is taken from those sciences within which these attributes are missing. The natural scientist remains separate from the objects of his observation, and, despite the acknowledgment of the possibility of mutual influence between observer and observed, there remains the basic category differentiation. Furthermore, the simple ability to put these words together in a meaningful sentence distinguishes me, as a man, from those objects of science that most resemble me, the higher animals. By the process of writing a sentence, I am choosing what

I create; I am not merely reacting to external stimuli, at least in a sense readily amenable to prediction.

In summary terms, the *subjective* elements of our discipline are defined precisely within the boundaries between the positive, predictive science of the orthodox model on the one hand and the speculative thinking of moral philosophy on the other—hence, the chapter's title. For our purposes, I define *moral philosophy* as discourse that embodies an explicit denial of the relevance of scientific explanation. Note that this approach does not require a categorical rejection of the relevance of empirically testable, positive hypotheses concerning certain aspects of human behavior commonly labeled "economic." Nor does the approach rule out the relevance of normative moral philosophy. The approach emphasizes, instead, the existence and the importance of the area between empirical science and moral philosophy. It denies that these categories of thought span the universe of relevance. On this point, I think that my own professor, Frank Knight, and Ludwig von Mises would have been in substantial agreement. Both would have been extremely critical of the modern economists who seek to rule out any nonempirical economics as nonscientific and, by inference, normative. Both these seminal thinkers would have been comfortable with a science of subjective economics, although they might have differed somewhat on the relevance of any other part of our discipline.

II. Adam Smith and Classical Economics

Classical economics has been almost universally interpreted as an attempted, and ultimately failed, effort to derive an objective and predictive theory of the relative values of commodities. The central features are perhaps best exemplified in Adam Smith's famous deer-beaver illustration, which I shall use here. Smith's hypothesis was that one beaver would "naturally" exchange for two deer in that setting where two days of labor are required to kill a beaver and one day of labor to kill a deer. I want to ask the following question: Even if we grant all the required presuppositions of the Smith model, do we then derive a genuinely predictive theory of the relative values of beaver and deer? Or do there remain necessarily subjective elements in the inclusive explanatory model, even within such an extremely restricted setting?

The required presuppositions are familiar. Deer and beaver must be "goods" to all potential consumers and producers: labor must be a "bad." Labor is the only productive resource, and units of labor are completely homogeneous. Further, each commodity must be producible at constant returns. But we must recall that Adam Smith was seeking to explain *exchange* values. The restrictions of the model, even if fully realized, do not explain the emergence of exchange, and, in the strict sense, no exchange would take place in the setting postulated. If the input ratio is two for one, precepts for rationality suggest that each behaving unit will attain an equilibrium adjustment when the two-for-one ratio is equated to a two-for-one valuation ratio for the two goods. There is no subjective element in the analysis, as I have deliberately limited the scope for the term *subjective* here.

Adam Smith and classical economics were not, however, interested in explaining individual behavioral adjustment. Smith was interested in explaining *exchange* values. And, to explain these, he had to explain the emergence of exchange itself. To do so, he must have incorporated an additional presupposition not listed. The productivity of labor when specialized must be higher than when unspecialized. Smith's emphasis on the importance of the division of labor suggests, of course, that this presupposition was indeed central to his explanatory model. But why would exchange emerge in the first place? Here Smith resorted to man's "propensity to truck, barter, and exchange one thing for another."[1] The critical role of this propensity in Smith's analysis has been too much neglected in interpretations of his work. But with this propensity, Smith places a subjective element at the heart of the whole explanatory model. He quite explicitly contrasts the actions of man with the animals in this respect when he says that "nobody ever saw a dog make a fair and deliberate exchange of one bone for another with another dog."[2]

In some preexchange setting, the exercise of the "propensity to truck" — behavior that must necessarily have been different in kind from that which had been reflected in established patterns (and, hence, predictable scientifically, at least within stochastic limits) — allowed man to discover the advantages of specialization and to create the institutions of exchange within which relative values of commodities come to be settled. The person who initially imagines some postspecialization, postexchange state and who acts to bring such a state into existence must engage in what I shall here call "active" choice. He must do more than respond predictably to shifts in the constraints that are exogenously imposed on him.

An economy (if indeed it could be called such) in which all persons respond to constraints passively and in which no one engages in active choice could never organize itself through exchange institutions. Such an economy would require that the constraints be imposed either by nature or by beings external to the community of those participants who are the passive responders. In either case, such an economy would be comparable in kind to those whose participants are the "animal consumers" examined by John Kagel and Raymond Battalio, and their coworkers.[3]

Even at the level of Adam Smith's most elementary discourse, there are two interpretations that may be placed on his analysis. If Smith is read as relatively unconcerned about the emergence of exchange institutions, and if he is assumed simply to have postulated the existence of specialization, it may be argued that his aim was to present a positive, predictive theory of the relative values of commodities. On the other hand, if Smith is read as primarily or centrally concerned with explaining how exchange institutions emerge, he becomes a thoroughgoing subjectivist in that he resorts to that particular propensity that distinguishes man from other animals. There could be no predictive science concerning the exercise of this propensity, since to predict here would imply that the direction of all future exchanges would be conceptually knowable at any point in time.

The two interpretations of Smith's basic analysis differ in their *explananda*. The first involves an explanation, or attempted explanation, of relative exchange values of commodities. The second involves an explanation of exchange institutions themselves. That which can be predicted (conceptually) can be explained with an objective or scientific theory. That which cannot be predicted can be explained (understood) only by a subjective theory. If this basic methodological duality had been accepted at the outset, much confusion in the history of economic doctrine, then and now, might have been avoided. Subjective economics, properly, even if strictly, defined, occupies an explanatory realm that is mutually exclusive with that properly occupied by positive economics. If this much is granted, however, the relative significance of the two realms of discourse for the inclusive understanding of human interaction becomes clear. Positive or predictive economics becomes largely exercise in triturating the obvious; subjective economics can offer insights into the dynamics through which a society of persons who remain free to choose in a genuine sense develops and prospers.

In this article, I shall illustrate this basic argument by reference to somewhat misguided and at least partially confused efforts to emphasize the subjective elements in economic theory, broadly defined. I shall discuss the so-called subjective-value revolution and its transformation into the modern neoclassical synthesis. I shall discuss also the dimensionality of economic theory to show that the dimensionality problem should be considered separately from that of operationality of theory. A discussion of the particular Austrian variant of neoclassical economics, as exemplified notably in the works of Mises, follows with particular emphasis on his insistence of the praxeological foundations of the discipline. The following section discusses the potential applicability of subjective and objective economic theory, and I shall offer a provisional explanation for the relative dominance of the latter in the postclassical century. Finally, I shall summarize the argument and draw some inferences for the direction of research.

III. The Subjective-Value Revolution of the 1870s and the Subsequent Neoclassical Synthesis

As noted previously, classical economic theory was widely interpreted as an attempt to derive a predictive theory of the relative values of commodities.[4]

Classical economics was acknowledged to have failed in such an attempt. Emphasis came to be placed on the specific difficulties that could not be satisfactorily met with the classical models. The diamond-water paradox remained; the classical effort to explain relative exchange value by objectively measurable costs of production could not survive.

The so-called subjective-value revolution, presented in various ways in the early 1870s by Jevons, Menger, and Walras, was explicitly aimed at resolution of the prevailing difficulties in the classical explanation of exchange values. The early contributions here demonstrated that relative values depend on schedules of evaluation on both sides of the markets for goods, on demand and supply. But we must ask a question here that has not, to my knowledge, been frequently posed. To what extent does the economic theory of Jevons, Menger, and Walras, or their neoclassical successors, embody genuine subjective economics as I have defined this term? Despite its label as the subjective-value revolution in economic theory, are there any necessarily subjective elements in the inclusive explanatory models that were offered in place of the discarded classical edifice?

I suggest that the label *subjective* may be misleading in application to this theory of exchange values, notably so as the initial contributions were redeveloped and refined into the neoclassical synthesis of the twentieth century. The marginal-utility theory of the 1870s embodied the central notion that values are determined at the appropriate margins of evaluation and that the locations of the margins are relevant. The diamond-water paradox was thereby resolved satisfactorily. But there is nothing in the whole analytical framework here to suggest that the evaluation schedules (those of demand and supply), which simultaneously interact to determine the location of the margins and hence exchange values, are not, themselves, *objectively determinate,* at least in a conceptual sense. There is nothing in neoclassical economic theory that precludes the universalized existence of simple reaction patterns of behavior on the part of all persons in the economy, reaction patterns that, even if more complex, are still analogous to those that might empirically describe the behavior of rats. Once individual-utility functions are formally specified, individuals whose behavior is thereby depicted cannot choose differently. Choice, as such, cannot remain in any such formulation.

I am not suggesting here that the objectification of the solution to the problem of determining relative exchange values of goods (and bads) was necessarily central to neoclassical theory. It was not. The earlier classical effort was aimed to provide a single, and simplistic, objective measure of relative exchange values that might be both readily understood and empirically estimated. The neoclassical effort, in contrast, was primarily aimed at resolving difficulties at the level of logical coherence and rigor. There was a shift of emphasis from attempts to provide empirical bases for measurement toward attempts to offer understanding of the whole logical structure of economic interaction. For the latter purpose, the issues involved in making empirical estimates or predictions about relative exchange values do not take on critical significance. These issues tend to be overshadowed by those concerning the derivations of proofs of the existence of solutions to the complex interdependencies that the economy embodies. That the empirical measurability or predictability of exchange values does not occupy center stage in orthodox neoclassical theory should not, however, be taken as evidence that, conceptually, such measurability is categorically impossible. The focus of neoclassical economic theory, in comparison with classical, is shifted from empirical estimates to analyses of structures, but there is nothing directly in neoclassical theory that implies the absence of conceptual predictability. If utility and production relationships are ascertainable, solutions exist and are determinate. It is meaningful in this context to make an attempt to compute equilibrium prices.

IV. The Dimensionality and Data of Economic Theory

My purpose in this section is to clarify possible confusion and ambiguity that may arise from my somewhat restricted definition of subjective economics and from my claim that the term subjective-value revolution as applied to the contribution of the 1870s, may be, in this context, misleading.

It is necessary to distinguish carefully between the definition of the dimensions of the space within which the operations of economic theory are performed and the operationality of the theory itself. My narrowly restricted definition of subjective economic theory is relevant only to the second of these subjects. As I have limited the term here, subjective economic theory embodies those elements of explanation of the economic process that cannot be operationalized in the orthodox sense of predictive science. For those elements of economic theory that can be operationalized, however, I have advanced no presumption whatever about the dimensionality of the space.

Confusion necessarily arises at this point between the claim that any economic theorizing must take place within a subjective-value dimension and the totally different claim that, because of the subjective dimensionality, an operational theory is not possible. The first of these claims must be accepted. Economic theory is surely concerned with evaluations, with values. It is totally misleading to think of physical dimensionality here. Goodness and badness are qualities that are assigned to physical things, to commodities or services, by personal evaluations.

The naive and simplistic efforts by the classical economists to derive a predictive theory of relative exchange values tended to obscure the value dimension and generated the absurdity that commodities may be produced by commodities, somehow independently of the evaluation put on these by persons. In the sense that it emphasized and brought to full realization the essential value dimension, it is appropriate to label the 1870s effort as a subjective-value revolution. But, as I have noted, this corrective shift in implied dimensionality of the space for the application of economic theory carries with it no direct implication for the potential operationality of the theory itself. Indirectly, of course, there is the obvious implication that only if economic theory applies within a value dimension could there arise any issue of nonoperationality. Subjective economics could hardly be discussed in any analysis of variables in pure-commodity space. On the other hand, however, there is nothing in the value dimension itself that logically prohibits the derivation of a fully operational science. Whether or not such analysis is possible depends not on dimensionality but instead on the possible uniformity of valuations over persons.

A related source of confusion involves the informational requirements that a thoroughgoing recognition of the value dimensionality of economics places on any putative scientist who seeks to derive empirically testable hypotheses. F. A. Hayek, in particular, has emphasized the value dimensionality of economic theory and the informational implications of this attribute for the organization of society.[5] Markets utilize information efficiently; they do not require extensive centralization of information about individual evaluations. And, indeed, the informational requirements for a centrally planned economy may be practically insurmountable. There is nothing in the basic Hayekian insight, however, that precludes the possible derivation of a set of conceptually refutable hypotheses about the evaluations of all persons over all goods and services.

In earlier works I have stressed the subjectivity of costs, and I have tried to show how errors arise in applications of economic theory when this basic dimensionality is overlooked.[6] In the restricted classification scheme that I have suggested in this article, however, there is nothing in my analysis of cost, as such, that precludes the derivation of a set of conceptually refutable hypotheses, which is, of course, the criterion of a predictive theory. Costs are, of course, related to choices, but if there are sufficient data on the environment of a past choice and if the chooser's behavior is, in some sense, predictable on the basis of observed uniformities, choices may be judged ex post facto. Practically, the subjective-value dimension of economic behavior may make enforcement of any cost-price rule impossible, but such application of the predictive science cannot be deemed conceptually impossible.

VI. Mises and Praxeology

Mises explicitly denied that economic theory can be operational in the orthodox meaning of this term. Economic theory was, for Mises, necessarily a priori; it offered a pure logic of choice. In taking this extreme position methodologically, Mises seemed to be aware that attempts to force economic theory into the straitjacket imposed by the requirements for predictive science must, at the same time, deny to persons who act the possibility of making genuine choices.

I shall confess here that I have never been able to appreciate fully the Misesian emphasis on praxeology or "the science of human action."[7] Central to this conception is the purposefulness of all human action. Man acts always with a purpose; he seeks to replace a state of relative dissatisfaction with one of relative satisfaction. However, an observer can never get inside anyone else; he can never know what a person's purpose is. Hence, there is no way, even conceptually, to predict what action will be taken in any particular circumstance. A person chooses that which he chooses, and when he so chooses, he must anticipate that the chosen course of action will yield a net increment to his satisfaction. Although he may err, we can never infer, ex post facto, that he acted irrationally.

At its most general, this Misesian theory of choice is totally nonoperational. It can "explain" any conceivable course of action that a person might be observed to take; the obverse is, of course, that the theory can really "explain" nothing at all. Mises himself did not worry about nonoperationality as such, presumably because his reliance on introspection provided him with a basis for sorting out meaningful from meaningless explanations. To return to the Adam Smith illustration, Mises could claim to have explained why exchange institutions emerged from the vision of some person who imagined the mutual advantages of specialization and exchange. Mises could also explain the relative values of deer and beaver quite simply as those exchange ratios that emerge from the purposeful choice behavior of participants in the exchange process, whose acts of participation or nonparticipation are themselves purposeful.

Misesian economic theory becomes strictly subjective economics in my earlier definition of the term. But my basic criticism of Mises is that he claimed far too much for the subjective-economics domain. He seemed to want to preempt the whole territory when he totally rejected the existence of any relevant domain for what I have called positive or predictive objective economic theory. This somewhat overzealous extension of methodological frontiers may be at least partially responsible for the relatively limited reception that the ideas of Mises have had among economists, catholically classified.

The basic Mises conception of praxeology seems flawed in that it appears to incorporate two quite distinct sorts of human action, one of which may be analyzed scientifically and empirically in the orthodox sense. Consider two examples: (1) A man is walking along a road; he sees a car approaching; he jumps to the side of the road to avoid being run down. His action here is purposeful. It is surely aimed at removing a potential state of dissatisfaction and replacing it by one that is preferred. (2) A man is walking along a road barefooted. His feet are sore. He sees some cowhide and he imagines the possibility of shoes. He acts to make the shoes from cowhide. (My thanks to Israel Kirzner for this example.) This action is purposeful, and it, like the first, is surely aimed at replacing a state of dissatisfaction (sore feet) with one that is preferred.

But Misesian praxeology, as I understand it, would seem to include both examples within the realm of human action that theory seeks to analyze and to explain. I submit, however, that they are categorically distinct. The first action need not reflect conscious, active, or creative choice; it can be interpreted as an animal-like response to a change in the external environment. It is reflective of behavior that might have been scientifically predicted. It is the sort of action that could describe the behavior of rats as well as men. By evident and sharp contrast, an animal could never take the second sort of creative action, which becomes uniquely human.[8] The Misesian praxeological umbrella that seems to encompass both sorts of action does not allow the sophisticated discrimination that must be made between the two. Indeed the Misesian emphasis on treating all human action as if it were like the second example tends to foster a critical response that involves the danger of neglect of the very type of action that subjective economics properly emphasizes.[9]

VII. The Mutually Exclusive Domains for Economic Theory

There are patterns of human behavior in economic interaction that are subject to conceptual prediction about which empirically testable hypotheses may be derived. There is a legitimate domain for predictive economic theory. Or, to put my point differently but somewhat more dramatically, in some aspects of their economic behavior, with appropriate qualifications, men are indeed like rats.[10] They are essentially passive responders to economic stimuli; they react; they do not choose. They are programmed, whether genetically or culturally, to behave in potentially predictable ways to specific modifications in the constraints that they face. The scope for this predictive theory of economic behavior is enormously extended when it is acknowledged that it is the behavior of some average or representative member of a group that is to be predicted here, not the particularized behavior of an individual.

The recognition of the domain of an operationally meaningful economic theory does not carry with it any implication concerning the practical usefulness of this theory in making predictions in the real world and/or in using such predictions to control man's behavior in that reality. There remains the awesome gap between the science that embodies conceptually refutable hypotheses and that science that embodies definitive refutation or corroboration. The familiar distinctions between the human and the nonhuman sciences involving controls on experiments arise here, along with the informational problems noted briefly earlier. Nonetheless, ultimate empirical content remains in the theory, regardless of actual testability, and the elaboration of the structure of relationships can add to our understanding of economic reality.

There are also aspects of human action that cannot be subjected to explanation in an operationally meaningful theory of economics. Any attempt to derive even conceptually refutable hypotheses about such action would amount to epistemological confusion. I have labeled this domain that of subjective economics or subjective economic theory. The objects for analysis are the *choices* of persons, which cannot be genuine choices and at the same time subject to prediction. Theory or analysis can be of explanatory value in this domain without the attribute of operationality in the standard sense. Theory can add to our understanding *(verstehen)* of the process through which the economic world of values is created and transformed. Subjective economics offers a way of thinking about economic process, a means of imposing an intellectual order on apparent chaos without inferentially reducing the status of man, as a scientific object, to something that is not, in kind, different from that of animals.[11]

The limits of this vision of economic process must be recognized, however, along with its advantageous insights. Subjective economic theory can be of little assistance in an explanation or understanding of the allocation of values or in predicting general responses to changes in constraints imposed on actors. Since this theory advances no claim to prediction, it can, at best, suggest that any predictions made will likely prove to be wrong, indeed must be wrong to the extent that its own domain of choice is allowed operative range.

The purpose of the explanatory exercise determines the appropriate domain of economic theory to be employed. If this purpose is that of control of the economy through some manipulation of the constraints within which persons respond, the first domain of positive, predictive economic theory is the only one that holds out any scope for assistance. To the extent that this theory can isolate predicted response patterns to shifts in imposed constraints (to an increase or decrease in taxes, for example), those persons who participate in making political decisions (who may, of course, also be members of the group whose reaction behavior is being predicted by the economists) make their choices among alternative constraints on the basis of better information. The predictions of the economists have value, and this value commands a price. It is, therefore, not at all surprising that the efforts of economists shifted toward the predictive-science domain during the century-long period of increasing controls over national economies. Faith in the efficacy of such predictive science for assistance in controlling the economy perhaps reached its apogee in the 1960s, after which skepticism emerged from its dormancy. The very failures of the predictive science of economics suggest the necessity of allowing for the existence of that domain of human action not amenable to scientistic explanation.

As the purpose of inquiry shifts toward understanding the sources of value creation with some ultimate objective of encouraging the establishment and maintenance of an environment within which human choices are allowed to take place relatively free of imposed constraints, we should expect economists to direct more of their attention to the domain of subjective economic theory.

VIII. Of Rats and Men

I have found a discussion of the methodology of subjective economics impossible without first defining what I have called the "domain," and my discussion here has been almost exclusively limited to definitional issues. After considerable intellectual floundering, my proposed classification of the two domains of economic theory emerged from a consideration of the very interesting laboratory experiments of rats and pigeons that have been conducted by Kagel, Battalio, and their colleagues. It seemed evident to me that this experimental work was scientific in a sense fully analogous with that carried out by our noneconomist peers in the natural sciences. And yet, as this work has revealed, rats have been shown to choose rationally, to respond predictably to stimuli, to react to "prices," and in many respects to behave as true (even if simple) "economic men." It is possible to derive demand and supply schedules for rats. That part of economic theory, therefore, that analyzes human behavior of the sort that is also evidently descriptive of rat behavior must be categorized as a genuinely predictive science.

The residual aspects of human action that are not reducible to ratlike responses to stimuli, even in the much more complex human variants, define the domain for a wholly different, and uniquely human, science — one that cannot, by its nature, be made analogous to the positive-predictive sciences of the orthodox paradigm.

There is surely room for both sciences to exist in the more inclusive rubric that we call economic theory. We must acknowledge that in many aspects of their behavior, men conform to laws of behavior so that such behavior becomes subject to scientifically testable prediction and control through the external manipulation of constraints. But we must also acknowledge that men can choose courses of action that emerge only in the choice process itself. Men create value by the imagination of alternatives that do not exist followed by the action that implements the possibilities imagined.[12]

Perhaps the methodology of subjective economics, once the definition of its domain is accepted, can best be advanced by a deliberate attempt to sweep out thought patterns that are carried over from its positivist counterpart. I cannot, in this concluding section, discuss such steps in particular, but one example indicates my meaning. It has been suggested that subjective economic theory necessarily draws attention to the elementary fact that choices are made under conditions of uncertainty. Any attempt, however, to carry over the modern analysis of individual choice under uncertainty to the genuine choice making that is the subject of subjective economic theory reflects intellectual confusion. How can anything remotely resembling a probabilistic calculus be applied to choices that are among alternatives that only come into being through the act of choice itself? The human beings whose choices occupy the thoughts of G.L.S. Shackle could never be reduced to the status of rats, even superintelligent ones.[13] In my view, no economist other than Shackle works exclusively within the domain of subjective economic theory, as I have defined it here.

Any methodological advance must build on the work of Shackle. But as many scholars have already found, the next steps are not easy. The advances themselves will, of course, be genuine choices in the full Shackleian sense. They cannot be predicted. But there is surely some relationship between the objects of attention and the imaginative results that emerge. So long as modern economists devote their considerable intellectual energies and imaginative skills, to the search for empirically testable regularities in human conduct, they will succeed in extending the scope of applicability for the man-as-rat metaphor to describe economic theory. To the extent that modern economists use their own imaginations in efforts to understand more fully those aspects of human action that reflect man's own distinctive imaginative ability to choose his own reality, we can expect new insights about the process of economic interaction to emerge.

Notes

I am indebted to Pamela Brown and Karen Vaughn for helpful comments. Precursory ideas to those developed in this chapter are present in J. M. Buchanan, "General Implications of Subjectivism in Economics" and "Natural and Artifactual Man," *What Should Economists Do?* (Indianapolis: Liberty Press, 1979).

1. Adam Smith, *Wealth of Nations,* (New York: Modern Library Edition, 1937), p. 13.

2. Ibid.

3. See John H. Kagel et al., "Demand Curves for Animal Consumers," *Quarterly Journal of Economics* 96 (February 1981): 1–16.

4. This statement should be qualified to limit its relevance to the core problem of economic theory, that of explaining how an economy allocates resources and distributes product. Classical economics has been differently interpreted as offering a theory of economic development or growth.

5. F. A. Hayek, "Economics and Knowledge," *Economica* 4 (1937): 33–54.

6. J. M. Buchanan, *Cost and Choice* (Chicago: Markham, 1969).

7. Thomas Nagel's fascinating review of Brian O'Shaughnessy's two-volume book suggests that at least some of the attention of modern analytic philosophers is turning to what seems to be a Miseslike a priori conception of human action. See Thomas Nagel, "The Self from Within," review of Brian O'Shaughnessy, *The Will: A Dual Aspect Theory,* vols. 1 and 2 (Cambridge: Cambridge University Press, 1980), in *London Times Literary Supplement,* 27 March 1981, pp. 327–28.

8. I ignore the tool-using action of some primates. My purpose is conceptual classification rather than ethology.

9. My criticism of the Mises-Austrian position in this section (although it was developed independently before I knew about Nozick's paper) closely parallels that taken by Robert Nozick in part 2 of his paper, "On Austrian Methodology," *Synthese* 36 (1977): 353–92, especially pp. 361–69. For an informative critique that is somewhat differently directed, see Willy Meyer, "Erkenntnistheoretische Orientierungen und der Charakter des ökonomischen Denkens," in *Zur Theorie marktwirtschaftliche Ordnungen,* eds. E. Streissler and C. Watrin (Tübingen: Mohr, 1980), especially pp. 82–91.

10. The qualifications refer to the obvious differences in the complexity of response patterns as between man and rat. I am not saying that men are like rats in any descriptive sense. My purpose, to repeat, is conceptual classification, not accuracy in description.

11. The work of Israel Kirzner exemplifies subjective economic theory in the sense defined here. Few critics could argue that Kirzner's discussion of entrepreneurship and the role of the entrepreneur in the competitive economic process is not explanatory in the ordinary meaning of the term. See Israel Kirzner, *Competition and Entrepreneurship* (Chicago: University of Chicago Press, 1973).

12. Methodologically, it is important to insist that the two domains be treated as mutually exclusive. Unless this precept is strictly adhered to, the operational status of the predictive theory may become meaningless. Suppose that an hypothesis derived from this theory is empirically refuted. The theorist cannot be allowed to fall back on an essentially subjective-economics explanation to the effect that utility functions have shifted, that persons have exercised genuine choice. He should, instead, be forced to acknowledge the falsification of his hypothesis about behavioral reality. To resort to presumed shifts in the reality itself while holding to the central hypothesis is methodologically illegitimate.

For a fascinating discussion of a related problem that arises in the relationship between moral and predictive theory, see David Levy, "Rational Choice and Morality: Economics and Classical Philosophy," December 1979, mimeo.

13. Among Shackle's many books, see, in particular, *Epistemics and Economics* (Cambridge: Cambridge University Press, 1972) and *Imagination and the Nature of Choice* (Edinburgh: Edinburgh University Press, 1979).

Part II.
INDIVIDUAL CHOICES AND SOCIAL
OUTCOMES

6.

Politics, Policy, and the Pigovian Margins

Since Sidgwick and Marshall, and notably since Pigou's *The Economics of Welfare*, economists have accepted the presence or absence of external effects in production and consumption as a primary criterion of market efficiency. When private decisions exert effects that are external to the decision maker, "ideal" output is not obtained through the competitive organization of economic activity even if the remaining conditions necessary for efficiency are satisfied. The market "fails" to the extent that there exist divergences between marginal private products and marginal social products and/or between marginal private costs and marginal social costs. This basic Pigovian theorem has been theoretically refined and elaborated in numerous works, but its conceptual validity has rarely been challenged.[1] The purpose of this paper is to bring into question a fundamental implication of this aspect of theoretical welfare economics, namely, the implication that externalities are either reduced or eliminated by the shift of an activity from market to political organization. I shall try to show that this implication will stand up to critical scrutiny only under certain highly restricted assumptions about human behavior in modern political systems. When these restrictive assumptions are modified, the concept of divergence between marginal "social" product (cost) and marginal private product (cost) loses most of its usefulness.[2]

"Imperfection" and "failure" are descriptive nouns that tell something about the operation of the organism, the activity, or the organization that is under discussion. These words, and others like them, are meaningful only if the alternative states of "perfection" and "success" are either specifically described or are assumed to be tacitly recognized by participants in the discussion. In the analysis of market organization, the "perfectly working" order has been quite carefully defined. The necessary conditions for Paretian optimality are now a part of the professional economist's stock-in-trade, and these conditions are known to be satisfied only when all of the relevant costs and benefits resulting from an action are incorporated into the calculus of the decision maker that selects the action. By contrast with this state of perfection, almost all ordinary or real-world markets are "imperfect," in greater or lesser degree. Most private decisions exert external effects. So far, so good. If this were the end of it, however, there would be little point in all of the effort. Economists must imply or suggest that the imperfectly working organization is, in fact, "perfectible": that is, they must do so if they are to justify their own professional existence. The analysis of an existing social order must, almost by the nature of science itself, imply that some "improvement" in results can be produced by changes that can be imposed on the variables subject to social control.

Such improvements in the organization of economic activity have, almost without exception, involved the placing of restrictions on the private behavior of individuals through the implementation of some *political* action. The various proposals that have been advanced by economists are sufficiently familiar to make a listing at this point unnecessary. They run the gamut from the relatively straightforward tax-subsidy schemes of Marshall to the more sophisticated and highly intricate proposals for multi-part pricing, counter-speculation, collective simulation of ideal market processes, and many other intriguing methods designed to promote and to insure the attainment of economic efficiency. Indeed, economists tend to be so enmeshed with efficiency notions that it seems extremely difficult for them to resist the ever-present temptation to propose yet more complex gimmicks and gadgets for producing greater "efficiency." In almost every case, and often quite unconsciously, the suggested improvement is assumed to be within the realm of the genuinely attainable. And, if some skeptic dare raise a question on this point, the economist is likely to respond to the effect that his task is not that of the politician, that he does not appropriately concern himself with the political feasibility or workability of his proposals. But if political obstacles to realization are not, in fact, discussed, the implication is clear that the proposals which are advanced are attainable as a result of some conceivable politically imposed modifications in the institutional framework within which decisions are made. It seems fully appropriate to charge welfare economists, generally, with an implicit acceptance of this implication of their analyses. If this were not the case, it is difficult to see why, for example, William J. Baumol should have attempted to construct a theory of the state, of collective action, on the basis of the externality argument,[3] why K. W. Kapp should have entitled his work, *The Social Costs of Private Enterprise*,[4] and why Francis Bator should have called his recent summary analysis, "The Anatomy of Market Failure."[5]

I shall not be concerned here with the analysis of market imperfection or failure, as such. The primary criticism of theoretical welfare economics (and economists) that is advanced in this article is that its failure to include analyses of similar imperfections in realistic and attainable alternative solutions causes the analysis itself to take on implications for institutional change that are, at best, highly misleading. To argue that an existing order is "imperfect" in comparison with an alternative order of affairs that turns out, upon careful inspection, to be unattainable may not be different from arguing that the existing order is "perfect."[6] The existence of demonstrated imperfection in terms of an unattainable state of affairs should imply nothing at all about the possibility of actual improvement to an existing state. To take this step, considerably more is required than the preliminary analysis of "ideal output." This is not to suggest, of course, that the preliminary analysis is not essential and important.

I shall try to show that, with consistent assumptions about human behavior in both market and political institutions, any attempt to replace or to modify an existing market situation, admitted to be characterized by serious externalities, will produce solutions that embody externalities which are different, but precisely analogous, to those previously existing. Indeed, the Pigovian analysis lends itself readily to the analysis of political imperfection.

I

In order to analyze political processes in a manner that is even remotely similar to the methods of economic theory, great simplification and abstraction are required. To the political scientist, accustomed as he is to working with more "realistic" models of human behavior, the simplified models with which the economist must analyze political institutions can only seem to be grossly inadequate caricatures of the operation of complex organizational structures. This rather sharp methodological gap between the two social sciences incorporated in "political economy" provides an important reason why the political scientist has not filled, and could hardly be expected to fill, the analytical void left open by the incompleteness of welfare economics.

I shall assume the existence of a community composed of separate individuals in which all collective decisions are reached by a voting rule of simple majority with universal suffrage. More complex, and realistic, models introducing representation, political parties, leadership, etc., could be employed but without significantly altering the conclusions reached. Almost any political order described by the term, "democratic," in the modern Western usage of this term may, for present purposes, be simplified into this extreme model of "pure" democracy. Characteristics of the political structure may modify the majority equivalent in the simple model.

That is to say, a model of two-thirds or three-fourths majority may be more appropriate to the analysis of some political structures under certain conditions than the simple majority model. However, this quantitative variation in the voting rule equivalent does not affect the conclusions of this paper. Each particular rule, save that of unanimity, leads to conclusions that are identical to those reached in the simple majority model. The magnitude of the distortions produced is, of course, affected by the voting rule. The analysis here is concerned solely with indicating the direction of these effects, not with their magnitude. A distinction among the various "majority equivalents" is not, therefore, necessary.

In the first model, the orthodox assumptions of positive economics will be retained insofar as these concern individual motivation and action. Private individuals are assumed to be sufficiently informed and rational to conduct the required calculus and to reach decisions on the basis of a comparison of private costs and benefits at the relevant margins. No considerations of the "public" or the "social" interest are assumed to enter into this individual calculus within the relationship in question except insofar as this should coincide with individual interest. In determining his voting behavior on each issue confronted by the group, the individual is assumed, quite simply, to act in that manner which he considers to advance his own interest. The model embodies, therefore, a rather straightforward extension of the behavioral assumptions of orthodox economic theory, as a predictive, explanatory theory, to political choice making.

If no institutional restrictions are placed on this majority-rule model of the collective choice process, the characteristics of the "solution" should be intuitively clear. The minimum-size effective or dominating coalition of individuals, as determined by the voting rule, will be able to secure net gains at the expense of the other members of the political group. These gains, secured through the political process, will tend to be shared symmetrically (equally) among all members of the dominant coalition. In the simple majority-rule model, this involves, in the limit, fifty-plus percent of the total membership in the dominating coalition and fifty-minus percent of the total membership in the losing or minority coalition. That such a solution will, in fact, tend to emerge under the conditions of the model seems hardly subject to question. It is helpful, however, to note that such a solution, and only such, satisfies fully the Von Neumann-Morgenstern requirements for solutions to n-person games which, of course, all political "games" must be.[7]

It is useful to apply the familiar Pigovian calculus to this model of political behavior. To the individual member of the effective majority, the political process provides a means through which he may secure private gain at the expense of other citizens. In determining the margins to which political activity shall be extended, the individual member of the dominant coalition will include in his calculus a share of the net benefits from public activity that will be larger than the offsetting individualized share or proportion of the net costs of the activity. In the calculus of the individuals effectively making the final collective decision, marginal private benefits will tend to exceed marginal social benefits and/or marginal private costs will tend to fall short of marginal social costs. The distortions produced are, therefore, precisely analogous, in opposing directions, to those present in the market solution characterized by the familiar Pigovian divergences. In essence, the value of a political vote in this model lies in its potential power to impose external costs on other members of the group. Externalities must be present in any solution reached by the voting process under all less-than-unanimity rules. If the possible "perfectibility" of market organization is to be determined under these conditions, it is clearly necessary to compare two separate imperfections, in each of which significant divergences of the Pigovian sort may exist at the individualized margins of decision making. Since there will be nothing in the collective choice process that will tend to produce the "ideal" solution, as determined by the welfare economist, the presence or absence of a Pigovian marginal divergency in the market solution, even of sufficient seriousness to warrant concern, provides in itself no implication for the desirability of institutional change.[8]

II

This conclusion holds so long as consistency in individual behavior patterns over market and voting processes is retained, independently of the specific motivation that may be assumed to direct this behavior. The oversimplified model of Part I may be criticized on the grounds that individuals do not act in the way postulated: that is, they do not follow their own interests when they participate in the formation of social decisions for the community. Several responses might be advanced to such criticism, but it is not the purpose of this article to defend the validity, methodologically or otherwise, of the self-interest assumption about behavior. The relevant response to the charge of unrealism at this point is surely the frank admission that, of course, individuals do not always act as the model of Part I postulates. A model is a construction that isolates one element of behavior and, upon this, the analyst may erect conceptually refutable hypotheses. The model of majority rule in the simple pure democracy is not different in this respect from the competitive model of economic theory. Both models isolate that part of human behavior that does reflect the rational pursuit of private gain by individuals in particular institutional relationships, and both models fail to the extent that individuals do not, in fact, behave in this fashion in the relationships under consideration.[9]

Any number of models of individual behavior can be constructed. The only real limitation lies, ultimately, in the testing of the predictions made. It will not be necessary, however, to develop any large number of additional and complex models to illustrate the central point of this note. One additional extremely simple model will suffice for this purpose. In this second model, I shall drop the assumption that individuals, in both their market and in their political behavior, act in pursuit of their own narrowly defined self-interest. Instead, I now postulate that individuals act in the other extreme: I assume that each individual, in all aspects of his behavior, tries to identify himself with the community of which he is a member and to act in accordance with his own view of the overall "public" or "social" interest. Each member of the group tries to act in the genuine interest of the whole group as this is determined for him through the application of some appropriately chosen Kantianlike rule of action.

The results are again almost intuitively clear. Since each member of the group acts on the basis of identifying his own interest with that of the larger group, no deliberate exploitation of minority by majority can take place through the political process regardless of the voting rule that is applied. Differences that may arise, and which must be resolved by voting, stem solely from differences in individual conceptions of what the group interest on particular issues is. The Pigovian-type marginal divergences between private and social costs or benefits disappear from the individual calculus in this model of behavior. It is in application to market, rather than to political, behavior that this model seems somewhat unorthodox. Under the assumptions of the model, the individual in his market behavior will also try to identify himself with the group as a whole and to act in accordance with what he considers to be the "public" interest. If his chimney pours out smoke that soils his neighbors' laundry, he will assess these costs as if they were his own in reaching a decision concerning the possible introduction of a smoke-abatement device. The familiar analysis of welfare economics simply does not apply. Each individual decision maker does, in fact, attempt to balance off "social" benefits against "social" costs at the margin. While, as in the collective sector, differences may arise among members of the group concerning the proper definition of social benefits and social costs, these differences cannot be interpreted in the standard way. The Pigovian divergence between marginal private product and marginal social product disappears in both the market and the political organization of activity in this universal benevolence model. The policy conclusions are, however, identical with those reached from the use of the extreme self-interest model. If chimneys smoke, or if the majority is observed to impose discriminatory taxes on the minority, these facts carry with them no implications for institutional changes. In this case, they must represent the decision makers' estimates of genuine community interest. Neither "real" nor "apparent" externalities can, in themselves, provide grounds for suggesting organizational changes.

III

From the analysis of these two extreme and contrasting models of human behavior, the inference is clear that so long as individuals are assumed to be similarly motivated under market and under political institutions there can be no direct implications drawn about the organizational structure of an activity on the basis of a Pigovianlike analysis of observed externalities. The orthodox implication of Pigovian welfare economics follows only on the assumption that individuals respond to *different* motives when they participate in market and in political activity. The only behavioral model appropriate to the Pigovian analysis is that which has been called "the bifurcated man." Man must be assumed to shift his psychological and moral gears when he moves from the realm of organized market activity to that of organized political activity and vice versa. Only if there can be demonstrated to be something in the nature of market organization, as such, that brings out the selfish motives in man, and something in the political organization, as such, which, in turn, suppresses these motives and brings out the more "noble" ones, can there be assumed to exist any "bridge" between the orthodox externality analysis and practical policy, even apart from problems of specific policy prescription.

The characteristics of the organizational structure within which choices must be made may affect the nature of the value system upon which individual action is based. It seems probable that the individual in his voting behavior will tend to choose among alternatives on the basis of a somewhat broader and more inclusive value scale than that which will direct his behavior in the making of market choices. One reason for this is that, in political behavior, the individual is made fully conscious of the fact that he is choosing *for* the whole group, that his individual action will exert external effects on other members of the group, that he is acting "socially." In his market behavior, on the other hand, the external effects of individual choice are sensed only indirectly by the chooser.[10] But this recognition that the individual value scale may be, to some extent, modified by the institutional structure within which choice is exercised is quite different from accepting the idea that the motivation for individual action is wholly transformed as between two separate structures. While it may be acknowledged as "realistic" to assume that the model of individual choice based on self-interest motivation, the "economic" model, is somewhat more applicable to an analysis of markets than of voting processes, this is far removed from accepting the applicability of the universal benevolence model for the latter. At most, the influence of the different organizational structures, as such, on motivation would seem to be conceptually represented by a reasonably narrow distance on some motivational spectrum. If, at the elementary stages of analysis, a choice must be made between that conception of behavior that assumes this possible institutionally generated difference to be absent or negligible (models that I have called consistent) and the conception that assumes wholly different behavioral patterns solely due to the institutional structure, the first alternative seems obviously to be preferred. Yet, as I have shown, it is the second, and clearly extreme, conception of human behavior that is implicit in much of the discussion of Pigovian welfare economics.

This assumption of behavioral dichotomy, as opposed to behavioral consistency, is most openly expressed in the early literature on socialism, especially that of the Christian and Fabian varieties. The criticism of the market order of affairs was often made by referring to the pursuit of private gain, and the case for socialism was based on the replacement of this pursuit of private gain by that of public good. Although this rather naive conception has perhaps lost some of its appeal since World War II, it continues to be implied in much of the popular discussion. While this is not in itself surprising, it does seem notable that the analytical structure based on this conception of human behavior should have remained largely unchallenged in the scientific literature.[11]

IV

Up to this point the discussion has been concerned with the most general case in which no limitations are placed on the activities that may be organized through the political process. Can the implications of the Pigovian welfare analytics be rescued by restricting the movement of the political-institutional variables? If collective action can take place only within prescribed limits, which can be assumed to be fixed by constitutional rules, a model may be constructed in which the policy implications of the Pigovian type of analysis do not run into immediate conflict with reasonable assumptions concerning human motivation. To accomplish this result, however, the range of possible political action must be restricted to such an extent as to make the analysis practically worthless.

Let it be assumed that constitutional rules dictate that all human activity shall be organized privately and voluntarily except that which involves the provision of genuinely collective goods and services. These are defined as those goods and services which, when a unit is made available to one individual member of the group, an equal amount, one unit, is also made available to each other member of the group. These goods and services are completely indivisible. Let it be further assumed that the constitution states that the provision of such goods and services, if politically organized, shall be financed by taxes that are levied on the "marginal benefit principle." That is to say, each individual shall be required to contribute a "tax-price" that is exactly proportional to his own marginal rate of substitution between the collective good and money (all other goods). This marginal tax will be different for different individuals in the group because, although the good is genuinely collective, the relative marginal utility of it will vary from individual to individual.

If the provision of such a good or service should be organized privately rather than collectively, and if individuals are assumed to be motivated by self-interest considerations, the market solution will be characterized by the presence of significant externalities. The individual, acting privately, will take into account only that share of total marginal benefit or product that he expects to enjoy. By comparison, he will take into account the full amount of the marginal costs which, by hypothesis, he must bear individually. In other words, he cannot exclude other members of the group from the enjoyment of the benefits provided by the good: but there is no way that he may include these other members of the group in the payment of the costs. This market organization produces, therefore, the familiar result; the private calculus of individuals embodies the Pigovian divergence at the margins of decision. Compared to a Pareto-optimal situation, relatively too few resources will be devoted to the provision of the common good or service.

Under this situation, a shift in organization from the private or market sector to the collective sector will, under the conditions specified, tend to eliminate the Pigovian divergence, even if the self-interest motivation of individual action is retained. If the individual, in making a political or voting choice concerning the possible marginal extension of the provision of the collective good or service, is required to include in his calculus a share of the total marginal cost of the extension that is proportional to his individualized share of the total marginal benefits provided by the extension, a "solution" will tend to be produced by political choice that will meet all of the necessary conditions for Pareto optimality. If the total marginal costs of extending the activity fall short of the total marginal benefits, individuals will not be in equilibrium and they will, accordingly, vote to extend the activity. At the "solution," all of the necessary conditions are satisfied, and total incremental benefits equal total marginal costs. No externalities exist.[12]

The reason for this result is not difficult to understand. By imposing the restriction that the individual voter must pay for the marginal unit of the collective good or service in proportion to the marginal benefit enjoyed, it is insured that the individual's private calculus becomes a miniature reflection of the aggregate or "social" calculus that would be made by an omniscient, benevolent despot acting in the interests of all persons in the community. The individual voter cannot, because of the restrictions on the model, impose external costs on others in the group through the political process. In his private voting decision he will recognize that additional units of the collective good will yield benefits to others than himself. But he will, under the self-interest assumption, not be influenced by these spillover benefits at all. There are, however, also spillover marginal costs that the provision of the additional units of the collective good will impose on his fellows, and the neglected external benefits will tend to offset these neglected external costs.

This highly restricted model has several interesting features. First of all, note that the sharp difference in result as between the market and the political solution emerges only if the self-interest assumption about human motivation is consistently adopted and applied. If, by contrast, the universal benevolence assumption is introduced, the market organization and the political organization will tend to produce similar results, as in the earlier analyses. Secondly, if the self-interest assumption is adopted, the political result in the restricted model here will tend to be identical under *any* voting rule. Any rule will, under the constitutional restrictions imposed, tend to produce a solution that satisfies all of the necessary conditions for Pareto optimality. The single individual acting as a dictator, the simple majority, and the rule of unanimity: each of these will tend to produce the same results. These separate rules for making political decisions only become important because they reflect differences in the ability of some members of the group to impose costs on other members, an ability that is specifically eliminated by the constitutional restrictions postulated.

It is not, of course, surprising to find that the Pigovian analysis has relevant policy implications only for the provision of genuinely collective (perfectly indivisible) goods and services. Indeed, the statement that externalities exist in any private market solution is one means of stating that genuinely collective elements characterize the activity under consideration. This restricted model indicates clearly, however, that the good must be wholly collective if the implications of the Pigovian analysis are to apply. If an activity is only quasicollective, that is to say, if it contains elements that are privately divisible as well as collective elements, the political solution must also involve externalities. The restricted model analyzed here is perhaps even more useful in pointing up the extremely limited tax scheme that is required for the analysis to apply at all. Even for those goods and services that are wholly collective in nature, the provision of them through the political process will produce Pigovianlike externalities at the margin unless taxes are collected on the basis of marginal benefits. In the real world, very few, if any, goods and services are wholly collective. And even if these few could be isolated, they would not be financed by taxes levied on this principle of incremental benefits enjoyed. Such a principle is not only politically unimaginable in modern democracy: it is also conceptually impossible. Its application would require that the taxing authorities be able to determine, in advance, all individual preference functions. It must be concluded, therefore, that the restricted institutional model in which the implications of the standard externality analysis might apply is nothing but a conceptual toy. In the real world, political results must embody externalities to the extent that individuals follow self-interest in their capacities as collective decision makers: individuals are able, by political means, to impose costs on other individuals.

V

In Part III it was demonstrated that the generalized implications of the Pigovian analysis could be supported only on the adoption of a highly questionable conception of human motivation. In Part IV it was demonstrated that these implications would be drawn from a consistent motivational model only if this model should be so highly restricted as to make the analysis of little practical value. It is much easier, however, to explain the reasons for economists neglecting to examine these aspects of their analysis than it is to justify their neglect. As Knut Wicksell suggested many years ago, most economists are content with assuming the presence of a benevolent despot. Insofar as their analysis points toward policy at all, as it must, the improvements in efficiency advanced are assumed to be attainable within the realm of the politically possible. The almost universal neglect of the imperfections that might arise from the political attempts at applying the economists' efficiency criteria represents a serious deficiency in the work of welfare economists and economists generally. To shy away from considerations of the politically feasible has been deemed an admirable trait, but to refuse to examine the politically possible is incomplete scholarship.

Notes

Although independently developed, this paper draws upon and extends certain ideas that have been developed in a larger work undertaken in collaboration with Gordon Tullock. See *The Calculus of Consent* (Ann Arbor: University of Michigan Press, 1962). I should acknowledge Tullock's indirect as well as his direct influence on the general ideas presented in this paper.

1. The current work of my colleague, Ronald Coase, should be mentioned as a notable exception. Coase's criticism of the Pigovian analysis concerns the implications of externality for resource allocation. For a preliminary statement of Coase's position see R. H. Coase, "The Federal Communications Commission," *Journal of Law and Economics*, 2 (1959), especially pp. 26–7. A more complete statement appears in "The Problem of Social Cost," *Journal of Law and Economics*, 3 (1960).

2. It should be noted that I shall not be concerned with the conceptual ability of welfare economists to make specific policy prescriptions, a problem that has been central to much of the modern discussion. It is now widely acknowledged that welfare economics, as such, can provide few guides to positive policy making in a specific sense. But the analysis continues to be employed for the purposes of demonstrating the existence of market failure. If, as J. de V. Graaff suggests, "*laissez-faire* welfare theory" was "largely concerned with demonstrating the optimal properties of free competition and the unfettered price system," it is surely equally accurate to suggest that modern welfare theory has been largely concerned with demonstrating that these conclusions are invalid: that is, that competitive markets do not satisfy the necessary conditions for optimality. Graaff's own work is, perhaps, the most elegant example. See his *Theoretical Welfare Economics*, (1957), p. 170.

3. William J. Baumol, *Welfare Economics and the Theory of the State*, (1952).

4. K. W. Kapp, *The Social Costs of Private Enterprise*, (1950).

5. Francis Bator, "The Anatomy of Market Failure," *Quarterly Journal of Economics*, 72 (1958), pp. 351–79.

6. Frank Knight's statement that "to call a situation hopeless is equivalent to calling it ideal" may be reversed. To call a situation ideal is merely another means of calling it hopeless: that is, not perfectible.

7. J. Von Neumann and O. Morgenstern, *Theory of Games and Economic Behavior* (third ed., 1953), p. 264.

8. I am not suggesting that deliberate exploitation of minority by majority need be the only purpose of collective activity, even in this polar model. The point is rather that, independently of the motivation for collective activity, majority-rule institutions of decision making create opportunities within which Pigovianlike externalities may arise. There will, of course, arise situations in which the self-interest of the individual dictates the collectivization of an activity in order that the application of general rules to *all* members of the group can be effected. It is precisely in such cases that, conceptually, unanimity may replace majority rule as the decision device, and the propositions of modern welfare economics become fully appropriate. But so long as majority rule prevails, the "political externalities" are present, whether these be purposeful or ancillary to collective action designed to accomplish other ends.

9. Care must be taken to distinguish between the self-interest assumption, as the basis for a "logic of choice" and the self-interest assumption as the basis of a

predictive, explanatory theory of human action. In the first sense, all action of individuals must be based on self-interest, and it becomes meaningless to discuss alternative models of behavior. The pure logic of individual choice is not without value, but it should be emphasized that the argument of this article employs the second version of the self-interest assumption. If conceptually refutable hypotheses are to be developed, the behavior of choice-making individuals must be externally observable in terms of measurable criteria of choice. In the market relationship, this degree of operational validity is often introduced by stating that the minimal requirement is that individuals, when confronted with choice, choose "more" rather than "less." But "more" or "less" take on full operational meaning only when they become measurable in something other than subjective utility of the choosers. The "measuring rod of money" must be allowed to enter before the generalized logic of choice can produce even so much as the first law of demand.

10. For a further discussion on these points see my "Individual Choice in Voting and the Market," *Journal of Political Economy*, 62 (1954), pp. 334–43.

11. The behavioral inconsistency here has been, of course, indirectly recognized by many writers. However, the only explicit reference to the private-cost social-cost analysis, to my knowledge, is contained in the paper by William H. Meckling and Armen A. Alchian, "Incentives in the United States," *American Economic Review*, 50 (1960), pp. 55–61, and, even here, the reference is only a passing one.

12. This solution is that which has been rigorously defined by Paul A. Samuelson in "The Pure Theory of Public Expenditure," *Review of Economics and Statistics*, 36 (1954), pp. 386–88; "Diagrammatic Exposition of a Theory of Public Expenditure," *Review of Economics and Statistics*, 37 (1955), pp. 350–56.

7.

Externality

WITH WILLIAM CRAIG STUBBLEBINE

Externality has been, and is, central to the neoclassical critique of market organization. In its various forms—external economies and diseconomies, divergencies between marginal social and marginal private cost or product, spillover and neighborhood effects, collective or public goods—externality dominates theoretical welfare economics, and, in one sense, the theory of economic policy generally. Despite this importance and emphasis, rigorous definitions of the concept itself are not readily available in the literature. As Scitovsky has noted, "definitions of external economies are few and unsatisfactory."[1] The following seems typical:

> External effects exist in consumption whenever the shape or position of a man's indifference curve depends on the consumption of other men.
> [External effects] are present whenever a firm's production function depends in some way on the amounts of the inputs or outputs of another firm.[2]

It seems clear that operational and usable definitions are required.

In this paper, we propose to clarify the notion of externality by defining it rigorously and precisely. When this is done, several important, and often overlooked, conceptual distinctions follow more or less automatically. Specifically, we shall distinguish marginal and inframarginal externalities, potentially relevant and irrelevant externalities, and Pareto-relevant and Pareto-irrelevant externalities. These distinctions are formally developed in Section I. As we shall demonstrate, the term "externality," as generally used by economists, corresponds only to our definition of Pareto-relevant externality. There follows, in Section II, an illustration of the basic points described in terms of a simple descriptive example. In Section III, some of the implications of our approach are discussed.

It is useful to limit the scope of the analysis at the outset. Much of the discussion in the literature has been concerned with the distinction between *technological* and *pecuniary* external effects. We do not propose to enter this discussion since it is not relevant for our purposes. We note only that, if desired, the whole analysis can be taken to apply only to technological externalities. Secondly, we shall find no cause for discussing production and consumption externalities separately. Essentially the same analysis applies in either case. In what follows, "firms" may be substituted for "individuals" and "production functions" for "utility functions" without modifying the central conclusions. For expositional simplicity only, we limit the explicit discussion to consumption externalities.

I

We define an external effect, *an externality,* to be present when,

(1) $u^A = u^A (X_1, X_2, \ldots, X_m, Y_1)$.

This states that the utility of an individual, A, is dependent upon the "activities," $(X_1, X_2, \ldots, X_m)$, that are exclusively under his own control or authority, but also upon another single activity, Y_1, which is, by definition, under the control of a second individual, B, who is presumed to be a member of the same social group. We define an *activity* here as any distinguishable human action that may be measured, such as eating bread, drinking milk, spewing smoke into the air, dumping litter on the highways, giving to the poor, etc. Note that A's utility may, and will in the normal case, depend on other activities of B in addition to Y_1, and also upon the activities of other parties. That is, A's utility function may, in more general terms, include such variables as $(Y_2, Y_3, \ldots, Y_m; Z_1, Z_2, \ldots, Z_m)$. For analytical simplicity, however, we shall confine our attention to the effects of one particular activity, Y_1, as it affects the utility of A.

We assume that A will behave so as to maximize utility in the ordinary way, subject to the externally determined values for Y_1, and that he will modify the values for the X's, as Y_1 changes, so as to maintain a state of "equilibrium."

A marginal externality exists when,

(2) $u^A_{Y_1} \neq 0$.

Here, small u's are employed to represent the "partial derivatives" of the utility function of the individual designated by the super-script with respect to the variables designated by the subscript. Hence, $u^A_{Y_1} = \partial u^A / \partial Y_1$, assuming that the variation in Y_1 is evaluated with respect to a set of "equilibrium" values for the X's, adjusted to the given value for Y_1.

An inframarginal externality holds at those points where,

(3) $u^A_{Y_1} = 0$,

and (1) holds.

These classifications can be broken down into economies and diseconomies: a marginal external economy existing when,

(2A) $u_{Y_1}^A > 0$,

that is, a small change in the activity undertaken by B will change the utility of A in the same direction; a marginal external diseconomy existing when,

(2B) $u_{Y_1}^A < 0$.

An inframarginal external economy exists when for any given set of values for $(X_1, X_2, \ldots, X_m)$, say, $(C_1, C_2, \ldots, C_m)$,

(3A) $u_{Y_1}^A = 0$, and $\int_0^{Y_1} u_{Y_1}^A \, dy_1 > 0$.

This condition states that, while incremental changes in the extent of B's activity, Y_1, have no affect on A's utility, the total effect of B's action has increased A's utility. An inframarginal diseconomy exists when (1) holds, and, for any given set of values for $(X_1, X_2, \ldots, X_m)$, say, $(C_1, C_2, \ldots, C_m)$, then,

(3B) $u_{Y_1}^A = 0$, and $\int_0^{Y_1} u_{Y_1}^A \, dy_1 < 0$.

Thus, small changes in B's activity do not change A's level of satisfaction, but the total effect of B's undertaking the activity in question is harmful to A.

We are able to classify the effects of B's action, or potential action, on A's utility by evaluating the "partial derivative" of A's utility function with respect to Y_1 over all possible values for Y_1. In order to introduce the further distinctions between *relevant* and *irrelevant* externalities, however, it is necessary to go beyond consideration of A's utility function. Whether or not a relevant externality exists depends upon the extent to which the activity involving the externality is carried out by the person empowered to take action, to make decisions. Since we wish to consider a single externality in isolation, we shall assume that B's utility function includes only variables (activities) that are within his control, including Y_1. Hence, B's utility function takes the form,

(4) $u^B = u^B (Y_1, Y_2, \ldots, Y_m)$.

Necessary conditions for utility maximization by B are,

(5) $u_{Y_1}^B / u_{Y_j}^B = f_{Y_1}^B / f_{Y_j}^B$,

where Y_j is used to designate the activity of B in consuming or utilizing some numéraire commodity or service which is, by hypothesis, available on equal terms to A. The right-hand term represents the marginal rate of substitution in "production" or "exchange" confronted by B, the party taking action on Y_1, his production function being defined as,

(6) $f^B = f^B(Y_1, Y_2, \ldots, Y_m)$,

where inputs are included as activities along with outputs. In other words, the right-hand term represents the marginal cost of the activity, Y_1, to B. The equilibrium values for the Y_i's will be designated as $\overline{Y}_i$'s.

An externality is defined as *potentially relevant* when the activity, to the extent that it is actually performed, generates *any* desire on the part of the externally benefited (damaged) party (A) to modify the behavior of the party empowered to take action (B) through trade, persuasion, compromise, agreement, convention, collective action, etc. An externality which, to the extent that it is performed, exerts no such influence is defined as *irrelevant*. Note that, so long as (1) holds, an externality remains; utility functions remain interdependent.

A potentially relevant marginal externality exists when,

(7) $u^A_{Y_1}\Big|_{Y_1 = \overline{Y}_1} \neq 0.$

This is a potentially relevant marginal external economy when (7) is greater than zero, a diseconomy when (7) is less than zero. In either case, A is motivated, by B's performance of the activity, to make some effort to modify this performance, to increase the resources devoted to the activity when (7) is positive, to decrease the quantity of resources devoted to the activity when (7) is negative.

Inframarginal externalities are, by definition, irrelevant for small changes in the scope of B's activity, Y_1. However, when large or discrete changes are considered, A is motivated to change B's behavior with respect to Y_1 in all cases *except* that for which,

(8) $u^A_{Y_1}\Big|_{Y_1 = \overline{Y}_1} = 0,$ and

$u^A(C_1, C_2, \ldots, C_m, \overline{Y}_1) \geq u^A (C_1, C_2, \ldots, C_m, Y_1),$ for all
$Y_1 \neq \overline{Y}_1.$

When (8) holds, A has achieved an absolute maximum of utility with respect to changes over Y_1, given any set of values for the X's. In more prosaic terms, A is satiated with respect to Y_1.[3] In all other cases, where inframarginal external economies or diseconomies exist, A will have some desire to modify B's performance; the externality is potentially relevant. Whether or not this motivation will lead A to seek an expansion or contraction in the extent of B's performance of the activity will depend on the location of the inframarginal region relative to the absolute maximum for any given values of the X's.[4]

Pareto relevance and irrelevance may now be introduced. The existence of a simple desire to modify the behavior of another, defined as potential relevance, need not imply the ability to implement this desire. An externality is defined to be Pareto-relevant when the extension of the activity may be modified in such a way that the externally affected party, A, can be made better off without the acting party, B, being made worse off. That is to say, "gains from trade" characterize the Pareto-relevant externality, trade that takes the form of some change in the activity of B as his part of the bargain.

A marginal externality is Pareto-relevant when[5]

(9) $\quad (-)\, u^A_{Y_1}/u^A_{X_j} > [u^B_{Y_1}/u^B_{Y_j} - f^B_{Y_1}/f^B_{Y_j}]_{Y_1 = \bar{Y}_1}$ and when $u^A_{Y_1}/u^A_{X_j} < 0$, and
$u^A_{Y_1}/u^A_{X_j} > (-)\, [u^B_{Y_1}/u^B_{Y_j} - f^B_{Y_1}/f^B_{Y_j}]_{Y_1 = \bar{Y}_1}$ when $u^A_{Y_1}/u^A_{X_j} > 0$.

In (9), X_j and Y_j are used to designate, respectively, the activities of A and B in consuming or in utilizing some *numéraire* commodity or service that, by hypothesis, is available on identical terms to each of them. As is indicated by the transposition of signs in (9), the conditions for Pareto relevance differ as between external diseconomies and economies. This is because the "direction" of change desired by A on the part of B is different in the two cases. In stating the conditions for Pareto relevance under ordinary two-person trade, this point is of no significance since trade in one good flows only in one direction. Hence, absolute values can be used.

The condition, (9), states that A's marginal rate of substitution between the activity, Y_1, and the *numéraire* activity must be greater than the "net" marginal rate of substitution between the activity and the *numéraire* activity for B. Otherwise, "gains from trade" would not exist between A and B.

Note, however, that when B has achieved utility-maximizing equilibrium,

(10) $\quad u^B_{Y_1}/u^B_{Y_j} = f^B_{Y_1}/f^B_{Y_j}$.

That is to say, the marginal rate of substitution in consumption or utilization is equated to the marginal rate of substitution in production or exchange, i.e., to marginal cost. When (10) holds, the terms in the brackets in (9) mutually cancel. Thus, potentially relevant marginal externalities are also Pareto-relevant when B is in utility-maximizing equilibrium. Some trade is possible.

Pareto equilibrium is defined to be present when,

(11) $(-)u^A_{Y_1}/u^A_{X_j} = [u^B_{Y_1}/u^B_{Y_j} - f^B_{Y_1}/f^B_{Y_j}]$, and when $u^A_{Y_1}/u^A_{X_j} < 0$, and
$u^A_{Y_1}/u^A_{X_j} = (-)[u^B_{Y_1}/u^B_{Y_j} - f^B_{Y_1}/f^B_{Y_j}]$ when $u^A_{Y_1}/u^A_{X_j} > 0$.

Condition (11) demonstrates that marginal externalities may continue to exist, even in Pareto equilibrium, as here defined. This point may be shown by reference to the special case in which the activity in question may be undertaken at zero costs. Here Pareto equilibrium is attained when the marginal rates of substitution in consumption or utilization for the two persons are precisely offsetting, that is, where their interests are strictly opposed, and *not* where the left-hand term vanishes.

What vanishes in Pareto equilibrium are the Pareto-relevant externalities. It seems clear that, normally, economists have been referring only to what we have here called Pareto-relevant externalities when they have, implicitly or explicitly, stated that external effects are not present when a position on the Pareto optimality surface is attained.[6]

For completeness, we must also consider those potentially relevant inframarginal externalities. Refer to the discussion of these as summarized in (8) above. The question is now to determine whether or not, *A*, the externally affected party, can reach some mutually satisfactory agreement with *B*, the acting party, that will involve some discrete (nonmarginal) change in the scope of the activity, Y_1. If, over some range, any range, of the activity, which we shall designate by ΔY_1, the rate of substitution between Y_1 and X_j for *A* exceeds the "net" rate of substitution for *B*, the externality is Pareto-relevant. The associated changes in the utilization of the *numéraire* commodity must be equal for the two parties. Thus, for external economies, we have

$$(12) \quad \frac{\Delta u^A}{\Delta Y_1} \Big/ \frac{\Delta u^A}{\Delta X_j} > (-) \left[\frac{\Delta u^B}{\Delta Y_1} \Big/ \frac{\Delta u^B}{\Delta Y_j} - \frac{\Delta f^B}{\Delta Y_1} \Big/ \frac{\Delta f^B}{\Delta Y_j} \right]_{Y_l = \bar{Y}_1},$$

and the same with the sign in parenthesis transposed for external diseconomies. The difference to be noted between (12) and (9) is that, with inframarginal externalities, potential relevance need not imply Pareto relevance. The bracketed terms in (12) need not sum to zero when *B* is in his private utility-maximizing equilibrium.

We have remained in a two-person world, with one person affected by the single activity of a second. However, the analysis can readily be modified to incorporate the effects of this activity on a multiperson group. That is to say, *B*'s activity, Y_1, may be allowed to affect several parties simultaneously, several *A*'s, so to speak. In each case, the activity can then be evaluated in terms of its effects on the utility of each person. Nothing in the construction need be changed. The only stage in the analysis requiring modification explicitly to take account of the possibilities of multiperson groups being externally affected is that which involves the condition for Pareto relevance and Pareto equlibrium.

For a multiperson group $(A_1, A_2, \ldots, A_n)$, any one or all of whom may be externally affected by the activity, Y_1, of the single person, B, the condition for Pareto relevance is,

$$(9\text{A}) \quad (-)\sum_{i=1}^{n} u_{Y_1}^{A_i}/u_{X_j}^{A_i} > [u_{Y_1}^{B}/u_{Y_j}^{B} - f_{Y_1}^{B}/f_{Y_j}^{B}]_{Y_1 = \bar{Y}_1} \text{ when } u_{Y_1}^{A_i}/u_{X_j}^{A_i} < 0, \text{ and,}$$

$$\sum_{i=1}^{n} u_{Y_1}^{A_i}/u_{X_j}^{A_i} > (-)[u_{Y_1}^{B}/u_{Y_j}^{B} - f_{Y_1}^{B}/f_{Y_j}^{B}]_{Y_1 = \bar{Y}_1} \text{ when } u_{Y_1}^{A_i}/u_{X_j}^{A_i} > 0.$$

That is, the summed marginal rates of substitution over the members of the externally affected group exceed the offsetting "net" marginal evaluation of the activity by B. Again, in private equilibrium for B, marginal externalities are Pareto-relevant, provided that we neglect the important element involved in the costs of organizing group decisions. In the real world, these costs of organizing group decisions (together with uncertainty and ignorance) will prevent realization of some "gains from trade" – just as they do in organized markets. This is as true for two-person groups as it is for larger groups. But this does not invalidate the point that potential "gains from trade" are available. The condition for Pareto equilibrium and for the inframarginal case summarized in (11) and (12) for the two-person model can readily be modified to allow for the externally affected multiperson group.

II

The distinctions developed formally in Section I may be illustrated diagrammatically and discussed in terms of a simple descriptive example. Consider two persons, A and B, who own adjoining units of residential property. Within limits to be noted, each person values privacy, which may be measured quantitatively in terms of a single criterion, the height of a fence that can be constructed along the common boundary line. We shall assume that B's desire for privacy holds over rather wide limits. His utility increases with the height of the fence up to a reasonably high level. Up to a certain minimum height, A's utility also is increased as the fence is made higher. Once this minimum height is attained, however, A's desire for privacy is assumed to be fully satiated. Thus, over a second range, A's total utility does not change with a change in the height of the fence. However, beyond a certain limit, A's view of a mountain behind B's property is progressively obscured as the fence goes higher. Over this third

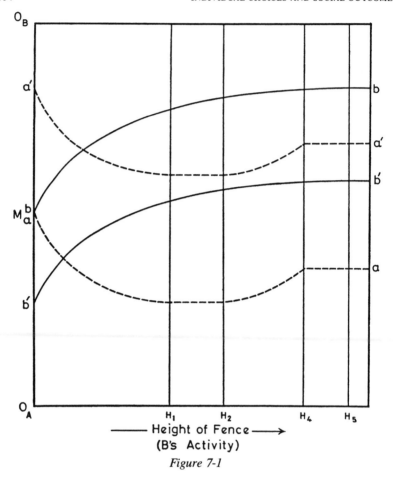

Figure 7-1

range, therefore, A's utility is reduced as the fence is constructed to higher levels. Finally, A will once again become wholly indifferent to marginal changes in the fence's height when his view is totally blocked out.

We specify that B possesses the sole authority, the only legal right, to construct the fence between the two properties.

The preference patterns for A and for B are shown in Fig. 7-1, which is drawn in the form of an Edgeworthlike box diagram. Note, however, that the origin for B is shown at the upper left rather than the upper right corner of the diagram as in the more normal usage. This modification is necessary here because only the *numéraire* good, measured along the ordinate, is strictly divisible between A and B. Both must adjust to the same height of fence, that is, to the same level of the activity creating the externality.

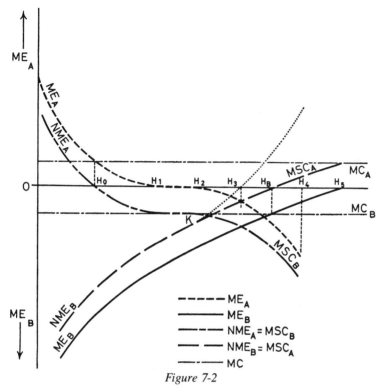

Figure 7-2

As described above, the indifference contours for A take the general
shape shown by the curves aa, $a'a'$, while those for B assume the shapes,
bb, $b'b'$. Note that these contours reflect the relative evaluations, for A
and B, between money and the activity, Y_1. Since the costs of undertaking
the activity, for B, are not incorporated in the diagram, the "contract
locus" that might be derived from tangency points will have little relevance except in the special case where the activity can be undertaken at
zero costs.

Fig. 7-2 depicts the marginal evaluation curves for A and B, as derived
from the preference fields shown in Fig. 7-1, along with some incorporation of costs. These curves are derived as follows: Assume an initial
distribution of "money" between A and B, say, that shown at M on Fig.
7-1. The marginal evaluation of the activity for A is then derived by
plotting the negatives (i.e., the mirror image) of the slopes of successive
indifference curves attained by A as B is assumed to increase the height
of the fence from zero. These values remain positive for a range, become
zero over a second range, become negative for a third, and, finally, return
to zero again.[7]

B's curves of marginal evaluation are measured downward from the upper horizontal axis or base line, for reasons that will become apparent. The derivation of B's marginal evaluation curve is somewhat more complex than that for A. This is because B, who is the person authorized to undertake the action, in this case the building of the fence, must also bear the full costs. Thus, as B increases the scope of the activity, his real income, measured in terms of his remaining goods and services, is reduced. This change in the amount of remaining goods and services will, of course, affect his marginal evaluation of the activity in question. Thus, the marginal cost of building the fence will determine, to some degree, the marginal evaluation of the fence. This necessary interdependence between marginal evaluation and marginal cost complicates the use of simple diagrammatic models in finding or locating a solution. It need not, however, deter us from presenting the solution diagrammatically, if we postulate that the marginal evaluation curve, as drawn, is based on a single presumed cost relationship. This done, we may plot B's marginal evaluation of the activity from the negatives of the slopes of his indifference contours attained as he constructs the fence to higher and higher levels. B's marginal evaluation, shown in Fig. 7-2, remains positive throughout the range to the point H_5, where it becomes zero.

The distinctions noted in Section I are easily related to the construction in Fig. 7-2. To A, the party externally affected, B's potential activity in constructing the fence can be assessed independently of any prediction of B's actual behavior. Thus, the activity of B would,

(1) exert marginal external economies which are potentially relevant over the range OH_1;

(2) exert inframarginal external economies over the range H_1H_2, which are clearly irrelevant since no change in B's behavior with respect to the extent of the activity would increase A's utility;

(3) exert marginal external diseconomies over the range H_2H_4 which are potentially relevant to A; and,

(4) exert inframarginal external economies or diseconomies beyond H_4, the direction of the effect being dependent on the ratio between the total utility derived from privacy and the total reduction in utility derived from the obstructed view. In any case, the externality is potentially relevant.

To determine Pareto relevance, the extent of B's predicted performance must be determined. The necessary condition for B's attainment of "private" utility-maximizing equilibrium is that marginal costs, which he must incur, be equal to his own marginal evaluation. For simplicity in Fig. 7-2, we assume that marginal costs are constant, shown by the curve, MC. Thus, B's position of equilibrium is shown at H_B, within the range of marginal external diseconomies for A. Here the externality imposed by B's behavior is clearly Pareto-relevant: A can surely work out some means of compensating B in exchange for B's agreement to reduce the scope of the activity—in this example, to reduce the height of the fence between the two properties. Diagrammatically, the position of Pareto equilibrium is shown at H_3 where the marginal evaluation of A is equal in absolute value, but negatively to the "net" marginal evaluation of B, drawn as the curve NME_B. Only in this position are the conditions specified in (11) satisfied.[8]

III

Aside from the general classification of externalities that is developed the approach here allows certain implications to be drawn, implications that have not, perhaps, been sufficiently recognized by some welfare economists.

The analysis makes it quite clear that externalities, external effects may remain even in full Pareto equilibrium. That is to say, a position may be classified as Pareto-optimal or efficient despite the fact that, at the marginal, the activity of one individual externally affects the utility of another individual. Fig. 7-2 demonstrates this point clearly. Pareto equilibrium is attained at H_3, yet B is imposing marginal external diseconomies on A.

This point has significant policy implications for it suggests that the observation of external effects, taken alone, cannot provide a basis for judgment concerning the desirability of some modification in an existing state of affairs. There is not a prima facie case for intervention in all cases where an externality is observed to exist.[9] The internal benefits from carrying out the activity, net of costs, may be greater than the external damage that is imposed on other parties.

In full Pareto equilibrium, of course, these internal benefits, measured in terms of some *numéraire* good, net of costs, must be just equal, at the margin, to the external damage that is imposed on other parties. This equilibrium will always be characterized by the strict opposition of interests of the two parties, one of which may be a multiperson group.

In the general case, we may say that, at full Pareto equilibrium, the presence of a marginal external diseconomy implies an offsetting marginal *internal* economy, whereas the presence of a marginal external economy implies an offsetting marginal *internal* diseconomy. In "private" equilibrium, as opposed to Pareto equilibrium, these net internal economies and diseconomies would, of course, be eliminated by the utility-maximizing acting party. In Pareto equilibrium, these remain because the acting party is being compensated for "suffering" internal economies and diseconomies, that is, divergencies between "private" marginal costs and benefits, *measured in the absence of compensation.*

As a second point, it is useful to relate the whole analysis here to the more familiar Pigovian discussion concerning the divergence between marginal social cost (product) and marginal private cost (product). By saying that such a divergence exists, we are, in the terms of this paper, saying that a marginal externality exists. The Pigovian terminology tends to be misleading, however, in that it deals with the acting party to the exclusion of the externally affected party. It fails to take into account the fact that there are always two parties involved in a single externality relationship.[10] As we have suggested, a marginal externality is Pareto-relevant except in the position of Pareto equilibrium; gains from trade can arise. But there must be two parties to any trading arrangement. The externally affected party must compensate the acting party for modifying his behavior. The Pigovian terminology, through its concentration on the decision making of the acting party alone, tends to obscure the two-sidedness of the bargain that must be made.

To illustrate this point, assume that A, the externally affected party in our model, successfully secures, through the auspices of the "state," the levy of a marginal tax on B's performance of the activity, Y_1. Assume further that A is able to secure this change without cost to himself. The tax will increase the marginal cost of performing the activity for B, and, hence, will reduce the extent of the activity attained in B's "private" equilibrium. Let us now presume that this marginal tax is levied "correctly" on the basis of a Pigovian calculus; the rate of tax at the margin is made equal to the negative marginal evaluation of the activity to A. Under these modified conditions, the effective marginal cost, as confronted by B, may be shown by the curve designated as MSC_B in Fig. 7-2. A new "private" equilibrium for B is shown at the quantity, H_3, the same level designated as Pareto equilibrium in our earlier discussion, if we neglect the disturbing interdependence between marginal evaluation and marginal costs. Attention solely to the decision calculus of B here would suggest, perhaps, that this position remains Pareto-optimal under these revised circumstances, and that it continues to qualify as a position of Pareto equilibrium. There is no divergence between marginal private cost and marginal social cost in the usual sense. However, the position, if attained in this manner, is clearly neither one of Pareto optimality, nor one that may be classified as Pareto equilibrium.

In this new "private" equilibrium for B,

(13) $u_{Y_1}^B/u_{Y_j}^B = f_{Y_1}^B/f_{Y_j}^B - u_{Y_1}^A/u_{X_j}^A,$

where $u_{Y_1}^A/u_{X_j}^A$ represents the marginal tax imposed on B as he performs the activity, Y_1. Recall the necessary condition for Pareto relevance defined in (9) above, which can now be modified to read,

(9B) $(-) u^A_{Y_1}/u^A_{X_j} > [u^B_{Y_1}/u^B_{Y_j} - f^B_{Y_1}/f^B_{Y_j} + u^A_{Y_1}/u^A_{X_j}]_{Y_1 = \bar{Y}_1}$, when $u^A_{Y_1}/u^A_{X_j} < 0$,

and $u^A_{Y_1}/u^A_{X_j} > (-)[u^B_{Y_1}/u^B_{Y_j} - f^B_{Y_1}/f^B_{Y_j} + u^A_{Y_1}/u^A_{X_j}]_{Y_1 = \bar{Y}_1}$, when $u^A_{Y_1}/u^A_{X_j} > 0$.

In (9B), $\bar{Y}_1$ represents the "private" equilibrium value for Y_1, determined by B, after the ideal Pigovian tax is imposed. As before, the bracketed terms represent the "net" marginal evaluation of the activity for the acting party, B, and these sum to zero when equilibrium is reached. So long as the left-hand term in the inequality remains nonzero, a Pareto-relevant marginal externality remains, despite the fact that the full "Pigovian solution" is attained.

The apparent paradox here is not difficult to explain. Since, as postulated, A is not incurring any cost in securing the change in B's behavior, and, since there remains, by hypothesis, a marginal diseconomy, further "trade" can be worked out between the two parties. Specifically, Pareto equilibrium is reached when,

(11A) $(-)u^A_{Y_1}/u^A_{X_j} = [u^B_{Y_1}/u^B_{Y_j} - f^B_{Y_1}/f^B_{Y_j} + u^A_{Y_1}/u^A_{X_j}]$ when $u^A_{Y_1}/u^A_{X_j} < 0$, and

$u^A_{Y_1}/u^A_{X_j} = (-)[u^B_{Y_1}/u^B_{Y_j} - f^B_{Y_1}/f^B_{Y_j} + u^A_{Y_1}/u^A_{X_j}]$ when $u^A_{Y_1}/u^A_{X_j} > 0$.

Diagrammatically, this point may be made with reference to Fig. 7-2. If a unilaterally imposed tax, corresponding to the marginal valuation of A, is placed on B's performance of the activity, the new position of Pareto equilibrium may be shown by first subtracting the new marginal cost curve, drawn as MSC_B, from B's marginal evaluation curve. Where this new "net" marginal evaluation curve, shown as the dotted curve between points H_3 and K, cuts the marginal evaluation curve for A, a new position of Pareto equilibrium falling between H_2 and H_3 is located, neglecting the qualifying point discussed in Note 8.

The important implication to be drawn is that full Pareto equilibrium can never be attained via the imposition of unilaterally imposed taxes and subsidies until all marginal externalities are eliminated. If a tax-subsidy method, rather than "trade," is to be introduced, it should involve bilateral taxes (subsidies). Not only must B's behavior be modified so as to insure that he will take the costs externally imposed on A into account, but A's behavior must be modified so as to insure that he will take the costs "internally" imposed on B into account. In such a double tax-subsidy scheme, the necessary Pareto conditions would be readily satisfied.[11]

In summary, Pareto equilibrium in the case of marginal externalities cannot be attained so long as marginal externalities remain, until and unless those benefiting from changes are required to pay some "price" for securing the benefits.

A third point worthy of brief note is that our analysis allows the whole treatment of externalities to encompass the consideration of purely collective goods. As students of public finance theory will have recognized, the

Pareto equilibrium solution discussed in this paper is similar, indeed is identical, with that which was presented by Paul Samuelson in his theory of public expenditures.[12] The summed marginal rates of substitution (marginal evaluation) must be equal to marginal costs. Note, however, that marginal costs may include the negative marginal evaluation of other parties, if viewed in one way. Note, also, that there is nothing in the analysis which suggests its limitations to purely collective goods or even to goods that are characterized by significant externalities in their use.

Our analysis also lends itself to the more explicit point developed in Coase's recent paper.[13] He argues that the same "solution" will tend to emerge out of any externality relationship, regardless of the structure of property rights, provided only that the market process works smoothly. Strictly speaking, Coase's analysis is applicable only to inter-firm externality relationships, and the identical solution emerges only because firms adjust to prices that are competitively determined. In our terms of reference, this identity of solution cannot apply because of the incomparability of utility functions. It remains true, however, that the basic characteristics of the Pareto equilibrium position remain unchanged regardless of the authority undertaking the action. This point can be readily demonstrated, again with reference to Fig. 7-2. Let us assume that Fig. 7-2 is now redrawn on the basis of a different, legal relationship in which A now possesses full authority to construct the fence, whereas B can no longer take any action in this respect. A will, under these conditions, "privately" construct a fence only to the height H_0, where the activity clearly exerts a Pareto-relevant marginal external economy on B. Pareto equilibrium will be reached, as before, at H_3, determined, in this case, by the intersection of the "net" marginal evaluation curve for A (which is identical to the previously defined marginal social cost curve, MSC, when B is the acting party) and the marginal evaluation curve for B.[14] Note that, in this model, A will allow himself to suffer an internal marginal diseconomy, at equilibrium, provided that he is compensated by B, who continues, in Pareto equilibrium, to enjoy a marginal *external* economy.

Throughout this paper, we have deliberately chosen to introduce and to discuss only a single externality. Much of the confusion in the literature seems to have arisen because two or more externalities have been handled simultaneously. The standard example is that in which the output of one firm affects the production function of the second firm while, at the same time, the output of the second firm affects the production function of the first. Clearly, there are two externalities to be analyzed in such cases. In many instances, these can be treated as separate and handled independently. In other situations, this step cannot be taken and additional tools become necessary.[15]

Notes

1. Tibor Scitovsky, "Two Concepts of External Economies," *Journal of Political Economy*, 62 (1954), p. 143.

2. J. de V. Graaff, *Theoretical Welfare Economics* (Cambridge: 1957), p. 43 and p. 18.

3. Note that, $u_{Y_1}^A|_{Y_1 = \bar{Y}_1} = 0$, is a necessary, but not a sufficient, condition for irrelevance.

4. In this analysis of the relevance of externalities, we have assumed that B will act in such a manner as to maximize his own utility subject to the constraints within which he must operate. If, for any reason, B does not attain the equilibrium position defined in (5) above, the classification of his activity for A may, of course, be modified. A potentially relevant externality may become irrelevant and vice versa.

5. We are indebted to Mr. M. McManus of the University of Birmingham for pointing out to us an error in an earlier formulation of this and the following similar conditions.

6. This applies to the authors of this paper. For discussion of external effects when we have clearly intended only what we here designate as Pareto-relevant, see James M. Buchanan, "Politics, Policy, and the Pigovian Margins," *Economica*, 26 (1962), pp. 17–28, and, also, James M. Buchanan and Gordon Tullock, *The Calculus of Consent* (Ann Arbor: 1962).

7. For an early use of marginal evaluation curves, see J. R. Hicks, "The Four Consumer's Surpluses," *Review of Economic Studies*, 11 (1943), pp. 31–41.

8. This diagrammatic analysis is necessarily oversimplified in the sense that the Pareto equilibrium position is represented as a unique point. Over the range between the "private" equilibrium for B and the point of Pareto equilibrium, the sort of bargains struck between A and B will affect the marginal evaluation curves of both individuals within this range. Thus, the more accurate analysis would suggest a "contract locus" of equilibrium points. At Pareto equilibrium, however, the condition shown in the diagrammatic presentation holds, and the demonstration of this fact rather than the location of the solution is the aim of this diagrammatics.

9. Cf. Paul A. Samuelson, *Foundations of Economic Analysis* (Cambridge, Mass.: 1948), p. 208, for a discussion of the views of various writers.

10. This criticism of the Pigovian analysis has been developed by R. H. Coase in "The Problem of Social Cost," *Journal of Law and Economics*, 3 (1960), pp. 1–44.

11. Although developed in rather different terminology, this seems to be closely in accord with Coase's analysis. Cf. R. H. Coase, loc. cit.

12. Paul A. Samuelson, "The Pure Theory of Public Expenditure," *Review of Economics and Statistics*, 36 (1954), pp. 386–89.

13. R. H. Coase, loc. cit.

14. The H_3 position, in this presumably redrawn figure, should not be precisely compared with the same position in the other model. We are using here the same diagram for two models, and, especially over wide ranges, the dependence of the marginal evolution curves on income effects cannot be left out of account.

15. For a treatment of the dual externality problem that clearly shows the important difference between the separable and the nonseparable cases, see Otto Davis and Andrew Whinston, "Externalities, Welfare, and the Theory of Games," *Journal of Political Economy*, 70 (1962), pp. 241–62. As the title suggests, Davis and Whinston utilize the tools of game theory for the inseparable case.

8.

Public and Private Interaction Under Reciprocal Externality

WITH GORDON TULLOCK

Market organization fails to produce results that satisfy the necessary conditions for Pareto optimality when Pareto-relevant externalities remain in equilibrium. This statement is tautological, but it accurately reflects the content of significant portions of theoretical welfare economics. From this statement, a second, and quasitautological one emerges. Given the presence of Pareto-relevant externalities in market equilibrium, collectivization *could* modify the results so as to guarantee the attainment of the Pareto welfare surface. There are no grounds for disagreement here, although, of course, the following less familiar statement is also indisputable. Given the presence of Pareto-relevant externalities in political equilibrium, marketization *could* modify the results so as to guarantee that the welfare surface is reached.

We propose to extend the analysis of both market organization and collective organization in the presence of a specific sort of externality relationship. We shall demonstrate that this extension introduces complications that are not normally considered, despite their importance for any comparative evaluation of the two organizational alternatives. We limit the analysis to those activities which involve reciprocal externalities. That is to say, the behavior of a single unit in a group exerts external effects on remaining members of the group, while, at the same time, the behavior of any other single unit in the group exerts external effects on the first unit.[1] Since the argument for collectivization rests largely on the presence of significant external economies, we shall consider only this case, neglecting external diseconomies. Given any activity that is characterized by relevant reciprocal external economies, private or market organization will result in the simultaneous undertaking of the activity by many persons. If a municipal government does not exist for the performance of such functions, private citizens will, independently, hire guards and night watchmen, vaccinate their dogs against rabies, install fire protection devices, plant flowers in the spring, keep boulevards clear of snow in winter, send their children to school, paint their own houses, feed the birds. The list could be lengthened readily. It is clear that, in many such activities, the private behavior of each person may exert relevant external economies on some or all of the other persons in the community.

There may or may not exist a determinate equilibrium as a result of the interaction of individuals responding independently in activities of this sort. This equilibrium, if it exists, may involve a greater or smaller resource outlay than that which is necessary to satisfy the necessary conditions for Pareto optimality.[2] The mutual adjustment process under independent behavior must be carefully examined before the efficacy of market organization can be compared with that of collectivization.

I. Private and Collective Adjustments

Market Adjustment

Consider a simple example. Immunization against communicable disease protects the individual who takes the shots, but, at the same time, it reduces the likelihood that others in the community catch the disease. If all persons other than one in a community are protected, the remaining member is unlikely to get the disease for the simple reason that there is no one from whom he may catch it. A situation of this sort under a world-of-equals model is represented diagrammatically in Fig. 8-1.

First, consider a discrete case in which it is assumed that one shot provides complete protection to the person who takes it over some relevant time period. If an individual does not get a shot, his chances of contracting the disease decrease as the numbers of others in the community who are inoculated increase. The disease is assumed to be painful; it "costs" something, but it is not fatal. Also, assume that being inoculated costs something. The vertical axis of Fig. 8-1 measures costs, in dollars, either of being inoculated or the properly computed expected dollar equivalent of the pain and inconvenience of getting sick. Conceptually, one can think of the latter as the current insurance premium on a policy providing complete indemnification of illness from the disease.[3] On the horizontal axis is measured the percentage of the population in the group that is inoculated; the group is assumed to be closed. The cost, to an individual, of getting a shot is shown by *OB*. The expected cost of the disease, to the individual, is indicated by the curve, *I,* which may be labeled the "curve of external economies."

If all private decisions are to be made simultaneously, no position of stable equilibrium is present in this simple system. Initially, given the

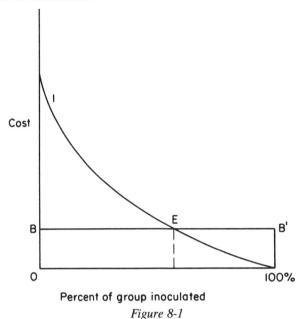

Figure 8-1

costs as depicted in Fig. 8-1, all members of the group purchase inoculations. And, once having done so, all members seek to change their decisions. If it is assumed that immunity lasts for one period only, the simultaneous adjustment model would produce a cyclical swing between full inoculation and no inoculation. The model produces quite different results if the reasonable assumption is made that individuals make decisions in some temporal sequence, even though they may remain, for relevant purposes, essentially identical. In other words, one need assume only that "someone acts first." Under these conditions, individuals will continue to purchase inoculations so long as the discounted or expected costs of getting the disease exceed the costs of the shot. Equilibrium is reached at point *E* in Fig. 8-1. Note that, in this position, persons who are inoculated and those who are not are in roughly equivalent situations. Those who purchase insurance policies pay premiums equal to the costs of the inoculations.

Point *E* represents a position of group equilibrium, when each individual acts independently. Note that, although individuals act independently of each other, they do take into account the presence of external economies in their behavior. The location of the individual along curve *I* depends, not on his own behavior, but on that of all others in the group. This location becomes the basis for his own decision. There is, of course, no means of identifying which individuals will become immunized and which will not.

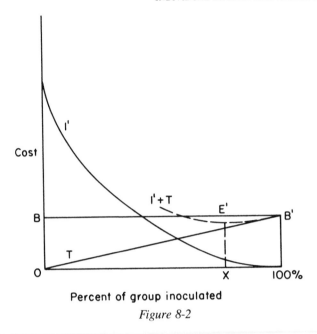

Percent of group inoculated
Figure 8-2

Collective Adjustment

The position of group equilibrium attained under private adjustment must be compared with that which would be attained under collectivization, provided the underlying conditions of the model are not changed. Assume, as before, that all members of the group are identical for relevant purposes. How will collectivization of the activity affect the two cost functions confronted by the single individual, as drawn in Fig. 8-1? Since individuals are assumed equal in this model, tax financing will impose on each person an equal charge. Hence, one can derive a tax-cost function, T, which runs from O to B' in Fig. 8-2. Only if each person in the whole group is inoculated will the tax cost per person equal the cost of purchasing one shot privately.

Under collectivization, it is assumed that the group, as a group, decides upon the percentage of the total number to be inoculated and that, once this decision is made, individuals to be immunized are chosen in some random fashion. Thus, regardless of the collective decision, an individual stands some chance of being in the immunized group. This fact must be taken into account in deriving the external economies curve under collectivization. For each level of inoculation for the group, it will be possible to compute the expected costs of the disease, costs that will become relevant to the individual as he participates in the collective decision process.[4] Because of some positive probability that he will be in the immunized group, at any percentage level, the external economies curve under collectivization, drawn as I' in Fig. 8-2, will lie below the analogous curve, I, in Fig. 8-1 throughout its range, assuming that the basic parameters of the model remain unchanged.

By utilizing the two cost functions in Fig. 8-2, I' and T, it becomes possible to depict the position of group equilibrium under collective organization. This position is *not* indicated by the intersection of these two curves. These are total cost curves, and, in the collectivization model, as different from the private-adjustment model, the individual is able, through some political voting procedure, to choose the position for the "group." The optimal position, for the individual, is indicated by the low point in the curve of total cost, $I' + T$, which is derived by the vertical summation of the two components.[5] This "solution" is to the right of and below the position of equilibrium attained under private provision. In other words, collectivization produces both a greater degree of immunization and a lower cost per person than that which would be present under independent or market adjustment.

There is, of course, nothing at all startling about this result, which is strictly orthodox. The construction introduced does, however, allow attention to be focused on one or two features of the model that are not usually taken into account. Note that, even in ideal collective equilibrium, marginal external economies remain. What are eliminated are the Pareto-relevant externalities, not all externalities. Secondly, the model draws attention to the question as to why the ideal or optimal solution is not achieved under independent adjustment. Return to the insurance premium version. Why does the rational insurance firm not subsidize some of its own clients, encouraging them to be inoculated? If there is only one firm, it could clearly increase profits by carrying out such subsidization to the point where the same amount of immunization that is present under collectivization would be achieved. One firm might, of course, go further and exploit its monopoly position. However, even if there should be a number of insurance firms, each would find it profitable to subsidize inoculation to some extent. One need not, however, rely on the insurance version of the model. Without insurance against the disease, it remains rational for individuals to "bribe" others in the group, each other, to secure inoculation, so long as Pareto-relevant externalities remain. It is, of course, the costs of organizing such bribes or compensations among large groups, and not the presence of externalities, per se, that provide the legitimate basis for collectivization.

Market for Externalities

Such cost barriers to the organization of interpersonal markets point up a rather curious development in the theory of markets. Economists have often assumed that markets work perfectly for the exchange of goods and services, but that markets do not work at all for the exchange of those activities generating external effects. If, in fact, markets should work "perfectly" in a more inclusive sense, all gains from trade would be eliminated, including those that exist, by definition, when Pareto-relevant externalities are present. "Optimal" results are guaranteed by "perfect" markets in this broader model of trade. In the real world, of course, markets work, more or less, for the exchange of goods and services and for the exchange of externalities. The difference is one of degree, not of kind. Side payments for externalities do exist, and institutions are continually emerging to internalize these. Cost barriers to the organization of such interpersonal markets are more severe than those present for ordinary commodity and service markets, but these costs are not necessarily insurmountable.[6]

Distributional Equity

The model suggests yet another important point that often tends to be overlooked. As the cost functions are drawn in Fig. 8-2, collectivization, if ideally operative, will involve only some share of the total population securing inoculation. In the real world, this result may not be forthcoming. Generally accepted standards of equity may, in such instances, require that all persons be inoculated, or that inoculations be made free to all who choose voluntarily to take them. Under the assumptions made, these alternatives would produce the same results; everyone would be inoculated. Note that this solution will not represent any improvement over private provision. All persons will be inoculated; more resources will be devoted to vaccine and clinics; insurance costs will be zero; taxes will be high. Given any bias toward individual freedom of choice, this solution will be less satisfactory than private market adjustment. As compared with "ideal" immunization, this equity solution involves a relative overextension whereas the private adjustment process involves a relative underextension. The cost equivalence between these two inefficient results stems, of course, from the assumption that shots are available at constant costs. If increasing costs should characterize this service, the equity solution would be inefficient, even for the totalitarian. With decreasing costs, the equity solution would always be the efficient one.

The practical implication of this point is that it may be necessary, in order to achieve tolerable efficiency under collective organization, to devise some means of choosing those members of the total population who are to be directly benefited. This means must not appear to violate generally accepted standards of nondiscrimination. The desired results may be broadly attained by certain class distinctions, such as, for example, that only children or the aged shall be immunized. Alternatively,

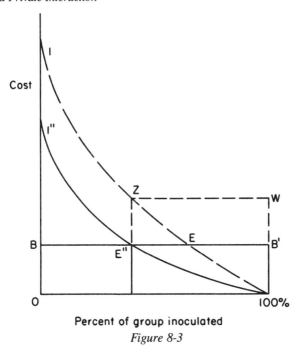

Cost

Percent of group inoculated

Figure 8-3

direct-user pricing could be introduced; inoculations could be made freely available to all who choose to pay a direct-user charge. This charge would be set at a level that would generate approximately the optimal outcome. In any case, either administrative rules or direct-user pricing must, if introduced, be substantially "correct." If not, there may arise particular institutional diseconomies that would have to be taken into account in any comparative evaluation of public and private organization.

Collectivization without Relevant Externality

One useful benchmark case that is not normally considered, but which will be helpful, involves the collectivization of an activity that is not characterized by relevant externality in market organization. Suppose, for example, that through some error, inoculation against the communicable disease is not collectivized but that, instead, the medical treatment of the disease is. (The current practice of the National Health Service in Great Britain, which provides free hospital care but charges small fees for drugs, may be a partially applicable real-world example.) The situation is depicted in Fig. 8-3, where the underlying conditions are assumed the same as before. The expected cost of the disease is reduced for the individual, since treatment is provided "free"; the external economies curve becomes I'', which is clearly lower than I in Fig. 8-1 (drawn as dotted in Fig. 8-3), and may be, although it will not necessarily be, lower than I' in Fig. 8-2. The cost of inoculation is not changed. Hence, independent adjustment will produce group equilibrium at E''. Note that, under this scheme, there will be fewer inoculations and more disease than under wholly private organization. Each individual will, however, bear the same direct cost as under wholly private provision. The tax costs of treatment are wholly excess. The amount of these costs, for the group, is shown by the rectangle, $E''ZWB'$. This result need not be surprising. Treatment of disease is "free," and the individual adjusts his behavior to this fact. Since there are, by assumption, no relevant external economies involved in treatment, per se, only full-cost user pricing could eliminate the inefficiency under these arrangements. But, of course, such pricing would undermine the rationale for the collectivization.

The particular details of the example are not important. It should be noted, however, that when an activity that generates no significant external effects is collectivized, some distortion in resource use will necessarily result, unless goods and services are distributed through a system of voluntary purchases at market prices. This point is a familiar and obvious one, but it does represent one side of the whole externality-collectivization discussion that tends to be sidetracked. Arguments for decollectivization based on government failure in such cases are on all fours with arguments for demarketization based on market failure.

Excess Burden of Taxation

To this point, as is normal with economists who discuss topics such as these, we have assumed that tax-supported collective activities are financed with zero excess burden. If one is to complete the catalogue of externalities that must be relevant to any decision among alternative organizational forms, this element must be incorporated in the model. It is widely accepted that any tax, other than a purely hypothetical lump-sum construction, modifies the conditions for choice of the individual and, therefore, distorts his behavior to some extent. This possibility can be introduced into the simple geometrical model without difficulty. In Fig. 8-4, Fig. 8-2 is reproduced, only here allowance is made for some excess burden of taxation. The tax curve, T, is shifted upward to, say, T'. This, in turn, shifts the total cost curve, $I' + T'$, upward, and, with the configuration as drawn, this shifts the "optimal" position to the left. If the excess burden involved with raising tax revenues is sufficiently large, the final results achieved under collectivization may actually be less "efficient" than those achieved under market adjustment, despite the admitted presence of noninternalized and relevant reciprocal external economies in the latter. The implication is clear that the size of the excess burden of taxation

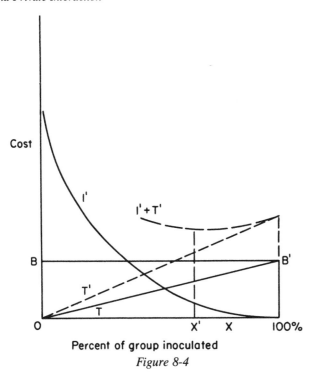

Percent of group inoculated

Figure 8-4

should, in fact, be considered along with the other externalities in any choice of organization.

This point, like the others, is an obvious one. However, it seems rarely to have been made explicit in the discussion. Cost-benefit analysis, which is now becoming a popular pastime, has developed with very little attention being paid to the excess burden that might be involved in raising given revenue sums through taxation.

II. Multiple Alternatives

Market Adjustment with Multiple Alternatives:
    The Unequal Distribution Case

In the simple model introduced in the first section, it has been assumed that each individual confronts only two alternatives of choice. He either gets inoculated or he does not. In the more general case, many alternatives will be open to him. Staying within the immunization model for the

	a_0	a_1	a_2	a_3	a_4
b_4	30 70 / 0 30	12 62 / 10 22	4 64 / 20 24	2 72 / 30 32	0 80 / 40 40
b_3	50 86 / 0 50	22 67.5 / 10 32	8 63 / 20 28	4 68 / 30 34	0 72 / 40 40
b_2	62 96 / 0 62	27 70 / 10 37	12 64 / 20 32	5 63 / 30 35	0 64 / 40 40
b_1	70 110 / 0 70	29 78 / 10 39	13 70 / 20 33	5.5 67.5 / 30 35.5	0 62 / 40 40
b_0	75 150 / 0 75	30 110 / 10 40	14 96 / 20 34	6 86 / 30 36	0 70 / 40 40

Figure 8-5

sake of expositional continuity, one can think of the individual either doing nothing, getting one shot, two shots, three shots, etc. Each additional shot will provide him with additional protection against disease and also generate external benefits for his fellows, but never reduce his risk to zero. Infantile paralysis vaccinations provide a partially applicable real-world example here. The reciprocal externality relationship is assumed to extend over the whole range of possible action open to each member of the group.

One means of illustrating this model is provided in the matrix of Fig. 8-5. Here for consideration is a two-person group only, consisting of individuals A and B. Each person can either get no shots or any number of shots up to a maximum of four per time period, producing a twenty-five cell matrix. For convenience, payoffs are measured negatively in terms of costs; hence, each "player" will attempt to minimize his relevant payout. In each matrix cell several entries are included. These are to be read as follows: In the upper left-hand corner of each cell is the expected cost of the disease computed from the probability of contracting it and the cost of suffering it once contracted. For simplicity, this may again be considered as the cost of an insurance premium per period. In the lower left-hand corner of each square is the cost of inoculations, assumed to be $10 per shot. These two costs are summed in the lower right-hand corner of each cell, giving the total cost to the individual, who is A in the payout matrix shown. Individual A will attempt to minimize the figure in the lower right-hand corner. Again for simplicity in exposition, it is assumed that A and B are identical in relevant respects. This makes the matrix confronting B the transpose of that confronting A. Thus, for example, the

figure in the lower right-hand corner of the cell, a_3b_1, gives a total cost to
A of \$35.50. This must be the same as the total cost to B in the cell b_3a_1.
One can in this way compute the costs to B in each cell. Adding these to
those for A, one obtains a total social cost figure, which is entered in the
upper right-hand corner of each cell.

Consider now the adjustment process under private organization.
Assume that no elements of strategic behavior are present, an assumption
that will be justified later. Under these conditions, each person will purchase two shots per period. If, for any reason, some cell other than (a_2b_2)
is found to exist, one or both of the individuals will find it advantageous
to shift his own behavior. Note, however, that the social optimum is
located at (a_4b_1) or (a_1b_4). In this case, total costs can be minimized (total
benefits maximized, by a significantly unequal distribution of) services
between the two persons. It is, of course, obvious that this particular
result stems from the values assigned in the matrix illustration. The result
is interesting, nevertheless, for it suggests one possibly important basis
for collectivization that is seldom discussed. It is possible that the reciprocal external economies are such that only through collective organization can a sufficiently *unequal* distribution of services be implemented, so
as to achieve efficiency. In this instance, collectivization allows a specific
technological improvement in distribution to be made that is not possible
under private provision. This seems reasonably common with some real-
world public services. Police do not patrol every street with the same
intensity. The national defense establishment concentrates its services at
strategic points.

Market Adjustment with Multiple Alternatives:
    The Equal Distribution Case

Despite the importance of the unequal distribution of services in securing
overall efficiency in particular situations, it will be profitable to return to
the equal-distribution model since it is slightly more amenable to analysis.
Continue to assume that individuals in the group are substantially identical. A matrix similar to that of Fig. 8-5, but with different payoffs, is
shown in Fig. 8-6. Note that here each person would be motivated to take
one shot, but neither would take a second, since he could not expect the
other person to do likewise. However, if the two parties could make an
agreement, each would be better off with both parties taking two shots.
This is, of course, the traditional reciprocal external economies case,
presented here as a version of the prisoners' dilemma game. Note, however, that if inoculation should be collectivized, with services being made
free to individuals, that is, with the receipt of services wholly divorced
from tax payments, both A and B would take four shots. This position is

B \ A	a_0	a_1	a_2	a_3	a_4
b_4	13 58 X 0 13	8 61 10 18	2 63 20 22	0 70 30 30	0 80 z 40 40
b_3	15 52 X 0 15	10 55 10 20	3 56 20 23	2 64 30 32	0 70 40 40
b_2	21 50 X 0 21	12 49 o 10 22	4 48 o 20 24	3 56 30 33	1 63 40 41
b_1	26 56.5 0 26	15 50 X 10 25	7 49 o 20 27	5 55 30 35	3 61 40 43
b_0	30 60 0 30	19.5 56.5 10 29.5	9 50 X 20 29	7 52 30 37	5 58 40 45

Figure 8-6

less desirable than that reached under private adjustment, given the pay-offs of the matrix. Such free provision of partially divisible services leads individuals to extend consumption to the point where marginal evaluation is zero, resulting in excessive utilization.[7]

Five cells in the matrix of Fig. 8-6 are marked with X's. These represent simply the best situations for A, given each possible choice on the part of B. Note that the configuration of these A *optima* cells has specific characteristics. Its general direction is north-northwest, with the total costs for A becoming lower and lower as movement is made in this general direction. Call this locus of low points for A "the river," or "A's river," since one can think of these X cells as the locus of the lowest points on the third dimensional cost surface of the matrix.

Three other cells on the matrix are marked with o's. These make up the set of positions that show lower social costs than a_1b_1, the position of independent adjustment equilibrium. The cell, a_2b_2, marked o', is the single "optimum," but for both individuals in the group, either of the o cells would be preferable to the private equilibrium position. This whole set may be called the "social provision area."

Continuous Variation

It is relatively easy to shift from the matrix illustration that incorporates discrete and discontinuous alternatives to the more familiar case of continuous variation. Fig. 8-7 simply converts relationships similar to those in Fig. 8-6 to the continuous case. The "river" now becomes a smooth curve. Private equilibrium is shown by the intersection of the river, labeled R,

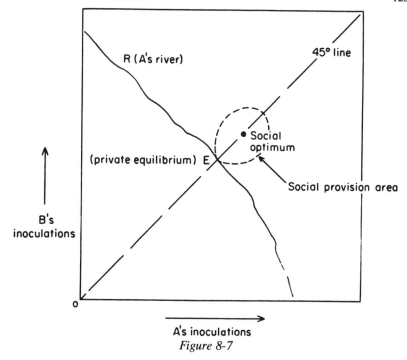

Figure 8-7

with a 45-degree line drawn from the origin. The 45-degree line is, of course, the result of the assumption of identical persons and equal distribution of the activity. For *B,* it would be possible also to draw in a river curve, which would be the transpose of that drawn in for *A* under the stated restrictions. The two rivers would, of course, both cut the 45-degree line in the same point, labeled *E,* in Fig. 8-7.

This construction has the advantage of facilitating the shift from the two-person case to the *n*-person case without difficulty. So long as one retains the assumption that all persons are identical in relevant respects, the analysis is not modified. On the one axis we simply measure the activity of "all others than *A.*" Given appropriately defined scales, one can still utilize the 45-degree line construction. Any point along this line represents equal consumption of the service by all members of the *n*-person group.

In the two-person model, we have assumed, arbitrarily, that individuals did not engage in strategic bargaining behavior. The basis for this assumption can now be clarified, and with this assumption, two-person models may be used to attain results applicable to *n*-person groups. In an *n*-person group, a single individual, say *A,* will realize that the behavior of the *n*-1 others in the group will influence his own utility. Recognizing this externality, he will adjust his own behavior to it. He will not, however, consider

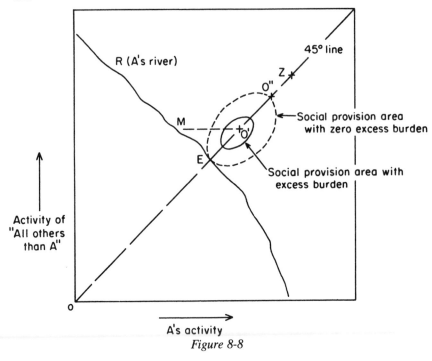

Figure 8-8

his own action to be sufficiently important as to influence the aggregate behavior of others. Hence, rational behavior consists in his adjusting or adapting his own activity to the situation in which he finds himself. This is, of course, fully analogous to the standard assumption concerning behavior of the individual buyer or seller in competitive markets.

Fig. 8-8 illustrates the *n*-person model. This is identical with Fig. 8-7 except for the fact that "all others than *A*" are substituted for *B*. *A*'s river may be drawn in, as before, and the position of group equilibrium under private adjustment, *E*, remains determined by the intersection of the river and the 45-degree line. This position will not be optimal. If joint action is possible, there must be points to the northeast of *E* that are preferable to *E*, for *A* and also for all others in the group. Topologically, the "river" represents the locus of low points on the third-dimensional cost surface, as this is confronted by *A*, acting independently. Remaining members in the group will confront similar cost surfaces, upon which similar "rivers" can be traced. The final position will be determined by the independent action of each person. Joint action is required to shift into the preferred area, which we have called the area of "social provision." Each point in this set is lower on the cost surface than *E*, for *A* and for everyone else in the group. But each point is dominated, for *A* and for everyone else, by points along the river, if independent adjustment is allowed.

Excess-Burden Qualification

The excess-burden qualification must be incorporated into the geometrical model. If collectivization necessarily involves the imposition of taxes that have allocative-incentive effects, the "social provision" area is smaller in size than that which is indicated under the assumption of zero excess burden (shown by the dashed-circle area in Fig. 8-8). It is possible, of course, that the external costs imposed by tax collection would eliminate altogether any net advantages of collectivization. However, the illustration is deliberately drawn to suggest that, even with some positive excess burden of taxation, a social provision area remains, as shown by the area enclosed by the solid line in Fig. 8-8. Any position within this area represents some improvement, for A and all other members of the group, over E. A single optimal position, within this area, is shown at O'. This position will be located along the 45-degree line, from our assumption of equal distribution of the activity or service.

Rationing Difficulties

Again we emphasize that there is nothing particularly new in this construction. It does help to point to some of the complicating features that must be taken into account. Refer to the area of social provision shown in Fig. 8-8. The shift from private organization, which would attain position E, to collective or political organization, is efficient only if the group can insure a final location within the preferred area. There are, however, two separate problems that must be surmounted before such insurance is present. First of all, as previously suggested for the discrete case, unless either administrative controls or price rationing are introduced, collectivization may result in an excessive utilization of available facilities. Suppose, for example, that government finances the activity in question from general tax revenues, and, to stay with the example, then makes immunization shots free to all who want them in whatever quantity desired. The adoption of this "needs" approach to budgeting, which is not at all uncommon in real-world fiscal experience, would surely lead to some position such as that shown by Z in Fig. 8-8, a position that may clearly be less desirable than E.

This problem becomes serious only insofar as individuals are able, by their utilization of a collectively provided service, to reduce the quantity available for others. Hence, for a purely collective good, defined in the strict Samuelson sense, this problem need not arise. It is known, however, that few goods or services are wholly indivisible. Most collective services embody both divisible and indivisible elements. To remain within the social provision area, therefore, something other than the mere collectivization of an activity must be introduced. The various administrative schemes for carrying out the necessary rationing are familiar. Police protection is provided generally, but a policeman cannot be asked to stand in front of every house. Firemen will respond to calls if fire breaks out, but only on occasion will they take pet cats out of trees, and severe fines are imposed for false alarms. Normally, only certain types of rubbish are picked up by municipal garbage collectors.

This first problem of keeping government efficient has been traditionally recognized in the theory of public finance. A time-honored principle states that governments cannot, efficiently, give away services for which the demand is price-elastic over some range between cost price and zero. The treatment of the problem here is couched in different terms, but remains basically within the orthodox tradition.

Chiseling under Collectivization

The second problem of government efficiency also brings up a familiar issue in price theory, which, to our knowledge, has not been developed with respect to the provision of public goods or services. The price theory analogue here is the enforcement of cartel agreements. Each partner to an agreement has an opportunity to "chisel," and, thereby, to secure differential profits for himself, although he recognizes that, if all parties to the agreement do the same, everyone will be damaged.[8] Competitive pressures are usually held to be sufficiently strong to guarantee that chiseling will take place in large-number groups until and unless severe sanctions are in some fashion imposed against all potential price-cutters.

The same analysis is clearly applicable to the problem of remaining within the area of efficient social provision under collectivization of an activity. Refer to Fig. 8-8. Note that, by the construction of the river, A will be motivated, always, to move in an east-west direction (the only way that he can move) so as to reach the lowest point on his cost surface. Assume now that the activity has been collectivized, and that the optimal position O' has been reached. Individual A finds himself located at O', on the 45-degree line. Clearly, if he retains any freedom of private action he would find it preferable to shift to point M, the lowest point in the plane cut horizontally through O'. If he should succeed in reaching M, he will be better off than at O'. But, since we assume that all individuals act similarly, the group will eventually end up again at E, where all will be worse off than at O'. In fact, they will be worse off than they were initially since they will be bearing the excess burden of providing part of the activity in question by taxation.

Wagner's Law of Increasing Government Activity

The point made in the previous paragraph is worth developing in some detail since it provides one explanation of Wagner's law of ever-increasing government activity. The question that arises is how and why will the individual shift from the social provision area? If the activity is collectivized, the individual will, presumably be subjected to some coercive levy of taxes. Hence, he will not be able, by his own independent action, to reduce his own share of the cost of providing services for the group. If he were allowed purely private adjustment, he could shift to point *M* and reduce costs. Since he cannot do so, he will have no incentive to shift from *O'* to *M*. No problem of chiseling arises.

If the activity in question should be wholly independent of other activities within the adjustment possibilities of the individual, no process analogous to chiseling will take place. There would be no incentive for the individual to break the implicit agreement that collectivization enforces. It is known, however, that many separate activities, whether these are publicly or privately organized, are interdependent for the individual's decision calculus. Remaining within the immunization example, at *E,* the position of private equilibrium, assume that the individual is fully adjusted to the external actions of other persons. He will secure the indicated number of shots; he will also take certain other actions that may be closely related to direct immunization. Assume these include the maintenance of certain standards of sanitation in the treatment of garbage. Now assume that the immunization program in the community is collectivized, and the individual shifts to position *O'*. While he will have no incentive to modify his consumption of the service, assuming coercive tax payments along with ideal rationing schemes, he will not be in equilibrium with respect to those privately purchased services that are related to immunization. If, as has been assumed, individual *A* is in full equilibrium at *E*, then at *O'* he will find that he has an unnecessarily high level of sanitation. He will be able to, and he will have an incentive to, reduce his private spending on sanitation. As a result of this adjustment process, all individuals will find that position *O'*, with respect to immunization from the disease, is no longer optimal. The effect of the private adjustment process is to increase the value of the external economies from direct immunization. Hence, position *O'*, assumed to be optimal in relation to a determinate level of closely related activities, assumes nonoptimal properties. The group, despite the fact that it has collectivized inoculations, remains in an external-economies dilemma. Thus, there is an incentive to expand the immunization further, to, say, *O''*. The whole area of social provision shifts to the northeast, but this is not drawn in Fig. 8-8. Once again a private adjustment process will take place, and, for the same reason, rational individual behavior in collective choice will further increase the level of the activity. The spiral-like process will continue, with public expenditures rising and private expenditures falling until some position is reached where the interdependence between immunization and other activities under the private control of the individual becomes insignificantly small.

If the excess burden resulting from public provision is taken into account, the possibility that the ultimate outcome may be undesirable is increased. Returning to Fig. 8-8, suppose that the society has previously moved from E to O', and then that private adjustment has taken place in other activities, making an extension of government provision desirable. For the move to O'' to be taken, it is only necessary that the *additional* excess burden be less than the gain expected. The process of adjustment may, through this effect, remove the net benefit from public provision. In order to avoid this result, the following steps would have to be taken: Before making each adjustment, not only the excess burden would have to be taken into account, but also the predicted private adjustment to each new arrangement of services.

Practical illustrations of the relationship noted here are surely abundant in emerging municipalities. Without collective fire protection devices, homeowners buy fire extinguishers and introduce private sprinkler systems. Once collective fire departments are installed, these individual devices are not replaced. Rational homeowners, and potential owners, depend upon municipally supplied protection, once it is provided, and, because they do so, investment in further expansion of municipal protection becomes necessary. In established municipalities it can be predicted that increased efficiency could be achieved by some substitution of individual or private fire protection devices for collective protection, provided that the institutional means could be found through which such a substitution would be possible. There would probably be a greater return, at the margin, from investment in more and better locks than in an addition to the police force.

In these illustrations, collectively supplied services stand in some substitute relationship to privately supplied services. This seems the most realistic case, although complementarity could also be present. The provision of a public park may, for example, encourage people to expand their private purchases of picnic supplies and equipment. This, in turn, makes them desire more picnics, for which some greater investment in public parks may be necessary. The outcome is the same; a spiral-like expansion of public expenditures until all of the secondary adjustments in private behavior produce some overall equilibrium.

Intergovernmental Applications

The mechanism of adjustment analyzed here can be applied without difficulty to intergovernmental fiscal relationships. It is commonly observed that when the federal government begins to supplement state expenditures for particular functions, there seems an inexorable tendency for state-local expenditures to be totally replaced by federal. This is, of course, readily explained by the fact that states and localities adjust to their own optimal levels, creating as they do still further need for expansion in federal outlay. Viewed in this light, matching provisions on the various conditional grants-in-aid may be seen as one device aimed at keeping state-local behavior restricted so as to guarantee that some position in the social provision area is maintained for the particular function. The matching grant would be analogous to an administrative requirement that all warehouses provide private sprinkler systems, even after the organization of a municipal fire department.

III. Collectivization and Growth

To be sophisticated in the mid-1960s, any discussion on matters remotely economic must, at some point, introduce the effects of the model on growth or the effects of growth on the model. Does the fact of growth affect the decision as to whether particular activities should, on efficiency grounds, be publicly or privately organized? There seems to be agreement on the fact that growth does modify the conditions of the problem, but there is also widespread disagreement as to the direction that the influence takes. It will be instructive to apply the models developed in this article to this issue.

Return to the matrix illustration contained in Fig. 8-6. Assume that, as growth takes place, personal incomes rise. With higher personal income levels, the money values for the opportunity costs of getting the disease increase. If, for purposes of this example, one can assume that these costs consist solely in time lost from the earning of salaries, a doubling of personal incomes will tend to double opportunity costs of illness. The number in the upper left-hand corner in each matrix cell of Fig. 8-6 can then be doubled. Let it also be assumed that the costs of inoculations do not increase, but remain at $10 per shot. Fig. 8-9 incorporates the necessary changes from Fig. 8-6, changes that are due to growth in the manner postulated.

The rather dramatic change in results can best be noted by examining the cells marked with the Xs in the two matrices. Fig. 8-9 exhibits column dominance; regardless of what action B takes, A will find it advantageous to take two shots. Since the matrix confronted by B is merely the transpose of that facing A, he will also take two shots. Private adjustment will, therefore, attain the social optimum. There exists no position that is socially superior to the cell marked X', the position of private equilibrium. There is no social provision area.

B \ A	a_0	a_1	a_2	a_3	a_4
b_4	26 76 0 26	16 72 10 26	4 66 (X) 20 24	0 70 30 30	0 80 40 40
b_3	30 74 0 30	20 70 10 30	6 62 (X) 20 26	4 68 30 34	0 70 40 40
b_2	42 80 0 42	24 68 10 34	8 56 (X') 20 28	6 62 30 36	2 66 40 42
b_1	52 102 0 52	30 80 10 40	14 68 (X) 20 34	10 70 30 40	6 72 40 46
b_0	60 120 0 60	40 102 10 50	18 80 (X) 20 38	14 74 30 44	10 76 40 50

Figure 8-9

Note that the external economies are not eliminated by the fact of income growth; these continue to exist as before. What the change has accomplished is the conversion of external economies that were Pareto-relevant, at the private equilibrium solution of Fig. 8-6, into external economies that are not Pareto-relevant, at the private equilibrium solution of Fig. 8-9. Individual A's situation continues to be affected by B's level of immunization; the more shots B takes, the better off A finds himself. Total costs for A fall as he moves north along any column of the matrix. The same holds for B, of course, in the transpose matrix; "rivers still run downhill." In the equilibrium position, X', in Fig. 8-9, however, A and B cannot, by mutual agreement, attain any other position that is preferred to X'. Each person would be willing to contribute up to \$2 for either his own or his fellow's securing an additional shot. But this leaves a \$6 deficit when benefits are compared with the \$10 cost.

The matrix of Fig. 8-9 represents, of course, only one simple numerical example that is deliberately constructed to make the point desired. The result derived can be made generally applicable if it is carefully applied. So long as the process of economic growth and development serves to increase the opportunity costs arising from failure of individuals to act privately more than it serves to increase the private cost of the activity itself, there will surely be some tendency for the independent or private adjustment equilibrium to shift toward the social optimum in the process, "optimum" being defined by the standard Paretian criteria. The external economies become less relevant as the society becomes more affluent. At some point in the process of development, these may become irrelevant, and, if they do, the activity should be returned to private organization providing it has been previously collectivized.

Practical examples are available to illustrate these general results. It is probably correct to say that the external or spillover benefits argument for governmental or collective support for elementary schooling becomes less and less relevant as the average level of income in a community rises. The case for socialized medicine was not so strong in 1964 as it would have been in 1938, on pure efficiency grounds, other elements of the problem remaining unchanged.

For completeness, it should be noted that the process of economic growth could make the external economies more significant in certain cases. If, for example, as personal incomes double, and opportunity costs of disease double (as between the situation in Fig. 8-6 and that in Fig. 8-9), the costs of inoculations should also double, the external economies remaining relevant. What is important here is the relationship between the opportunity costs (the benefits) of the action generating reciprocal external effects and the direct costs of carrying out the activity. With economic progress, it seems reasonable to suppose that the former should increase more rapidly than the latter, although peculiar circumstances may alter this relationship.

The analysis is not intended to suggest that, considered overall, the aggregate collectivization of the economy need decrease as economic development proceeds. Other elements of change surely introduce differ-ent, and to an extent, offsetting factors. It seems safe to say that the external economies argument for expansion in the public sector will diminish over time, as this argument suggests. However, there will prob-ably arise other interrelationships among persons, for the most part exter-nal diseconomies, which will require additional collective action in order for tolerable efficiency to be achieved. This may be summarized by saying that, as people get richer, they need to rely less and less on their neighbors to cooperate in securing the indivisible benefits of possible joint activities, but they may need to rely more and more on some collective mechanism to prevent themselves, and their neighbors, from imposing mutually unde-sirable costs on each other. In its broadest sense, "congestion" replaces "cooperation" as the underlying motive force behind collective action.

Analytically, external diseconomies and external economies are basi-cally equivalent. There are important implications for the trend of public expenditure totals over time, however, if the thesis here is accepted. The collective action required in the case of Pareto-relevant external disecon-omies can often be carried out by the introduction of simple administrative rules. Municipalities can simply prohibit transistor radios on public beaches, for example. By contrast, if the same municipality desires to see that all its schoolchildren get hot school lunches, it will normally expend funds to provide such lunches. It could, of course, simply require that all children purchase hot lunches. But distributional considerations prevent

	a_0	a_1	a_2	a_3	a_4
b_4	13 55.5 (2.5) X 0 13 (40) (42.5)	8 59.5 (1.5) 10 18 (40) (41.5)	2 62.5 (.5) 20 22 (40) (40.5)	0 70 (0) 30 30 (40) (40)	0 80 (0) 40 40 (40) (40)
b_3	15 48.5 (3.5) X 0 15 (30) (33.5)	10 52.5 (2.5) 10 20 (30) (32.5)	3 53.5 (1.5) 20 23 (30) (31.5)	2 63 (1) 30 32 (30) (31)	0 70 (0) 40 40 (30) (30)
b_2	21 45.5 (4.5) X 0 21 (20) (24.5)	12 45.5 (3.5) 10 22 (20) (23.5)	4 46 (2) 20 24 (20) (22)	3 54.5 (1.5) 30 33 (20) (21.5)	1 62 (1) 40 41 (20) (21)
b_1	26 46 (10) 0 26 (10) (20)	15 42.5 (7.5) X 10 25 (10) (17.5)	7 43 (6) 20 27 (10) (16)	5 50 (5) 30 35 (10) (15)	3 57 (4) 40 43 (10) (14)
b_0	30 45 (15) B 0 30 (0) (15)	20 43 (13) B 10 30 (0) (13)	9 39.5 (10.5) XB 20 29 (0) (10.5)	7 44.5 (7.5) B 30 37 (0) (7.5)	5 51 (6.5) B 40 45 (0) (6.5)
B / A	a_0	a_1	a_2	a_3	a_4

Figure 8-10

the extension of administrative rules to the external economies side comparative with their application on the diseconomies side.

IV. Nonsymmetrical Reciprocity

A World of Unequals

There remains the task of extending the models so as to make them apply to a social group that contains persons who are *unequal* in respects relevant to the reciprocal externality relationships under consideration. As before, it is useful to begin with a two-person matrix illustration. Fig. 8-10 duplicates Fig. 8-6 in payouts confronting Individual A. Let us now assume that, instead of being equal with A, Individual B is, relatively, poor. The monetary value of benefits (opportunity costs) to B is, therefore, lower for B than for A. For simplicity, assume these to be one-half those for A. The matrix confronted by B is, in this case, no longer the simple transpose of that confronted by A, but instead is the transpose with the figures in the upper left-hand corner of each cell reduced by one-half.

The payouts actually confronting B are shown in Fig. 8-10 in the bracketed figures. Assume that the price of getting the shots remains the same as before.

The optimum values for A remain unchanged, as is shown by the cells marked by X's. Note, however, that the behavior of B will be substantially different. As the figures are computed for the example, B finds himself in a position of row dominance. Regardless of what A does or might do, B will not find it advantageous to get any immunization on his own. The cells marked with the B's trace the optimum values for B over all possible actions of A. In this case, cell a_2b_0 becomes the private adjustment equilibrium. Note, also, that this is the collective or social optimum under the revised set of payoffs. This result need not, of course, be a general one. It does indicate, however, that private adjustment may, in fact, generate the socially optimum solution, even in the presence of reciprocal external economies.

Discriminatory Pricing

When the world of unequals is introduced, and especially when the collectivization alternative is examined, the assumption that individuals will be confronted with uniform prices for the services in question becomes highly unreal. The poor may be allowed to purchase services at lower prices than the rich. One could, somewhat realistically in the particular example of medical care, assume that the private suppliers of inoculations made shots available to the poor at lower prices than to the rich. This would, of course, modify the private adjustment solution. This pricing change may or may not shift the solution closer to that which satisfied the necessary conditions for Pareto optimality. The relationship of the change to the Pareto frontier would depend upon the precise nature of the reciprocal externality in reference to the particular form of discrimination introduced.

Discrimination in Tax Prices

A more interesting, and applicable, model, for the purposes of this discussion, is that which assumes the service to be collectivized, with the financing of the combination of services provided carried out on the basis of some familiar pattern of taxation. Suppose, for example, that the payout situation confronting A and B is that shown in Fig. 8-10. However, the activity will now be under collective organization, and the direct outlay for inoculations is to be financed by the levy of a proportional income tax. Assume that A has an income that is double that for B. Hence, out of each aggregate outlay, A will pay two-thirds, and B only one-third. The results of this change are shown in Fig. 8-11.

	a_0	a_1	a_2	a_3	a_4
b_4	13 55.4 (2.5) X 26.6 39.6 (13.3) (15.8)	8 59.4 (1.5) 33.3 41.3 (16.6) (18.1)	2 62.5 (.5) 40 42 (20) (20.5)	0 69.9 (0) 46.6 46.6 (23.3) (23.3)	0 79.9 (0) 53.3 53.3 (26.6) (26.6)
b_3	15 48.5 (3.5) X 20 35 (10) (13.5)	10 52.4 (2.5) 26.6 36.6 (13.3) (15.8)	3 54.4 (1.5) 33.3 36.3 (16.6) (18.1)	2 63 (1) 40 42 (20) (21)	0 69.9 (0) 46.6 46.6 (23.3) (23.3)
b_2	21 45.4 (4.5) B 13.3 34.3 (6.6) (11.1)	12 45.5 (3.5) B 20 32 (10) (13.5)	4 45.9 (2) BX 26.6 30.6 (13.3) (15.3)	3 54.4 (1.5) 33.3 36.3 (16.6) (18.1)	1 62 (1) 40 41 (20) (21)
b_1	26 45.9 (10) 6.6 32.6 (3.3) (13.3)	15 42.4 (7.5) C 13.3 28.3 (6.6) (14.1)	7 43 (6) X 20 27 (10) (16)	5 49.9 (5) 26.6 31.6 (13.3) (18.3)	3 56.9 (4) 33.3 36.3 (16.6) (20.6)
b_0	30 45 (15) 0 30 (0) (15)	20 42.9 (13) 6.6. 26.6 (3.3) (16.3)	9 39.4 (10.5) XO' 13.3 22.3 (6.6) (17.1)	7 44.5 (7.5) B 20 27 (10) (17.5)	5 51.4 (6.5) B 26.6 31.6 (13.3) (19.8)

B / A

Figure 8-11

The figures in the upper left-hand corner of each cell are the same as shown in Fig. 8-10, since the opportunity costs of the disease have not changed. Similarly, the figures in the upper right-hand corner of each cell are not changed. Neither opportunity costs nor direct costs have been modified, for the group as a whole. For each cell, however, the distribution of direct costs has been modified. Note, for example, cell $a_0 b_1$; under the private adjustment situation, B pays $10 for one shot; A pays nothing since he gets no shots. However, in the proportional income tax model, for this same physical activity, B will pay only one-third of the total cost of $10, while A will pay two-thirds. The figures in the lower right-hand corner of each cell, indicating individual cost totals, are changed appropriately to reflect this modification in the allocation of direct costs.

It is clear that the individually desired positions will be modified by this imposed change in the allocation of costs. Individual adjustment is not, of course, possible since it is assumed that the activity is now collectivized. It is useful in evaluating the collective result that may emerge, however, to trace through the positions of individual optima under these modified conditions. The cells marked X trace out the positions that A would choose, given each level of B's activity. Similarly, the B cells trace out the same thing for B.

Now assume that both persons must agree on any collective solution, but that some constitutional rule requires proportional taxation. The position of political equilibrium in this case is that indicated by cell a_1b_1, marked as C. This may be shown by examining the process through which agreement is reached. Clearly, both persons would agree to move from a_0b_0, the no-activity cell, to a_1b_1. However, at least one person would object to any moves beyond this, in any direction. Note, however, that the political equilibrium solution is not the social optimum under the revised payoffs. This is shown, as in Fig. 8-10, in the cell, b_0a_2, marked O' in Fig. 8-11.

There is nothing especially new in this conclusion. Collective organization should not be expected to produce optimal results unless the structure of tax prices should be such as to guarantee that the Pareto conditions are satisfied. And it should be evident that it would be, indeed, highly unlikely that the distribution of total taxes on the basis of any of the familiar institutions of taxation would produce optimal results. The model is helpful in that it does indicate the necessary correspondence between the structure of tax prices and the political solution that might emerge.

In a more realistic setting, larger groups would have to be considered, along with different political rules for reaching collective decisions. The two-man model can be applied to a limited, but helpful, extent in this connection. Suppose, for example, that the poor were in the majority, and that majority rule prevailed, although the constitutional requirement of proportional taxation remained in force. In this case, a solution approximating that shown at a_0b_2 would be predicted. On the other hand, should the rich be in the majority under similar circumstances, cell a_2b_0 could be predicted as the result. It is, of course, pure circumstance that the latter would be, in the configuration of the numerical example, the socially most desirable result.

V. Conclusion

In this paper we have attempted to examine, with the aid of some very simple examples and some very elementary models, the adjustment process in the presence of reciprocal external economies. Several points have been developed which have not, possibly, been adequately recognized in the more hurried discussions of external economies and diseconomies. The importance of the social decision concerning the basic organizational structure of activities generating reciprocal external economies cannot be underestimated. Perhaps the major single point to be gained from this paper is that there are many more complications relevant to this social decision than might appear upon cursory examination. The results have been primarily negative; it is far easier to indicate that certain solutions fail to produce the ideally desired results than it is to indicate alternative institutional arrangements that will do so. Perhaps the greatest single need for improved analysis in theoretical political economy is for somewhat more careful recognition and analysis of the institutional processes through which people, publicly or privately, carry on economic activities.

Notes

1. For a definition of an externality, and for a careful distinction between a Pareto-relevant and a Pareto-irrelevant externality, see James M. Buchanan and William C. Stubblebine, "Externality," *Economica,* 29 (November 1962), pp. 371–84. For an important paper that introduces some of the complications of the reciprocal externality case, and for a paper further developing some ideas related to those treated here, see Otto Davis and Andrew Whinston, "Externalities, Welfare, and the Theory of Games," *Journal of Political Economy,* 70 (June 1962), pp. 241–62, and Davis and Whinston, "Some Foundations of Public Expenditure Theory" (unpublished ms.) Turvey summarizes the developments in Ralph Turvey, "On Divergencies Between Social Cost and Private Cost," *Economica,* 30 (August 1963), pp. 309–13.

2. For a demonstration of the point that private adjustment may generate a greater than optimal outlay, see James M. Buchanan and M. Z. Kafoglis, "A Note on Public Goods Supply," *American Economic Review,* 52 (June 1963), pp. 403–14.

3. If the world-of-equals assumption should be relaxed, there would, of course, be a different external economies curve for each person. This complicating factor would not change the basic conclusions of the analysis.

4. Note that this "external economies" curve is analogous to that derived in the private adjustment model, but that it is not identical. For each level of collective immunization it would be possible to derive a whole curve that would be identical in construction to that in Fig. 8-1. In this context, the curve in Fig. 8-1 is drawn on the basis of zero collective immunization. The composite "external economies" curve in Fig. 8-2, I', traces out a locus of points on a whole family of such curves, drawn for each level of collective immunization.

5. The constructions here are similar to those that have been employed by James M. Buchanan and Gordon Tullock in their analysis of political voting rules, *The Calculus of Consent* (Ann Arbor: University of Michigan Press, 1962).

6. Ronald H. Coase, "The Problem of Social Cost," *The Journal of Law and Economics,* 3 (October 1960), pp. 1–44.

7. The leaders of the Soviet Union, presumably on ideological grounds, distribute bread at prices far below costs, and they often discuss making bread "free." This practice has led to weird, but predictable, results, including the feeding of

cattle on bread rather than grain. Even the secret police have not been able to force consumers to behave in a Marxian manner toward bread.

8. G. Warren Nutter in "Duopoly, Oligopoly, and Emerging Competition" (unpublished manuscript) has recently developed a generalized "theory of chiseling" that does much to clarify the standard economic-theory treatment.

9.

L.S.E. Cost Theory in Retrospect

In his paper, "Economics And Knowledge," Hayek scarcely mentioned "cost." Nonetheless he provides indirectly the strongest argument for attempting to focus the attention of modern economists on the elementary meaning of cost. Hayek emphasized the differences, in principle, between the equilibrium position attained by a single rational decision maker in his own behavioral adjustments, given his preference function and the constraints that he confronts, and the equilibrium potentially attainable through the interaction of many persons. To Hayek the latter "is not an equilibrium in the special sense in which equilibrium is regarded as a sort of optimum position."

Despite Hayek's warning, since the 1930s, when the London School of Economics (L.S.E.) tradition in cost theory was developed, economists have increasingly analyzed equilibrium states in terms of their optimality or nonoptimality properties, defined by criteria for maximizing some objective function. It is somewhat paradoxical that Robbins, whose contributions to London cost theory cannot be questioned, should also have been at least partially responsible for the drift of modern economic theory toward the mathematics of applied maximization, variously elaborated, and away from the analysis of exchange processes. In *The Nature and Significance of Economic Science*,[1] Robbins supplied the methodological paradigm within which modern microeconomics has been developed. Elementary textbooks throughout the world soon came to define "economics" in terms of "the economic problem," the allocation of scarce resources among alternative ends. So defined, the "problem" faced by the individual on the desert island, the Crusoe so familiar to us all, is, at base, quite similar to that faced by the society or the community of persons. The paradigm was somewhat differently put, but with the same effect, by Paul A. Samuelson in his influential *Foundations of Economic Analysis,* when he stated:

> They [meaningful theorems in diverse fields of economic affairs] proceed almost wholly from two types of very general hypotheses. The first is that *conditions of equilibrium are equivalent to the maximization (minimization)* of some magnitude.[2] [Italics supplied.]

The increasing conceptual quantification in economic theory was almost necessarily accompanied by increasing conceptual "objectification." Once the magnitude to be maximized is symbolically defined, attention is quite naturally diverted to the manipulation of the symbols and away from the initial leap into presumed objectivity itself. The increasing conceptual quantification need not have introduced confusion save for the simultaneous developments in theoretical welfare economics. Within what Hayek called the "Pure Logic of Choice," the formal theory of utility maximization, mathematical rigor has offered aesthetic satisfaction to the sophisticated without loss of explanatory potential. More importantly, the increasingly elegant and formalistic content of general equilibrium theory, and notably its emphasis on existence proofs and stability conditions, yields pleasure to the talented, criteria to the critical, and convictions to some who have remained unconvinced about the overall efficacy of market order.

So long as the object for discussion, and for theorizing, is either the individual decision maker or the interactions of separate decision makers *in markets,* no harm is done and perhaps some good is added by conceptual objectification. Confusion arises only when the properties of equilibrium, as defined for markets, are transferred as criteria of optimization in *nonmarket* or political settings. It is here that the critical distinction between the equilibrium of the single decision maker and that attained through market interaction, the distinction stressed by Hayek, is absolutely essential to forestall ambiguity and analytical error. The theory of social interaction, of the mutual adjustment among the plans of separate human beings, is different in kind from the theory of planning, the maximization of some objective function by a conceptualized omniscient being. The latter is equivalent, in all respects, to the problems faced by Crusoe or by any individual decision maker. But this is not the theory of markets, and it is artificial and basically false thinking that makes it out to be. There are properties or characteristics of equilibria in markets that seem superficially to be equivalent to those attainable by the idealized optimization carried out by the planner. But shadow prices are not market prices, and the opportunity costs that inform market decisions are not those that inform the choices of even the omniscient planner. These appear to be identical only because of the false objectification of the magnitudes in question.

This is what the great debate on socialist planning in the 1930s was all about, comment to the contrary notwithstanding. And modern economic theorists measure their own confusion by the degree to which they accept the alleged Lange victory over Mises, quite apart from the empirical record since established. The central issue in this debate should not have been the possibility or impossibility of socialist calculation. All the participants were wrong in concentrating on this. The difference in data confronted by decision makers in different institutional settings is quite sufficient to prove that the properties of market equilibrium cannot in the nature of things be duplicated under nonmarket institutional structures. This is not of course to say that "efficiency," defined in a different but legitimate planning sense, cannot be defined in an ideal-type socialist model. Of course it can. But it is a wholly different "efficiency" framework that is involved here, informed by the marginal-value estimates of the planner and not by the participants in markets.

I think that it is legitimate to trace the sources of error to fundamental misconceptions in the theory of opportunity cost, misconceptions that the London (and Austrian) scholars were attempting to clarify, and which later I tried similarly to rectify with my little book, *Cost and Choice*, in 1969.[3] Unfortunately neither the London contribution nor my book seems to have exerted much effect on mainstream thinking in economic theory.

But I am getting ahead of my story. As I noted above, the increasing conceptual quantification, and objectification, of economic theory need not have sown confusion without the accompaniment of developments in theoretical welfare economics. Precisely at the time that methodologists were effective in formalizing economic theory within a more rigorous maximization framework, interest in "market failure" rather than "market success" was at its peak, and, with this, interest in the extension of economic theory to socialist organization became widespread. The Robbins definition of the allocation problem, with its implied emphasis on the universality of scarcity, supported such an extension. It was predictable that economists, trained professionally to analyze market equilibria, and increasingly adept at formalizing the maximization paradigm, should begin to discuss planning problems and solutions as if these required the same set of tools as those applicable to market phenomena. In retrospect it seems singularly unfortunate that the institutionalists should have lost favor precisely when their emphasis on and expertise in the functioning of organizational-institutional structures, and the impact of differing structures on behavior of decision makers, might have, with some intrusion of analysis, yielded their highest marginal product in effective critical scholarship. Instead, the mathematically sophisticated analytics of such scholars as Hotelling were allowed to go unchallenged despite their vulnerability in this most fundamental sense. And young economists everywhere learned to appreciate the beauty of the mathematical models of what they called "an economy." Theirs was not the role of skeptic, and to question quantification and objectification itself quickly came to be the mark of eccentricity rather than excellence.

Is it any wonder that, in the idealized fully quantifiable and fully objectifiable "economy" that commanded all attention, the market itself should come to be regarded as a "mechanism," as an "analogue computing device," to be legitimately treated as one among several alternative means of allocating resources, to be evaluated comparatively in terms of some criteria of accomplishment? And so it should be in such a world.

The quest for objectivity is eternal and perhaps praiseworthy, but what has modern scholarship to offer where the classical economists tried and failed? There seems little harm in speculating about the properties of an economy whose only scarce resource is a homogeneous glob of something (putty clay or Little Abner's schmoos) that may be instantly convertible into any one of a large number of final goods upon which consumers place value. In this setting the cost of any one good becomes the displaced physical alternative, measurable separately in any one of the other n goods potentially available from the single homogeneous source. If a unit of good X uses up twice as much of the scarce resource as a unit of good Y, the cost of X is properly defined as 2Y, and the cost of Y as one-half X. In such a model it is meaningful to consider the planner's problem of maximizing output, defined in values or prices of goods, from the single scarce input. The norms of theoretical welfare economics can be applied directly to this purpose. The omniscient planner can solve his maximization problem quite simply by setting the prices of goods at their relative marginal costs, arbitrarily choosing one good as *numéraire*. As the final consumers adjust quantities demanded to the announced set of prices, the value of total output, denominated the *numéraire*, will be maximized.

Nor need we limit analysis of such a conjectural economy to the planner's problems. As an alternative speculative exercise we may suppose that our homogeneous glob of scarce resource (putty clay or schmoos) is initially and arbitrarily parcelled out among persons under a private-property-rights arrangement. By assumption, the individual owners are completely indifferent as to just what set of final goods their own assigned input becomes in the transformation. These owners are motivated solely by their own desire for final goods, command over which is measured by income, denominated in some commonly agreed *numéraire* good. The only difference between this model and the one described earlier is that this one "works on its own," once private property rights are defined and protected. The scarce resource will be allocated among uses; final goods will be "produced"; prices will be set. The "market" equilibrium that emerges will in this case be equivalent in all respects to the solution of the maximization problem posed for the planner in the earlier model. Prices will equal marginal costs, not because some hidden planner has now drawn on the norms of welfare economics, but because this equality is descriptive of the end of the trading process. If this equality is not satisfied, further gains from trade would be possible; potentially realizable surplus would remain unexploited. Not only can we deduce the equivalence in results between these two models on some a priori basis. We could also *observe* such equivalence in an objectively verifiable sense.

I do not think it a caricature to describe modern economic theory as being grounded on the two conjectural models that I have briefly sketched, and on the equivalence between their "equilibrium-optimality" properties. Viewed in this simplistic perspective, however, the models paradoxically suggest that economic theory has advanced little, if at all, over that advanced almost two centuries earlier by the classical economists. In one respect at least, the classical writers were more honest in their efforts. They sought to explain relative prices by relative-input ratios of homogeneous labor. They fell short precisely because the deficiency in their common objective standard for measurement was revealed for all to see. This prompts the question as to why modern theorists have been so much more successful in concealing the fundamental flaw in their structure; "Camouflage by complexity" provides only a part of the answer here. The classical economists failed because their standard for measurement was demonstrably deficient, but also because their logical structure was not complete. One must read much into classical structure if any general-equilibrium theory of markets is to be discerned. They did not close the circle, and the lacunae in their essentially one-sided explanatory model provided the source for the familiar normative critique associated with Marx. The circle was completed by the subjective-value theorists, by the Marshallian synthesis, and, more explicitly, by the Walrasian theory of general equilibrium. These several contributions represent a major conceptual advance over classical economic analysis by criteria of logic and coherence. But the logical symmetry achieved in explaining the workings of the economic process was secured at a cost which is reflected by drainage of empirical, objective content. The classical economists offered us a positive-predictive theory of relative prices; this theory was falsified. But the neoclassical model contained no comparable predictive hypotheses; there was no externally measurable standard which allowed the scientist to make predictions from observable data. This postclassical theory described an interaction process and allowed the identification of certain properties of equilibrium positions. But there was nothing upon which the economist could have based objective predictions about relative-price formation.

This was surely sensed by Alfred Marshall as witnessed by his lingering adherence to classical models, and the desire for some restoration of predictive content offers a motivation for his time-period analysis. Frank Knight was also unwilling to disregard fully the classical precepts, and, despite his affinity with some of the Austrians, students of students of students of Knight continue to learn, and to learn well, the lessons of the deer and beaver. The reaction of the Austrians was quite different. They seemed quite willing to jettison the putative objective content of the classical hypotheses. The full implications of this may not have been recognized by the early Austrians, but in Mises and his followers economic theory is explicitly acknowledged to be wholly nonobjective. Intellectual tidiness rather than empirical or explanatory content seemed to be the purpose of both earlier and latter-day Walrasians.

As I have suggested above, confusion emerged only when 1) theorists overlooked the absence of objective content in neoclassical and general equilibrium analysis, *and* 2) when they attempted to utilize the properties of market equilibrium as norms for the optimizing solutions of problems posed in nonmarket institutional settings. The presence or absence of objective content assumed instrumental significance only when the planner was introduced, whether in the administration of state or public enterprises (piecemeal or in toto) or in levy of corrective taxes and/or subsidies on production in markets. The control or correction of allocation requires that norms be invoked, and these norms must come from somewhere. The presumption of modern economic theory that such norms are readily identifiable must be attributed to the acceptance of the paradigm one-resource model sketched above.

In any plausibly realistic market process, however, only prices have objective content. This being so, how can prices be settled by reference to "costs" or to anything else? It will be useful to discuss briefly the precise relationships between prices and "costs" in full market equilibrium. (In this treatment I shall follow closely the discussion in *Cost and Choice,* page 85.)

In full market equilibrium expected marginal benefit for each participant will be equal to marginal opportunity cost, both measured in terms of the person's subjective valuation. All persons confront uniform relative prices for goods; this is a necessary condition for the absence of further gains from trade. Since each participant is in full behavioral equilibrium, it follows that each person must also confront the same marginal cost. As a demander the individual adjusts his purchases to insure that marginal benefit equals price. Hence the anticipated marginal benefits of a good, again measured in the *numéraire*, are equal for all demanders. As a supplier the individual adjusts his sales to insure that anticipated opportunities forgone, marginal opportunity cost, equals price. Hence marginal opportunity cost in the *numéraire* is equal for all suppliers.

Prices tend to equal marginal opportunity costs in market equilibrium. But costs here are fully analogous to marginal benefits. Only prices have objective, empirical content. Neither the marginal valuations of demanders nor the marginal costs of suppliers can be employed as a basis for determining or setting prices. The reason is that both are brought into equality with prices by behavioral adjustments on both sides of the market. Prices are not brought into equality with some objectively measurable phenomena on either the demand or supply side.

The implications of this basic, and in one sense, elementary fact for applying economic theory's tools to the making of control decisions for a wholly or partially socialized institutional structure have not been fully recognized, even by those who have partially escaped the dominance of the single-resource model. To an extent the blame for this lies in the failure of the London economists, and of the latter-day Austrians, to develop a full-blown "subjectivist economics" that commands intellectual respect while seeming to retain explanatory relevance. Mises and his followers have been too prone to accept the splendid isolation of arrogant eccentrics to divorce their teaching too sharply from mainstream interests, and too eager to launch into polemic: epistemological, methodological, ideological. Certain members of the London group, although profoundly influenced by the Austrians via both Hayek and Robbins, had the merit of maintaining more practical interest in business decision problems. But unfortunately their interest was too pedestrian to allow them to attempt the "grand design" that might have been produced from the cost-theory foundations which they developed.

As a result, we find Hayek (and Mises even more emphatically) talking largely to the disciples of the Austrian faith, and alongside we find Coase, Edwards, Thirlby, and Wiseman taking up the cudgels against orthodoxy in detailed and particularistic applications. In their later papers both Thirlby and Wiseman seemed to recognize the grander implications but both men were perhaps discouraged by their failure to secure acceptance of their particularistic arguments, discouraged to the extent that neither made the attempt to draft the "treatise" that seemed to be required, and which still seems to offer challenge.

Perhaps the most significant L.S.E. impact on modern economics has come through an indirect application of opportunity-cost theory rather than through an undermining of basic cost conceptions. "Marginal social cost," enthroned by Pigou as a cornerstone of applied welfare economics, was successfully challenged by R. H. Coase a quarter-century after his initial work on cost. His now classic paper on social cost,[4] which reflects essentially the same cost theory held earlier, succeeded where the more straightforward earlier attack on the marginal-cost pricing norm – attacks by Coase himself, by Thirlby and by Wiseman – apparently failed. Nonetheless the still provisional success of Coase's modern challenge should be noted. As this is written, in mid-1972, the implications of Coase's attack on the Pigovian concept of social cost for the elementary textbook discussions of opportunity cost have not yet been realized. Advanced textbooks, and notably those written in what may loosely be called the

"Chicago-Virginia" tradition, devote some space to the "Coase theorem," but the standard chapters on cost in these same textbooks remain as if the more fundamental critique in the Coase paper had never been published.[5]

A primary purpose of this summary of doctrinal developments has been to emphasize the general importance of the theory of opportunity cost, and the London contributions to the development of a fundamentally correct theory which has not yet come to inform mainstream thinking in economics. The significance may, I fear, be hidden from those who glance only at the volume's title, *L.S.E. Essays on Cost*, and whose subjective image of "cost" calls up carefully specified algebraic functions, sharply etched geometrical figures, or actual numbers carried to at least two decimal points in accountants' worksheets. Such an image may unfortunately be reinforced by a superficial survey of titles of some of the independent essays included here. Coase, Edwards, and Thirlby, in some of the papers reprinted here, were interested in practical problems faced by business decision makers in business administration as such. They were attempting to use economic theory in this severely practical setting, to apply opportunity-cost notions to the problems faced in everyday economic choices. In this effort the London economists did not themselves fully appreciate the uniqueness and originality of their approach. To an extent they looked on themselves as writing down, in the context of practical-problem situations, what "everyone knew" about cost, at least everyone around L.S.E. during the period in question.

As the norms drawn from the description of competitive equilibrium came to be presented more and more as "rules" for socialist planners, and "marginal-cost pricing" was elevated into a paradigm for the management of public enterprise, the significance of getting the elementary confusions identified, and with this the relative importance and uniqueness of the London approach, came to be recognized. Both Thirlby and Wiseman, in the most recently published papers in this volume, recognized the depth of mainstream intellectual error, but their plaints were largely ignored. One reason perhaps lies in the fact that the critique of orthodoxy is too fundamental; to accept fully the implications of the theory of opportunity cost that is implicit in these essays requires the modern economist to throw overboard too much of his invested intellectual capital. How can we write the elementary textbooks and teach the elementary course if we cannot draw the standard cost curves? How can we carry out benefit-cost analysis and pretend that we are assisting in social decision making? How can we say anything at all about managing nationalized public enterprises?

What is so "revolutionary" in the theory of opportunity cost that threatens the very foundations of modern applied economics? I do not propose to develop my own interpretation and application of the theory. I have done the latter in *Cost and Choice*. But brief elaboration of the central argument may offer some support to my assertions about significance. The basic idea is at once extremely simple and profound. *Cost* is inherently linked to *choice*. This notion did not of course originate with the economists associated with the L.S.E. in the 1930s or before or since. As students of Frank Knight learned, elements of the correct theory of opportunity cost are found in Adam Smith's deer-and-beaver model. Even before the subjective-value revolution, Francesco Ferrara in Italy was sharply critical of classical theory on opportunity-cost grounds.[6] The opportunity-cost conception was explicitly developed by the Austrians, by the American, H. J. Davenport, and the principle could scarcely have occupied a more central place than it assumed in P. H. Wicksteed's *Common Sense of Political Economy*.[7] This book was independently influential at L.S.E., and it properly deserves mention here.

At the L.S.E. there was the beginning and the widening recognition of the implications of elementary opportunity-cost theory for applications of economics. Almost all professional economists, old and new, can provide a rough working definition of opportunity cost that is tolerably acceptable for pedagogic purposes. But very few economists, new or old, have been consistent. Almost none of them beyond the London-Austrian axis has recognized just what his own definition suggests for the application of his discipline.

Simply considered, cost is the obstacle or barrier to choice, that which must be got over before choice is made. Cost is the underside of the coin, so to speak, cost is the displaced alternative, the rejected opportunity. Cost is that which the decision maker sacrifices or gives up when he selects one alternative rather than another. Cost consists therefore in his own evaluation of the enjoyment or utility that he anticipates having to forgo as a result of choice itself. There are specific implications to be drawn from this choice-bound definition of opportunity cost:

1. Cost must be borne exclusively by the person who makes decisions; it is not possible for this cost to be shifted to or imposed on others.

2. Cost is subjective; it exists only in the mind of the decision maker or chooser.

3. Cost is based on anticipations; it is necessarily a forward-looking or *ex ante* concept.

4. Cost can never be realized because of the fact that choice is made; the alternative which is rejected can never itself be enjoyed.

5. Cost cannot be measured by someone other than the chooser since there is no way that subjective mental experience can be directly observed.

6. Cost can be dated at the moment of final decision or choice.[8]

In any general theory of choice cost must be reckoned in a *utility* rather than in a *commodity* dimension. From this it follows that the opportunity cost involved in choice cannot be observed and objectified and, more importantly, it cannot be measured in such a way as to allow comparisons over wholly different choice settings. The cost faced by the utility-maximizing owner of a firm, the value that he anticipates having to forgo in choosing to produce an increment to current output, is not the cost faced by the utility-maximizing bureaucrat who manages a publicly owned firm, even if the physical aspects of the two firms are in all respects identical. As the London economists stressed, cost is that which might be avoided by not making choice. In our example the private owner could avoid the explicit incremental outlay *and* the incremental profit opportunity should he fail to produce the output increment. The socialist manager, by our assumptions, could avoid the same objective consequences by taking the same course of action. These consequences could be measured in monetary terms. But the opportunity cost relevant to choice making must be translated into a utility dimension through a subjective and personal evaluation. The private owner may evaluate the objectively measurable consequences of choice quite differently from the bureaucrat, although both are utility-maximizers.

I am not suggesting that the contributors to the London tradition in cost theory fully appreciated and understood all the implications of their own conception, nor that even now they would endorse my interpretation of this conception. I suggest only that their several papers mark a beginning of such appreciation, that they reflect an early critical questioning of aspects of modern economic theory, a questioning that is more urgently needed in the 1970s than it was when they wrote.

While the contribution of the L.S.E. group of economists should be emphasized, the constructive content of their work should not be exaggerated. Taken as a whole, the London effort is largely negative in its impact. Properly interpreted, it demonstrates major flaws in the applications and extensions of economic theory. But there is little in this work which assists us in marrying "subjectivist" and "objectivist" economic theory. Few modern economists would be willing to go all the way with the latter-day Austrians and convert economics into a purely logical exercise. Most of us want to retain, and rightly so, positive and predictive content in the discipline, to hold fast to the genuine "science" that seems possible. To accomplish this, however, *homo economicus* must be returned to scientific respectability, and economists must learn to accept that hypotheses may be falsified. Finally, and more importantly, we must try to construct meaningful, if limited, norms for decision making in nonmarket institutional structures. In competitive markets prices tend to equal marginal costs, but do we want to *make* prices equal "marginal costs" in nonmarket settings, when we fully realize that marginal costs can only be objectified by the arbitrary selection of some artificially homogenized measure? Do we really want to make one beaver exchange for only two deer when poisonous snakes abound near the beaver dams? Of course not! But how do we know that the snakes are there? Because the beaver hunters think they are?

Notes

I am indebted to my colleagues, Thomas Borcherding and Gordon Tullock for helpful comments.

1. L. Robbins, *The Nature and Significance of Economic Science* (London: 1932).

2. Paul A. Samuelson, *Foundations of Economic Analysis* (Cambridge, Mass.: 1947), p. 5. Samuelson's Nobel lecture provides evidence that his own position has not substantially changed. See "Maximum Principles in Analytical Economics," *American Economic Review,* 62 (June 1972), pp. 249–62.

3. James M. Buchanan, *Cost and Choice* (Chicago: 1969).

4. R. H. Coase, "The Problem of Social Cost," *Journal of Law and Economics* 3 (October 1960), pp. 1–44.

5. This summary of the impact of the London cost theory should include mention of G. L. S. Shackle. Although Shackle does not specifically present his ideas in opportunity-cost terms, his whole approach to decision is fully consistent with that developed by the London theorists. Shackle was both directly and indirectly associated closely with the London group. For Shackle's most appropriate treatment of decision, see his *Decision, Order and Time in Human Affairs* (Cambridge: 1961).

6. See James M. Buchanan, *Fiscal Theory and Political Economy* (Chapel Hill, N.C.: 1960), pp. 27–30, for a summary treatment. One of my own projects is a critical analysis of Ferrara's work, with a view toward making his contribution more widely known to English-language readers.

7. P. H. Wicksteed, *Common Sense of Political Economy* (London: 1910).

8. For a detailed discussion of each of these attributes of opportunity cost see James M. Buchanan, *Cost and Choice*, chap. 3.

10.

Rights, Efficiency, and Exchange: The Irrelevance of Transaction Cost

I. Introduction

Economists commence analysis with utility functions and production functions as defining attributes of choosing-acting entities. Interdependencies among utility and production functions of separate persons and units provide the origins of exchanges, which become the central subject matter for economists' attention. Interdependencies that remain outside exchanges, uncompensated transfers of positive and negative values, become externalities in the economists' lexicon. One of the contributions of the property-rights, law-economics research of the last three decades has been the focus of economists' attention on the necessity of including legal-institutional constraints along with resource constraints in any analysis of economic interaction.

Lawyers commence analysis with legal rights assignments as defining attributes of potential litigants. Differential evaluation of rights by separate persons and units give rise, in the legal setting for analysis, to exchanges in rights, which are equivalent to the exchanges that the economists analyze. Predation or invasion of rights, whether actual or potential, gives rise to appeals to the protective capacity of the state, or, with uncertainty in rights definition, to potential litigation. Note that the economists' conception of externalities bears no direct relation to the legal invasion of rights. Persons may impose economic harms or benefits, without payment or exaction of compensation, while confining behavior within spheres of legally defined rights. Lawyers, as well as economists, have come to recognize, however, that well-defined rights can facilitate exchanges.[1]

Ambiguity remains on the question of whether or not legally permissible impositions of harms (and/or benefits) of a person (persons) on another (others) generate inefficiency in resource utilization in a setting where rights are well-defined and contracts are enforced and in which all persons can enter into voluntary exchanges. In such a setting, *will resources necessarily move toward their most highly valued uses?*

The central argument in Coase's seminal 1960 paper, "The Problem of Social Cost,"[2] is that voluntary exchange in well-defined rights provides a sufficient condition for allocative efficiency. Coase amended this central proposition by what has been widely interpreted as a "zero transactions costs" qualifier, which, as I shall demonstrate, weakened the force of his argument.[3] Robert Cooter raised the question explicitly in his 1982 paper, "The Cost of Coase."[4] He argued that allocative efficiency is guaranteed by voluntary exchanges of rights only in fully competitive environments, and that strategic bargaining behavior will emerge as a source of potential resource wastage in noncompetitive interactions. In the absence of some externally imposed rule for dividing the purely distributional gains, there is no assurance that exchanges in rights will shift the economy toward the Pareto efficiency frontier and maintain a position on the frontier once reached.

My purpose in this paper is to exorcise the ambiguity here, an ambiguity that emerges from confusion on elementary conceptual principles, and a confusion that is shared, at least to some degree, by the Coasians as well as their critics. I shall demonstrate that consistent application of a *subjectivist-contractarian* perspective offers genuine clarification along several dimensions of the law-economics intersection.[5]

II. A Contractarian Reconstruction of the Coase Theorem

Coase was primarily interested in showing, through a series of both hypothetical and historical examples, that freedom of exchange and contract will insure that resources are allocated to their most highly valued uses, that if the assignment of rights is clear, parties involved in actual or potential interdependence will have incentives to negotiate among themselves and exchange rights to the disposition over resources so long as differential evaluations are placed on those rights of disposition. Put in externality language, Coase was essentially arguing that all Pareto-relevant externalities would tend to be eliminated in the process of free exchange-contract among affected parties.[6]

It is unfortunate that Coase presented his argument (through the examples) largely in terms of presumably objectively measurable and independently determined harm and benefit relationships. In his formulation, these relationships become *identical* in the perception of all parties to any potential exchange of rights.[7] Hence, the unique "efficient" (benefit maximizing or loss minimizing) allocation of resources exists and becomes determinate conceptually to any external observer. The efficacy of free exchange of rights in attaining the objectively determined "efficient" outcome becomes subject to testing by observation. The exchange process, in this perspective, is itself evaluated in terms of criteria applied to the outcomes that the process is observed to produce. There are values inherent in allocations that exist quite independently of the means through which these allocations are generated.

Despite his own earlier contribution to what may be called the subjectivist theory of opportunity cost,[8] Coase's position on the independent determinacy and existence of an "efficient" allocation of resources is not clear. Both his use of the numerical examples and his introduction of the transactions-costs proviso suggest that Coase was, indeed, applying outcome criteria to results of the exchange process rather than limiting his attention to the process itself. To the extent that Coase does apply outcome criteria for allocative efficiency, however, his whole analysis, along with that of his many favorable interpreters, becomes vulnerable to the critique mounted by Cooter and others, who suggest that elements of confusion have been introduced by thinking that transactions costs involve only communication-information difficulties. In fact, parties to bargains in small-number settings with distributive as well as allocative implications have strategic reasons to conceal their preferences and, in large-number settings, all parties may have free-rider motivations, independently of any communication-information failures. In both of the latter cases, voluntary exchange would not seem to guarantee the attainment of the Pareto-efficiency frontier, and for reasons not well defined within the transactions-costs rubric. Interpreted in terms of satisfying outcome criteria for efficiency, the Coase theorem fails in noncompetitive settings; free exchange and contract among parties does not necessarily generate an allocation of resources to their most highly valued uses. "Social value" is not necessarily maximized; "externalities" that are Pareto-relevant may remain in full trading equilibrium.

The Coasian, who remains at the same time an objectivist for whom an "efficient" resource allocation exists independently of the process of its generation, will have difficulty responding satisfactorily to the critique advanced by Cooter and others who make similar arguments. Parties to potential exchanges who are rational maximizers of expected utilities may fail to reach the presumed objectifiable Pareto-efficiency frontier. "Gains from trade" may remain after the parties conclude their bargaining sessions; resources may remain in uses that yield relatively lower values than they might yield in alternative uses.

If, however, the whole Coase analysis is interpreted in subjectivist-contractarian (or, if preferred, Austrian-Wicksellian) terms, the critique can be shown to be without substance. If the only source of valuation of assets or resource claims is the revealed choice behavior of parties to potential exchanges, there is no means through which an external observer can determine whether or not trade, as observed, stops short of some idealized norms. If a person, A, is observed to refuse an offer of $X for asset, T, that person, A, must be presumed to place a value on T in excess of $X. That asset, in A's usage, must be yielding a value or benefit more than $X. The fact that some portion of the imputed subjective value of T, to the current owner, A, may be based on his estimates as to the real preferences (valuations) of B, the potential purchaser, is totally irrelevant. In the institutional setting implicitly postulated here, in which A and B are isolated parties to potential exchange, the absence of a consummated exchange of the asset, T, demonstrates that this asset remains in its most highly valued use. "Efficiency" in resource use, *given the institutional setting,* is insured so long as A and B remain free to make the exchange or to refuse to make it.

Note that the invariance version of the Coase theorem is *not* valid in this perspective. The contractarian approach suggests that free exchange among parties will guarantee that resources remain in their most highly valued uses, but it does imply that the ownership or liability patterns, the assignment of legal rights, may affect the allocation that emerges in small-number settings, and quite apart from the acknowledged relevance of income effects. A switch in the assignments of ownership rights in my example, from A to B with respect to the initial ownership of the asset, T, may well result in the retention of the asset by B, and, therefore, in a usage different from that to which A might have put the asset with the earlier ownership assignment.

III. Is What Is Always Efficient?

The contractarian reconstruction of the Coase theorem outlined in Section II may seem, at the outset, vulnerable to the charge that, so interpreted, the theory becomes a tautology.[9] If there is no objective criterion for resource use that can be applied to outcomes, as a means of indirectly testing the efficacy of the exchange process, then so long as exchange remains open and so long as force and fraud are not observed, that upon which agreement is reached is, by definition, that which can be classified to be efficient.[10] In this construction, how can inefficiency possibly emerge?

In a paper published initially in 1959,[11] I suggested that agreement is the only ultimate test for efficiency, but that the test need not be confined in application to the allocative results or outcomes generated under explicitly existing or defined institutional-structural rules. The agreement test for efficiency may be elevated or moved upward to the stage of institutions or rules, as such. Agreement on a change in the rules within which exchanges are allowed to take place would be a signal that patterns of outcomes reached or predicted under the previously existing set of rules are less preferred or valued than the patterns expected to be generated under the rule-as-changed. Hence, the new rule is deemed more efficient than the old. The discussion and agreement on the change in the rules here is analogous to the trade that takes place between ordinary traders in the simple exchanges made under postulated rules.

With a change in the rule or institution, however, the pattern of outcomes reached through within-rule trades or exchanges would be expected to be different from that attained under the rules that existed prior to the change. This suggests only that any allocation of resources that is to be classified as "efficient" depends necessarily on the institutional structure within which resource utilization-valuation decisions are made.[12] This implication creates no difficulty for the subjectivist-contractarian who does not acknowledge the uniqueness of the resource allocation that is properly classified to be efficient.

The position I am advancing here may be clarified by reference to the familiar prisoners' dilemma. The contractarian is not put in the role of denying that such dilemmas exist. Indeed his diagnosis may suggest that such dilemmas characterize many areas of social interaction. Consider, then, how the contractarian-subjectivist would approach the prisoners' dilemma. Take the most familiar, and original, example, where two prisoners are presented with the classic alternatives, and allowed no communication with each other. Here, the outcome predicted, and possibly observed, to emerge may be classified as "presumably inefficient" for the set of prisoners considered as a group because they are not allowed to make explicit exchanges. If they are, instead, allowed to communicate, one with another, and to make *binding-enforceable contracts,* they would never remain in the "both confess" trap. They would exchange binding commitments not to confess, and this result, as observed, would be classified properly as "efficient," again for the set of prisoners treated as the relevant group.

The dilemma, as such, may, however, be an efficient institution for forcing prisoners to confess. That is to say, the subset of the population made up of prisoners only may not be the set relevant for a political-collective evaluation of the institution. In the more inclusive community, the test for whether or not that institution which removes the option of binding contracts among prisoners is efficient would depend on the attainment or nonattainment of community-wide consensus on change to some alternative institution.

IV. Transactions Costs

I have not introduced transactions costs as a possible barrier to the attainment of allocative efficiency through voluntary exchanges anywhere in the above discussion. And, as I noted earlier, the thrust of Coase's argument is weakened by the insertion of the transactions-costs qualification or proviso. There is no meaning of the term "allocative efficiency" in an idealized zero transactions-costs setting under the subjectivist-contractarian perspective. Such "efficiency" assumes meaning only if an objectivist conceptualization of resource use is implicitly postulated. Resources will, of course, be differently allocated by voluntary exchanges of rights in differing institutional settings, as noted above, but to say this is to do nothing more than to say that persons will behave differently under differing constraints.

To the extent that trade is free to all parties in an interaction, and all parties have well-defined rights, resources will move toward their most highly valued uses without qualification. To the extent that potential traders are coerced, either by prohibitions on their ability to make enforceable contracts or by the imposition of noncompensated transfers, no conclusions about value-maximizing resource use can be drawn because the rules permit no test.[13] The only criterion available, that of prior agreement on the transfers of value, is explicitly replaced as a decision rule, although it remains as the valid test.

In this Section, I propose to discuss three broadly defined categories of problems that are often placed in the transactions-costs rubric, and I shall show how these putative barriers to allocative efficiency are readily incorporated into a coherent subjectivist-contractarian argument.

Information-Communication Constraints

Transactions costs are perhaps most familiarly discussed as arising from some failure of parties to potential exchange to attain access to information on proffered terms of trade or to communicate their own offers effectively to other traders. Hence, or so the orthodox argument might run, if potential traders could be better informed and be made better able to communicate one with another, now unconsummated trades might be worked out, generating increments in value, insuring greater efficiency in resource use. If "efficiency" is defined as that pattern of resource use reached through voluntary exchanges *after* the new information-communication setting is in place, then, of course, the prior-existing allocation is *now* "inefficient." But in the postulated initial setting, there was a different information-communication environment. Given the then-existent constraints under which traders behaved, the prior allocation was "efficient."

Whether or not a shift in information-communication constraints is, in itself, an efficient or Pareto-superior change can be determined only by applying some criterion that remains *internal* to the set of potential traders. If the initial constraints are deemed to be "inefficient," potential traders will, themselves, find it advantageous to invest resources in efforts to shift them.

Consider a simple example. There are two totally isolated villages, Adam and Smith, with no communication with each other. In one village, two deer exchange for one beaver. In the other, two beaver exchange for one deer. In the setting of isolation, the allocative results are efficient provided that trade is free in each village. If the isolation between the villages is not itself efficient, it will be to the advantage of a trading entrepreneur in one village or the other to seek out means of breaking the trading barrier. Profits from arbitrage will attract such behavior as will be required to remove differentials in the terms of trade and to generate differing patterns of resource use, if the shift is such as to confer net benefits. It is misleading to suggest that the initial setting of isolation prevented efficient resource utilization because of the transactions-cost barrier. Voluntary exchange must be defined to include entrepreneurial trading effort which will emerge to insure that all gains-from-trade in breaking down information-communication constraints are exhausted.

To the extent that the constraints that exist are *artificially* imposed, via the auspices of political-governmental agency, the activities of entrepreneurial traders that might otherwise generate an optimal breakdown of barriers may be prevented or inhibited. In the presence of observed artificial constraints the allocative patterns can be labeled as "presumably inefficient," since trade is not allowed to take place.

Free Rider Constraints

The question of the possible efficacy of removing existing governmental-political constraints, or of imposing new ones, shifts analysis to the second familiar source of alleged barriers to resource utilization, a source that is often swept within the transactions-cost qualification, but is more specifically discussed under the "free rider" rubric. In large-number settings, the individual participant has little or no incentive to initiate action designed to yield benefits for all members of the community, to secure information about alternatives, and to be concerned about enforcement of community-wide agreements. There may exist complex exchanges that might be agreed to by all participants, but it is to the advantage of no single person or small group to assume the leadership role in the design and implementation of such potential agreements.

This setting differs from that discussed under the information-communication rubric in that individual entrepreneurial efforts cannot here be depended on to search out productive shifts in institutional arrangements due to the absence of residual claimancy. In my 1959 paper, I suggested that the proper role for the normative political economist was that of discovering potential rules changes that might yield general benefits and then of presenting these changes as *hypotheses* subject to the Wicksellian contractual-consensus test. If, when presented a suggested change in rules, agreement among all potentially interacting parties is forthcoming, the hypothesis is corroborated. The previously existing rule is proven inefficient. If disagreement emerges on the proposed rules change, the hypothesis is falsified. The existing rule is classified as Pareto-efficient. And, given this institutional setting, any outcomes attained under free and open exchange processes are to be classified as efficient.

It is useful at this point to introduce the classic externality case from welfare economics, the setting in which ordinary economic activity within well-defined legal rights imposes noncompensated damages on a sufficiently large number of persons so as to insure failure of a bargained solution due to free-rider motivation.[14] Can "uncorrected" outcomes in this setting be labeled to be efficient? Consistent application of the contractarian perspective must attach the efficiency label here, so long as all members of the relevant community remain free to make intervening offers and bids to those traders whose activity is alleged to generate the spillover harms. There is no overtly coercive overriding of individual claims. The fact that, given the institutional structure postulated, outcomes are reached through an exchange-contract process open to all entrants is the criterion for efficiency of those outcomes, the only one that is available without resort to some objectivist standard.

Note, however, that this classification of such "noncorrected" outcomes in the alleged large-number externality situation as "efficient" is not equivalent to taking some Panglossian attitude toward the set of arrangements that generates such outcomes. The institutional structure may *not* be efficient, and the political economist may hypothesize that agreement can be secured on some realignment of rights (including required compensations to those who might be asked to give up valued claims) that will allow potentially damaged parties in the interaction to possess rights of veto over specified in-market activity of the ordinary sort.

In the contractarian perspective, to say that free and open exchange tends to insure that resources flow to their most highly valued uses means only that such uses are relevant to the institutional structure in being. It is not to say that the unfettered market under any and all assignments of rights is the most "efficient" institution. These are two wholly different propositions that have become confused because of the failure to make the distinction between the objectivist and the subjectivist perspective on allocative processes.

It is necessary to distinguish carefully between agreement or unanimity as a *test* for an "efficiency-enhancing trade" and unanimity as a *decision rule*. This distinction tends to be neglected in analyses of simple exchanges organized through market processes, largely because the decision rule that effectively operates coincides with the ultimate test for the results of that rule. Within a specific legal order, if entry is free, market exchanges are made under an implicit rule of unanimity.[15] If A and B voluntarily agree to an exchange, and if C remains free to offer possibly differing terms to either party, there is no outcome that does not pass the consensus test. The outcome attained can be classified as "efficient" because it reflects agreement among all parties, and the decision rule or institution that allows such outcome patterns to be generated can be classified to be "efficient" if there is no consensus to be reached on any possible change.

With "public good" or "public goods" in the standard meaning, however, it may be impossible that market exchanges, made voluntarily within well-defined assignment of rights, will generate patterns of results that are preferred by participants. Given the assignment of rights, and given the institution of exchange, the outcomes reached may still be classified to be "efficient." But the institution of voluntary exchange, as ordinarily understood, may not, in this case, be "efficient" because there may emerge general agreement upon a change in institutional structure. Explicit political or governmental decision rules may be accepted by all parties as being preferred to the decision rules of the market. That political-governmental decision rule upon which agreement is reached, however, may *not* require consent of all parties to reach particular outcomes, either explicitly or implicitly. That is to say, the "efficient" decision rule may be such that specific outcomes need not meet the consensus test.[16]

Consider an example. Suppose that there is general agreement upon a constitutional rule that specifies that police services shall be politicized and that decisions on the organization and financing of these services shall be made by majority voting rules in an elected legislature. By the fact of general agreement, this *institution* is efficient. There is no change upon which everyone affected might agree. Within the operation of the rule or institution, however, there is no basis for presuming that particular outcomes are "efficient" in the contractarian perspective. A majority coalition may impose its preferences on the members of the minority. And, given the legal order which may prohibit side payments, resources may well be allocated to uses that are valued less highly than they might be in alternative uses. There is simply no means of making the required test for efficiency or inefficiency within the rule or institution as it operates.

The majority-rule setting here is analogous to that discussed earlier under the prisoners' dilemma. For the inclusive community, a rule that places captured prisoners in isolation and prevents binding contracts, may be "efficient," despite its evident presumed inefficiency to the subset of prisoners themselves. With majority rule, or any less than unanimity rule, for political-governmental decisions, the decision structure may itself be "efficient" while at the same time the particular outcomes attained under the structure may be presumed inefficient, at least in some situations, for those who are directly coerced. To introduce "transactions costs" as a barrier to the attainment of efficiency in this generalized free-rider context seems to confuse rather than to clarify the complex set of issues involved.

Strategic Behavior

The third source of alleged inefficiency in resource utilization, also sometimes included in the broadly defined transactions-costs basket, is summarized under the rubric, *strategic behavior.* Cooter concentrated his critique of the Coase theorem on this element, in the sense previously noted.

The strategic-behavior setting differs from the two previously analyzed. As Cooter correctly indicates, the alleged barrier to possible agreement among potential traders or bargainers arises in small-number, noncompetitive settings not from any necessary informational or communication failure that might be profitably eliminated by arbitrage. And, since the numbers of potential interacting parties are small, there is no free-rider motivation for behavior. In this setting, how can criteria for improvement be derived internally from the parties?

Here there is a direct analogue to the large-number setting in the sense that any modification of the structure of interaction becomes a "public good" for all parties. Hence, in a strict two-person interaction where both parties expect to engage in a whole sequence of similar potential interactions, they may acknowledge the wastefulness of investment in strategic bargaining. In such a case, they would agree on an arbitration procedure or rule which might take the form of the appointment of an external or third-party adjudicator along with a commitment to accept the terms laid down. Again, as in all other settings, the test for efficiency in the institutional rule is agreement among affected parties.

In a more inclusive context, if all members of the relevant political community recognize that many of them will be placed in small-number bargaining settings on occasion, as either buyer or seller in potential exchanges, there may possibly emerge some general agreement on political-legal rules that reduce the potential profitability of strategic investment. Such rules may involve the promotion of competitive environments for exchanges of rights, since competition, actual and potential, dramatically restricts the scope for strategic behavior. Note, however, that such an agreement would not be based putatively on any perception that competition produces an objectifiably meaningful efficient allocation of resources. The agreement itself becomes the test as to whether or not competitive arrangements are more "efficient" than the alternative arrangements in being.

V. Competition as a Device or as a Determinant

As the last remarks suggest, there are two profoundly different conceptions of competition and the competitive process that emerge from the objectivist perspective on the one hand and from the subjectivist-contractarian perspective on the other. In the former, there exists an efficient allocation of resources independently of any process through which it is generated. From this supposition, it follows that institutional arrangements may be directly evaluated in terms of their relative success or failure in attaining the desired pattern of resource use. Normative argument in support of competitive institutions emerge, in this perspective, only because such institutions are judged to be relatively superior "devices," "instruments," or "mechanisms" in generating independently derived results. Where competitive institutions do not seem to exist, as defined by some independently derived structural criteria (e.g., number of firms in an industry, concentration ratios, etc.), there emerges a normative argument for direct intervention with voluntary exchange process as a means of moving results toward the externally derived allocative norm or ideal. Small-number bargaining settings (bilateral monopoly, isolated exchanges, locationally specific assets) necessarily fail to guarantee efficiency due to the presence of incentives for strategic behavior. Governmental action in monitoring the bargains struck in all such settings seems a normative consequence of the analysis.

In the subjectivist-contractarian perspective, "efficiency" cannot be said to exist except as determined by the process through which results are generated, and criteria for evaluating patterns of results must be applied only to processes. In this perspective, voluntary exchanges among persons, within a competitive constraints structure, generate efficient resource usage, which is determined only as the exchanges are made. Competitive institutions, in this perspective, are not instruments to be used to generate efficiency. They are, instead, possible structures, possible rules or sets of rules, that may emerge from generalized agreement. If such institutions do not emerge from a consensus operating via politically orchestrated exchanges, those alternative arrangements that may be observed to persevere must themselves be judged to be "efficient," and, within these structures, patterns of voluntary exchange outcomes may also be so classified.[17] The role of the political order, of law, or government, is to facilitate agreement on institutional arrangements, and to police rights assigned under such agreements. There is no role for specific governmental monitoring of bargains anywhere in the picture.

I should acknowledge at this point that it is difficult for anyone trained in economics in this century to hold consistently to the perspective that I have laid out in this paper. What is government's role, for example, in the case of natural monopoly, which operates "inefficiently" under the orthodox perspective and thereby seems to warrant political-governmental intrusion into the exchanges that might be made between the monopolist and his potential customers? No such normative inference can follow from a consistent application of the contractarian perspective. At best, the hypothesis may be advanced to the effect that consensus should emerge on a scheme to "buy out" existing owners of such monopolized resources (opportunities) and to replace their operation with governmental-political management, based on some cost-based pricing rules. But the subjectivist will also acknowledge that costs are not independently determinate, in which case such operating rules become absurd. At best, the hypothesis must be for a scheme that would compensate the monopoly owners and replace them with governmental agents. Modern public choice theory has put the nod to "public interest" idealizations of the behavior of such agents. In some final analysis, the subjectivist-contractarian must be hypothetically pragmatic in all those cases that seem to have been the bread-and-butter of conventional normative political economy, welfare economics, and, now, law-and-economics. He may, with little fear of analytical ambiguity, strongly urge that alternative sets of rules be presented and tested in the political exchange process. And he may, of course, utilize his specialist talents in the design and predicted operation of such alternative arrangements. He should not, however, ever be allowed to take the arrogant stance of suggesting that this or that set of institutions is or is not more "efficient."[18]

VI. Conclusions

In this paper, I have tried to support the following propositions:

1. Given the institutions within which behavior is constrained, voluntary exchanges among traders in a legal market order tend to insure that resources flow to and remain in their most highly valued uses;

2. the most highly valued uses of resources depend on the institutional setting within which voluntary exchanges take place;

3. institutions are, themselves, variables subject to change, and agreement among persons who operate within institutional constraints is fully analogous to voluntary exchange within established rules;

4. the several so-called "transactions costs" barriers to "efficiency" in resource allocation can be more appropriately analyzed in the context of hypotheses about institutional reform;

5. the ultimate test for institutional reform remains that of agreement among affected parties.

I have shown that these propositions follow consistently from a subjectivist-contractarian perspective on the behavior of persons within well-defined institutional structures as well as on their behavior in modifying such structures. The perspective allows a functional role for the political economist to be well-defined. The propositions place the now-famous Coase theorem in a position that renders it much less vulnerable to its objectivist critics. At the same time, however, the implication that what is, is always efficient is avoided.

Analysis must be based squarely on the recognition that persons are simultaneously "trading" at several levels. They are considering voluntary exchanges within institutional rules that they treat, for purposes of such within-rule calculus, as fixed. Given the institutions of the market or private sector, resources tend to be flowing to their most highly valued uses, although care should be taken here to state this proposition in terms of the continuously equilibrating properties of the system rather than in terms of any achieved equilibrium. At the same time, however, the same persons are engaged in nonmarket or political "trades," within the defined political order that exists. In this set of interactions, economic resources need *not* be moving toward their most highly valued uses because, under the decision rules of the political order, persons may be permitted to effectuate resource transfers without the voluntary agreement, explicit or implicit, of all affected parties. The political decision rule, as contrasted with the market decision rule, offers no test of the results that it acts to generate.

At the same time that they act within defined market and political rules, persons are considering "trades" that may involve changes in these decision rules, or institutional structures, themselves. There will be, at this level, forces generated by utility-maximizing considerations that move the rules-structure toward that which is "efficient." The patterns of resource use generated under less-than-unanimity decision rules in the political order, which embody no presumption of value maximization for the reasons noted, may offer reasons for considering shifts toward the market order, which does generate results that may be presumed to be value-maximizing. However, other reasons may well dominate any such comparative institutional calculus. Consistency requires that the contractarian apply the same criterion for institutional efficiency that he applies to allocative efficiency within institutions. That which is efficient is that upon which all potentially affected parties agree, explicitly or implicitly. While the absence of the unanimity rule in politics does give some basis for the generalized hypothesis that, where they are substitutes, individuals would agree to replace politicized arrangements with market or marketlike arrangements, this must remain strictly a hypothesis subject to the agreement test.

My whole analysis in this paper has been based in the presupposition that, in both the market and the political order, rights are well-defined. With reference to constitutional reform in particular, however, basic uncertainties in the assignment of rights may inhibit agreement on rules changes. Persons who remain uncertain as to just what rights they do possess in a politicized economy cannot consider rationally based plans for exchanges in these rights. Those members of politically organized groups who seem politically advantaged under existing rules will not agree to constitutional reform without compensation, and those who might otherwise be willing to pay such compensation may not do so because they do not acknowledge the rights of those to whom such payments would have to be made. It is in this whole area of potential political-constitutional "exchange" that the problems of modern Western societies are acute, and it is to the analyses of these problems that scholars in the broadly defined law-economics, property-rights, public-choice subdisciplines should turn increasing attention.

Notes

I am indebted to A. J. Culyer, David Levy, Viktor Vanberg, and Karen Vaughn for helpful comments on an earlier draft.

1. A by-product of law-economics analysis has been the proposition that the definition of rights should reflect some underlying economic efficiency norm. I shall not discuss this norm here, but my analysis suggests that the norm enters the analysis quite differently under the conception of efficiency herein advanced.

2. R. H. Coase, "The Problem of Social Cost," *Journal of Law and Economics*, 3 (October 1960), pp. 1–44.

3. Coase did not refer to transactions costs, as such. The qualifying statement that has been interpreted in zero transactions-cost terms is as follows: "and the pricing system works smoothly (strictly this means that the operation of a pricing system is without cost)." Ibid., p. 2.

4. Robert Cooter, "The Cost of Coase," *Journal of Legal Studies*, 11 (January 1982), pp. 1–34.

5. I have elaborated this perspective in earlier writings. See, in particular, James M. Buchanan, *Freedom in Constitutional Contract* (College Station: Texas A&M University Press, 1978).

6. This sentence summarizes the central argument made in James M. Buchanan and William Craig Stubblebine, "Externality", *Economica*, 29 (November 1962),

pp. 371–84. In writing that paper, Stubblebine and I considered ourselves to be developing an argument that was wholly consistent with Coase's, even if we also recognized that our approach was basically contractarian, whereas his was not explicitly defined. Coase, who had been a colleague at the University of Virginia, did not, however, like the Buchanan-Stubblebine paper, presumably because he strenuously objected to any usage of the term "externality." Also, however, his objection may have stemmed from the ambiguity in perspective that I emphasize in this paper.

7. For an analysis of a setting in which potential traders differ in their evaluation of benefits and/or harms, see James M. Buchanan and Roger L. Faith, "Entrepreneurship and the Internalization of Externality," *Journal of Law and Economics* (March 1981), pp. 95–111.

8. See R. H. Coase, "Business Organization and the Accountant," in *L.S.E. Essays on Cost*, ed. James M. Buchanan and G. F. Thirlby (New York: New York University Press, 1981), pp. 95–134.

9. Cooter, op. cit., pp. 14–15.

10. Note that this statement does not require any presumption about the knowledge possessed by potential participants in the interaction process. An alternative formulation of the Coasian perspective may be advanced in which the presumption of shared knowledge of institutional results is critical to the allegedly tautological character of the Coasian propositions. In his interesting paper, which ties together several strands of modern theory, T. K. Rymes seems to advance this alternative formulation. See T. K. Rymes, "Money, Efficiency, and Knowledge," *Canadian Journal of Economics* (November, 1979), pp. 575–89.

11. See James M. Buchanan, "Positive Economics, Welfare Economics, and Political Economy," *Journal of Law and Economics,* 2 (October 1959), pp. 124–38, reprinted in James M. Buchanan, *Fiscal Theory and Political Economy* (Chapel Hill: University of North Carolina Press, 1969), pp. 105–24. Also see David Levy, "Is Observed Monopoly Always Efficient?" (mimeographed: Center for Study of Public Choice, 1982); A. J. Culyer, "The Quest for Efficiency in the Public Sector: Economists versus Dr. Pangloss," (mimeographed: University of York, September 1982).

12. On this point, see W. C. Stubblebine, "On Property Rights and Institutions," in *Explorations in the Theory of Anarchy,* ed. Gordon Tullock (Blacksburg: Center for Study of Public Choice, 1972), pp. 39–50. Also see James M. Buchanan, "The Relevance of Pareto Optimality," *Journal of Conflict Resolution,* 7 (December 1962), pp. 341–54, reprinted in James M. Buchanan, *Freedom in Constitutional Contract*, op. cit., pp. 215–34.

13. Interpreted in these terms, the Coase qualifying statement, cited in note 3 above, should have been "the pricing (exchange) system works without interference."

14. For an analysis of this setting in a more general context, see James M. Buchanan, "The Institutional Structure of Externality," *Public Choice,* 14 (Spring 1973), pp. 69–82.

15. On this point, see James M. Buchanan, "Individual Choice in Voting and the Market," *Journal of Political Economy,* 62 (August 1954), pp. 334–43. Reprinted in James M. Buchanan, *Fiscal Theory and Political Economy* (Chapel Hill: University of North Carolina Press, 1960), pp. 90–104. Also, see Ludwig von Mises, *Human Action* (New Haven: Yale University Press, 1949), p. 312.

16. For elaboration, see James M. Buchanan and Gordon Tullock, *The Calculus of Consent* (Ann Arbor: University of Michigan Press, 1962).

17. I seek no quarrel at this point with the evolutionists who argue that institutions emerge from the historical process of development without any explicit

constitutional-political agreement having been made. So long as rights are well-defined and enforced, the institutional evolution meets the criterion of implicit unanimity analogously to the market process more narrowly defined. And the continued acceptance of institutional forms itself suggests the presumption that these forms meet the efficiency test.

Wegehenkel has specifically related the process of evolutionary change in an economy to the transaction-costs discussion. While accepting the orthodox meaning of the Coase theorem, Wegehenkel argues that the evolutionary process, generated by entrepreneurial effort, pushes the economy continually in the direction of transactions-costs reduction. See Lothar Wegehenkel, *Gleichgewicht, Transaktionskosten und Evolution* (Tübingen: Mohr, 1981).

18. It should be evident from my argument that there is no justification at all for judicial introduction of the putative efficiency norm, presumably to be imposed independently of the political process. On this, see James M. Buchanan, "Good Economics—Bad Law," *Virginia Law Review*, 60 (Spring 1974), pp. 483–92, reprinted in James M. Buchanan, *Freedom in Constitutional Contract*, op. cit., pp. 40–49.

Part III.
INDIVIDUAL AND COLLECTIVE CHOICE

11.

Social Choice, Democracy, and
Free Markets

Kenneth Arrow's provocative essay, *Social Choice and Individual Values*,[1] has stimulated a great deal of comment and discussion during the years since its publication. Reviewers and discussants have been primarily concerned with those formal aspects of Arrow's analysis which relate to modern welfare economics. This concentration, which is explained by both the stated purpose of the work and the tools with which it is developed, has resulted in the neglect of the broader philosophical implications of the essay.[2] In this article I propose to examine the arguments of Arrow and his critics within a more inclusive frame of reference. This approach reveals a weakness in the formal analysis itself and demonstrates that some of the more significant implications drawn from the analysis are inappropriate.

I shall first review briefly Arrow's argument, in order to isolate the source of much of the confusion which has been generated by it. Following this, I shall raise some questions concerning the philosophical basis of the concept of social rationality. In the next section I shall attempt to show that the negative results of Arrow's analysis as applied to voting represent established and desirable features of the decision making process embodied in constitutional democracy. From this it follows that if the conditions required by Arrow were satisfied, certain modifications in the underlying institutional structure would become imperative. Finally, I shall develop the argument that the voting process is fundamentally different from the market when the two are considered as decision making processes rather than as bases for deriving social welfare functions. Here it will be demonstrated that the market does produce consistent choices and that the market does not belong in the category of collective choice at all.

I. Arrow's Conditions for the Social Welfare Function

Arrow first defines his problem as that of constructing an ordering relation for society as a whole which will also reflect rational choice making. This construction requires the establishment of a weak ordering relation among alternative social states. He then defines the social welfare function as a *process* or rule which, for each set of individual orderings ... *states* a corresponding social ordering" (italics mine).[3] The language is extremely important here, and the use of the word "process" seems singularly unfortunate. This usage has apparently been the source of the confusion, which is present in both the original essay and most of the criticism, between the definition of the social welfare function and the actual *processes* of choice: voting and the market. As will be shown, the decision-making *process* may produce consistent choice, even though the *rule* which *states* the social ordering from the individual values may not exist.

Having defined the social welfare function, Arrow proceeds to set up the conditions which are necessary to insure that it will be based on individual values. These conditions have received the bulk of attention in the discussion of Arrow's work and are so generally familiar that they may be merely listed here. They include the requirements that (1) the function shall not be imposed; (2) it shall not be dictated by any one individual; (3) if one individual prefers one social alternative to another and everyone else is indifferent between the two, the preferred alternative shall not stand lower in the social ordering; and (4) irrelevant social alternatives shall not affect the ranking of relevant alternatives.[4]

Having set up these necessary conditions, Arrow develops his General Possibility Theorem,[5] which states that, if there are at least three alternatives, every social welfare function satisfying the rationality conditions along with requirements (3) and (4) above must violate the condition either of nonimposition or of nondictatorship. The theorem is proved to be applicable to the method of majority decision *as a welfare function* and to the market *as a welfare function*. It is inapplicable only when there exists unanimous agreement among all individuals concerning alternative social states, when the required majority of individuals possesses identical orderings of social alternatives, or when individual orderings are characterized as "single-peaked." Since each of these possibilities appears somewhat remote, the weight of Arrow's argument is to the effect that the individual values which are implicit in the normal decision-making mechanisms of society do not provide methods of deriving social welfare functions that are neither imposed nor dictatorial. So far, so good. But Arrow extends the argument to say that these ordinary decision-making mechanisms do not allow rational social choice.[6] Now this is a horse of quite a different color, with which the Arrow argument should not legitimately concern itself at all. Arrow is not at all clear as to which of these two animals he is chasing. The title of his essay implies that he is concerned with decision-making processes, and he begins his work by reference to the democratic means of decision making — voting and the market.

He states his General Possibility Theorem in terms of "moving from individual tastes to social *preferences*" (italics mine).[7] Yet he slips almost imperceptibly into the terminology of social ordering relations or social welfare functions when he sets up his required conditions. He fails to see that his *conditions, properly interpreted, apply only to the derivation of the function and do not apply directly to the choice processes.*[8] As will be shown in Section III, this distinction is not important in application to voting, and this appears to be the root of some of the difficulty. As will be shown in Section IV, when the market is considered, this distinction is fundamental. It will be proved that the existence of an Arrow social welfare function is not a necessary condition for consistent decision making.

Unfortunately, but understandably, the Arrow argument has been widely interpreted in the erroneous sense of proving that the decision-making processes are irrational or inconsistent.[9] To the critics and reviewers of his analysis, almost without exception, Arrow appears to have subjected voting and the market to the test for rationality and to have found both these processes wanting.

II. The Concept of Social Rationality

It is difficult to know exactly what is meant by "rational social choice" in the Arrow analysis. Social rationality appears to imply that the choice-making processes produce results which are indicated to be "rational" by the ordering relation, that is, the social welfare function. But why should this sort of social rationality be expected? Certainly not because it is required for the derivation of the function in the first place. The mere introduction of the idea of social rationality suggests the fundamental philosophical issues involved. Rationality or irrationality as an attribute of the social group implies the imputation to that group of an organic existence apart from that of its individual components. If the social group is so considered, questions may be raised relative to the wisdom or unwisdom of this organic being. But does not the very attempt to examine such rationality in terms of individual values introduce logical inconsistency at the outset? Can the rationality of the social organism be evaluated in accordance with any value ordering other than its own?

The whole problem seems best considered as one of the "either-or" variety. We may adopt the philosophical bases of individualism in which the individual is the only entity possessing ends or values. In this case no question of social or collective rationality may be raised. A social value scale as such simply does not exist. Alternatively, we may adopt some variant of the organic philosophical assumptions in which the collectivity is an independent entity possessing its own value ordering. It is legitimate to test the rationality or irrationality of this entity only against this value ordering.[10]

The usefulness of either of these opposing philosophical foundations may depend upon the type of problems to be faced.[11] But the two should always be sharply distinguished, and it should be made clear that any social value scale may be discussed only within an organic framework. Once this approach is taken, the question as to whether or not the social value scale may be based on individual values may properly be raised,[12] and the individual orderings of all possible social states may be the appropriate starting point in the construction of a social ordering that is to be based on individual values. But the appropriateness of such individual orderings for this purpose does not depend on the fact that these are sufficient to allow the ordinary decision-making processes to function.

Voting and the market, as decision-making mechanisms, have evolved from, and are based upon an acceptance of, the philosophy of individualism which presumes no social entity. These processes are related only indirectly to the individual values entering into any welfare function. This was true even in the pre-Robbins state of welfare economics. The measurability and comparability of utility did provide a means by which individual psychological attributes could be amalgamated into a conceptual social magnitude. The social welfare function of the utilitarians was based, in this way, on components imputable to individuals. But the welfare edifice so constructed was not necessarily coincident with that resulting from the ordinary choice-making processes. It was made to appear so because the utilitarians were also individualists[13] and, in one sense, philosophically inconsistent.

Arrow's work, correctly interpreted, consists in rigorously proving that the individual orderings of alternatives which are sufficient to allow the decision-making processes to function produce no such measuring stick as was provided by the measurability of utility. The overthrow of such measurability destroyed the conceptual social welfare function; there are no longer any units of account.[14] Arrow's analysis appears to consist, however, in proving that the decision-making processes themselves define no social welfare function, that is, do not produce rational social choice. And here the implication is strong that this is true only when an ordinal concept of utility is substituted for a cardinal concept. Actually, the decision-making processes do not produce rational social choice, even in the utilitarian framework, until and unless certain restrictive assumptions are made.

If social rationality is defined as producing results indicated as rational by the welfare function, that is, maximizing total utility in the utilitarian framework, a market decision is socially rational only if individuals are rational and individual utilities are independent. A voting decision is socially rational only if individual voting power is somehow made proportional to individual utility. Cardinal utility allowed the economist to construct a social welfare function from the individual utilities; it did nothing to insure that market or voting choices were socially rational. Here the distinction between a rational choice process and an acceptable social welfare function becomes evident.

The proper approach to social welfare functions appears to begin with the frank admission that such functions are social, not individual, and therefore are of a fundamentally different philosophical dimension from individual values or from individualistically oriented decision-making processes. It seems meaningless to attempt to test such choice processes for social rationality. But if the idea of acceptable social welfare functions and of social or collective rationality is completely divorced from the decision-making processes of the group, what is there left of the Arrow analysis? It is still possible to test these processes for consistency;[15] but consistency or rationality in this sense must not be defined in terms of results obtainable from a social ordering. Consistency must be defined in terms of satisfying "the condition of rationality, as we ordinarily understand it."[16] This implies only that choices can be made (are connected) and that the choices are transitive. The implications of the Arrow argument appear to be that such consistency of choice, could it be achieved, would be a highly desirable feature of decision making. I shall attempt in the following section to show that possible inconsistency of collective choice as applied to voting is a necessary and highly useful characteristic of political democracy.

III. Majority Decision and Collective Choice

The reaching of decisions by majority vote provides the simplest example of voting. In the historical and philosophical context, majority decision evolved as a means through which a social group makes collective choices among alternatives when consensus among the individuals comprising the group cannot be attained. Correctly speaking, majority decision must be viewed primarily as a device for breaking a stalemate and for allowing some collective action to be taken. A decision reached through the approval of a majority with minority dissent has never been, and should never be, correctly interpreted as anything other than a provisional or experimental choice of the whole social group. As a tentative choice, the majority-determined policy is held to be preferred to inaction,[17] but it is not to be considered as irrevocable. The fact that such decisions may be formally inconsistent provides one of the most important safeguards against abuse through this form of the voting process.[18] If consistency were a required property of decision, majority rule would not prove acceptable, even as a means of reaching provisional choices at the margins of the social decision surface.

One of the most important limitations placed upon the exercise of majority rule lies in the temporary or accidental nature of the majorities. One social alternative may be chosen during a legislative session, but a new and temporary majority may reverse the decision during the same or the next session. A majority may reject C in favor of B, and then select A over B, but still select C over A when put to yet another test. The obvious result of this so-called "paradox" of voting is that the social group cannot make a firm and definite choice among the alternatives offered.[19] Thus the voting process does not necessarily produce consistency of choice, and, within the Arrow framework, the individual rankings required for voting cannot be translated by the economist into a satisfactory social welfare function. The implication is that both these results are undesirable; the transitivity property is not present.

But, certainly, majority rule is acceptable in a free society precisely because it allows a sort of jockeying back and forth among alternatives, upon none of which relative unanimity can be obtained. Majority rule encourages such shifting, and it provides the opportunity for any social decision to be altered or reversed at any time by a new and temporary majority grouping. In this way, majority decision making itself becomes a means through which the whole group ultimately attains consensus, that is, makes a genuine social choice. It serves to insure that competing alternatives may be experimentally and provisionally adopted, tested, and replaced by new compromise alternatives approved by a majority group of ever changing composition. This is democratic choice process, whatever may be the consequences for welfare economics and social welfare functions.

The paradox is removed, and majority rule produces consistent choices, in the formal sense, if the individual components of a majority possess identical orderings of all social alternatives. If, for example, Joe and Jack both prefer A to B to C, and Tom prefers C to B to A, Joe and Jack can always outvote Tom and adopt A. The selection of A would represent definite and irreversible choice as long as the individual orderings remain unchanged. This is one of the situations in which Arrow's General Possibility Theorem would not hold; a social welfare function may be derived, and the implication appears to be that such a situation would prove a more desirable one than that in which inconsistency is present. In one of the most revealing statements in his essay Arrow says: "Suppose it is assumed in advance that a majority of individuals will have the same ordering of social alternatives.... Then the method of majority decision will pick out the agreed-on ordering and make it the social ordering. Again all the ... conditions will be satisfied. These results reinforce the suggestion ... that like attitudes toward social alternatives are needed for the formation of social judgments."[20] The above statement also shows that Arrow is primarily interested in individual values as the units of account to be used in deriving social welfare functions. It is the collective rationality with which he is concerned; his approach includes no consideration of individual values as ends as well as means.

If one examines the choices made in this case of identical majority orderings, it becomes evident that collective rationality or consistency is secured here only at a cost of imposing a literal "tyranny of the majority." Minorities under such conditions could no longer accept majority decisions without revolt. If there should exist policy areas in which specific majority groupings possess identical orderings of social alternatives, it would become necessary to impose additional restraints upon the exercise of majority decision. This was one of the considerations which led Wicksell to advocate the adoption of the principle of unanimity in the approval of tax bills. He reasoned that in the imposition of taxes the given majority in power would tend to be too cohesive and would, therefore, be able permanently to impose its will on the minority.[21]

The form in which Arrow states his condition of nondictatorship is closely related to the point discussed above. This condition, as applied to group decision, states that no one individual must dictate the choice without regard to the values of other individuals.[22] From the individual minority member's point of view, however, the acceptance of irrevocable majority decision is not different from the acceptance of irrevocable authoritarian decision. In either case the choice is dictated to the individual in question, since his values are overruled in the decision making. If one thinks in terms of individual values as ends, "dictated to" seems a more meaningful concept than "dictated by."

The reason that majority rule proves tolerably acceptable and individual authoritarian dictatorship does not lies not in the many versus the one. It is because ordinary majority decision is subject to reversal and change, while individual decision cannot readily be made so. With identical majority orderings, the majority would, of course, always choose the same leaders, and this advantage of majority rule would be lost. It is not evident that we should summarily reject the rule of one individual if we could be assured that every so often a new dictator would be chosen by lot and that everyone's name would be in the lottery.

The attempt to examine the consistency of majority voting requires the assumption that individual values do not themselves change during the decision-making process. The vulnerability of this assumption in the general case has been shown by Schoeffler.[23] Individual values are, of course, constantly changing; so a postdecision ordering may be different from a predecision ordering. The assumption of constancy may, however, be useful in certain instances. For example, the assumption of given tastes in the decision making represented by the market is essential for the development of a body of economic theory. But the extension of this assumption to apply to individual values in the voting process disregards one of the most important functions of voting itself.[24] The definition of democracy as "government by discussion" implies that individual values can and do change in the process of decision making. Men must be free to choose, and they must maintain an open mind if the democratic mechanism is to work at all. If individual values in the Arrow sense of orderings of all social alternatives are unchanging, discussion becomes meaningless. And the discussion must be considered as encompassing more than the activity prior to the initial vote. The whole period of activity during which temporary majority decisions are reached and reversed, new compromises appear and are approved or overthrown, must be considered as one of genuine discussion.

In a very real sense collective choice cannot be considered as being reached by voting until relatively unanimous agreement is achieved. Insofar as the attainment of such consensus is impossible, it is preferable that the actual choice processes display possible inconsistency to guaranteed consistency. The molding and solidifying of individual values into fixed ordering relations sufficient to make ordinary majority voting fit the Arrow conditions for consistency would mean the replacement of accepted democratic process by something clearly less desirable. The danger that such solidification will take place becomes more imminent as functional economic groups, subjecting members to considerable internal discipline, seek to institutionalize individual values.

The unanimity requirement need not imply that consistent choice can never be reached by voting. Relatively complete consensus is present in the social group on many major issues, and the securing of such consensus need not involve the concept of a Rousseau-like general will. As Arrow points out,[25] the unanimity required may be reached at several levels. There may exist relatively general support of the framework within which change shall be allowed to take place, that is, the constitution. This in itself insures that a genuine attempt will be made to attain consensus on controversial issues and, more importantly, to insure that the changes which are made are introduced in an orderly and nonrevolutionary manner. This relative consensus on procedure, however, will exist only so long as majorities on particular issues do not solidify; in other words, as long as ordinary decision making may be formally inconsistent.

IV. Collective Choice and Free Markets

In his discussion Arrow fails to make any distinction between voting and the market mechanism as decision-making processes, and he specifically defines both as "special cases of the more general category of collective social choice."[26] He is led to this conclusion because he is unable to define a satisfactory social welfare function from the individual orderings required for either process. In the consideration of voting, it is a relatively simple step to discard the social rationality or social welfare function implications and to utilize the Arrow conditions in testing the consistency of the choice process. When this is done, it is found that ordinary majority rule does not necessarily produce consistent choices. Thus the voting process serves neither as a basis for deriving a social welfare function in the Arrow sense nor as a means of producing consistent choices if tested by the Arrow conditions. When the market is considered, however, a different result arises when the process is tested for consistency of choice from that which is forthcoming when one seeks to derive a social welfare function. A necessary condition for deriving a social welfare function is that all possible social states be ordered *outside* or *external to* the decision-making process itself. What is necessary, in effect, is that the one erecting such a function be able to translate the individual values (which are presumably revealed to him) into social building blocks. If these values consist only of individual orderings of social states (which is all that is required for either political voting or market choice), this step cannot be taken. This step in the construction of a social welfare function is the focal point in the Arrow analysis. This is clearly revealed in the statement: "The relation of known preference or indifference is clearly transitive, but it is not connected since, for example, *it does not tell us* how the individual compares two social alternatives, one of which yields him more of one commodity than the second, while the second yields him more of a second commodity than the first" (italics mine).[27]

By the very nature of free markets, however, the only entity required to compare two social alternatives when a choice is actually made is the individual. And, since individual orderings are assumed to be connected and transitive,[28] the market mechanism does provide a means of *making consistent choices* as long as individual values remain unchanged. If, given this constancy in individual tastes (values), the economic environment is allowed to change, consistency requires only that the same social state result always from similar environmental changes. Of course, there is no way of telling what a market-determined result will be (even if we know the individual orderings) except to wait and see what the market produces. The market exists as a means by which the social group is able to move from one social state to another as a result of a change in environment without the necessity of making a collective choice. The consistency of the market arises from what Polanyi has called the system of "spontaneous order" embodied in the free enterprise economy. The order "originates in the independent actions of individuals."[29] And, since the order or consistency does originate in the choice process itself, it is meaningless to attempt to construct the ordering. We should not expect to be told in advance what the market will choose. It will choose what it will choose.

The market does not establish the optimum social state in the sense that individuals, if called upon to vote politically (act collectively) for or against the market-determined state in opposition to a series of alternatives, would consistently choose it. This may or may not be an important conclusion, depending on the value-judgment made concerning the appropriateness of majority approval as the criterion of optimum collective choice. But the essential point here is that the market does not call upon individuals to make a decision collectively at all. This being the case, market choice is just as consistent as, and no more consistent than, the individual choice of which it is composed.

V. Summary

It is necessary to distinguish between the problem of deriving a social welfare function from the individual orderings required for the operation of the decision-making processes of our society and the problem of testing these processes themselves for consistency. I have shown that the failure to make this distinction clear is the source of much of the confusion surrounding the Arrow analysis. A second distinction must be made between social or collective rationality in terms of producing results indicated by a social ordering and the consistency of choice produced by the mechanisms of decision making. If rationality is taken to mean only that the choice making is consistent, the Arrow analysis shows that voting may be inconsistent. But I have argued that possible inconsistency is a necessary characteristic of orderly majority rule. The market, on the other hand, has been shown to produce consistent choice, in spite of the fact that a "satisfactory social welfare function" cannot be derived from the individual rankings implicit in the market mechanism.

The consistency of market choice is achieved without the overruling of minority values, as would be the case if ordinary political voting were made consistent. Therefore, in a very real sense, market decisions are comparable to political decisions only when unanimity is present. The question as to what extent this lends support to the utilization of the market as the decision-making process when it is a genuine alternative to voting opens up still broader areas of inquiry which cannot be developed here.[30]

Notes

I am indebted to Marshall Colberg and Jerome Milliman of Florida State University and to Proctor Thomson of the University of Chicago for helpful comments and suggestions.

1. Kenneth Arrow, *Social Choice and Individual Values* (New York: John Wiley & Sons, 1951).

2. Little's stimulating review article and, to a somewhat lesser extent, Rothenberg's subsequent critique provide partial exceptions to this general statement. See I. M. D. Little, "Social Choice and Individual Values," *Journal of Political Economy,* 60 (1952), pp. 422–32; and Jerome Rothenberg, "Conditions for a Social Welfare Function," *Journal of Political Economy,* 61 (1953), pp. 389–405.

3. Arrow, op. cit., p. 23.

4. For the most concise listing of these conditions, see William Baumol's review in *Econometrica,* 20 (1952), p. 110.

5. Arrow, op. cit., p. 59.

6. Arrow, op. cit., p. 59.

7. Ibid.

8. Little objects to Arrow's failure to draw a distinction between the social welfare function and the decision-making process on quite different grounds from those advanced here. His objections are primarily centered on Arrow's labeling the ordering as a "social welfare function" rather than merely as the resultant of the decision-making process (Little, op. cit., pp. 427–30). He thus fails, along with Arrow, to make the necessary distinction between an ordering of social states possessing certain properties and a decision-making process which is consistent, that is, rational.

Rothenberg, on the other hand, explicitly defines the results of the choice process as the social welfare function (Rothenberg, op. cit., p. 400). He fails, however, to trace through the effects of this definition on the Arrow analysis.

9. See, e.g., J. C. Weldon, "On the Problem of Social Welfare Functions," *Canadian Journal of Economics and Political Science,* 18 (1952), pp. 452–64.

10. By his statement that "every value judgment must be someone's judgment of values" (Little, op. cit., p. 427), Little appears fully to accept what I have called the "individualistic assumptions" and, in doing so, to deny the possible existence of an organic social unit. In his critique Rothenberg seems to adhere to the organic conception, when he states that "social valuation as opposed to solely individual valuation is an existential reality" (Rothenberg, op. cit., p. 397).

11. The point involved here is closely related to a central problem in the pure theory of government finance. The whole body of doctrine in this field has suffered from the failure of theorists to separate the two approaches. See James

M. Buchanan, "The Pure Theory of Government Finance: A Suggested Approach," *Journal of Political Economy,* 57 (1949), pp. 496–505.

12. Whether or not the degree of dependence on individual values is or is not a good criterion of appropriateness for a social ordering depends, in turn, on one's own value scale. We may or may not agree with Rothenberg when he says that consensus is required for a good social welfare function (Rothenberg, op. cit., p. 398).

13. Cf. Lionel Robbins, *The Theory of Economic Policy in English Classical Political Economy* (London: Macmillan & Co., Ltd., 1952), p. 182.

14. Several of the attempts to modify Arrow's conditions in such a way as to define an acceptable social welfare function involve, in one form or another, a revival of the interpersonal comparability of utility. See Murray Kemp and A. Asimakopulos, "A Note on Social Welfare Functions and Cardinal Utility," *Canadian Journal of Economics and Political Science,* 18 (1952), pp. 195–200; Leo Goodman and Harry Markowitz, "Social Welfare Functions Based on Individual Rankings," *American Journal of Sociology,* 58 (1952), pp. 257–62; Clifford Hildreth, "Alternative Conditions for Social Orderings," *Econometrica,* 21 (1953), pp. 81–95.

15. Cf. Little, op. cit., p. 432.

16. Arrow, op. cit., p. 3.

17. For a discussion of the basis for majority decision see Robert A. Dahl and Charles B. Lindblom, *Politics, Economics, and Welfare* (New York: Harper & Bros., 1953), pp. 43f.

18. Throughout this section the term "inconsistency" will be used in the formal sense without specific reference to the question of time dimension. This is admissible if it is assumed that all individuals have sufficient knowledge of alternatives to enable each to rank all alternatives and if it is assumed further that neither these individual orderings nor the available alternatives change over time. These assumptions, which are central to the Arrow analysis, allow the time dimension of the voting paradox to be neglected. When knowledge of alternatives is not perfect, however, and when the individual orderings do change over time (cf. below) or the alternatives presented vary, the concept of inconsistency itself becomes extremely vague. The argument of this section is applicable, however, whether or not the conditions required for the formal analysis are satisfied.

19. Dahl and Lindblom accept fully this interpretation of the paradox when discussing it in specific reference to Arrow's work. They also dismiss the logical difficulty involved in the paradox as "minor" and "not an empirical observation of a common difficulty." In this latter respect, they apparently fail to see that the potential intransitivity property of ordinary majority voting provides a means of removing one of the greatest of all difficulties in the structure of majority rule (op. cit., pp. 422f).

20. Op. cit., p. 74.

21. Knut Wicksell, *Finanztheoretische Untersuchungen* (Jena: Gustav Fischer, 1896), p. 122.

22. Arrow, op. cit., p. 30.

23. Sidney Schoeffler, "Note on Modern Welfare Economics," *American Economic Review,* 42 (1952), p. 880–87.

24. The difference in the validity of the constancy assumption in these two situations is stressed by L. J. Richenburg in his review of Duncan Black and R. A. Nevins, *Committee Decisions with Complementary Valuation,* in *Economic Journal,* 63 (1952), p. 131.

25. Op. cit., pp. 90 f.

26. Op. cit., p. 5.

27. Arrow, op. cit., p. 61.

28. Ibid., p. 34.

29. Michael Polanyi, *The Logic of Liberty* (Chicago: University of Chicago Press, 1951), p. 160.

30. So far as I know, the differences between the market and political voting as choice processes have never been clearly and precisely analyzed. I hope to explore some of these differences in a forthcoming paper.

12.

Individual Choice in Voting and the Market

This paper will compare individual choice in the political voting process and in the market process, with both considered as ideal types. A substantial portion of the analysis will be intuitively familiar to all social scientists, since it serves as a basis for a large part of political theory, on the one hand, and economic theory, on the other. Perhaps as a result of disciplinary specialization, however, the similarities and the differences between these two methods of individual decision making in liberal society are often overlooked. The state of things is illustrated in the prosaic "one-dollar-one-vote" analogy, which is, at best, only partially appropriate and which tends to conceal extremely important differences.

It is necessary to emphasize the limitations of this analysis. No attempt will be made to compare market choice and voting choice in terms of the relative efficiency in achieving specified social goals or, in other words, as means of *social* decision making. Many comparisons of this sort have been made. In the great debate over the possibility of rational socialist calculation, the discussion has been concerned primarily with the workability of political decision-making processes when one is confronted with the social criterion of economic efficiency. The issue has been framed, appropriately, in terms of the relative efficiency of centralized and decentralized decision making. Collective choice implies centralized choice, whatever the process of choosing; hence the market has been compared with the whole subset of political choice processes ranging from pure democracy to authoritarian dictatorship.

This paper will compare the *individual* choices involved in the price system and in a single form of centralized decision making — pure democracy. The individual act of participation in the choice process will be the point of reference. The comparison does not, of course, imply that these two processes will be presented as genuine alternatives to the individual, even in their somewhat less pure forms. A more complete understanding of individual behavior in each process should, however, provide some basis for deciding between the two, if and when they do exist as alternatives.

The following distinctions between individual choice in voting and the market will be discussed: (1) the degree of certainty, (2) the degree of social participation, (3) the degree of responsibility, (4) the nature of the alternatives presented, (5) the degree of coercion, and, finally, (6) the power relations among individuals. Quite obviously, these distinctions are somewhat arbitrarily isolated from one another, and, in a broad sense, each implies others. After these are discussed, some attention will be given to their influence on the selection of voting or the market as a decision-making process for the social group.

I

It will be assumed that the individual chooser possesses the same degree of knowledge concerning the results of alternative decisions in the polling place that he does in the marketplace.[1] It is essential that this assumption be made at this stage, in order that the first important distinction, that of the degree of certainty, between individual choice in voting and individual choice in the market may be made clear.

In market choice the individual is the acting or choosing entity, as well as the entity for which choices are made. In voting, the individual is an acting or choosing entity, but the collectivity is the entity for which decisions are made. The individual in the market can predict with absolute certainty the direct or immediate result of his action. The act of choosing and the consequences of choosing stand in a one-to-one correspondence.[2] On the other hand, the voter, even if he is fully omniscient in his foresight of the consequences of each possible collective decision, can never predict with certainty which of the alternatives presented will be chosen. He can never predict the behavior of other voters in the polling place. Reciprocal behavior prediction of this sort becomes a logical impossibility if individual choice is accepted as meaningful.[3] This inherent uncertainty confronting the voter can perhaps be classified as genuine uncertainty in the Knightian sense; it is not subject to the application of the probability calculus.

This uncertainty must influence to some degree the behavior of the individual in choosing among the possible social alternatives offered to him. Whereas the chooser in the market,[4] assumed to know what he wants, will always take the attainable combination of goods and services standing highest on his preference scale, the voter will not necessarily, or perhaps even probably, choose the alternative most desirable to him. The actual behavior of the voter must be examined within the framework of a theory of choice under uncertainty. As is well known, there is no fully acceptable theory of behavior here, and there are some students of the problem who deny the possibility of rational behavior in uncertain conditions.[5]

II

The second fundamental difference in the two choice processes is found in the sense or degree of participation in social decision making. In the market the individual is confronted with a range of commodities and services, each of which is offered at a given price. Individually, the buyer or seller considers both the range of alternatives and the set of prices to be beyond his power to alter.[6] He is able, therefore, to assume himself apart from, or external to, the social organization which does influence the alternatives made available. He is unconscious of the secondary repercussions of his act of choice which serve to alter the allocation of economic resources.[7] The individual tends to act *as if* all the social variables are determined outside his own behavior, which, in this subjective sense, is nonparticipating and therefore nonsocial.[8] The influence of the individual's actual behavior on the ultimate social decision made has no impact upon such behavior.[9]

The individual in the polling place, by contrast, recognizes that his vote is influential in determining the final collective choice; he is fully conscious of his participation in social decision making. The individual act of choosing is, therefore, social, even in a purely subjective sense.

The sense of participation in social choice may exert important effects on the behavior of the individual. It seems probable that the representative individual will act in accordance with a different preference scale when he realizes that he is choosing for the group rather than merely for himself. There are two reasons for this. First, his identification will tend to be broadened,[10] and his "values" will be more likely to influence his ordering of alternatives, whereas in market choice his "tastes" may determine his decision.[11] As an example, the individual may cast a ballot-box vote for the enforcement of Prohibition at the same time that he visits his bootlegger, without feeling that he is acting inconsistently. Even if the individual's welfare horizon is not modified in a shift from market to voting choice, or vice versa, there is a second, and perhaps equally important, reason for a rearrangement of his preference scale and hence for some difference in behavior. The individual's ranking of alternatives in market choice assumes no action on the part of other individuals in specific correspondence to his own. In voting, the choice is determined from a ranking of alternative situations in each of which the position of the individual is collectively determined for him and for *all* other individuals in the group.[12] As an example of this difference, businessmen in a perfectly competitive industry marketing a product with an inelastic demand may vote to approve governmentally imposed production limitations, while, if left to operate independently, they would have no incentive to restrict production. A further example may be used to illustrate the case in which both these effects on individual choice may be operative. A man who in the unregulated market economy would construct a billboard advertising his product might vote for the abolition of billboards because he considers such action preferable in terms of group welfare and/or because his own interests will be better served by such collectively imposed action.

III

The difference in the individual's sense of social participation has its obverse, however, which may be introduced as a third distinction between the voting and market processes. Since voting implies collective choice, the responsibility for making any particular social or collective decision is necessarily divided. This seems clearly to affect the individual's interest in the choosing process. Since a decision is to be made in any case, the single individual need not act at all; he may abstain from voting while other individuals act.

The responsibility for market decisions is uniquely concentrated on the chooser; there can be no abstention. There is a tangible benefit as well as a cost involved in each market chooser's decision, while there is neither an immediately realizable and certain benefit nor an imputable cost normally involved in the voter's choice.[13] This difference tends to guarantee that a more precise and objective consideration of alternative costs takes place in the minds of individuals choosing in the market. This does not suggest, however, that the greater precision in the consideration of alternatives by individuals in the market implies that the costs and benefits taken into account are necessarily the proper ones from the social point of view.[14]

It seems quite possible that in many instances the apparent placing of "the public interest" above mere individual or group interest in political decisions represents nothing more than a failure of the voters to consider fully the real costs of the activity to be undertaken. It is extremely difficult to determine whether the affirmative vote of a nonbeneficiary individual for a public-welfare project implies that he is either acting socially in accordance with a "nobler" ordering of alternatives or is estimating his own self-interest in accordance with a "collective-action" preference scale, or whether it suggests that he has failed to weigh adequately the opportunity costs of the project.

The difference in responsibility provides a basis for Mises's argument that an individual is "less corruptible" in the market.[15] This might plausibly be advanced without necessarily contradicting the claim that ballot-box choice, if uncorrupted, is made in accordance with a more inclusive and modified value scale. A somewhat related point has been made by Spengler when he says that there is, in voting as compared with the market, "the tendency of the individual (especially when he is a part of a large and disciplined organization) more easily to lose . . . political than economic autonomy."[16]

IV

A fourth distinction, and perhaps one of the most important, between individual choice in voting and the market lies in the nature of the alternatives offered to the individual in each case. Choice implies that alternatives are mutually conflicting; otherwise, all would be chosen, which is equivalent to saying that none would be chosen. It is in the precise way in which the alternatives mutually conflict that the voting process must be sharply distinguished from the market mechanism.

Alternatives of market choice normally conflict only in the sense that the law of diminishing returns is operative. This is true at the level both of the individual chooser and of the social group. If an individual desires *more* of a particular commodity or service, the market normally requires only that he take *less* of another commodity or service. If all individuals, through their market choices, indicate that *more* resources should be devoted to the production of a particular commodity, this requires only that *less* resources be devoted to the production of other commodities.

Alternatives of voting choice are more normally mutually exclusive, that is, the selection of one precludes the selection of another. This, too, is true at the level both of the individual chooser and of the whole system. The individual voter normally faces mutually exclusive choices because of the indivisibility of his vote. Group choices tend to be mutually exclusive by the very nature of the alternatives, which are regularly of the "all-or-none" variety.

For the individual, market choice amounts to the allocation of an unspecialized and highly divisible resource (income-yielding capacity) among a range of alternatives. On the other hand, few voting schemes include means which enable an individual to break his total voting strength down into fractional parts. The attribute of scarcity has never been applied to voting strength; an additional vote is granted to each individual when each new collective decision is made. In order for market choice to be made similar to voting in this respect, each individual would be required to devote his whole capacity in each market period to one commodity or service. If only the buying side is taken into account, this means that the consumer's whole expenditure should be on one commodity. It seems clear that this feature of the choice process can itself affect the nature of the alternatives presented. If the individual were required to spend the whole of his income on one commodity, market alternatives would tend to become mutually exclusive and to become severely limited in number and variety. Most of the normally available goods and services would disappear from the marketplaces.

The major share of the difference in the nature of the alternatives presented in the two choice processes must, however, be attributed to fundamental differences in the objects of choice themselves. In a very real sense many voting choices can never be made in the market because they are inherently more difficult, involving, as they do, considerations which cannot be taken into account effectively by the individual choosing only for himself. The choice to be made is normally among two or more alternatives, only one of which may be chosen, with its very selection precluding the selection of the others. Even if the results of the voting were to be based upon the proportionate number of votes cast for each alternative, combinations or composite solutions of the market type would not be possible in most cases. Inherent in the market solution, by contrast, is choice among an almost infinite number of *combinations* of goods and services, in each of which some of almost every conceivable good and service will be included.[17] As a result of this difference, individual choice in the market can be more articulate than in the voting booth.

V

There follows directly from the difference in the nature of alternatives an extremely important fifth distinction between the voting process and the market process as faced by the individual choice maker. If production indivisibilities may be disregarded (they would not be present in the ideally competitive world), each dollar vote in the market becomes positively effective[18] to the individual, not only in providing him with a unit of the chosen commodity or service, but also in generating changes in the economic environment. In either of these senses a dollar vote is never overruled; the individual is never placed in the position of being a member of a dissenting minority.[19] When a commodity or service is exchanged in the market, the individual chooses from among *existing* alternatives; at the secondary stage, of which he is unconscious, his behavior tends to direct economic resources in a specific manner.

In voting, the individual does not choose among *existing* but rather among *potential* alternatives, and, as mentioned earlier, he is never secure in his belief that his vote will count positively. He may lose his vote and be placed in the position of having cast his vote in opposition to the alternative finally chosen by the social group. He may be compelled to accept a result contrary to his expressed preference. A similar sort of coercion is never present in market choice. It has been argued that pressure toward social conformity "compels those outvoted to make an expenditure against their will."[20] While it is no doubt true that both the individual's earning and expenditure patterns are conditioned to a large degree by the average patterns of his social group, the distinction between this indirectly coercive effect involved in the social urge to conform and the direct and unavoidable coercion involved in collective decision seems an extremely important one.

If the assumption of production divisibility is relaxed, some modifications of this conclusion must be made. Given the presence of indivisibility, the individual's dollar vote may be overruled at the secondary stage of the market-choice process. On the buying side, if the consumer's dollar vote is not accompanied by enough other votes to maintain the production of the particular good or service, it may be "lost," and at this stage, the buyer may be in a position apparently equivalent to that of the ballot-box supporter of the losing side of an issue. On the selling side, if there are not enough final demand dollar votes to warrant production of those commodities or services embodying the individual's productive contribution, then the attempt to convert productive services into generalized purchasing power on former terms may be thwarted. But in each case, at the initial or primary stage of the market process, the individual's expressed choice is never overruled. The buyer would never have possessed the opportunity to choose, had not the commodity or service been existent in the market; and the seller of productive services would have never been able to develop particular skills, had not a derived demand for those skills been present. And since the one-to-one correspondence between the act of choice and its result is the only condition directly influencing the individual's behavior, there can never be present the sense of directly losing one's market vote. There may, of course, arise a sense of regret when the consumer returns to the marketplace and finds a desired commodity no longer available and when the individual no longer is able to market productive services previously adapted to particular uses. The consumer may also regret that certain desired goods have never been placed in the market in the first place, and the individual seller may be concerned that there has never existed a ready market for his peculiar talents. This sort of regret does not, however, apply uniquely to market choice. It applies equally to political voting, and it does not, therefore, constitute the market's equivalent of the "lost" ballot-box vote. It is true that there may be commodities and services not offered for sale which the individual would be willing to purchase, but there may also be many potential alternatives never presented for a vote which an individual might desire to support.

VI

Each of the five preceding distinctions in the individual participation in voting and market choice is present even when the relative power positions of individuals are made equivalent in the two processes, that is, when there is absolute equality in the distribution of income-earning capacity among market choosers. All these distinctions tend, therefore, to be neglected in the simple "one-dollar-one-vote" analogy, which concentrates attention only upon the difference in the relative power of individuals. Market choice is normally conducted under conditions of inequality among individuals, while voting tends, at least ideally, to be conducted under conditions of equality.

The essential point to be emphasized in this connection is that the inequalities present in market choice are inequalities in individual power and not in individual freedom, if care is taken to define freedom and power in such a way as to maximize the usefulness of these two concepts in discussion. As Knight has suggested, it seems desirable for this reason to define freedom somewhat narrowly as the absence of coercion and unfreedom as the state of being prevented from utilizing the normally available capacities for action.[21]

VII

There remains the task of evaluating the foregoing differences in the position of the individual chooser in voting and in the market, with a view toward determining the relative appropriateness of the two choice processes for the social group when they are, in fact, possible alternatives. If rationality in individual behavior is considered a desirable feature of a choice process,[22] there would appear to be several reasons for claiming that market choice should be preferred. The greater degree of certainty seems clearly to produce more rational behavior; the uniquely centered responsibility tends to work in the same direction. Even if voting and the market are genuinely alternative means of making choices in a particular situation (thereby eliminating the inherent difficulties in voting choice when this is the only alternative), the difference in the divisibility of voting tends to make market choices finer and more articulate. The fact that market choice tends to embody greater rationality in *individual behavior* than does voting choice does not suggest that market choice tends to produce greater social rationality.[23]

The market should also be preferred as a choice process when individual freedom is considered in isolation. The absence of negative results of individual choices and, therefore, of the direct coercion which requires that the individual accept unchosen alternatives makes for a greater degree of freedom in market choice.

On the other hand, voting should perhaps be preferred to the market when individual motivation in choice is the attribute examined. Voting choice does provide individuals with a greater sense of participation in social decision making, and, in this way, it may bring forth the "best" in man and tend to make individuals take somewhat more account of the "public interest." This attribute of the voting process has probably been somewhat neglected by liberal students and somewhat overemphasized in importance by socialists. It should be noted, however, that, even if this proves to be an important difference, voting will produce consistent or "rational" *social* choice only if men are able to agree on the ultimate social goals.[24] If men are not able to agree on what is genuine morality, the adoption of a choice process in which they act more morally cannot be justified on this ground.[25]

It is in the power structure among individuals antecedent to choice that the market may, and most often does, prove acceptable. Political voting is characterized by an alternative power structure which may be deemed preferable to that of the market. And the selection of the one-for-one power relation among individuals appears to carry with it the selection of voting over market choice. If, however, the market power structure can be effectively modified independently of the choice process, this apparent advantage of political voting need not be present.

It should be noted that the fundamental decision to modify the power structure, as well as the extent of such modification, clearly must be made by the ballot box. And in this type of decision especially it is essential that individuals act in accordance with a value ordering which is somewhat different from that motivating individual market choice. After a redistributive decision for the group is made, it must be further decided whether a particular choice shall be made by the market or by political voting. This decision on process must also be made by means of the ballot box. In this decision the market should be rejected only if individual market choices are considered by voters to produce a social state less desirable than that which is produced by individual voting choices.

The selection of the choice process, if the redistributive decision can be made separately, will depend to a large degree upon the relative positions of the various social goals in the value scales of individuals comprising the voting group. If consistency in individual behavior and individual freedom are highly regarded relative to other values, the market will tend to be favored. If, on the other hand, the somewhat vague, even though meaningful, concept of "social welfare" is the overriding consideration, voting choice may be preferred. But even here, if the individual's expressed interest is judged to be the best index of social welfare, the market may still be acceptable as a choice process (this was essentially the position of the utilitarians).

The selection of the choice process will also depend on whether or not the voters consider their own self-interest to be better served individualistically or collectively. If the "collective-action" preference scale allows the required majority of individuals to attain a more esteemed position than does the "individual-action" preference scale, voting choice will be selected regardless of the ranking of social goals. In this case it might be irrational for an individual to choose the market process, even though his behavior in the market, once this process was selected by the group, would be more rational than his behavior in the voting booth. The electorate should select the ballot box over the marketplace in those areas where individually determined market acts tend to produce results which are in conflict either with those which a large group of voters estimate to be their own or the "social welfare," and where the conflict is significant enough to warrant the sacrifice both of the individual freedom and the individual rationality involved.

Insofar as market choice must be made under imperfectly competitive conditions[26] and voting choice under conditions of less than "pure" democracy, the analysis of individual behavior in each process must be appropriately modified and the conclusions reached earlier changed accordingly. No attempt will be made here to extend the analysis in this direction.

VIII

A major source of confusion in the discussion of economic policy stems from the failure to distinguish carefully between the selection of the power structure among individual choosers and the selection of the choice mechanism. This arises from the more fundamental failure to define freedom in such a way that market freedom and market power may be differentiated conceptually.[27] In many real-world situations the market power structure cannot be effectively modified independently, that is, a redistributive decision cannot be made in isolation. It is, nevertheless, essential for analytical clarity that this ideational distinction be made.

The separation of the power structure and the decision-making process is less inclusive and less complex than the similar and more commonly encountered distinction between the "income" and the "resource" aspects of economic policy. The problem of selecting the desirable structure of power relations among individuals in the market is, of course, equivalent to the income problem broadly considered. The "resource" side of the "income-resource" dichotomy introduces an evaluation of policy in terms of the social criteria of economic efficiency, and these aspects of the market mechanism tend to be emphasized. The "choice" side of the "power-choice" dichotomy which has been developed here tends to concentrate attention upon individual behavior in making choices, and it tends to emphasize the greater range of freedom allowed the individual, as well as the greater degree of individual rationality in market choice.

Notes

I am indebted to Marshall Colberg, Jerome Milliman, and Vincent Thursby for helpful comments and suggestions.

1. This is a simplifying assumption; there is reason for believing that the individual possesses a greater knowledge of alternatives in the market. This is due, first, to the greater continuity of market choice and, second, to the difference in the degree of knowledge required to compare alternatives in each case. The latter difference has been stressed by Hayek. See F. A. Hayek, "Individualism: True and False," *Individualism and Economic Order* (Chicago: University of Chicago Press, 1948); and Robert A. Dahl and Charles E. Lindblom, *Politics, Economics, and Welfare* (New York: Harper & Bros., 1953) p. 63.

2. Cf. Kenneth J. Arrow, "Alternative Approaches to the Theory of Choice in Risk-Taking Situations," *Econometrica,* 19 (1951), p. 405.

3. Cf. Frank H. Knight, "Economic Theory and Nationalism," *The Ethics of Competition* (London: Allen & Unwin, 1935), p. 340.

4. The device of considering productive services as negatively desired and hence carrying negative prices enables both the buying and the selling activity of the individual to be encompassed in "market choice."

5. See Arrow, op. cit., for an excellent summary of the various theories of choice under uncertainty.

6. Cf. Ludwig von Mises, *Human Action: A Treatise on Economics* (New Haven: Yale University Press, 1940), p. 312.

7. The fact that individual behavior in the market sets off reactions which are not recognized or intended by the actor, but which do control society's utilization

of resources, is stressed in a somewhat different context by Dahl and Lindblom, op. cit., pp. 99–102. They are concerned with the "spontaneous field control" exerted over the individual in this manner. "Control" in this sense, however, is no different from that imposed by the natural environment or any other set of forces external to the individual (see Sec. V).

8. For a definition of social action see Max Weber, *The Theory of Social and Economic Organization*, trans. A. M. Henderson and Talcott Parsons (New York: Oxford University Press, 1947), p. 88.

9. It has been advanced as a merit of the price system that it does place the individual in a position of adapting his behavior to the anonymous forces of the market without at the same time feeling that he can participate in changing these forces. On this point see Hayek, op. cit., p. 24.

Market behavior can, of course, become "social" if the individual is made to realize the secondary repercussions of his action. Exceptional cases of such realization may be present even in the perfectly competitive economy, e.g., "buyers' strikes."

10. Dahl and Lindblom, op. cit., p. 422.

11. Cf. Kenneth J. Arrow, *Social Choice and Individual Values* (New York: John Wiley & Sons, 1951), p. 82.

12. Cf. William J. Baumol, *Welfare Economics and Theory of the State* (Cambridge: Harvard University Press, 1952), p. 15; Trygve Haavelmo, "The Notion of Involuntary Economic Decisions," *Econometrica*, 18 (1950), pp. 3, 8.

13. On this point see Alfred C. Neal, "The 'Planning Approach' in Public Economy," *Quarterly Journal of Economics*, 54 (1940), p. 251.

14. In cases where spillover effects are significant, the costs taken into account by the individual in the market will clearly exclude some important elements of social costs (positive or negative) which should be considered in the making of a social decision (see Dahl and Lindblom, op. cit., p. 419.)

15. Ludwig von Mises, *Socialism* (new ed.; New Haven: Yale University Press, 1951), p. 21.

16. J. J. Spengler, "Generalists versus Specialists in Social Science: An Economist's View," *American Political Science Review*, 44 (1950), p. 378.

17. The market is thus the only system of proportional representation which will likely work at all. See Clarence Philbrook, "Capitalism and the Rule of Love," *Southern Economic Journal*, 19 (1953), p. 466.

18. A decision to sell productive services may be considered as a vote for generalized purchasing power (i.e., dollars), and thus may be considered positively effective if the sale is consummated.

19. For an excellent summary discussion of this point, see Von Mises, *Human Action: A Treatise on Economics*, p. 271.

20. Dahl and Lindblom, op. cit., p. 424. A similar position is taken in Howard Bowen, *Toward Social Economy* (New York: Rinehart & Co., 1948), p. 44.

21. See Frank H. Knight, "The Meaning of Freedom," in *The Philosophy of American Democracy*, ed. Charles M. Perry (Chicago: University of Chicago Press, 1943), p. 64; "Conflict of Values: Freedom and Justice," in *Goals of Economic Life*, ed. Dudley Ward (New York: Harper & Bros., 1953), pp. 207, 226. For supporting views see Michael Polanyi, *The Logic of Liberty* (Chicago: University of Chicago Press, 1951), p. 159; E. F. Carritt, *Morals and Politics* (London: Oxford University Press, 1953), pp. 195 f.

22. Rationality in individual behavior is defined in the normal manner, that is, the individual is able to rank alternatives, and such ranking is transitive.

23. It is on this basis that Dahl and Lindblom appear to reject the argument that market choice is more rational (op. cit., chap. 15). They do so because they

are concerned with rationality in the social sense, defined as that action which maximizes the achievement of certain postulated social goals. If rationality is defined purely in terms of individual behavior, their argument appears to support that of this paper, although they seem explicitly to deny this at one point. *Ibid.*, p. 422.

24. Cf. Arrow, *Social Choice and Individual Values.*

25. If they cannot agree, the possible irrationality of collective choice may be a desirable rather than an undesirable feature, since rationality could be imposed only at the cost of minority coercion. See James M. Buchanan, "Social Choice, Democracy, and Free Markets," *Journal of Political Economy,* 62 (1954), p. 114–23.

26. Imperfections include, of course, the presence of such monetary and structural factors as may lead to unemployment.

27. This constitutes one of the major weaknesses in Dahl and Lindblom's otherwise excellent comparison of voting and the market. Op. cit., pp. 414–27.

13.

Foreword to *The Politics of Bureaucracy*

"It is not from the benevolence of the butcher, the brewer, or the baker, that we expect our dinner, but from their regard to their own interest." This statement is, perhaps, the most renowned in the classic book in political economy, Adam Smith's *Wealth of Nations*. From Smith onwards, the appropriate function of political economy, and political economists, has been that of demonstrating how the market system, as a perfectible social organization, can, and to an extent does, channel the private interests of individuals toward the satisfaction of desires other than their own. Insofar as this cruder instinct of man toward acquisitiveness, toward self-preservation, can be harnessed through the interactions of the market mechanism, the necessity for reliance on the nobler virtues, those of benevolence and self-sacrifice, is minimized. This fact, as Sir Dennis Robertson has so eloquently reminded us, gives the economist a reason for existing, and his "warning bark" must be heeded by those decision makers who fail to recognize the need for economizing on "love."

Despite such warning barks (and some of these have sounded strangely like shouts of praise) the politicians for many reasons have, over the past century, placed more and more burden of organized social activity on political, governmental processes. As governments have been called upon to do more and more important things, the degree of popular democratic control over separate public or governmental decisions has been gradually reduced. In a real sense, Western societies have attained universal suffrage only after popular democracy has disappeared. The electorate, the ultimate sovereign, must, to an extent not dreamed of by democracy's philosophers, be content to choose its leaders. The ordinary decisions of government emerge from a bureaucracy of ever-increasing dimensions. Nongovernmental and quasi-governmental bureaucracies have accompanied the governmental in its growth. The administrative hierarchy of a modern corporate giant differs less from the federal bureaucracy than it does from the freely contracting tradesman envisaged by Adam Smith.

This set, this drift, of history toward bigness, in both "public" and in "private" government, has caused many a cowardly scholar to despair and to seek escape by migrating to a dream world that never was. It has caused other "downstream" scholars to snicker with glee at the apparent demise of man, the individual. In this book, by contrast, Tullock firmly grasps the nettle offered by the modern bureaucratic state. In effect, he says: "If we must have bureaucratic bigness, let us, at the least, open our eyes to its inner workings. Man does not simply cease to exist because he is submerged in an administrative hierarchy. He remains an individual, with individual motives, impulses, and desires." This seems a plausible view of things. But, and surprisingly, we find that few theorists of bureaucracy have started from this base. Much of administrative theory, ancient or modern, is based on the contrary view that man becomes as a machine when he is placed within a hierarchy, a machine that faithfully carries out the orders of its superiors who act for the whole organization in reaching policy decisions. Tullock returns us to Adam Smith's statement, and he rephrases it as follows: "It is not from the benevolence of the bureaucrat that we expect our research grant or our welfare check, but out of his regard to his own, not the public interest."

Adam Smith and the economists have been, and Tullock will be, accused of discussing a world peopled with evil and immoral men. Men "should not" be either "getting and spending" or "politicking." Such accusations, and they never cease, are almost wholly irrelevant. Some social critics simply do not like the world as it is, and they refuse to allow the social scientist, who may not like it either, to analyze reality. To the scientist, of course, analysis must precede prescription, and prescription must precede improvement. The road to Utopia must start from here, and this road cannot be transversed until here is located, regardless of the beautiful descriptions of yonder. Tullock's analysis is an attempt to locate the "here" in the real, existing, world of modern bureaucracy. His assumptions about behavior in this world are empirical, not ethical. He is quite willing to leave the test of his model to the reader and to future scholars. If, in fact, men in modern bureaucracy do not seek "more" rather than "less," measured in terms of their own career advancement, when they are confronted with relevant choices, Tullock would readily admit the failure of his model to be explanatory in other than some purely tautological sense.

When it is admitted, as all honesty suggests, that some individuals remain individuals, even in a bureaucratic hierarchy, Tullock's analysis assumes meaning. It provides the basis for discussing seriously the prospects for improving the "efficiency" of these bureaucratic structures in accomplishing the tasks assigned to them. There are two stages in any assessment of the efficiency of organizational hierarchies, just as there are in the discussions of the efficiency of the market organization. First, there must be a description, an explanation, a theory, of the behavior of the individual units that make up the structure. This theory, as in the theory of markets, can serve two purposes and, because of this, methodological confusion is compounded. Such an explanatory, descriptive, theory of individual behavior can serve a normative purpose, can provide a guide to the behavior of an individual unit which accepts the objectives or goals postulated in the analytical model. In a wholly different sense, however, the theory can serve a descriptive, explanatory function in a positive manner, describing the behavior of the average or representative unit, without normative implications *for* behavior of any sort. This important distinction requires major stress here. It has never been fully clarified in economic theory, where the contrast is significantly sharper than in the nascent political theory that Tullock, and a few others, are currently attempting to develop.

The analogy with the theory of the firm is worth discussing in some detail here. This theory of the firm, an individual unit in the organized market economy, serves two purposes. It may, if properly employed, serve as a guide to a firm that seeks to further the objectives specified in the model. As such, the theory of the firm falls wholly outside economics, political economy, and, rather, falls within business administration or managerial science. Essentially the same analysis may, however, be employed by the economist as a descriptive theory that helps the student of market organization to understand the workings of this system which is necessarily composed of individual units.

Tullock's theory of the behavior of the individual "politician" in bureaucracy can be, and should be, similarly interpreted. Insofar as such units, the "politicians," accept the objectives postulated—in this case, advancement in this administrative hierarchy—Tullock's analysis can serve as a "guide" to the ambitious bureaucrat. To think primarily of the analysis in this light would, in my view, be grossly misleading. Instead the analysis of the behavior of the individual politician should be treated as descriptive and explanatory, and its validity should be sought in its ability to assist us in the understanding of the operation of bureaucratic systems generally.

Once this basic theory of the behavior of the individual unit is constructed, it becomes possible to begin the construction of a theory of the inclusive system, which is composed of a pattern of interactions among the individual units. By the nature of the systems with which he works, administrative hierarchies, Tullock's "theory of organization" here is less fully developed than is the analogous "theory of markets." A more sophisticated theory may be possible here, and, if so, Tullock's analysis can be an important helpmate to whoever chooses to elaborate it.

Finally, the important step can be taken from positive analysis to normative prescription, not for the improvement of the strategically oriented behavior of the individual unit directly, but for the improvement in the set of working rules that describe the organization. This step, which must be the ultimate objective of all social science, can only be taken after the underlying theory has enabled the observer to make some comparisons among alternatives. The last half of this book is primarily devoted to the development of such norms for "improving" the functioning of organizational hierarchies.

Tullock's "politician" is, to be sure, an "economic" man of sorts. No claim is made, however, that this man, this politician, is wholly descriptive of the real world. More modestly, Tullock suggests (or should do so, if he does not) that the reference politician is an ideal type, one that we must recognize as being always a part of reality, although he does not, presumably, occupy existing bureaucratic structures to the exclusion of all other men. One of Tullock's primary contributions, or so it appears to me, lies in his ability to put flesh and blood on the bureaucratic man, to equip him with his own power to make decisions, to take action. Heretofore, theorists of bureaucracy, to my knowledge, have not really succeeded in peopling their hierarchies. What serves to motivate the bureaucrat in modern administrative theory? I suspect that one must search at some length to find an answer that is as explicit as that provided by Tullock. Because explicit motivation is introduced, a model containing predictive value can be built, and the predictions can be conceptually refuted by appeal to evidence. It is difficult to imagine how a "theory" of bureaucracy in any meaningful sense could be begun in any other way.

By implication, my comments to this point may be interpreted to mean that Tullock's approach to a theory of administration is an "economic" one, and that the most accurate shorthand description of this book would be to say that it represents an "economist's" approach to bureaucracy. This would be, in one sense, correct, but at the same time such a description would tend to cloud over and to subordinate Tullock's second major contribution. This lies in his sharp dichotomization of the "economic" and the "political" relationships among men. Since this book is devoted almost exclusively to an examination of the "political" relationship, it has little that is "economic" in its content. It represents an economist's approach to the political relationship among individuals. This is a more adequate summary, but this, too, would not convey to the prospective reader who is unfamiliar with Tullock's usage of the particular words the proper scope of the analysis. I have, in the discussion above, tried to clarify the meaning of the economist's approach. There remains the important distinction between the "economic" and the "political" relationship.

This distinction is, in one sense, the central theme of the book. In a foreword, it is not proper to quarrel with an author's usage, but synonyms are sometimes helpful in clearing away ambiguities. Tullock distinguishes, basically, between the relationship of *exchange,* which he calls the economic, and the relationship of *slavery,* which he calls the political.

I use bold words here, but I do so deliberately. In its pure or ideal form, the superior-inferior relationship is that of the master and the slave. If the inferior has no alternative means of improving his own well-being other than through pleasing his superior, he is, in fact, a "slave," pure and simple. This remains true quite independently of the particular institutional constraints that may or may not inhibit the behavior of the superior. It matters not whether the superior can capitalize the human personality of the inferior and market him as an asset. Interestingly enough, the common usage of the word "slavery" refers to an institutional structure in which exchange was a dominant relationship. In other words, to the social scientist at any rate, the mention of "slavery" calls to mind the exchange process, with the things exchanged being "slaves." The word itself does not particularize the relationship between master and slave at all. Thus, as with so many instances in Tullock's book, we find no words that describe adequately the relationships that he discusses. Examples, however, serve to clarify. Would I be less a "slave" if you, as my master, could not exchange me, provided only that I have no alternative source of income? My income may depend exclusively on my pleasing you, my master, despite the fact that you, too, may be locked into the relationship. "Serfdom," as distinct from "slavery" may be a more descriptive term, especially since Tullock finds many practical examples for his analysis in feudal systems.

The difficulty in explaining the "political" relationship in itself attests to the importance of Tullock's analysis, and, as he suggests, the whole book can be considered a definition of this relationship. The sources of the difficulty are apparent. First of all, the "political" relationship is not commonly encountered in its pure form, that of abject slavery as noted above. By contrast, its counterpart, the economic or exchange relationship, is, at least conceptually, visualized in its pure form, and, in certain instances, the relationship actually exists. This amounts to saying that without quite realizing what we are doing, we think of ourselves as free men living in a free society. The economic relationship comes more or less naturally to us as the appropriate organizational arrangement through which cooperative endeavor among individuals is carried forward in a social system. Unconsciously, we rebel at the idea of ourselves in a slave or serf culture, and we refuse, again unconsciously, to face up to the reality that, in fact, many of our relationships with our fellows are "political" in the Tullockian sense. Only this blindness toward reality can explain the failure of modern scholars to have developed a more satisfactory theory of individual behavior in hierarchic structures. This also explains why Tullock has found it necessary to go to the Eastern literature and to the discussions in earlier historical epochs for comparative analysis.

Traditional economic analysis can be helpful in illustrating this fundamental distinction between the economic and the political relationship. A

seller is in a purely economic relationship with his buyers when he confronts a number of them, any one of which is prepared to purchase his
commodity or service at the established market price. He is a slave to no
single buyer, and he need "please" no one, provided only that he performs
the task for which he contracts, that he "delivers the goods." By contrast,
consider the seller who confronts a single buyer with no alternative buyer
existent. In this case, the relationship becomes wholly "political." The
price becomes exclusively that which the economist calls "pure rent"
since, by hypothesis, the seller has no alternative use to which he can put
his commodity or service. He is, thus, at the absolute mercy of the single
buyer. He is, in fact, a "slave" to this buyer, and he must "please" in order
to secure favorable terms, in order to advance his own welfare. Note here
that the domestic servant who contracts "to please" a buyer of his services
may, in fact, remain in a predominantly economic relationship if a sufficient number of alternative buyers for his services exist whereas the
corporation executive who supervises a sizable number of people may be
in a predominantly political relationship with his own superior. To the
economist, Tullock provides a discussion of the origins of economic rent,
and a theory of the relationship between the recipient and the donor of
economic rent.

Tullock's distinction here can also be useful in discussing an age-old
philosophical dilemma. When is a man confronted with a free choice?
The traveler's choice between giving up his purse and death, as offered to
him by the highwayman, is, in reality, no choice at all. Yet philosophers
have found it difficult to define explicitly the line that divides situations
into categories of free and unfree or coerced choices. One approach to a
possible classification here lies in the extent to which individual response
to an apparent choice situation might be predicted by an external observer.
If, in fact, the specific action of the individual, confronted with an apparent choice, is predictable within narrow limits, no effective choosing or
deciding process could take place. By comparison, if the individual
response is not predictable with a high degree of probability, choice can
be defined as being effectively free. By implication, Tullock's analysis
would suggest that individual action in a political relationship might be
somewhat more predictable than individual action in the economic relationship because of the simple fact that, in the latter, there exist alternatives. If this implication is correctly drawn, the possibilities of developing
a predictive "science" of "politics" would seem to be inherently greater
than those of developing a science of economics. Yet we observe, of
course, that economic theory has an established and legitimate claim to
the position as being the only social science with genuine predictive value.
The apparent paradox here is explained by the generality with which the
economist can apply his criteria for measuring the results of individual

choice. Through his ability to bring many results within the "measuring rod of money," the economist is able to make reasonably accurate predictions about the behavior of "average" or "representative" men; behavior that, in individual cases, stems from unconstrained, or free, choices. Only through this possibility of relying on representative individuals can economics be a predictive science; predictions about the behavior of individually identifiable human beings are clearly impossible except in rare instances. By contrast, because his choice is less free, the behavior of the individual politician in a bureaucratic hierarchy can be predicted with somewhat greater accuracy than the behavior of the individual in the marketplace. But there exist no general, quantitatively measurable, criteria that will allow the external observer to test hypotheses about political behavior. There exists no measuring rod for bureaucratic advancement comparable to the economist's money scale. For these reasons, hypotheses about individual behavior are more important in Tullock's analysis, and the absence of external variables that are subject to quantification makes the refutation of positive hypotheses difficult in the extreme. For assistance here, Tullock introduces a simple, but neglected, method. He asks the reader whether or not his own experience leads him to accept or to reject the hypotheses concerning the behavior of the politician in bureaucracy.

Tullock makes no attempt to conceal from view his opinion that large hierarchical structures are, with certain explicit exceptions, unnecessary evils, that these are not appropriate parts of the good society. A unique value of the book lies, however, in the fact that this becomes more than mere opinion, more than mere expression of personal value judgments. The emphasis is properly placed on the need for greater scientific analysis. Far too often social scientists have, I fear, introduced explicit value judgments before analysis should have ceased. Ultimately, of course, discussion must reduce to values, but when it does so it is done. If the indolent scholar relies on an appeal to values at the outset, his role in genuine discussion is, almost by definition, eliminated.

The bureaucratic world that Tullock pictures for us is not an attractive one, even when its abstract character is recognized, and even if the reference politician of that world is not assigned the dominant role in real life. Those of us who accept the essential ethics of the free society find this world difficult to think about, much less to discuss critically and to evaluate. External events however force us to the realization that this is, to a large extent, the world in which we now live. The ideal society of freely contracting "equals," always a noble fiction, has, for all practical purposes, disappeared even as a norm in this age of increasing collectivization: political, economic, and philosophical.

Faced with this reality, the libertarian need not despair. The technology of the twentieth century has made small organizations inefficient in many respects, and the Jeffersonian image of the free society can never be realized. However, just as the critics of the laissez-faire economic order were successful in their efforts to undermine the public faith in the functioning of the invisible hand, the new critics of the emerging bureaucratic order can be successful in undermining an equally naive faith in the benevolence of governmental bureaucracy. Tullock's analysis, above all else, arouses the reader to an awareness of the inefficiencies of large hierarchical structures, independently of the presumed purposes or objectives of these organizations. The benevolent despot image of government, that seems now to exist in the minds of so many men, is effectively shattered.

Genuine progress toward the reform of social institutions becomes possible when man learns that the ideal order of affairs is neither the laissez-faire dream of Herbert Spencer nor the benevolent despotism image of an "economy under law" espoused by W. H. Ferry of the Center for the Study of Democratic Institutions. Man in the West, as well as in the East, must learn that governments, even governments by the people, can do so many things poorly, and many things not at all. If this very simple fact could be more widely recognized by the public at large (the ultimate sovereign in any society over the long run), a genuinely free society of individuals and groups might again become a realizable goal for the organization of man's cooperative endeavors. We do not yet know the structure of this society, and we may have to grope our way along for decades. Surely and certainly, however, man must cling to that uniquely important discovery of modern history, the discovery of man, the individual human being. If we abandon or forget this discovery, and allow ourselves to be drawn along any one of the many roads to serfdom by false gods, we do not deserve to survive.

14.
An Economic Theory of Clubs

The implied institutional setting for neoclassical economic theory, including theoretical welfare economics, is a regime of private property, in which all goods and services are privately (individually) utilized or consumed. Only within the last two decades have serious attempts been made to extend the formal theoretical structure to include communal or collective ownership-consumption arrangements.[1] The "pure theory of public goods" remains in its infancy, and the few models that have been most rigorously developed apply only to polar or extreme cases. For example, in the fundamental papers by Paul A. Samuelson, a sharp conceptual distinction is made between those goods and services that are "purely private" and those that are "purely public."[2] No general theory has been developed which covers the whole spectrum of ownership-consumption possibilities, ranging from the purely private or individualized activity on the one hand to purely public or collectivized activity on the other. One of the missing links here is "a theory of clubs," a theory of cooperative membership, a theory that will include as a variable to be determined the extension of ownership-consumption rights over differing numbers of persons.

Everyday experience reveals that there exists some most preferred or "optimal" membership for almost any activity in which we engage, and that this membership varies in some relation to economic factors. European hotels have more communally shared bathrooms than their American counterparts. Middle- and low-income communities organize swimming-bathing facilities; high-income communities are observed to enjoy privately owned swimming pools.

In this article I shall develop a general theory of clubs, or consumption ownership-membership arrangements. This construction allows us to move one step forward in closing the awesome Samuelson gap between the purely private and the purely public good. For the former, the optimal sharing arrangement, the preferred club membership, is clearly one person (or one family unit), whereas the optimal sharing group for the purely public good, as defined in the polar sense, includes an infinitely large number of members. That is to say, for any genuinely collective good defined in the Samuelson way, a club that has an infinitely large membership is preferred to all arrangements of finite size. While it is evident that some goods and services may be reasonably classified as purely private, even in the extreme sense, it is clear that few, if any, goods satisfy the conditions of extreme collectiveness. The interesting cases are those goods and services, the consumption of which involves some "publicness," where the optimal sharing group is more than one person or family but smaller than an infinitely large number. The range of "publicness" is finite. The central question in a theory of clubs is that of determining the membership margin, so to speak, the size of the most desirable cost and consumption sharing arrangement.[3]

I

In traditional neoclassical models that assume the existence of purely private goods and services only, the utility function of an individual is written,

(1) $U^i = U^i(X_1^i, X_2^i, \ldots, X_n^i)$,

where each of the X's represents the amount of a purely private good available during a specified time period, to the reference individual designated by the superscript.

Samuelson extended this function to include purely collective or public goods, which he denoted by the subscripts, $n + 1, \ldots, n + m$, so that (1) is changed to read,

(2) $U^i = U^i(X_1^i, X_2^i, \ldots, X_n^i; X_{n+1}^i, X_{n+2}^i, \ldots X_{n+m}^i)$.

This approach requires that all goods be initially classified into the two sets, private and public. Private goods, defined to be wholly divisible among the persons, $i = 1, 2, \ldots, s$, satisfy the relation

$$X_j = \sum_{i=1}^{s} X_j^i,$$

while public goods, defined to be wholly indivisible as among persons, satisfy the relation,

$$X_{n+j} = X_{n+j}^i.$$

I propose to drop any attempt at an initial classification or differentiation of goods into fully divisible and fully indivisible sets, and to incorporate in the utility function goods falling between these two extremes.

What the theory of clubs provides is, in one sense, a "theory of classification," but this emerges as an output of the analysis. The first step is that of modifying the utility function.

Note that, in neither (1) nor (2) is it necessary to make a distinction between "goods available to the ownership unit of which the reference individual is a member" and "goods finally available to the individual for consumption." With purely private goods, consumption by one individual automatically reduces potential consumption of other individuals by an equal amount. With purely public goods, consumption by any one individual implies equal consumption by all others. For goods falling between such extremes, such a distinction must be made. This is because for such goods there is no unique translation possible between the "goods available to the membership unit" and "goods finally consumed." In the construction which follows, therefore, the "goods" entering the individual's utility function, the X_j's, should be interpreted as "goods available for consumption to the whole membership unit of which the reference individual is a member."

Arguments that represent the size of the sharing group must be included in the utility function along with arguments representing goods and services. For any good or service, regardless of its ultimate place along the conceptual public-private spectrum, the utility that an individual receives from its consumption depends upon the *number of other persons with whom he must share its benefits*. This is obvious, but its acceptance does require breaking out of the private property straitjacket within which most of economic theory has developed. As an extreme example, take a good normally considered to be purely private, say, a pair of shoes. Clearly your own utility from a single pair of shoes, per unit of time, depends on the number of other persons who share them with you. Simultaneous physical sharing may not, of course, be possible; only one person can wear the shoes at each particular moment. However, for any finite period of time, sharing is possible, even for such evidently private goods. For pure services that are consumed in the moment of acquisition the extension is somewhat more difficult, but it can be made nonetheless. Sharing here simply means that the individual receives a smaller quantity of the service. Sharing a "haircut per month" with a second person is the same as consuming "one-half haircut per month." Given any quantity of final good, as defined in terms of the physical units of some standard quality, the utility that the individual receives from this quantity will be related functionally to the number of others with whom he shares.[4]

Variables for club size are not normally included in the utility function of an individual since, in the private-goods world, the optimal club size is unity. However, for our purposes, these variables must be explicitly included, and, for completeness, a club-size variable should be included for each and every good. Alongside each X_j there must be placed an N_j, which we define as the number of persons who are to participate as "members" in the sharing of good X_j, including the ith person whose utility function is examined. That is to say, the club-size variable, N_j, measures the number of persons who are to join in the consumption-utilization arrangements for good X_j over the relevant time period. The sharing arrangements may or may not call for equal consumption on the part of each member, and the peculiar manner of sharing will clearly affect the way in which the variable enters the utility function. For simplicity we may assume equal sharing, although this is not necessary for the analysis. The rewritten utility function now becomes,

(3) $U^i = U^i[(X_1^i, N_1^i), (X_2^i, N_2^i), \ldots, (X_{n+m}^i, N_{n+m}^i)].$[5]

We may designate a *numéraire* good, X_r, which can simply be thought of as money, possessing value only as a medium of exchange. By employing the convention whereby the lower case u's represent the partial derivatives, we get u_j^i/u_r^i, defined as the marginal rate of substitution in consumption between X_j and X_r for the ith individual. Since, in our construction, the size of the group is also a variable, we must also examine $u_{N_j}^i/u_r^i$, defined as the marginal rate of substitution "in consumption" between the size of the sharing group and the *numéraire*. That is to say, this ratio represents the rate (which may be negative) at which the individual is willing to give up (accept) money in exchange for additional members in the sharing group.

We now define a cost or production function as this confronts the individual, and this will include the same set of variables,

(4) $F = F^i[(X_1^i, N_1^i), (X_2^i, N_2^i), \ldots, (X_{n+m}^i, N_{n+m}^i)].$

Why do the club-size variables, the N_j's, appear in this cost function? The addition of members to a sharing group may, and normally will, affect the cost of the good to any one member. The larger is the membership of the golf club the lower the dues to any single member, given a specific quantity of club facilities available per unit time.

It now becomes possible to derive, from the utility and cost functions, statements for the necessary marginal conditions for Pareto optimality in respect to consumption of each good. In the usual manner we get,

(5) $u_j^i/u_r^i = f_j^i/f_r^i.$

Condition (5) states that, for the ith individual, the marginal rate of substitution between goods X_j and X_r in consumption, must be equal to the marginal rate of substitution between these same two goods in "production" or exchange. To this acknowledged necessary condition, we now add,

(6) $u^i_{N_j}/u^i_r = f^i_{N_j}/f^i_r$.

Condition (6) is not normally stated, since the variables relating to club size are not normally included in utility functions. Implicitly, the size for sharing arrangements is assumed to be determined exogenously to individual choices. Club size is presumed to be a part of the environment. Condition (6) states that the marginal rate of substitution "in consumption" between the size of the group sharing in the use of good X_j, and the *numéraire* good, X_r, must be equal to the marginal rate of substitution "in production." In other words, the individual attains full equilibrium in club size only when the marginal benefits that he secures from having an additional member (which may, and probably will normally be, negative) are just equal to the marginal costs that he incurs from adding a member (which will also normally be negative).

Combining (5) and (6) we get,

(7) $u^i_j/f^i_j = u^i_r/f^i_r = u^i_{N_j}/f^i_{N_j}$.

Only when (7) is satisfied will the necessary marginal conditions with respect to the consumption-utilization of X_j be met. The individual will have available to his membership unit an optimal quantity of X_j, measured in physical units and, also, he will be sharing this quantity "optimally" over a group of determined size.

The necessary condition for club size may not, of course, be met. Since for many goods there is a major change in utility between the one-person and the two-person club, and since discrete changes in membership may be all that is possible, we may get,

(7A) $\left. \dfrac{u^i_j}{f^i_j} = \dfrac{u^i_r}{f^i_r} > \dfrac{u^i_{N_j}}{f^i_{N_j}} \right|_{N_j=1} ; \left. \dfrac{u^i_j}{f^i_j} = \dfrac{u^i_r}{f^r} < \dfrac{u^i_{N_j}}{f^i_{N_j}} \right|_{N_j=2}$

which incorporates the recognition that, with a club size of unity, the right-hand term may be relatively too small, whereas, with a club size of two, it may be too large. If partial sharing arrangements can be worked out, this qualification need not, of course, be made.

If, on the other hand, the size of a cooperative or collective sharing group is exogenously determined, we may get,

(7B) $\left. \dfrac{u^i_j}{f^i_j} = \dfrac{u^i_r}{f^i_r} > \dfrac{u^i_{N_j}}{f^i_{N_j}} \right|_{N_j=k}$

Note that (7B) actually characterizes the situation of an individual with respect to the consumption of any purely public good of the type defined in the Samuelson polar model. Any group of finite size, k, is smaller than optimal here, and the full set of necessary marginal conditions cannot possibly be met. Since additional persons can, by definition, be added to the group without in any way reducing the availability of the good to other members, and since additional members, could they be found, would presumably place some positive value on the good and hence be willing to share in its costs, the group always remains below optimal size. The all-inclusive club remains too small.

Consider, now, the relation between the set of necessary marginal conditions defined in (7) and those presented by Samuelson in application to goods that were exogenously defined to be purely public. In the latter case, these conditions are,

(8) $\quad \sum_{i=1}^{s} (u^i_{n+j}/u^i_r) = f_{n+j}/f_r,$

where the marginal rates of substitution in consumption between the purely public good, X_{n+j}, and the *numéraire* good, X_r, summed over all individuals in the group of determined size, s, equals the marginal cost of X_{n+j}, also defined in terms of units of X_r. Note that when (7) is satisfied, (8) is necessarily satisfied, provided only that the collectivity is making neither profit nor loss on providing the marginal unit of the public good. That is to say, provided that,

(9) $\quad f_{n+j}/f_r = \sum_{i=1}^{s} (f^i_{n+j}/f^i_r).$

The reverse does not necessarily hold, however, since the satisfaction of (8) does not require that each and every individual in the group be in a position where his own marginal benefits are equal to his marginal costs (taxes).[6] And, of course, (8) says nothing at all about group size.

The necessary marginal conditions in (7) allow us to classify all goods only after the solution is attained. Whether or not a particular good is purely private, purely public, or somewhere between these extremes is determined only after the equilibrium values for the N_j's are known. A good for which the equilibrium value for N_j is large can be classified as containing much "publicness." By contrast, a good for which the equilibrium value of N_j is small can be classified as largely private.

II

The formal statement of the theory of clubs presented in Section I can be supplemented and clarified by geometrical analysis, although the nature of the construction implies somewhat more restrictive models.

Consider a good that is known to contain, under some conditions, a degree of "publicness." For simplicity, think of a swimming pool. We want to examine the choice calculus of a single person, and we shall

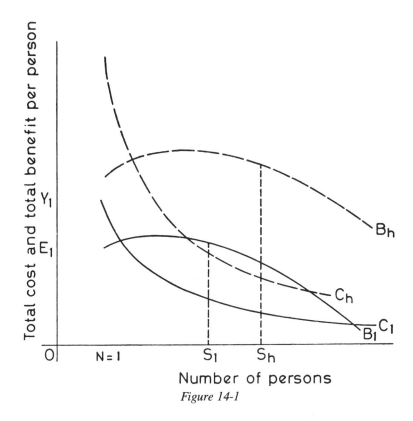

Figure 14-1

assume that other persons about him, with whom he may or may not choose to join in some clublike arrangement, are identical in all respects with him. As a first step, take a facility of one-unit size, which we define in terms of physical output supplied.

On the ordinate of Fig. 14-1, we measure total cost and total benefit per person, the latter derived from the individual's own evaluation of the facility in terms of the *numéraire*, dollars. On the abscissa, we measure the number of persons in possible sharing arrangements. Define the full cost of the one-unit facility to be Y_1, and the reference individual's evaluation of this facility as a purely private consumption good to be E_1. As is clear from the construction as drawn, he will not choose to purchase the good. If the single person is required to meet the full cost, he will not be able to enjoy the benefits of the good. Any enjoyment of the facility requires the organization of some cooperative-collective sharing arrangement.[7]

Two functions may now be traced in Fig. 14-1, remaining within the one-unit restriction on the size of the facility. A total benefit function and a total cost function confronting the single individual may be derived. As more persons are allowed to share in the enjoyment of the facility, of given size, the benefit evaluation that the individual places on the good will, after some point, decline. There may, of course, be both an increasing and a constant range of the total benefit function, but at some point congestion will set in, and his evaluation of the good will fall. There seems little doubt that the total benefit curve, shown as B_1, will exhibit the concavity property as drawn for goods that involve some commonality in consumption.[8]

The bringing of additional members into the club also serves to reduce the cost that the single person will face. Since, by our initial simplifying assumption, all persons here are identical, symmetrical cost sharing is suggested. In any case, the total cost per person will fall as additional persons join the group, under any cost-sharing scheme. As drawn in Fig. 14-1, symmetrical sharing is assumed and the curve, C_1, traces the total cost function, given the one-unit restriction on the size of the facility.[9]

For the given size of the facility, there will exist some optimal size of club. This is determined at the point where the derivatives of the total cost and total benefit functions are equal, shown as S_1 in Fig. 14-1, for the one-unit facility. Consider now an increase in the size of the facility. As before, a total cost curve and a total benefit curve may be derived, and an optimal club size determined. One other such optimum is shown at S_h, for a quantity of goods upon which the curves C_h and B_h are based. Similar constructions can be carried out for every possible size of facility; that is, for each possible quantity of good.

A similar construction may be used to determine optimal goods quantity for each possible size of club; this is illustrated in Fig. 14-2. On the ordinate, we measure here total costs and total benefits confronting the individual, as in Fig. 14-1. On the abscissa, we measure physical size of the facility, quantity of good, and for each assumed size of club membership we may trace total cost and total benefit functions. If we first examine the single-member club, we may well find that the optimal goods quantity is zero; the total cost function may increase more rapidly than the total benefit function from the outset. However, as more persons are added, the total costs to the single person fall; under our symmetrical sharing assumption, they will fall proportionately. The total benefit functions here will slope upward to the right but after some initial range they will be concave downward and at some point will reach a maximum. As club size is increased, benefit functions will shift generally downward beyond the initial noncongestion range, and the point of maximum benefit will move to the right. The construction of Fig. 14-2 allows us to derive an optimal goods quantity for each size of club; Q_k is one such quantity for club size $N = K$.

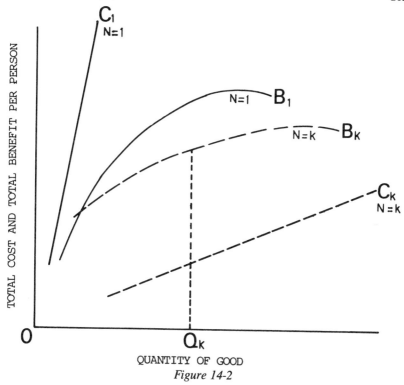

QUANTITY OF GOOD

Figure 14-2

The results derived from Figs. 14-1 and 14-2 are combined in Fig. 14-3. Here the two variables to be chosen, goods quantity and club size, are measured on the ordinate and the abscissa respectively. The values for optimal club size for each goods quantity, derived from Fig. 14-1, allow us to plot the curve, N_{opt}, in Fig. 14-3. Similarly, the values for optimal goods quantity, for each club size, derived from Fig. 14-2, allow us to plot the curve, Q_{opt}.

The intersection of these two curves, N_{opt} and Q_{opt}, determines the position of full equilibrium, G. The individual is in equilibrium both with respect to goods quantity and to group size, for the good under consideration. Suppose, for example, that the sharing group is limited to size, N_k. The attainment of equilibrium with respect to goods quantity, shown by Q_k, would still leave the individual desirous of shifting the size of the membership so as to attain position L. However, once the group increases to this size, the individual prefers a larger quantity of the good, and so on, until G is attained.

Fig. 14-3 may be interpreted as a standard preference map depicting the tastes of the individual for the two components, goods quantity and

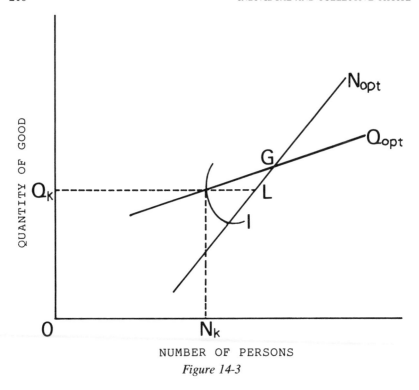

NUMBER OF PERSONS

Figure 14-3

club size for the sharing of that good. The curves, N_{opt} and Q_{opt}, are lines of optima, and G is the highest attainable level for the individual, the top of his ordinal utility mountain. Since these curves are lines of optima within an individual preference system, successive choices must converge in G.

It should be noted that income-price constraints have already been incorporated in the preference map through the specific sharing assumptions that are made. The tastes of the individual depicted in Fig. 14-3 reflect the postpayment or net relative evaluations of the two components of consumption at all levels. Unless additional constraints are imposed on the model, he must move to the satiety point in this construction.

It seems clear that under normal conditions both of the curves in Fig. 14-3 will slope upward to the right, and that they will lie in approximately the relation to each other as therein depicted. This reflects the fact that, normally for the type of good considered in this example, there will exist a complementary rather than a substitute relationship between increasing the quantity of the good and increasing the size of the sharing group.

This geometrical model can be extended to cover goods falling at any point along the private-public spectrum. Take the purely public good as

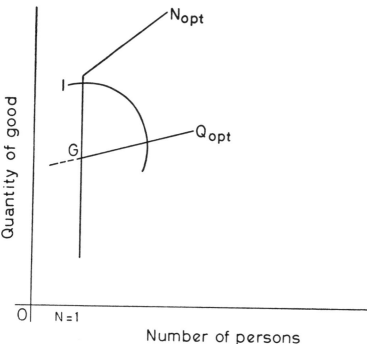

Number of persons

Figure 14-4

the first extreme case. Since, by definition, congestion does not occur, each total benefit curve, in Fig. 14-1, becomes horizontal. Thus, optimal club size, regardless of goods quantity, is infinite. Hence, full equilibrium is impossible of attainment; equilibrium only with respect to goods quantity can be reached, defined with respect to the all-inclusive finite group. In the construction of Fig. 14-3, the N curve cannot be drawn. A more realistic model may be that in which, at goods quantity equilibrium, the limitations on group size impose an inequality. For example, in Fig. 14-3, suppose that the all-inclusive group is of size N_k. Congestion is indicated as being possible over small sizes of facility, but, if an equilibrium quantity is provided, there is no congestion, and, in fact, there remain economies of scale in club size. The situation at the most favorable attainable position is, therefore, in all respects equivalent to that confronted in the case of the good that is purely public under the more restricted definition.

Consider now the purely private good. The appropriate curves here may be shown in Fig. 14-4. The individual, with his income-price constraints, is able to attain the peak of his ordinal preference mountain without the necessity of calling upon his fellows to join him in sharing arrangements. Also, the benefits that he receives from the good may be so exclusively his own that these would largely disappear if others were brought in to share them. Hence, the full equilibrium position, G, lies along the vertical from the $N = 1$ member point. Any attempt to expand the club beyond this point will reduce the utility of the individual.[10]

III

The geometrical construction implies that the necessary marginal conditions are satisfied at unique equilibrium values for both goods quantity and club size. This involves an oversimplification that is made possible only through the assumptions of specific cost-sharing schemes and identity among individuals. In order to generalize the results, these restrictions must be dropped. We know that, given any group of individuals who are able to evaluate both consumption shares and the costs of congestion, there exists some set of marginal prices, goods quantity, and club size that will satisfy (7) above. However, the quantity of the good, the size of the club sharing in its consumption, and the cost-sharing arrangements must be determined simultaneously. And, since there are always "gains from trade" to be realized in moving from nonoptimal to optimal positions, distributional considerations must be introduced. Once these are allowed to be present, the final "solution" can be located at any one of a subinfinity of points on the Pareto welfare surface. Only through some quite arbitrarily chosen conventions can standard geometrical constructions be made to apply.

The approach used above has been to impose at the outset a set of marginal prices (tax-prices, if the good is supplied publicly), translated here into shares or potential shares in the costs of providing separate quantities of a specific good for groups of varying sizes. Hence, the individual confronts a predictable set of marginal prices for each quantity of the good at every possible club size, independently of his own choices on these variables. With this convention, and the world-of-equals assumption, the geometrical solution becomes one that is relevant for any individual in the group. If we drop the world-of-equals assumption, the construction continues to hold without change for the choice calculus of any particular individual in the group. The results cannot, of course, be generalized for the group in this case, since different individuals will evaluate any given result differently. The model remains helpful even here, however, in that it suggests the process through which individual decisions may be made, and it tends to clarify some of the implicit content in the more formal statements of the necessary marginal conditions for optimality.[11]

IV

The theory of clubs developed in this paper applies in the strict sense only to the organization of membership or sharing arrangements where "exclusion" is possible. Insofar as nonexclusion is a characteristic of public goods supply, as Musgrave has suggested,[12] the theory of clubs is of limited relevance. Nevertheless, some implications of the theory for the whole excludability question may be indicated. If the structure of property rights is variable, there would seem to be few goods the services of which are nonexcludable, solely due to some physical attributes. Hence, the theory of clubs is, in one sense, a theory of optimal exclusion, as well as one of inclusion. Consider the classic lighthouse case. Variations in property rights, broadly conceived, could prohibit boat operators without "light licenses" from approaching the channel guarded by the light. Physical exclusion is possible, given sufficient flexibility in property law, in almost all imaginable cases, including those in which the interdependence lies in the act of consuming itself. Take the single person who gets an inoculation, providing immunization against a communicable disease. Insofar as this action exerts external benefits on his fellows, the person taking the action could be authorized to collect charges from all beneficiaries under sanction of the collectivity.

This is not, of course, to suggest that property rights will, in practice, always be adjusted to allow for optimal exclusion. If they are not, the "free rider" problem arises. This prospect suggests one issue of major importance that the analysis of this paper has neglected, the question of costs that may be involved in securing agreements among members of sharing groups. If individuals think that exclusion will not be fully possible, that they can expect to secure benefits as free riders without really becoming full-fledged contributing members of the club, they may be reluctant to enter voluntarily into cost-sharing arrangements. This suggests that one important means of reducing the costs of securing voluntary cooperative agreements is that of allowing for more flexible property arrangements and for introducing excluding devices. If the owner of a hunting preserve is allowed to prosecute poachers, then prospective poachers are much more likely to be willing to pay for the hunting permits in advance.

Notes

I am indebted to graduate students and colleagues for many helpful suggestions. Specific acknowledgement should be made for the critical assistance of Emilio

Giardina of the University of Catania and W. Craig Stubblebine of the University of Delaware.

1. It is interesting that none of the theories of socialist economic organization seems to be based on explicit cooperation among individuals. These theories have conceived the economy either in the Lange-Lerner sense as an analogue to a purely private, individually oriented social order or, alternatively, as one that is centrally directed.

2. See Paul A. Samuelson, "The Pure Theory of Public Expenditure," *Review of Economics and Statistics,* 36 (1954), pp. 387–89; "Diagrammatic Exposition of a Theory of Public Expenditure," *Review of Economics and Statistics,* 37 (1955), pp. 350–55.

3. Note that an economic theory of clubs can strictly apply only to the extent that the motivation for joining in sharing arrangements is itself economic; that is, only if choices are made on the basis of costs and benefits of particular goods and services as these are confronted by the individual. Insofar as individuals join clubs for camaraderie, as such, the theory does not apply.

4. Physical attributes of a good or service may, of course, affect the structure of the sharing arrangements that are preferred. Although the analysis below assumes symmetrical sharing, this assumption is not necessary, and the analysis in its general form can be extended to cover all possible schemes.

5. Note that this construction of the individual's utility function differs from that introduced in an earlier paper, where "activities" rather than "goods" were included as the basic arguments. See James M. Buchanan and William Craig Stubblebine, "Externality," *Economica,* 31 (1962), pp. 371–84. In the alternative construction, the "activities" of other persons enter directly into the utility function of the reference individual with respect to the consumption of all other than purely private goods. The construction here incorporates the same interdependence through the inclusion of the N_j's, although in a more general manner.

6. In Samuelson's diagrammatic presentation, these individual marginal conditions are satisfied, but the diagrammatic construction is more restricted than that contained in his earlier, more general model.

7. The sharing arrangement need not be either cooperative or governmental in form. Since profit opportunities exist in all such situations, the emergence of profit-seeking firms can be predicted in those settings where legal structures permit, and where this organizational form possesses relative advantages. (Cf. R. H. Coase, "The Nature of the Firm," *Economica,* 4 (1937), pp. 386–405.) For purposes of this article, such firms are one form of club organization, with cooperatives and public arrangements representing other forms. Generally speaking, of course, the choice among these forms should be largely determined by efficiency considerations.

8. The geometrical model here applies only to such goods. Essentially the same analysis may, however, be extended to apply to cases where "congestion," as such, does not appear. For example, goods that are produced at decreasing costs, even if their consumption is purely private, may be shown to require some sharing arrangements in an equilibrium or optimal organization.

9. For simplicity, we assume that an additional "membership" in the club involves the addition of one separate person. The model applies equally well, however, for those cases where cost shares are allocated proportionately with predicted usage. In this extension, an additional "membership" would really amount to an additional consumption unit. Membership in the swimming club could, for example, be defined as the right to visit the pool one time each week. Hence, the person who plans to make two visits per week would, in this modification, hold two memberships. This qualification is not, of course, relevant under

the strict world-of-equals assumption, but it indicates that the theory need not be so restrictive as it might appear.

10. The construction suggests clearly that the optimal club size, for any quantity of good, will tend to become smaller as the real income of an individual is increased. Goods that exhibit some "publicness" at low income levels will, therefore, tend to become "private" as income levels advance. This suggests that the number of activities that are organized optimally under cooperative-collective sharing arrangements will tend to be somewhat larger in low-income communities than in high-income communities, other things equal. There is, of course, ample empirical support for this rather obvious conclusion drawn from the model. For example, in American agricultural communities thirty years ago, heavy equipment was communally shared among many farms, normally on some single owner-lease-rental arrangement. Today, substantially the same equipment will be found on each farm, even though it remains idle for much of its potential working time.

The implication of the analysis for the size of governmental units is perhaps less evident. Insofar as governments are organized to provide communal facilities, the size of such units, measured by the number of citizens, should decline as income increases. Thus, in the affluent society, the local school district may, optimally, be smaller than in the poor society.

11. A note concerning one implicit assumption of the whole analysis is in order at this point. The possibility for the individual to choose among the various scales of consumption-sharing arrangements has been incorporated into an orthodox model of individual behavior. The procedure implies that the individual remains indifferent as to which of his neighbors or fellow citizens join him in such arrangements. In other words, no attempt has been made to allow for personal selectivity or discrimination in the models. To incorporate this element, which is no doubt important in many instances, would introduce a wholly new dimension into the analysis, and additional tools to those employed here would be required.

12. See R. A. Musgrave, *The Theory of Public Finance* (New York, 1959).

15.

An Individualistic Theory of
Political Process

The "theory" or "approach" presented in this paper represents an extension of the tools, methods, and procedures utilized by the economist to an analysis of politics. Like the political scientist, the economist studies social organization. But the economist does so, or should do so, differently. He studies the emergence of market and exchange relationships out of the choice processes of individual participants. Orthodox neoclassical economic theory gives a central position to the theory of individual choice behavior; and the textbooks normally begin with an analysis of individual demand for goods and services. Upon this theory of individual choice behavior, a theory of interaction among individuals and groups is constructed. The organization that comes into being as a result of individuals participating variously in exchange processes is called "the economy." This organization, this economy, as such, has no independent existence apart from the interaction of individual participants in it. It has no goals, no purposive intent.[1] It is properly a social organization, but it is not a social organism. The word *individualistic* in the title of this article is the opposite of the word *organismic,* and it classifies the approach taken in terms of methodology, not in terms of ideology.

In the individualistic approach, the polity is examined as a social organization in a manner similar to that in which the economy has traditionally been analyzed. The political structure is conceived as something that *emerges* from the choice processes of individual participants. This approach to politics is not, of course, novel. The whole of the contractarian tradition can, in one sense, be classified as falling within this approach. It nevertheless seems to be true that individual behavior in participating in and in determining the outcome of political process has been relatively neglected by political scientists. Many of these scholars continue to assume that, somehow and somewhere, there exists a "public interest" or "general interest" that is divorced from the interests of the individual participants. In their behavior in the economic process, private people, as consumers, workers, investors, and entrepreneurs, are assumed to have differing tastes, desires, and values. And the economy represents the institutional or organizational response to the need to satisfy simultaneously this manifold set of wants. By contrast, and with important exceptions, when individuals participate in the formation of social or collective decisions, they are assumed to be somehow identical. Political process has not been sufficiently examined as a means through which separate and differing individual and group interests come to be reconciled, although major contributions have been made in this country by the so-called Bentley school.

This school aside, political process has continued to be viewed as a means through which "right" or "correct" decisions are reached. Political decisions are, for the most part, still conceived as "truth judgments"; the primary task of political decision making becomes that of discovering the "true" public interest. When collective choices reduce to mutually exclusive, either/or, decisions, this "truth judgment" model has some validity. The basic issue is whether or not it is the appropriate model for analyzing the ordinary day-to-day operation of a democratic political structure. The approach to be developed here is based on the presumption that it is not, and that the political process in democratic society can best be examined by interpreting it as a means of reconciling divergent interests. The theory is one of "individualist democracy" as opposed to "idealist democracy," in the terms used by T. D. Weldon.[2]

The acceptance of this individualistic model as the appropriate one for analysis involves value judgment in two separate respects. As one who accepts the traditions of Western society, I think that we should treat the human individual as the basic philosophical entity, and that we should conceive the state as if it were ultimately derivative from individual consent. The second value judgment, which is more important for the purposes of this article, is a judgment about facts, a "characterizing value judgment," to use Nagel's term; it may be accepted independently of any judgment concerning the philosophy of the state. It involves the empirical judgment that political process can be "factored down" to the level of individual choices.

This statement need not, of course, involve the claim of exclusive, or even predominant, relevance for the individualistic model in making predictions about political decision processes. In the scientific house there are many mansions, and, in analyzing politics, there is surely room for alternative models. For some purposes, an organic model may be helpful; for others, a ruling-class or force theory of the state. And, in many instances, a model that bypasses the individual and begins with the interplay of group interests may yield fully satisfactory predictions. As base, it is claimed only that the model which derives the whole political process from the decisions made by individual persons, who are assumed to behave rationally, explains elements of politics that seem awkward in other models, by providing some "explanations" of reality that are not consistent with alternative theories.

At this point, a familiar methodological difficulty arises, one that caused a certain ambivalence in the more extensive treatment of this approach to politics that Gordon Tullock and I have published.[3] What is required of a "theory" of politics? There are two possible answers to this question. "Theory" may, first of all, be conceived of as a logical structure, an "explanation," which allows meaningful statements to be made and which helps to establish some uniformity in thinking without producing conceptually refutable hypotheses. At this level, which may be called that of "logical theory," all that is required in the individualistic model is that interests differ, and that individuals act in accordance with these separate interests. There is no need to examine the nature of these differences in individual and group wants. All that is required for the formal structure of a theory is the presumption that different individuals want to accomplish different things through the political mechanism. This "logical theory" of individualist democracy can be helpful in understanding the processes through which persons and groups compromise and reconcile their differences in a system of political order.

For a genuinely predictive theory of politics, however, more is needed. If by "theory" we mean the development of hypotheses about behavior in the political process that can be conceptually refuted by observation of real-world events, some additional constraints must be placed on the manner in which separate interests differ. The most familiar of these constraints, again taken from economics, is the hypothesis that individuals act in politics as they are assumed to act in the predictive theory of markets, so as to maximize their expected utility, and that their behavior in doing so is measurable in terms of some objectively identifiable magnitude such as personal income or wealth. In politics, this "positive" theory implies that individuals, and groups, act so as to further their economic positions. For example, California farmers vote for congressmen who vote for federal funds for irrigation projects; and owners of trucking firms vote for congressmen who vote for highway expenditure projects. Clearly, this hypothesis has at least *some* explanatory value. Alternative constraints on the pattern of individual differences could, of course, be imposed; hypotheses could be drawn, and the implications tested.

It should be emphasized that the acceptance of the individualistic approach to politics need not imply acceptance of the hypothesis that men and groups, even in a first approximation, act narrowly to further identifiable self-interest. As a logical theory of political behavior, the model is equally applicable to a world of altruists and to a world of egoists, although the testable hypotheses would, of course, sharply differ in the two cases. The logical construction can be applied even to a world of saints, so long as their separate visions of the "good society" differ. The model is inapplicable only to a world where separate individual interests really do not exist, but, instead, are somehow transcended in some supraindividual set of goals.

What contribution can the individualistic approach make to an understanding of politics? The underlying proposition is that individual interests differ. Starting from this, what happens to the "public interest?" Does it exist, and, if it does, how can individual interests be reconciled with it? The standard approach in political science seems to have been that of beginning with the "public interest," defined perhaps in terms of what the modern welfare economists refer to as a "social welfare function." The whole problem of "politics and morals," of "political obligation," arises out of attempts to get people to accept the "public interest" as their own. In other words, the reconciliation, if there is any, between private and public interests, must come about through some moral force that the latter exerts on individual behavior. Political behavior of the individual becomes, in this familiar approach, necessarily moral behavior.

This whole conception of politics is foreign to the approach that is summarized in this article. There exists no "social welfare function," no "public interest" as such in a society of freely choosing individuals, and there seems no reason to invent such a conception for analytical convenience. This does not imply, however, that political process reduces to a simple struggle for power among individuals and groups, which may be analyzed systematically and scientifically, but about which nothing can be said normatively. It is precisely at this stage that the individualistic model can rescue the "public interest," indirectly, through the essential separation between the constitutional and the operational stages of political decision. The clarification of this separation, and the implications that may be derived from an understanding of it, is the central contribution that the model can make to political theory.

It is necessary to distinguish sharply between day-to-day political decision making, where the struggle often does reduce simply to that among conflicting individual-group interests, and "constitutional" decision making, where individuals may be thought of as participating in choices on the set of rules under which subsequent day-to-day decisions are to be made. This second set of decisions, of choices, which may be called the "constitutional," is the important one, and, at this stage, it becomes possible to reconcile separate individual interests with something that could, with some legitimacy, be called the "public interest," were it not for the confusion that this particular usage might generate.

The center of attention becomes the mental calculus of the individual as he is confronted with a choice among alternative rules for the reaching of subsequent political decisions—that is to say, as he is confronted with a genuinely constitutional issue. The individual does not know, nor is he able to predict, what particular issues will be presented subsequent to the adoption of the rule. And, even if he can predict with some accuracy the sort of issues that may arise, he could hardly predict his own position vis-à-vis the other members of the group. Faced with such uncertainty, how does he proceed to choose among alternative rules? He must, in the nature of the case, try to select a rule that will work reasonably well for an unpredictable series of events and in terms of his own personal situation that he will assume to be more or less randomly distributed. Simple self-interest dictates that the individual try to rank alternative rules and institutions for collective decision making. The essential element here is the recognition that self-interest, at the level of decisions on rules or on institutions that are expected to remain in effect for long time periods, imposes on the individual an attitude and a behavior pattern that are not identical with those which the same self-interest would dictate in particular choices on specific political issues.

The members of the group may, of course, disagree on the rules, as they discuss these at the constitutional level of decision. A consensus on the ranking of alternative institutional schemes will not necessarily emerge. But it is precisely at this constitutional stage that discussion in some meaningful sense can take place. It is at this stage where analysis and argument can be helpful in resolving differences of opinion. No moral issue is introduced in this procedure; there is no dilemma that requires the individual to choose between furtherance of his own self-interest, as he perceives it, and some vague "public interest" as sensed by others than himself, with a view toward preserving social harmony. The reconciliation that is possible here is achieved through the fact that self-interest, as the individual himself perceives this, becomes less and less identifiable in any objectively measurable sense, for the individual is removed from the moment of pure conflict.

The analogy with the choosing of rules for an ordinary game is helpful, as my colleague, Rutledge Vining, has repeatedly emphasized. Consider the individual who participates in a poker game at the start of an evening's play. Rules under which play is to proceed are discussed and debated. No departure from pure self-interest is required for the individual to choose rules that will, in fact, be predicted to result in a reasonably "fair" game. Not knowing in advance how the cards will be distributed over a whole series of particular plays, the participant will, in his own interest, be motivated to choose rules that will make the game "fair," that is, "in the general interest of the group." Various players or prospective players may, of course, disagree on the precise content of the rules that are required to produce "fair" games. But these differences will be based, not so much

on differences in identifiable self-interest, but on differences in characterizing value judgments concerning the working properties of alternative
rules, that is to say, concerning the frequency distribution of predicted
outcomes. Ultimate agreement may not be possible, and the game may
not be played. But it seems that genuine compromise, genuine consensus,
is much more likely to result in this sort of situation than at that stage
where, by necessity and invention, individual positions come to be directly
opposed, one to the other.

At the constitutional level of discourse, unanimity or consensus becomes
important, not because there is something sacrosanct about unanimity per
se, but for the simple reason that it provides the *only* criterion through
which improvements in rules and institutions can, in fact, be judged
without the introduction of an explicit value scale. Lacking an explicit
social welfare function, there is no external or exogenous means of evaluating possible changes in the rules or institutions that describe an existing political structure. And, if agreement on possible changes in these
cannot be secured, how are the interests of the separate individuals or
groups to be weighed, one against the other? Agreement becomes the
only possible test, and if this does not, or cannot, exist, there is simply
nothing that can be said. Disagreement precludes any conclusion. But it
should be again emphasized that the standard arguments against the application of the unanimity rule do not apply with equal force at the constitutional level and at the operational level of choice. Where individual and
group interests are demonstrably in pure conflict, agreement is not possible, and some rule other than unanimity must normally be introduced to
resolve the issue. But where individual and group interests are not clearly
defined, where disagreement is based largely on conflicting interpretations concerning the working properties of alternative institutions, discussion and compromise leading to general agreement seem possible.

If observed agreement, or unanimity, provides the only criterion that
enables an evaluation of changes in the rules for making political decisions, the question of the starting point becomes important. What position
is in being, and what changes are to be considered? Obviously time is
wasted if discussion is limited to a hypothetical group of individuals
considering the original organization of a political society. The interpretation of the contract theory as applying to such a situation has, I think,
plagued much of the critical discussion concerning this theory, and it has
obscured the basic validity of the contract approach. A polity exists; it
seems best to start from an existing political entity which may best be
described in terms of the institutional-constitutional rules for reaching
decisions. What is to be sought, therefore, is a criterion for evaluating
changes in these existing rules. By saying that agreement or unanimity is
the only meaningful criterion in the individualistic context, I, of course,

stand accused of building into the model a defense of the status quo. The unique position given to this criterion seems to suggest that whatever exists, is "right," until and unless everyone agrees to make a change, emphasizing, of course, that changes in rules are the sort discussed.

Several points must be made in response to this entirely reasonable interpretation that may be placed on the approach to political process that has been sketched briefly here. In the first place, it should be noted that no statement at all is made or implied about what is or is not "right," "just," or "correct." The model is based on an explicit disavowal of any personal imputation of moral-ethical values into the system. Secondly, and more important, analysis must start from somewhere, and the existing set of rules and institutions is the only place from which it is possible to start. There is no implication that this position is personally desirable. But if we seek, dispassionately, to evaluate changes, there is no other place from which we may begin. Each and every one of us who looks at the existing political structure might prefer the world to be different from what it is now; but, until and unless general agreement can be reached on making changes, any modification of what exists must involve coercion of some persons by others.

And this means that some choice be made as to which individuals or groups are to be allowed to coerce others, a choice that simply cannot be made without the introduction of external value scales. This need not, of course, inhibit more general discussion. Value scales can be introduced on a personal and necessarily arbitrary basis, and statements can be made about "socially desired" changes in an existing set of rules. The steps are outside of the model of political process that can be properly called the "individualistic" model. But this is not equivalent to saying that these extraindividualistic models, and whatever theories or hypotheses they may produce, are somehow "improper." They are simply beyond the pale of this discussion.

Additional clarification may be forthcoming if we return to the poker game analogy. Assume that play has continued under an agreed-on set of rules for an hour, during which some participants have gained and others lost. A proposal is made to change the rules. The change considered must be from the existing set. Those proposing change may consider the rules wholly unfair and improper, but unless they are prepared to enforce their will on others, they can improve the rules only by securing agreement. Those who accumulated gains under the established rules will not necessarily be averse to reasonable proposals for change. Their positions on a future sequence of plays remain uncertain, and the fact that they have been gaining under one set of rules in no way insures that they will continue to do so. For these reasons, general agreement or consensus becomes possible on changes in rules for future play, as contrasted with the impossibility of agreement on some modified division of gains on a particular play. Clearly, proposals to change the rules of the game through general agreement belong to a different realm of discourse than proposals to change the results that have been generated under an existing set of rules, presumably in accordance with some externally determined value judgment.

Efforts to remain as clear as possible of externally imposed value judgments, to attempt to construct a theory of politics without interjecting interpersonal comparisons, may seem strained and tedious to political scientists. It should again be noted, however, that the approach here taken is derived from theoretical welfare economics. The unanimity criterion is merely the translation into political terms of the familiar Pareto criterion for evaluating changes in policy or in classifying positions.[4] Few economists have extended this criterion to the evaluation of rules or institutions, where it seems considerably more applicable than it does in connection with unique events.[5]

There is an important distinction that is of some significance in understanding the constitutional approach to political rules, one that follows directly from the economist's proclivity to consider human interaction in terms of exchanges. This is the distinction between a zero-sum and a positive-sum game, to use modern, and highly suitable, terminology. In other words, it is necessary to emphasize the difference between situations of pure conflict among individuals and groups and situations that include conflict but also embody mutual possibilities for gain. At the operational level of day-to-day politics, where interests of individuals and groups may be sharply identified and delineated, the pure-conflict or zero-sum model can yield useful explanations, as William Riker has demonstrated in his recent work on coalition formation.[6] At the constitutional level of decision, however, where selections must be made among alternative rules, and where individual and group interests are not clearly identified, the situation is not properly described by pure conflict models. Participation in the "great game of politics" must, on balance, be mutually beneficial to all parties, or else revolution would ensue. The game is best conceived as positive-sum. But the game analogy remains relevant. Conflict is not wholly eliminated, and "pure" cooperation (all players on the same side) does not describe the situation.

The ordinary exchange relationship seems to be the appropriate model at this level. Gains can be realized through reaching agreements, and these gains accrue to *all* parties to the relationship, although the distribution of these gains will depend on relative bargaining strengths. Perfect symmetry need not be a property of the result. Unless gains can be secured by *all* parties there is, of course, no possibility that a genuinely voluntary agreement can be attained. Ordinary exchanges, as well as ordinary games, are essentially voluntary because participants are free to withdraw from or to refrain from entering the association. Should the political relationship be viewed, at base, as essentially a voluntary one? That is, of course, the heart of the matter, and the individualistic approach or "theory" of politics comes down squarely on the affirmative side of this question. At the ultimate constitutional level, it seems difficult to talk about political organization unless the structure is assumed to be derived, in some way, from individual consent. If this is not accepted, the basis for any judgment becomes purely personal.

The discussion, to this point, has been devoted largely to presenting a frame of reference within which political process may be examined. The emphasis has been deliberate, for it is the shift in the frame of reference, and not the particulars of analysis, that is the important element in the individualistic approach. It remains, however, to discuss some of the implications that may be drawn from the approach.

It is perhaps evident that the approach is quite consistent with a pragmatic and pluralistic conception of existing political institutions. The test of an institution is whether or not it is predicted to work, not in a unique situation or in a unique period of time, but over a whole sequence of events, over a whole span of time. Workability is not, however, to be measured in terms of accomplishing specifically postulated goals for political action. Such goals are nonexistent in the model. Workability of an institution means the efficacy or efficiency of the institution in accomplishing, for the individual, those purposes or goals, unpredictable at any particular moment of time, that he may desire to achieve from collective action over a sequence of future periods.

Some predictions must be made concerning the adaptability of the institution under varying circumstances. The final estimation of the net efficiency of an institution involves both positive and negative accounts. The political rule or institution must be examined for its positive efficacy in promoting the results that the individual desires to see achieved through political process. But the same rule or institution must be examined also for its negative potentiality for promoting results or outcomes that the individual does not desire. Common sense suggests that different institutions or different rules will be recommended for different types of political decisions.

Tullock and I have analyzed one such institution—the simple majority voting rule—in part for its own intrinsic interest, and, in part, as illustrative of the sort of approach to the various political decision rules that the individualistic conception suggests.[7] Our approach implied that majority voting is not to be prejudged at the outset. It is one possible decision rule among many, and it must stand the test of efficiency when compared to alternative decision rules and institutions. What are the costs of allowing political decisions to be made by majority voting rules? What are the benefits? The point is that these familiar questions should be approached from the vantage point of the individual participant in political process, the citizen-voter-taxpayer-beneficiary. Clearly, if the decision involves choosing among predictable outcomes of a unique, once-and-for-all variety, the single individual could estimate the desirability or undesirability of majority voting rules quite simply by determining whether or not his own opinion is supported by a majority of his fellows. But again, it is not at this level or stage of decision that the rule itself should be evaluated. The individual should be conceived as participating in a "constitutional" decision that ultimately chooses majority rule, or some alternative, on the basis of its predicted effects in producing a whole sequence of outcomes, the particular configurations of which are largely unpredictable.

This "constitutional" choice among political rules and institutions can be subjected to rigorous general analysis that is helpful in indicating the elements that must enter into the individual's final decision. Let us return to the familiar questions concerning the benefits and costs to be expected under the institution of simple majority voting. The individual will recognize that, on a certain number of occasions, he will find himself in the minority, and that, on such occasions, he will be subjected to exploitation by the majority coalition; net costs will be imposed upon him. On the other hand, he will recognize that majority rule is one reasonably simple way of getting decisions made, of getting results accomplished through political process, without excessively high costs of decision. Weighing these two sides of the account, he may rationally choose majority rule as "optimal" for certain types of political decisions.

He may, however, reject majority rule for other types of political decisions; he may expect either some less-than-majority rule or some greater-than-majority rule to be more "efficient." His final choice among such rules or institutions will depend on a large number of factors. Prominent among these will be such things as the expected distribution of his own "interest" or "preference" as related to those of his fellows over the expected sequence of issues to be presented, and the expected intensity of this interest on particular sorts of issues. For many aspects of collective organization, where the important consideration becomes the general establishment and acceptance of some rule rather than no rule, the individual may, at the "constitutional" stage, quite rationally choose to delegate final authority to particular individuals in the group. For example, majority rule is obviously inefficient as a means of determining traffic regulations; this task is normally delegated to the bureaucratic apparatus. By contrast, for decisions that can significantly affect human life and property, the individual may choose to accept some "constitutional" constraint that requires greater-than-majority agreement. On such issues, he expects the intensity of his own interest to be such that majority rule will not be acceptable. The familiar constitutional protection to human rights can be "explained" in this way. At a more mundane level, the most familiar example of this sort of thinking is the requirement for variance in municipal zoning laws. Here, in many cases, some greater-than-majority agreement is required to approve proposed changes.

That majority voting is only one among many possibly efficient or inefficient institutions through which political choices are made in a rationally organized democratic structure is recognized in existing political institutions, as the few examples cited above suggest. But this fact seems to be less well-established in the literature of political analysis. The divergence here stems, in part, from the "truth judgment" approach to democratic choice that has been previously mentioned. If political decision structures are viewed, at base, as institutional means of arriving at "correct" decisions, rather than as means of simply reconciling differing individual and group interests, a wholly different conceptual framework of analysis is required. If this essentially nonindividualistic view of politics is accepted, the choice among decision-making institutions must be made on the basis of comparative efficiency in making decisions in terms of some externally established criteria.

Such an approach seems to provide the basis for arguments that decisions had best be left to "experts," to the bureaucrats, who will be able to choose "correctly" with greater efficiency. This is the current antithesis to the individualistic approach to democratic process, and the choice between these fundamentally opposed analytical models can only be made on the acceptance of explicit value judgment. If individual valuations and preferences are to be allowed to count—and this admittedly requires an explicit value judgment—and so long as individuals and groups differ in what they desire to see collectively accomplished, no conceivable computing technique can replace the constitutionally constrained institutions of representative democracy.

One additional implication of the individualistic approach to politics serves to sharpen its contrast with the "truth judgment" model. One of the fundamental "constitutional" decisions that any group must make concerns the appropriate areas of human activity that are to be subject to collective organization. How much collectivization is to be allowed? The answer to this question clearly depends, in the individualistic model, on the rules and institutions that are to prevail in the operation of the collectivized sector. The decisions as to the degree of collectivization and the choice among alternative decision-making institutions are interdependent. It becomes impossible to determine whether or not a particular activity should or should not be collectivized, on efficiency grounds, until the choice among decision rules is taken into account. This, too, is an obvious but important point that is often overlooked. Collectivization of an activity, say, education, may be highly desirable in a community that is to reach decisions under institutions of majority rule, but highly undesirable in a community that is subjected to dictatorial controls.

The "theory" of democratic political process that has been sketched in this article suggests a shift in research emphasis. There is required a painstaking and rigorous analysis of existing decision-making institutions in terms of their operation over periods of time and on numbers of issues sufficient to permit meaningful judgments to be made. Both in economics and in politics, attempts must be made to develop theories of institutional structures, and to test the hypotheses derived from these theories against real-world observations. The existing set of institutions surely includes some that are grossly inefficient, as well as others that are highly efficient, even within the limits of an individualistic model. Analysis can highlight these differences and explore the predicted working properties of alternative institutions. This research emphasis follows from an acceptance of the "efficiency" notion that emerges from the individualistic model. Efficiency is not to be defined independently of the choice calculus of the individual citizen as participant in political process.

Appendix

The "individualistic" approach to a theory of political process actually represents only one of several strands of recently converging research which, when taken together, promise significant contributions in the social sciences over the next decade. The theory of the firm, which is, of course, central to orthodox economic analysis, is only now being re-examined under the assumption that a business firm is not to be studied as a single person, but as an organization within which the several persons involved variously interact one with another. Bureaucratic structures, within or without government, are similarly under theoretical reappraisal, and the conflicts between individual and organizational goals and the impact of these conflicts on behavior and performance have come to be recognized as important elements of scientific investigation. And there are many other similar examples.

Contributions from organization theory, information theory, the theory of teams, statistical decision theory, game theory, learning theory, theoretical welfare economics, pure theory of government finance, and others point toward a fundamental revision of existing orthodoxy, and an emerging consensus on what may be called a general theory of social structures, which will surely include political organization as only one among an array of forms. These developments should help to break down the barriers among the disciplinary specializations in the social sciences, barriers which have been, at best, arbitrarily erected and maintained.

Notes

1. As Gunnar Myrdal pointed out in his fundamental methodological critique, many economists have erred in inferring "social" content in the results of the market economy, without making explicit value statements. See Gunnar Myrdal, *The Political Element in the Development of Economic Theory* (London: Routledge and Kegan Paul, Ltd., 1953).

2. T. D. Weldon, *States and Morals* (New York: McGraw-Hill Book Company, 1947).

3. James M. Buchanan and Gordon Tullock, *The Calculus of Consent: Logical Foundations of Constitutional Democracy* (Ann Arbor: University of Michigan Press, 1962).

4. This criterion states that a position is "optimal" or "efficient" when any change from that position will damage at least one person in the group. There are, of course, an infinite number of positions that may be classified as "optimal." The criterion is useful only for identifying "nonoptimal" positions. The same criterion may be applied to changes or proposals for change. If a move or change is such that at least one member in the relevant group is made "better off" while no one is made "worse off," the change is "optimal" in Pareto's sense. If a move or change damages at least one person, it is "nonoptimal." If an initial position is "nonoptimal," there must be at least one means of shifting to an "optimal" position in an "optimal" way. The relationship of this construction to the unanimity rule is a direct one once it is admitted that the only way in which an individual can be assured to be made "better off" is as a result of his own observed behavior in making choices.

5. For a discussion of this extension, see James M. Buchanan, "The Relevance of Pareto Optimality," *Journal of Conflict Resolution,* 6 (December, 1962), pp. 341–54.

6. William Riker, *The Theory of Political Coalitions* (New Haven: Yale University Press, 1962).

7. See Buchanan and Tullock, *The Calculus of Consent,* op. cit.

16.

Notes for an Economic Theory of Socialism

Economists have devoted considerable attention to the effects generated by market or private organization of the supply of goods and services that embody collective-consumption characteristics. Analysis of these effects makes up much of the content of modern public-goods theory. Rarely do we find the analysis turned on its head, so to speak, toward prediction of the effects generated by governmental organization of the supply of goods and services that are largely if not wholly "private," that is, fully divisible into separate and distinguishable units of consumption. When this relatively straightforward step is taken, the consequences of governmental or collective organization are readily demonstrable. The analysis is on all fours with its converse.

More than this, however, the analysis permits a satisfactory treatment of the relevant practical cases that involve the comparative efficiencies of private and government (market and political) organizational alternatives when goods and services possess both "publicness" and "privateness." Conceptually, the trade-offs between jointness efficiencies derived from collective consumption and the distributional efficiencies made possible by market-life quantity adjustments can be measured. More importantly, the analysis points toward quite specific policy norms with respect to the organization of the supply of partially divisible goods and services.[1]

The apparent reason for the neglect of this type of comparative analysis is found in economists' continuing but implicit assumption about the nature of collective or governmental organization. With little or no consideration of the implications of this assumption for the decision-making process itself, economists' standard models allow governments to distribute benefits unequally and at will. When politically supplied goods and services are privately divisible or partitionable among beneficiaries or consumers, no constraints are imposed on distribution.[2] Governments are assumed to be able, without cost, to distribute these among ultimate users in precisely the market pattern. Under this assumption, potential distributional inefficiencies of political organization are totally neglected.

In the models introduced here, *consumption uniformity* is postulated under political or collective provision, regardless of the descriptive characteristics of the goods and services provided. That is to say, once the provision of a good or service is politically organized, all persons in the political group share equally in the consumption benefits. This condition is necessarily satisfied when a good or service embodies technological characteristics that make divisibility among consumers impossible. One means of defining the polar case of a purely collective good is to say that no distributional problem is faced.[3] An alternative definition of the polar extreme states that consumption units to additional persons may be provided at zero cost. Note that, in this second definition, nothing is implied about the possibility or impossibility of divisibility. In effect, the analysis of this paper accepts the second definition in that full divisibility is assumed to be possible in all cases. In other words, distributional uniformity among consuming users is not imposed by the technological characteristics of the goods themselves. Instead, such uniformity tends to be produced as a consequence of the political decision-making process, at least so long as democratic structure remains ultimately in being. Democratic socialism, in any meaningful practical sense, is "about equality," and equal sharing is its centrally descriptive feature. The models of this paper do little more than to incorporate this feature systematically in efficiency comparisons among alternative organizational structures. In such comparisons, distributional inefficiencies arise when goods and services which could be differentially provided to consumers are uniformly provided unless, of course, individual preferences should be identical.

Illustrative examples may be helpful. If the pickup of garbage is politically organized, each resident of the community will tend to be provided with the same quantity of service (measured in number of pickups per week), regardless of his own quantity preferences. If education is governmentally organized, each family will be allowed access to the same quantity-quality of service independently of its own preferences.

I

Consider a two-man community. Individuals A and B find themselves under a marketlike organization that supplies the good X. In Fig. 16-1, the demand curves are shown by D_a and D_b. The price confronted by each man is P, and individually attained positions of equilibrium are shown at E_a and E_b. Each person attains equilibrium by adjusting quantity purchased to accord with his own preferences.

The problem is to examine the possible gains or losses from a shift to a collective organization for the supply of X. It is assumed that X is fully divisible in consumption as between A and B. By this is meant only that there is no spillover, externality, or nonexclusion in the consumption of

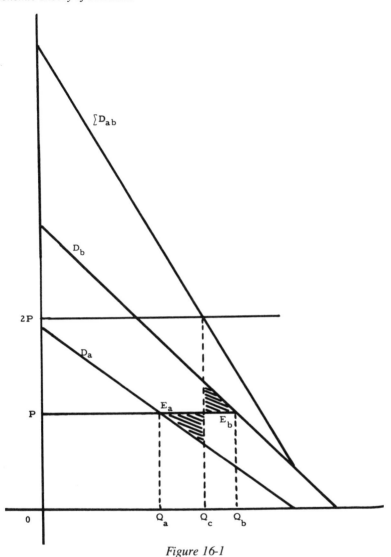

Figure 16-1

X. It is also assumed that neither person is interested in either the other's consumption of X or in the level of utility attained by the other. Uniformity in consumption is postulated under political or collective provision. Both A and B must consume the same quantity of X. If A is provided with one unit, then B must, and simultaneously, be provided with one unit. Trading or retrading outside the collective organization is assumed to be strictly prohibited.

The comparison lends itself to geometrical tools if the proper constructions are introduced. The collective good can be considered to be a two-component bundle containing two units of the market good X, with one being distributed to each person. Hence, the quantity dimension for examining demand-supply is two-unit bundles. The cost of providing such a bundle is now $2P$ which, as with the market good, is assumed to be unchanging over quantity. This dimensional conversion allows the individual market demand curves, D_a and D_b, to be treated as marginal evaluation curves for the collective good, now designated as XX, provided that income effect feedbacks are ignored.[4] In this way, A's evaluation of the two-unit bundle, XX, becomes equivalent to his evaluation of the one-unit good that he secures privately under the alternative market arrangements, since, of course, he secures only one unit in either case.[5]

If we now assume that there exists an omniscient and benevolent despot who is fully informed in modern welfare economics, and if we allow him to select the optimal collective "solution," he will add the two marginal evaluation curves vertically and set quantity at the point of intersection between the summed evaluation curve and the marginal cost curve.[6] In Fig. 16-1, this is shown at Q_c. As the construction indicates, there is a *welfare loss* in the shift from market to collective organization of supply. This loss is measured by the area of the two shaded triangles in Fig. 16-1, given the constraints of the model as defined. This welfare loss is exclusively distributional. It stems from the fact that A and B are required to consume uniform quantities of the good despite their differing evaluations placed on the good at the margins. If we assume that all demands are to be met jointly under these institutional arrangements, the conditions for optimality seem to be satisfied but the construction demonstrates that it remains more efficient in the large to allow for independent quantity adjustment. Note also that the welfare loss remains regardless of the cost-sharing arrangements, which have notbeen specified here.[7]

The demonstration that in this model there are excess costs of the collectivization of polar private goods suggests that offsetting cost-reducing elements must be present and sufficiently large to overcome the distributional inefficiencies before this organizational alternative becomes desirable. The cost-reducing element suggested is, of course, some departure from the polar case of zero advantage from joint consumption. Once this assumption is dropped, there may be possible gains to be secured from *joint,* rather than separate, consumption. The geometrical construction allows us to depict conceptually the degree or extent of "publicness" that is required to warrant organizational changes toward meeting demands jointly under the restrictive conditions outlined.

II

Consider Fig. 16-2, which duplicates Fig. 16-1 in several essential features. The cost of producing the two-unit bundle, XX, is now defined to be lower than double the cost of a one-unit bundle, X, by an amount R per unit, or to be $(2P - R)$. Independently considered, the technological improvement secured from joint supply involves a net welfare gain which may be measured by the upper shaded area, in Fig. 16-2. If this gain exceeds the area of the two triangles previously shown to measure the net welfare loss, the shift from all-market to all-governmental supply of the good is socially efficient under the restrictive conditions postulated. As the construction of Fig. 16-2 is designed to show, however, if only these polar organizational alternatives are considered, the market *may* remain the more efficient of the two, even when some jointness efficiencies exist. As Fig. 16-2 shows by inspection, there can be net losses in shifting from market to political provision. The "publicness" gains need not be sufficient to offset the distributional losses.

This result seems to embody a paradox of sorts, since institutional means should surely exist for exploiting fully all technological advantages, including those arising from jointness in consumption. The possibility that any attempt to exploit such advantages may involve welfare losses seems at odds with the economist's professional intuition. As previously noted, the result emerges because of the uniform consumption constraint. When this source of the paradox is recognized, there is suggested a search for institutional arrangements that will allow both the technological advantages of joint consumption and the distributional advantages of individual quantity adjustments to be secured.

Assume now that the benevolent despot instructs the two-person group to consume jointly the quantity Q'_a. Over this initial range of supply-demand, the full advantages of joint consumption are exploited, and there are no distributional costs. Assume further that the despot instructs B to pay a price of P per unit for this quantity, Q'_a. This guarantees that A will secure the full measure of society's gains over the initial range of joint consumption. This is indicated by the elongated lower shaded area below PE_a. Assume further that B is allowed to purchase supplementary quantities of one-unit bundles of the good as he desires through marketlike arrangements for supply. Under these conditions, B will extend his consumption purchases to E_b. At equilibrium, he will be securing Q'_a under joint supply arrangements with A and the additional amount, Q'_aQ_b, through a market. It is evident that, under this new institutional arrangement, B will find himself in precisely the same position as he is under full market organization. Since A will be better off, it must be concluded that the partial collectivization with market supplements is the best of the three alternative organizational arrangements examined to this point.

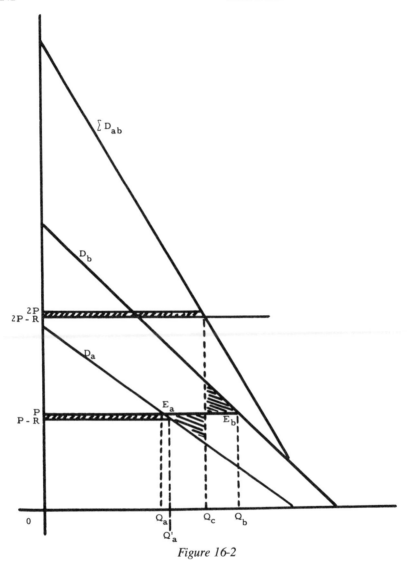

Figure 16-2

This solution also represents the most efficient organizational arrangement that is possible. There exists no means through which the remaining
technological gains from jointness in consumption may be secured without incurring larger distributional losses. This conclusion may continue
to contain apparent elements of paradox, however, because if considered
uncritically it appears to involve the violation of the familiar necessary
marginal conditions for efficiency in providing bundles of goods and

services containing uniform consumption components for each user. At Q'_a, the point at which joint consumption ceases, the summed marginal evaluation, shown by ΣD_{ab}, exceeds the marginal cost of production of the two-unit bundle, shown by $(2P - R)$. The familiar Samuelson requirement appears to suggest that joint consumption should be expanded to Q_c. However, when it is recognized that B can individually *supplement* the jointly supplied quantity through market arrangements at a price of P per unit, a generalization of the statement for the necessary marginal conditions can be shown to be satisfied only at Q'_a. Joint consumption of the quantity Q_c clearly violates rather than satisfies the general necessary marginal conditions for Pareto optimality.

To demonstrate this violation, it is useful to assume that individual A is the actual producer of both one-unit bundles of X and the two-unit bundles of XX. We continue to assume that these are produced at constant cost per unit of X.[8] Further assume that because of his strategic position as producer, A can choose the type of bundle; he can produce for either joint consumption or for independent private consumption. For purposes of analytical simplicity only, further assume that individual A is able to secure all gains from the possible advantages of joint provision. At Q'_a, the marginal cost of producing a two-unit bundle of XX is $(2P - R)$. The marginal cost to A, the producer, is, however, less than the marginal production cost because he, too, shares in the consumption. The supply price, or marginal cost of the two-unit bundle to B, the demander, is $(2P - R)$ less the evaluation that A himself places on this bundle. At Q'_a, this evaluation is equal to $(P - R)$. The marginal supply price to B at Q'_a is, therefore, $(2P - R) - (P - R)$, which is, simply, P. The marginal requirements met at Q'_a are that $D_b = P$, which is precisely the market equivalence. At Q'_a, the minimal supply price at which A will provide two-unit bundles is P. Beyond this quantity, however, A's own marginal evaluation becomes less than $(P - R)$. Therefore, the supply price of a two-unit bundle, as faced by B, will be higher than the supply price of a one-unit bundle provided exclusively for B's consumption, which remains at P. Since we have assumed that A is the supplier here who can also secure the full gains from joint-consumption if these exist, B's demand beyond Q'_a will be met by A's selling him one-unit rather than two-unit bundles.

The results do not depend on the particular assumption made about the sharing of the total gains from joint consumption. Individual B rather than A could have been allowed to secure all of the gains over inframarginal ranges of quantity. At the margin, however, optimality requires that the person who places the lowest evaluation on the good secure the full advantage of joint consumption. In all cases, efficiency requires that some critical quantity less than Q_c be provided for joint consumption and that the additional demands of B be met from supplementary private purchases.

III

The two-person geometrical construction may be extended to allow for any degree of jointness efficiency. It will be useful initially to consider the polar case of the purely collective or public good defined in the second sense noted earlier. Such a good is one for which the advantages of joint consumption are complete. The cost of supplying consumption units to *all* persons simultaneously is no higher than the cost of supplying consumption units to any one person individually or privately. Consider Fig. 16-3. It is assumed that the demand (marginal evaluation) curves remain the same as in the previous figures. Under the pure collective goods assumption, the cost of producing the two-unit bundle, XX, remains the same as the cost of producing the one-unit bundle, X; that is, P.

In this setting, efficiency requires that two-unit bundles be provided in the amount Q'_c. As the construction shows, neither person has an incentive to supplement this collective provision through his own independent or private purchases if these should be possible. And, more significantly, there are sizable welfare gains in shifting from market to collective provision in this instance.

The construction in Fig. 16-3 enables a limit to be determined for those situations in which joint consumption should be utilized in meeting *all* demands. In the two-person case depicted, assume now that the unit cost of supplying the one-unit bundle remains at P. If the gains from the simultaneous or joint provision of consumption units to both A and B are such that the two-unit bundle can be supplied at $(2P - R')$ or below, then *all* demands can be most efficiently met through joint consumption. Geometrically this limit is determined by the intersection of both D_b and P and ΣD_{ab} and $(2P - R')$ at the same quantity. The curve D_b must cut the line drawn horizontally from P at or to the left of the quantity, Q_c. In somewhat different terms, if individual B's preferred market purchase quantity does not *exceed* the optimally efficient joint-provision quantity, all demands can best be met jointly.

This general conclusion can be extended to show that there may be cases in which some demands should be met independently and nonjointly *even* when the jointness is complete in a technological sense. Instead of P, assume now that the one-unit bundle can be produced at a cost of P' per unit and that the advantages of jointness are complete so that $(2P - R'' = P'$. Assume that the demand curves remain as before. In this case, note that the condition defining the limit is met. D_b and ΣD_{ab} are coincident at the intersection with the horizontal drawn from P'. At any cost per unit (equivalent for one-unit and two-unit bundles by assumption here) below P', an amount, Q_m, should be supplied jointly with the additional quantity desired by B being met from independent provision. This result

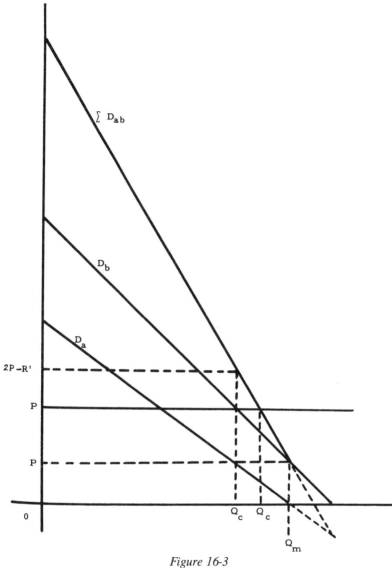

Figure 16-3

stems, of course, from the constructed extension of D_a into the ranges of negative evaluation. Beyond Q_m, B's demands should be met privately even in the case of a purely collective good because only in this manner can A's negative evaluations be avoided or made unnecessary.

IV

The next stage in the analysis is the obvious one of generalizing the results attained with the simplified two-person model to an n-person setting. The problem is more complex than the familiar one of stating the necessary marginal conditions for optimality or efficiency under assumed institutional or organizational invariance. The problem here is to include within a statement of the necessary conditions for efficiency some criterion for organizational form.

This may be done by stating a generalized rule that involves an either/or criterion:

The quantity of good or service provided jointly to all members of a group of n persons should be extended to the *minimal* amount that satisfies *either* (1) or (2) below:

(1) $\quad MC_{x_{1,2,\ldots n}} = \sum_{i=1}^{n} ME_{x_i}$

(2) $\quad MC_{x_{1,2,\ldots n}} - MC_{x_{1,2,\ldots s}} = \sum_{i=1}^{n} ME_{x_i} - \sum_{i=1}^{s} ME_{x_i},$

where $MC_{x_{1\ldots n}}$ indicates the marginal cost of supplying a single multicomponent "production unit" that contains n separate and equal consumption units, X, one of which is provided to each person in the inclusive group of size N.[9] The right-hand term in (1) indicates the marginal evaluations for a unit of X summed over all persons in N. In (2), S designates any group of persons of size smaller than N, including one-person groups.

If (1) is met, and if cost functions and utility functions are normal, then, at that quantity,

(1A) $\quad MC_{x_{1,2,\ldots n}} - MC_{x,\ldots s} \leq \sum_{i=1}^{n} ME_{x_i} - \sum_{i=1}^{s} ME_{x_i}$

which reduces to

(1B) $\quad MC_{x_{1,2,\ldots s}} \geq \sum_{i=1}^{s} ME_i.$

The statement (1B) indicates that no subgroup less than the whole membership in N finds it economically advantageous to supplement privately or through independent purchase the jointly provided quantity at which (1) is satisfied. All demands are met jointly under the efficient organizational arrangements.[10]

If, however, the rule is met by the satisfaction of (2) at the *minimal* quantity, it is implied that, at such quantity,

(2A) $\quad MC_{x_{1,2\ldots n}} < \sum_{i=1}^{n} ME_{x_i}$

and that

(2B) $\quad MC_{x_{1,2,\ldots s}} < \sum_{i=1}^{s} ME_{x_i}.$

The statement (2B) implies that independent or subgroup action on the part of some persons supplementary to the joint-provision quantity for the *n*-person group as defined by (2) is efficient. The necessary conditions for efficiency in the supplementary extension for the subgroup, which may itself be a collectivity, can be defined in a manner precisely equivalent to those laid down above for the more inclusive group. The subgroup *S* should provide the extended quantity jointly to the minimal limits where *either* (11) or (22) is satisfied,

$$(11) \quad MC_{x_{1,2,\ldots,s}} = \sum_{i=1}^{s} ME_{x_i}$$

$$(22) \quad MC_{x_{1,2,\ldots,s}} - MC_{x_{\ldots,t}} = \sum_{i=1}^{s} ME_{x_i} - \sum_{i=1}^{t} ME_{x_i}$$

where *T* is any group of persons less than *S*, including one-person groups.

This procedure can, of course, be extended to smaller and smaller groups. As the analysis clearly suggests, the most efficient organizational mix need not be either collective or joint provision for the whole group of *n* persons, some mixture of this and single person supplements through the market, or all persons purchasing from the market. The most efficient organizational arrangement might well be that *some* part of total demand be met by joint provision of consumption units to all *n* persons simultaneously, some part of total demand be met by joint provision of consumption units to all members of one or more subgroups of differing sizes, and *some* part of total demand be met by private or individualized purchases by single buyers. In the limit, of course, the conditions defined by (1) and (2) collapse to the same statements for the one-person subgroup.

V

The rules for stating the necessary conditions for both the optimal quantity of good and for the optimal organizational arrangement for its provision allows us to classify all goods and services into three mutually exclusive categories. If, for any good or service, condition (1) above is satisfied at a quantity below that which might satisfy (2), the good or service should be provided jointly for the simultaneous consumption of *all* persons in the community of *n* persons. If for all groups larger than one-person membership, the equivalent of condition (2) is met at a quantity below that which meets the equivalent of condition (1), efficiency requires that all demands be met through private and individualized purchases from some marketlike source, with independent quantity adjustments. Between these polar organizational extremes, there can be varying mixes between collective, cooperative, and private organizational arrangements that satisfy the efficiency norms outlined.

Since the size of the inclusive political community, N, is assumed to be exogenously determined here, it is evident from the analysis that a different classification will emerge in different-sized communities. If cost conditions are equivalent, the proportion of goods-services falling in the first category, where all demands are best met through joint provision to all members of the inclusive political community, will decline as N increases.

VI

The comparative analysis of organizational forms has relevance for policy choices. Since the restrictive requirement suggesting that all demands be met through joint provision for all members of the group in any given political community is not likely to be met in many cases, the efficiency argument for collective or governmental provision of *minimal* quantities of those goods and services that possess joint-consumption characteristics is strengthened. This conclusion applies particularly to those goods and services that are recognized to be partitionable among separate users, in whole or in part. Examples are educational services, health services, sanitation services.

There is an asymmetry in the analysis which should be explicitly recognized. It is assumed that individuals or subgroups smaller than the total membership of the political community can supplement the consumption provided by the larger unit through independent or marketlike sources more efficiently than similar groups could dispose of collectively provided consumption units through independent or marketlike outlets. This assumption seems acceptable on the basis of empirical observation. Private or cooperative supplementing of collective consumption can take place at reasonably low transactions costs; private or cooperative disposition of collectively supplied consumption units may involve prohibitive transactions costs. (In Los Angeles, private firms sell services that consist of removing garbage cans from back alleys and placing them on front streets where public pickups are made. It is not easy, however, to sell the services of half-empty garbage cans, and no such market is to be observed.)

Finally, I should emphasize that the whole analysis of this article is based on the assumption that collective decision making is itself ideally efficient. This amounts to saying that the comparison is among pure organizational alternatives. It can plausibly be argued that individuals and small groups adjust quantities to their own preferences with a high degree of efficiency. By no stretch of the imagination can a similar argument be advanced for collectively organized groups. Individual preferences are not revealed except through behavior, and the costs of securing multiperson agreement are sufficient to prevent effective groping toward collective efficiency. Decision rules must be adopted at some "constitutional" stage, and the working out of these rules may generate significant departures from efficient collective outcomes. Recognition of this tends to strengthen the argument of this paper. It has been demonstrated that, even when collective decision making is assumed to be ideally efficient, the most advantageous organizational arrangements for the provision of many goods and services embodying collective-consumption characteristics involve collectivization of only *some* part of the total supply along with the private or voluntary group supplementation of this supply from ordinary market sources. When the predicted inefficiency of collective decision making is taken into account, the argument for encouraging the maximal feasible usage of private or voluntary quantity adjustment becomes stronger. At a minimum, the analysis tends to undermine any arguments in favor of political prohibition of supplemental provision of goods and services, as witness the United States Postal System.[11]

Notes

This paper was directly stimulated by Yoram Barzel's recent contribution, which is, in turn, based on a model initially discussed by Gordon Tullock. See Yorum Barzel, "Two Propositions on the Optimum Level of a Producing Collective Goods," *Public Choice*, 6 (Spring 1969), pp. 31–38; and Gordon Tullock, "Social Cost and Governmental Action," *American Economic Review*, 59 (May 1969), pp. 189–97. Tullock's model is more completely developed in his *Private Wants, Public Means* (New York: 1970 Basic Books). This paper may be interpreted as a generalization of the Tullock-Barzel construction in the context of a more restricted model than either of these authors considered.

I am greatly indebted to Armen A. Alchian, University of California, Los Angeles, and to Charles Goetz, Virginia Polytechnic Institute, for helpful discussions during the critical stages of the development of my argument.

1. In a recent paper, J. G. Head and C. S. Shoup classify goods into three distinct categories depending on the relative efficiency of market and nonmarket modes of provision. Their analysis is primarily classificatory but they appear to compare the two organizational modes as mutually exclusive alternatives. They neglect the mixed alternatives treated in this paper. As I shall indicate, a broad three-part classification also emerges from my construction. The central difference between their approach and my own stems from their emphasis on the effects of inframarginal cost-sharing schemes. If this is neglected, as I have done in this paper, the analysis of Head and Shoup suggests that the relative efficiency of the different organizational forms would depend only on cost differentials; that is, on the presence or absence of jointness efficiencies. This would, in turn, imply that all goods for which such gains from joint consumption arise can be more advantageously provided as collective-consumption goods, income effects apart. Head and Shoup seem to neglect the distributional inefficiencies arising from collectively imposed uniformities in consumption. See J. G. Head and C. S. Shoup,

"Public Goods, Private Goods, and Ambiguous Goods," *Economic Journal,* 74 (September 1969), pp. 567–72.

2. Armen Alchian has suggested that the terms "partition" and "partitionable" be used to refer to the separation of consumption units of a good or service among persons. This allows the terms "division" and "divisibility" to retain their orthodox economic-theory meaning in reference to an absence of lumpiness in some physical-quantity dimension. While there is much to be said for this suggested terminology on grounds of semantic efficiency, the usage of the terms "divisibility" and "indivisibility" in public-goods theory seems to have been so widely adopted as to make such a change confusing at this stage. Ambiguity will, of course, continue to be present unless the precise context in which "divisibility" or "indivisibility" is introduced is specified.

3. For an elaboration of this point, see James M. Buchanan, *Demand and Supply of Public Goods* (Chicago: Rand McNally, 1968), chap. 9.

4. This essentially Marshallian escape route greatly facilitates straightforward presentation of the central argument without undermining its context. To the extent that income effects are relevant in determining the optimally preferred quantities of good at the margin, the ordinarymarket demand curves must be replaced by specific marginal evaluation curves that are, in turn, functionally related to the particular sharing arrangements assumed to be in force.

5. A similar sort of dimensional shift was used previously in James M. Buchanan, "A Public Choice Approach to Public Utility Pricing," *Public Choice,* 5 (Fall 1968), pp. 1–18.

6. Without the income-effect assumption made above, this solution is not unique but depends on the sharing arrangement over inframarginal units.

7. The welfare loss can best be seen by considering that, under political organization, each person pays an equal share in the cost of each unit supplied. The measure of the welfare loss by the two shaded triangles under other sharing schemes is more tedious to prove geometrically, but under the restrictions of the model such proof always remains possible.

8. The constant-cost assumption is required here because we allow one person to become the supplier. In a more general context, we need assume only that the actual production of the good or service, whether supplied/sold to governmental units, to subgovernmental collective groups, or to private individuals, is made available to them in such a manner as to insure that they remain price takers. That is to say, variations in quantities demanded cannot modify price per unit, either within a fixed or changing composition of consuming groups.

9. In the polar extremes of a purely private good, as defined here,

$$MC_{x_{1,2,\ldots n}} = MC_{x_1} + MC_{x_2} + MC_{x_3} + \ldots + MC_{x_n}$$

In the other polar extreme where jointness efficiency is complete,

$$MC_{x_{1,2,\ldots n}} = MC_{x_1} = MC_{x_2} = \ldots = MC_{x_n}$$

The notation here is a simplified form of that introduced in James M. Buchanan, "Joint Supply, Externality, and Optimality," *Economica,* 33 (November 1966), pp. 404–15. See, especially, p. 406, note 1.

10. This position has properties that are analogous to those that characterize a solution in the core of an *n*-person game. For an effort to relate public-goods theory to the concept of the core, although in a setting different from that of this paper, see Mark Pauly, "Clubs, Commonality, and the Core," *Economica,* 34 (August 1967), pp. 314–24.

11. I am indebted to Yoram Barzel, University of Washington, for this point.

Part IV.

THE ECONOMIST AS CONTRACTARIAN

17.

The Justice of Natural Liberty

I. Introduction

The 1976 bicentennial of the publication of Adam Smith's *The Wealth of Nations* occurs amid a still-accelerating discussion of the principles of justice, stimulated in large part by John Rawls. His catalytic book, *A Theory of Justice,* published in 1971,[1] has caused economists, along with other social scientists and philosophers, to devote more attention to "justice" in the first half-decade of the 1970s than in perhaps all of the preceding decades of this century combined. This discussion has been hailed as the return of political and social philosophy to its former status of intellectual interest and respectability. My purpose in this paper is to re-examine Adam Smith's norms for social order, notably for justice, and especially as these may be related to the modern post-Rawlsian discussion. I want, in particular, to evaluate Smith's "system of natural liberty" in terms of criteria for justice that are akin to those employed by Rawls.

In order to do this, it will first be necessary to define, as fully as is possible, Smith's underlying model or paradigm for social interaction, a paradigm that was influenced by the historical setting of Scotland in the 1770s. In addition, it will be useful to discuss briefly Smith's methodology. Once these steps are taken, we can outline Smith's ordering of the priorities for reform. From this we should then be able to suggest how a returned Adam Smith might view our society in 1976, and how his modern ordering of reform priorities might differ from those two centuries removed. This imagined Smithian stance may then be compared and/or contrasted with that of John Rawls. In a thesis that may be surprising, and especially to those who are only casually familiar with the works of each man, I shall demonstrate that the similarities outweigh the differences. A returned Adam Smith would be a long distance from the modern libertarian anarchists, and even from the espousal of the minimal state described by Robert Nozick.[2] But Rawls is also a long distance from the position which has been attributed to him, that of being a "defender of the liberal welfare state, somewhat modified in the direction of greater egalitarianism."[3] These philosophers would surely be closer to each other than either would be to the image that intellectual fashion has imposed upon him.

II. The Real and the Conceptual World of Adam Smith

Adam Smith was one of the leading figures of the Scottish Enlightenment, which suggests that his interests were in no way provincial. His intent in *The Wealth of Nations* was to offer a readily generalizable criticism of what he labeled the "policy of Europe." But he lived and worked, nonetheless, in eighteenth-century Scotland. Because his writings, and again notably *The Wealth of Nations,* retain so many elements of direct and current relevance, it is easy for the modern reader to neglect the necessary influences of time and place on his analysis as well as on his normative priorities.

What were the essential structural characteristics of the society that Adam Smith observed? Almost two centuries would elapse before a popular tract could condemn an "affluent society." The industrial revolution, with its technological counterpart, was in its very early and formative stages. Indeed its full achievements might never have become reality save for the impact of some of Smith's own ideas. The modern corporation was foreshadowed only in the government-sponsored international trading companies. Still largely agricultural, Britain was only becoming "a nation of shopkeepers."

The society that Smith observed was highly stable relative to that of our own century. This society was also very poor by twentieth-century standards; Smith's analysis was applied directly to what we would now call a "developing" or an "underdeveloped" society. The expansion in material goods generated by the technological revolution of the post-Enlightenment era was not predictable in 1776. Most men were born to live, work, and die in the same local community.

Some appreciation of this historical setting is helpful in any attempt to define Smith's working model for social interaction. Two central elements of this model or paradigm may be isolated here as important in understanding his conceptions of justice. The first of these involves what we should now call the utility of income to the individual. Smith did not use this terminology and he was not intellectually hidebound by the now dominant orthodoxy which largely neglects basic questions about the meaning of utility itself and then proceeds to impose a particular form on the utility function. Instead, Smith carefully distinguished between that which drives men to action—the promised or anticipated utility from an increasing stream of real goods and services or from a growing stock of assets—and that which measures the actual satisfactions secured subsequent to the receipt of such incremental flows and stocks. Beyond a certain level of real income (a level which was, nonetheless, presumably out of reach for the average or representative member of the working class), the anticipated marginal utility of income to an individual exceeds the realized marginal utility. This divergence constituted, for Smith, the great deception that was essential in driving the whole system, which acted to insure that self-interest would, in fact, generate increasing prosperity and economic growth.[4]

In some sense, therefore, differentials in measured or received incomes among individuals and among social classes or groups were, to Adam Smith, considerably less important than to his counterpart who inhabits the modern welfare state. Smith was not nearly so ready to translate these into differences in achieved satisfaction, happiness, or well-being. And who is to attribute naivete to Adam Smith in this respect? The balance is not on one side alone.

Smith expressed little or no normative concern with income differences among persons; he was primarily concerned with the absolute levels of income generated, and with the differences in these levels among time periods, that is, with growth. He did infer a direct relationship between the aggregate income generated for the whole society and the well-being of the laboring classes.

There is a second element of Adam Smith's model of social interaction that is helpful in evaluating his conceptions of justice. Smith did not assume or postulate significant differentials in capacities among human beings. The differences between the "philosopher and the street porter" were explained largely in terms of upbringing, training, and education. In the current debates, Smith would find himself arrayed squarely on the side of those who stress environmental factors and who play down the relevance of genetic endowments. Smith was also writing before Cairns and Mill had developed the economic theory of noncompeting groups. In his conceptual model, individual income differences (at least as regards wage or salary incomes) were explained largely in "equalizing" terms. That is to say, in an operative "system of natural liberty" the observed differences would be those that would be predicted to emerge when all persons freely exercised their choices among occupations and employments. By implication, at least for the members of the laboring class, in such a system all persons would be equally advantaged at the onset of making career and occupational choices.

III. The Scottish Method

A. L. Macfie makes the distinction between what he calls the Scottish method, characteristic of Adam Smith's approach to problems of social policy, and the scientific or analytical method, which is more familiar to modern social scientists.[5] In the former, the center of attention lay in the society as observed, rather than in the idealized version of that society considered as an abstraction. As I have suggested above, Smith did have an underlying model or paradigm for social interaction; he could scarcely have discussed reforms without one. But his interest was in making the existing social structure "work better," in terms of the norms that he laid down, rather than in evaluating the possible limitations of the structure as it might work ideally if organized on specific principles. Frank Knight suggested that critics of the free-enterprise system are seldom clear as to whether they object to the system because it does not work in accordance with its idealized principles or because it does, in fact, work in some approximation to these principles. There is no such uncertainty with respect to Adam Smith. He was critical of the economic order of his time because it did not work in accordance with the principles of natural liberty. He was not, and need not have been, overly concerned with some ultimate evaluation of an idealized structure.

Smith's methodology has been turned on its head by many modern scientists. The post-Pigovian theory of welfare economics has largely, if not entirely, consisted in a search for conceptual flaws in the workings of an idealized competitive economic order, conceived independently of the flawed and imperfect order that may be observed to exist. Partial correctives are offered in both the theory of the second best and in the still emerging theory of public choice, but the perfect-competition paradigm continues to dominate applied economic policy discussions. This methodological distinction is important in our examination of Smith's conception of justice. In one sense, Rawls's efforts in defining and delineating "a theory of justice" are akin to those of the neoclassical economists who first described the idealized competitive economy. (I am not, of course, suggesting that Rawls's attempt has had or will have comparable success or even that the basic subject matter is amenable to comparable analytical treatment.) By contrast, Smith saw no need for defining in great detail the idealized operation of a market system and for evaluating this system in terms of strict efficiency criteria. Similarly, he would have seen no need for elaborating in detail a complete "theory of justice," for defining those principles which must be operative in a society that would be adjudged to be "just." In comparing Smith with Rawls, therefore, we must somehow bridge the contrasting methodologies. We can proceed in either one of two ways. We can make an attempt to infer from Smith's applied discussion of real problems what his idealized principles of justice might have embodied. Or we can infer from Rawls's treatment of idealized principles what his particular applications of these might be in an institutional context. In what follows, I shall follow both these routes.

IV. Justice as Security

Adam Smith did not publish the book on jurisprudence that he had projected, although a student's notes from his lectures apparently include most of the material that might have been incorporated.[6] In these lectures, "justice" was listed as only one of the four great objects of law. In the section specifically on justice, Smith referred almost exclusively to the relatively narrow conception of security. "The end of justice is to secure from injury."[7] In this context, the treatment seems quite different from that of John Rawls, for whom "justice is the first virtue of social institutions."[8] But the difference can be exaggerated, even here. Smith explicitly calls attention to security as a necessary attribute of any well-functioning society, and he reflects common-sense usage of the term "justice" in his discussion. Rawls, two centuries later, takes this aspect of justice more or less for granted, and shifts his discussion to another level. He would, presumably, agree fully with Smith that any just society would also require security of person and property. Rawls's primary interest is "beyond justice" in the more restricted definition employed by Adam Smith.[9]

Their difference lies in the fact that Smith did not make a comparable extension. Distributive justice, in the modern meaning of this term, is largely neglected by Smith, at least in terms of explicit treatment. This is explained, in part, by Smith's underlying presuppositions about utility differences, noted above, and in part by the relatively greater importance appropriately assigned to economic development in the eighteenth-century setting. As I shall demonstrate, however, Smith's suggestions for policy reforms generate distributive results that may be reconciled readily with Rawlsian criteria. We need not accept Jacob Viner's interpretation that writers in the Scottish tradition were minimally interested in reform, in the modern meaning of this term.[10]

V. Natural Liberty

Adam Smith explicitly rejected a contractarian explanation for the emergence of government and for the obligation of persons to abide by law, preferring, instead, to ground both on the principles of authority and utility.[11] Furthermore, he did not recognize the possible value in using a conceptualized social contract as a benchmark or criterion for evaluating alternative political structures. However, his device of the "impartial spectator" serves this function and is in many respects akin to the conceptualized contract. Smith's norms for social order were not strictly utilitarian, in the Benthamite sense, and justice was an important attribute, justice which embodied the security to person and property previously noted but extended beyond this when his whole structure is considered.[12] Beyond security, Smith would have surely ranked "natural liberty" as his first principle of justice.

> To hurt in any degree the interest of any one order of citizens for no other purpose but to promote that of some other, is evidently contrary to that justice and equality of treatment which the sovereign owes to all different orders of his subjects.[13]

In several applied cases, he makes clear that violations of natural liberty are unjust.[14]

Before discussing these, however, it may be helpful to digress somewhat. Smith's great work, *The Wealth of Nations*, has been widely interpreted as being informed normatively by efficiency criteria. This emphasis is broadly correct, provided that the efficiency norm is not given exclusive place. Smith's purpose was to demonstrate how the removal of restrictions on free-market forces, how the operation of his "system of natural liberty," would greatly increase the total product of the economy and, more importantly, how this would generate rapid economic growth, thereby improving the lot of the laboring classes. What is often missing from this standard interpretation is Smith's corollary argument, sometimes implicit, to the effect that this system of natural liberty would also promote his ideal of justice. Failure to allow individuals to employ "their stock and industry in the way that they judge most advantageous to themselves, is a *manifest violation of the most sacred rights of mankind.*"[15] There was, to Smith, no trade-off between "efficiency" and "equity," in the more familiar modern sense. As a general principle of social order, the freedom of individual choice would produce efficiency; but it would also be a central attribute of any social order that was just.

My emphasis in this paper is on this aspect of Smith's argument because I want to compare his first principle of "natural liberty" with Rawls's first principle of "equal liberty." Smith's method forces us to look at his examples rather than to expect to find any elaborated discussion of the concept per se. The examples suggest that Adam Smith was by no means an eighteenth-century Robert Nozick, who conceived natural moral boundaries to individuals' rights and who claimed that any invasion of these rights was unjust. The Smithean system of natural liberty is not anarchy, either the Hobbesian war of each against all or the more confined Rothbard-Nozick setting where individuals mutually respect the boundaries of each other. "Boundary crossings," to employ Nozick's helpful terminology here, violate Smith's natural liberty in some cases but such violations must be assessed in essentially pragmatic terms. Smith's sanctioned violations of natural liberty were not invariant to the environmental setting in which individuals might find themselves.

Almost by necessity, we look at Smith's treatment from the vantage point of modern welfare economics. When we do so, his limits to the exercise of natural liberty seem to coincide surprisingly with those extensions of potentially warranted collective action that might be laid down by a careful and sophisticated application of externality analysis. To Smith, there is clearly an unwarranted invasion of natural liberty if an individual's (any individual's) freedom of choice is restricted when there are no demonstrable spillover damages on others in the community. On the other hand, Smith sanctioned interferences with individual freedom of choice when the exercise of such choices (for example, the building of walls that were not fireproof) "might endanger the security of the whole society."[16] Smith explicitly stated that such latter restrictions on individual choices may be "considered as in some respect a violation of natural liberty," but that such choices ought to be "restrained by the laws of all governments."[17]

Adam Smith distinguished between what we would now call pecuniary and technological externalities. His approved interferences with natural liberty extended only to those cases where genuine technological externality could be demonstrated, and he quite explicitly stated that possible pecuniary spillovers gave no cause for restrictions on trade.[18] It would, of course, be absurd to suggest here that Smith's final array of potentially justifiable interferences with the freedom of individual choices corresponds fully with that which might be produced by the modern welfare economist. Furthermore, his own array of examples of potentially warranted interferences with natural liberty would surely be different in 1976 from that of 1776. On balance, however, there seems no question but that Smith's implied analysis of potential restrictions on the freedom of individual market choices can be made reasonably consistent with modern efficiency analysis utilizing Pareto criteria for meaningful improvement. That is to say, even if Pareto optimality or efficiency is held up as the only relevant norm, many of Smith's particular examples would qualify. What is important for my purposes, however, is that Smith sanctioned interferences only when efficiency criteria overweighed those of justice, conceived here not in distributional terms at all, but in terms of the value of natural liberty. If we leave aside considerations of administration and enforcement, modern economic analysis would suggest the introduction of restrictions when overall efficiency is enhanced, with no explicit recognition of the necessary trade-off with individual freedom of choice. With Adam Smith, by contrast, any restriction on the freedom of individuals "may be said . . . [to be] a manifest violation of that natural liberty, which it is the proper business of law, not to infringe, but support."[19] Possible efficiency gains must, therefore, be reckoned against the costs in liberty, in "justice" in the broader sense here considered.

In evaluating his own work, there is some evidence that Adam Smith considered *The Wealth of Nations* to be a demonstration that the "system of natural liberty," which emerged more fundamentally from normative criteria of justice, could *also* meet efficiency criteria.[20] It is perhaps our relative overconcentration on his major treatise that causes modern interpreters to overlook the noneconomic, or more generally the nonutilitarian, foundations for the "natural system of perfect liberty and justice."[21]

VI. Rawls's Principle of Equal Liberty

Smith's principle may be compared with John Rawls's first principle of justice, that of "equal liberty," to which he assigns lexical priority over his second principle. These two principles or conceptions of liberty are, in practice, substantially equivalent although, strictly speaking, and perhaps surprisingly, Rawls must be classified as a more ardent laissez-faire theorist than Smith. This is due to Rawls's lexical ordering of the principle of equal liberty as prior to his distributive precept. Smith, in contrast, inserts a threshold before marginal trade-offs can be considered, a threshold beyond which invasions of apparent natural liberty might presumably be sanctioned. But their positions are similar in that neither Smith nor Rawls is utilitarian in the sense that final evaluation is reduced to a single standard. To Smith, the "impartial spectator" would not condone piecemeal interferences with natural liberty even if aggregate social production was thereby maximized. To Rawls, the maximization of expected utility is rejected as the objective, even behind a genuine veil of ignorance.

The principle of equal liberty, as presented by Rawls, is stated as follows:

> Each person is to have an equal right to the most extensive total system of equal basic liberties compatible with a similar system of liberty for all.[22]

In his discussion Rawls emphasizes the implications of this principle for political institutions (e.g., for equality of franchise, for freedom of speech and press), but he tends to neglect the comparable implications for economic institutions, which were, of course, central to Adam Smith's concern. In several places, Rawls does state that the principle of equal liberty suggests a market system, but he does not discuss particular examples or cases.[23] Nonetheless, any attempt to apply the Rawlsian principle must lead to a condemnation of many overt restrictions on individual choices that have been and may be observed in the real world. Particular interferences that would, in this way, be classified as "unjust" by Rawlsian criteria would correspond very closely to those which Smith classified in the same way. Consider only two of the most flagrant modern-day examples. The uniform minimum-wage regulations imposed by the Congress under the Fair Labor Standards Act, as amended, would clearly be "unjust" under either Rawlsian or Smithean criteria. Mutually agreeable contractual terms between unemployed persons (notably teenagers) and potential employers are prohibited, with an absence of comparable restrictions on others in society.[24] Or, consider the regulations of the Interstate Commerce Commission in restricting entry into trucking, clearly an invasion of the natural liberty of those who might want freely to enter this business as well as a violation of the principle of equal liberty. The listing could be readily extended to such institutions as tenure in universities, restrictive licensing of businesses and professions, prohibition or sumptuary taxation of imports, subsidization of exports, union shop restrictions in labor contracts, and many others.

It is unfortunate that Rawls did not see fit to discuss more fully the application of his first principle to such institutions, especially since his treatise and general argument have attracted such widespread attention from social scientists generally. Economists have continued to call attention to the inefficiency of these institutions, but, since Smith, they have rarely called attention to their fundamental injustice.[25] Had they, or Rawls, done so, these institutions might have proved more vulnerable to criticism than they have appeared to be.

Difficulties arise when we attempt to apply the Rawlsian principle of equal liberty to those restrictions on individual choices that might be plausibly defended on familiar externality grounds. As noted above, Smith's less constraining norm allows natural liberty to be violated under some circumstances, provided that the costs are properly reckoned. But Rawls's lexical ordering prevents this sort of trade-off, even with the insertion of an appropriate threshold. Consider, for a real-world example, the closing of the Saltville, Virginia, plant of the Olin Corporation in the early 1970s as a result of governmentally imposed water-quality standards. Local residents were left unemployed; long-term contractual agreements between these persons and Olin were terminated, clearly a restriction on liberties. Presumably, defense of this governmental action was based on the alleged benefits of improved water quality to the general population of the whole country. It does not seem possible to stretch Rawls's principle of equal liberty to cover such instances. The liberties of some persons were restricted for the alleged benefits of others, and without appropriate compensation. There was no trade-off with other liberties, as Rawls might have required; the defense could only have been advanced on utilitarian-efficiency grounds. To Rawls, this governmental action could only be classified as "unjust."[26]

Working from the principle of equal liberty alone, therefore, and keeping in mind the lexical priority assigned to this principle in his whole construction, we must conclude that John Rawls is far from the "defender of the liberal welfare state" that he has been made out to be, and, indeed, that his implied institutional structure for the economy closely resembles that which was first described by Adam Smith. Only a "system of natural liberty," a regime of effectively operating free markets, could meet Rawlsian requirements for "equal liberty," and, through these, for "justice."

VII. Distribution and Justice

Rawls has been misinterpreted in this respect because of his relative neglect in elaborating the implications of his first principle for economic institutions and, more importantly, because of his relative concentration on the second principle that he adduces, that which addresses the distribution of the social product. It is here that Adam Smith and John Rawls seem most apart, and Rawls explicitly discusses the system of natural liberty only to reject it in favor of what he terms the system of democratic equality.[27] But we need to see precisely wherein these two philosophers diverge. I shall try to demonstrate that, once their methodological differences are acknowledged and once their empirical presuppositions are fully exposed, there need be little variance in their assessments of reform priorities in a 1976 setting.

We can perhaps best commence by examining the distributional consequences of Adam Smith's system of natural liberty, under the empirical presuppositions that Smith himself adopted. In 1776, a very large part of the total population was made up of members of the laboring classes, and Smith did not think that inherent differences in capacities were significant. The economic position of an average or representative member of this group could best be improved by allowing markets freely to emerge and to operate, by removing all or substantially all restrictions on trade, and by eliminating all constraints on the flow of resources, human and non-human, among alternative uses. Such a system would predictably generate differences in incomes among different members of the laboring classes, but these would tend to equalize the relative advantages of different employments. Those who were not members of these classes, those employers who accumulated capital and utilized it productively in hiring labor, would secure differentially higher incomes from profits. But Smith makes it clear that it is precisely the attraction of such incomes which drives the whole process, which insures that the economy grows and prospers. Even here, however, Smith raises some questions about the efficacy of exceptionally high incomes from profits, and he warns against the tendency toward profligacy that such excesses create.[28] Smith is not clear on the possible allocative role played by rental incomes secured by landowners. Given his pre- but quasi-Ricardian model of the economy, he probably would not have been opposed to taxes on land rent.

There are distributional consequences of Smith's system, but, strictly speaking, the *distribution* of product among social classes or among members of any one class is clearly secondary to production, to securing maximal national income. This was to be accomplished by the removal of disincentives throughout the economy. The overriding objective was to increase the economic well-being of the members of the laboring classes while adhering to the precept of justice which the system of natural liberty represented.

At first glance, Smith's system seems a world apart from the Rawlsian setting, where the emphasis is on distribution, with production being largely neglected. The difference principle of distribution, appended lexically to that of equal liberty, states that inequalities in access to primary goods are acceptable in the just society only insofar as they are shown to be advantageous to the least-advantaged members of the community. But, in the empirical setting postulated for Adam Smith, what would an application of this Rawlsian difference principle have implied? An argument for a tax on land value might have been produced, along with an argument for taxation of excessively high incomes from profits, with a redistribution of proceeds generally to members of the laboring classes. Perhaps more importantly, from his discussion of the favorable effects of less restrictive laws of land ownership and transfer in the English as opposed to the Spanish and Portuguese colonies, we may infer that Smith would have supported legal reforms designed to open up prospects for greater mobility of persons between the land-owning and nonowning groups.[29] Such reform implications of his system could have been readily accepted by Smith, who might, however, have treated such reforms as being of slight importance compared with the more fundamental steps which involved the removal of governmental constraints on individual liberty.

Rawls projects the distributional issue to center stage perhaps because he presumes, empirically, that there exists only a relatively remote relationship between the pattern of income receipts, and of asset holdings, in society and the aggregate size of the total product. Furthermore, he seems to assume that there exists a distribution of natural or inherent capacities among persons, a distribution which tends to generate nonequalizing income-wealth differentials that carry with them neither economic nor moral justification. In the Rawlsian paradigm, the philosopher is not merely an educated porter.

The "system of natural liberty" that Rawls explicitly discusses, and rejects, is not that of Adam Smith.[30] Rawls uses this designation to refer to a system that embodies economic efficiency (Pareto optimality) as its only objective, and his critical remarks suggest that he does not impose the constraints that are made quite explicit in Smith. Rawls does not examine Smith's system in itself, but from his more general discussion we may infer that his central objection would be focused on the dependence of distributional outcomes on initial asset holdings, or initial endowments. Before treating this point in some detail, I re-emphasize that Rawls does not criticize the market-determined distribution of product, given the set of initial endowments, a source of much confusion in the continuing critique of social institutions.[31] His attention is concentrated, properly, on the premarket distribution of endowments to which, contrary to Nozick, Rawls attributes no moral qualities.

Adam Smith did not discuss the distribution of initial endowments, but for his system of natural liberty to meet the Rawlsian precepts for justice in the postulated Rawlsian setting, two conditions would have to be met. First, any deliberately imposed change in the basic institutions of society designed to bring about greater equality in initial endowments must be shown to worsen the position of the least advantaged. It does not seem likely that this condition could be fulfilled.[32] Even here, however, it should be recognized that the most glaring inequalities in initial endowments could scarcely arise in a genuine system of natural liberty. How many great family fortunes would exist had not the government employed its power to enforce and to police monopoly privileges? Secondly, there would have to be a direct relationship between the economic position of the least-advantaged members of society and the total income generated in the economy. This condition seems more likely to be met, regardless of how the "least-advantaged" members are to be defined, provided only that the difference principle is applied in a dynamic setting.[33] Institutional changes that tend to retard or to stifle economic growth seem likely to harm the position of the least-advantaged rather than to improve it, almost regardless of the motivation for such changes.[34]

I do not want to make Adam Smith and John Rawls seem to be more similar in their basic philosophical positions than a careful interpretation of their published works might warrant. Even when we take into account the historical and methodological distance between them, and even when we try to apply their criteria for justice in the converse empirical settings, we cannot legitimately infer a Smithean distributional interest comparable to Rawls. In 1976, a returned Adam Smith might or might not be an egalitarian of Rawlsian stripe. Because of his relative underemphasis on the relationship between material goods and human happiness, the most judicious evaluation suggests that Smith would not have been motivated to stress distributional inequities to the extent of Rawls. It also seems clear that, even in the affluence of 1976, Smith would have paid considerably more attention to the net benefits, measured in terms of both efficiency and justice, to be secured by a dismantling of restrictions on freedom of individual choices.

Finally I should note a possible difference in the implications of a commonly shared philosophical rather than empirical presupposition for normative discourse. Even if he should have recognized, empirically, that persons differ, and substantially so, in basic capacities, Adam Smith might well have argued that such inequalities have no place in, and in fact must be presumed away, in the process of designing a just and viable social order. The basic institutions of society must be based on the presumption that men are "equals" in some fundamental generic sense.[35] This is the attitude that clearly informs the United States Declaration of Independence, and the coincidence of dates between this and the publication of *The Wealth of Nations* is not merely historical accident. From this presumption or presupposition, undue concern with distributional outcomes might be considered to be, at base, aberrant. In this light, the onus would be on John Rawls to defend his concentration on the distributional principle as appended to the principle of equal liberty rather than on Adam Smith to defend his failure to make a comparable extension.

VIII. Conclusions

I have had several objectives in this paper. First of all, I have tried to show that Adam Smith's system of natural liberty, interpreted as his idealized paradigm for social order, embodies justice as well as economic efficiency. Indeed Smith may well have conceived his masterpiece to be an argument to the effect that the system which was acknowledged to embody justice could also be efficient. Secondly, I have attempted to compare Smith's first principle of natural liberty with John Rawls's first principle of equal liberty. Although I have not tried to examine an exhaustive list of examples here, a straightforward application of either of these principles implies significant restrictions on the propriety of governmental-political interference with the freedom of individuals to make their own economic decisions. My ultimate, and perhaps most important, purpose has been to use the timely discussion of Adam Smith's precepts for justice as a vehicle for correcting what has seemed to me a grossly neglected aspect of John Rawls's much-acclaimed and much-discussed book. Both Smith and Rawls are libertarians in that principles of liberty hold positions of priority in their orderings of objectives. Neither is utilitarian in the Benthamite or even in the more constrained Paretian sense of this term. The differences between Smith and Rawls lie in the fact that Smith's discourse is concentrated on the efficiency-producing results of natural liberty; the corollary attributes of justice are not stressed. And, for the several reasons noted, the distributional results are not explicitly evaluated against criteria of justice. On the other hand, Rawls treats liberty sketchily despite the lexical priority assigned to it, and he concentrates on the distributional qualities of an idealized social order. Translated into practical reform proposals, however, both philosophers accept an effectively operative market economy as a basic institution in any society that could be classified as just.

The differences in distributional emphasis are important, but I have showed that these are at least partially explained by differences in empirical and possibly philosophical presuppositions. One implication of the comparison should be that a libertarian position is not inconsistent with an egalitarian one, despite attempts to make these seem contradictory by both the libertarian-antiegalitarians and the collectivist-egalitarians. A strong defense of the liberties of individuals, which can only be secured in an operating market economy, may be joined with an equally strong advocacy for the reform of basic social institutions designed to produce greater equality among individuals in their initial endowments and capacities. This is how I interpret John Rawls's position, which comes close to that associated with Henry Simons,[36] whose explicit emphasis on free markets is clearly akin to that of Adam Smith. If my interpretation is accepted, the normative distance between Adam Smith and John Rawls is surely less than the sometimes careless comparisons of images would suggest.

Notes

I am indebted to my colleagues, Victor Goldberg, Nicolaus Tideman, Gordon Tullock, and Richard Wagner for helpful comments on earlier drafts.
1. John Rawls, *A Theory of Justice* (1971).
2. Robert Nozick, *Anarchy, State and Utopia* (1974).
3. Marc F. Plattner, "The New Political Theory," *Public Interest*, 40 (Summer, 1975) p. 120.
4. For the most direct statement on this, see Adam Smith, *The Theory of Moral Sentiments*, ed. E. G. West (1969), pp. 263–65.
5. A. L. Macfie, "The Individual in Society," *Papers on Adam Smith*, 19 (1967).
6. Adam Smith, *Lectures on Justice, Police, Revenue and Arms*, ed. Edwin Cannan (1896).
7. Ibid., p. 5.
8. Rawls, op. cit., p. 3.
9. Ibid., p. 7.
10. Jacob Viner, *Guide to John Rae's Life of Adam Smith*, p. 112, published with John Rae, *Life of Adam Smith* (Reprints of Econ. Classics, 1965).
11. Smith, *Lectures*, op. cit., pp. 11–13.
12. For a good discussion on this, see Macfie, op. cit., pp. 68–71.
13. Adam Smith, *The Wealth of Nations* (Modern Library ed.) p. 618 [hereinafter cited as *The Wealth of Nations*]. All subsequent references are to this edition.

Note the similarity of this statement of Smith to John Rawls's definition of the principle of equal liberty, cited below.

14. See *The Wealth of Nations* (on apprenticeship requirements), pp. 121–22; (on restrictions on migration), p. 141; (on entry restrictions), p. 497, as examples.

15. Ibid., p. 549 (italics supplied).

16. Ibid., p. 308.

17. Ibid.

18. See, in particular, *The Wealth of Nations*,, p. 342, where he rejects imposing restrictions on entry into retailing trades even "though they [shopkeepers] may so as to hurt one another."

19. Ibid., p. 308.

20. In Rae's citations from the notes of John Miller, one of Smith's best students, there is the following passage; "In the last of his lectures he examined those political regulations which are founded, not upon the principle of *justice* but that of *expediency,* and which are calculated to increase the riches, power, and prosperity of a state. Under this view he considered the political institutions relating to commerce, to finances, to ecclesiastical and military establishments. What he delivered on these subjects contained the substance of the work he afterwards published under the title of *An Inquiry into the Nature and Causes of the Wealth of Nations.*" Rae, op. cit., p. 55.

21. *The Wealth of Nations*, p. 572.

22. Rawls, op. cit., p. 250.

23. "I assume in all interpretations that the first principle of equal liberty is satisfied and that the economy is roughly a free market system," Ibid., p. 66.

24. Minimum-wage legislation would also be unjust by Rawls's second principle since the primary groups harmed are those who are least-advantaged, those with relatively low economic productivity.

25. F. A. Hayek, *The Constitution of Liberty* (1960). Hayek does not represent liberty or freedom as an attribute of "justice," but rather as an independent "source and condition of most moral values," p. 6. At one point, however, he does suggest that justice requires something akin to the Rawlsian principle of equal liberty, p. 99.

26. I do not suggest that the idealized Rawlsian constitution could not allow for escapes from the genuine externality-public goods dilemmas that fully independent private adjustments might produce. Such a constitution would require that such escapes be accomplished through more inclusive contractual agreements, which would, of course, embody compensations to those who might be harmed by change. My point in the text here is to indicate that the Rawlsian principle of equal liberty would not allow for governmentally imposed changes without compensation, regardless of the benefit-cost ratios.

27. Rawls, op. cit., pp. 65–75.

28. This aspect of Smith's argument is stressed by Rosenberg. See Nathan Rosenberg, "Some Institutional Aspects of *The Wealth of Nations*," *Journal of Political Economics,* 68 (1960), p. 557.

29. *The Wealth of Nations,* pp. 538–39.

30. Rawls, op. cit., pp. 65–75.

31. For my own explicit discussion of this point, see James M. Buchanan, "Political Equality and Private Property: The Distributional Paradox," in Proceedings of Conference on Markets and Morals, Battelle Institute, Seattle, May 1974.

32. An argument to this effect could be plausibly advanced with respect to certain of the more obvious proposals. One such argument that might possibly be extended in this way relates to the confiscatory taxation of inheritances. See

Gordon Tullock, "Inheritance Justified," *Journal of Law and Economics*, 14 (1971).

33. Critics of Rawls have pointed to the ambiguities that arise in defining "least-advantaged," and Rawls has acknowledged the difficulties involved when dynamic or intergenerational issues are introduced. Even if the "least-advantaged" are defined to be those members of society who are wholly nonproductive, growth-retarding policies will violate the difference principle if the intergenerational discount rate is sufficiently low. The indigent of the 1970s are in a better position than they would have been had a Rawlsian difference principle of justice been applied, without consideration of the intergenerational impact, in the 1870s.

34. The "quality of life" or environmental regulations that have now become widespread seem to offer the best examples. These institutional changes are acknowledged to have differentially harmed those who are in differentially disadvantaged economic positions. Quite apart from possible violations of the principles of equal liberty, these changes would have to be classified as unjust by the difference principle.

35. For a discussion of this presumption of fundamental equality, even in the context of empirical inequalities, see James M. Buchanan, *The Limits of Liberty: Between Anarchy and Leviathan* (1975), esp. pp. 11–12.

Rawls, of course, accepts this presumption in his basic contractarian derivation of the principles of justice. The presumption is not at issue here. The possible difference lies in the implications of this presumption for distributional norms.

Care must be taken to distinguish a presumption of equality in some "original position" and/or in some basic philosophical sense, and the elevation of distributional equality as an ideal attribute of the just society. Rawls is somewhat vulnerable on this count, especially because he derives his principles of justice from "fairness" notions. Insofar as "fairness" applies to the rules of games, by extension to ordinary games, it becomes questionable to speak of achieved or final equality as an ideal. This would amount to "condemning a footrace as unfair because someone has come out ahead." On this point, see Frank H. Knight, *The Ethics of Competition* (1935), p. 61.

36. See Henry Simons, *Economic Policy for a Free Society* (1948) and *Personal Income Taxation* (1938).

There are some ambiguities in Rawls which make my interpretation less persuasive than might appear. He does not seem to recognize the necessary relationship between an operative market economy and the dispersion of property ownership. For this reason, particular sections of his treatise may be interpreted as collectivist in flavor. See, especially, Rawls, op. cit., pp. 271–72. On balance, these seem to me to represent failures to follow through carefully the full implications of the first principle of equal liberty.

18.

Markets, States, and the Extent of Morals

Man acts within a set of institutional constraints that have developed historically: in part by sheer accident; in part by survival in a social evolutionary process; in part by technological necessity; in part by constructive design (correctly or incorrectly conceived). These constraints which define the setting within which human behavior must take place may, however, be inconsistent with man's capacities as a genuine "social animal." To the extent that moral-ethical capacities are "relatively absolute,"[1] there may be only one feasible means of reducing the impact of the inconsistency. Attempts must be made to modify the *institutions* (legal, political, social, economic) with the objective of matching these more closely with the empirical realities of man's moral limitations.

In a certain restricted sense, the observed behavior of the modern American is excessively "self-interested." Rather than hope for a "new morality," I shall focus on the potential for institutional reform that may indirectly modify man's behavior toward his fellows. Institutions may have been allowed to develop and to persevere that exacerbate rather than mitigate man's ever present temptation to act as if he is an island, with others treated as part of his natural environment. In a properly qualified sense, the latter pattern of behavior is the economist's "ideal," but the costs have not been adequately recognized.

Let me proceed by simple illustration. Consider two traders, each of whom is initially endowed with a commodity bundle. Gains from trade exist and cooperation through trade is suggested, but there arises the complementary conflict over the sharing of net surplus. As we extend the model by introducing additional traders, however, the conflict element of the interaction is squeezed out, and, in the limit, each trader becomes a pure price taker. "In perfect competition there is no competition," as Frank Knight was fond of emphasizing. (However, we must never lose sight of the elementary fact that this "economic ideal," including its most complex variants, presumes the existence of laws and institutions that secure private property and enforce contracts.)

Let me change the illustration and now assume that the same two persons find themselves in a genuine "publicness" interaction. (They are villagers alongside the swamp, to use David Hume's familiar example.) As before, there exist potential gains from trade, and these can be secured by agreement. Cooperation and conflict again enter to influence choice behavior, but here the introduction of more traders does nothing to squeeze down the range of conflict. Indeed, it does quite the opposite. Beyond some critical limit, each person will come to treat the behavior of others as part of the state of nature that he confronts as something wholly independent of his own actions.

Numbers work in opposing directions in the two cases. Under a set of laws and institutions that are restricted to the security of property and contract, the extension of the market in partitionable goods moves the efficiency frontier of the community outward. But, under the same laws and institutions, if there exist nonpartitionable interdependencies (public goods), an increase in the size of the group may move the attainable efficiency frontier inward.

I have introduced the familiar private goods–public goods comparison to illustrate my general argument to the effect that there are opposing behavioral implications involved in any extension in the membership of a community. The effects of group size on choice behavior, and, through this, on the normative evaluation of institutions, have not been sufficiently explored by economists, most of whom have remained content to concentrate on the formal efficiency properties of allocations. With relatively few exceptions they have worked with fixed-sized groups. And, even in 1978, most economic policy discussion proceeds on the implicit presumption that "government" is benevolently despotic.[2]

What is the orthodox economists' response when pure public goods are postulated? It is relatively easy to define the formal conditions that are necessary for allocative efficiency, but it is not possible to define the governmental process that might generate these results.[3] Work in public-choice theory has contributed to our understanding of how governmental processes actually operate, but this theory is, in a general sense, one of governmental failure rather than success.

Political scientists have objected to the imperialism of public-choice economists who extend utility-maximizing models of behavior to persons who act variously in collective-choice roles, as voters, as politicians, and as bureaucrats. These critics intuitively sense that a polity driven solely by utility maximizers (with empirical content in the maximand) cannot possibly generate an escape from the large number analogue to the prisoners' dilemma suggested in the simple example of a public-goods interaction. These critics have not, however, understood the basic causes for the general dilemma that modern collectivist institutions impose on citizens, politicians, and bureaucrats. Even more than the economists, orthodox political scientists have tended to ignore the possible effects of group or community size on individual behavior patterns.

Any political act is, by definition, "public" in the classic Samuelsonian sense. An act of voting by a citizen potentially affects a result that, once determined, will be applied to *all* members of the community. Similarly, an act by a legislator in voting for one tax rule rather than another becomes an input in determining a result that will define the environment for all members of the polity. Comparable conclusions extend to each and every act of a civil servant and to each decision of a judge.[4] Under what conditions could we predict that such political acts will provide public good? For instruction here, we can return directly to our elementary example. We should expect at least some such behavior to exhibit co-operative features in effectively small groups. We should not, and could not, expect persons who act politically to provide public good voluntarily in large-number settings.

We can reach this conclusion by economic analysis that incorporates standard utility-maximizing behavior on the part of all actors. My principal hypothesis, however, involves the possible inconsistency between man's *moral* capacities and the institutions within which he acts. Is not man capable of surmounting the generalized public goods dilemma of modern politics by moral-ethical principles that will serve to constrain his proclivities toward aggrandizement of his narrowly defined self-interest? It is here that my secondary hypothesis applies. The force of moral-ethical principle in influencing behavior is directly dependent on the size of community within which action takes place. Other things equal, the smaller the number of persons with whom a person interacts, the higher the likelihood that he will seem to behave in accordance with something akin to the Kantian generalization principle: in our terminology, that he will provide public good in his choice behavior.

Even this secondary hypothesis can be discussed in a way as to bring it within a utility-maximizing framework. The extent that a person expects his own behavior to influence the behavior of those with whom he interacts will depend on the size of the group. Hence, utility maximization in a small-number setting will not exhibit the observable properties of utility maximization in a large-number setting.[5] I want, however, to go beyond this strictly small group phenomenon of direct behavioral feedback. I want to introduce moral-ethical constraints in a genuine noneconomic context here. I propose to allow *homo economicus* to exist only as one among many men that describe human action, and, in many settings to assume a tertiary motivation role.

The precise dimension of human behavior that I concentrate on here is the location of the effective mix between the two motivational forces of economic self-interest and what I shall term "community."[6] I do not want to, and I have no need to, identify with any particular variant of nonself-interest: fellowship, brotherhood, Christian love, empathy, Kantian imperative, sympathy, public interest, or anything else. I want only to recognize the existence of a general motive force that inhibits the play of narrowly defined self-interest when an individual recognizes himself to be a member of a group of others more or less like himself. Robinson Crusoe could be motivated by nothing other than self-interest until Friday arrives. Once he acknowledges the existence of Friday, a tension develops and Crusoe finds that his behavior is modified. This tension exists in all human action, and observed behavior reflects the outcome of some resolution of the inner conflict. The institutional setting determines the size of community relevant for individual behavior. This influence of size is exerted both directly in the sense of limits to recognition, and indirectly in the relationship between a community's membership and its ability to command personal loyalties. Conceptually, the "structure of community" within which an individual finds himself can shift the location of behavior along a spectrum bounded on one extreme by pure self-interest and on the other by pure community interest within which the actor counts for no more than any other member.

The institutions (economic, geological, legal, political, social, technological), which define the sizes of community within which an individual finds himself, impose *external* bounds on possible behavior. Parallel to these external constraints there are also *internal* limits or bounds on what we may call an individual's moral-ethical community. There are, of course, no sharp categorical lines to be drawn between those other persons whom someone considers to be "members of the tribe" and those whom he treats as "outsiders." I make no such claim. I assert only that, for any given situation, there is a difference in an individual's behavior toward members and nonmembers, and that the membership lists are drawn up in his own psyche. This is not to say either that persons are uniform with respect to their criteria for tribal membership or that these criteria are invariant with respect to exogenous events. Clearly, neither of these inferences will hold. However the fact of behavioral discrimination is empirical and subject to test. I am not arguing normatively to the effect that individuals should or should not discriminate among other members of the human species, or even as between humans and other animals.

My colleague Tullock enjoys asking egalitarians whether or not they would extend their precepts for social justice to the people of Bangladesh. He gets few satisfactory answers. Why should precepts for distributive justice mysteriously stop at the precise boundaries of the nation-state? If one responds that they need not do so, that national boundaries are arbitrary products of history, then one is led to ask whether or not effective precepts of justice might stop short of such inclusive community, whether or not the moral-ethical limit for most persons is reached short of the size of modern nations.[7] At provincial or regional boundaries? At the local community level? The extended family? The clan? The racial group? The ethnic heritage? The church membership? The functional group?

What can a person be predicted to do when the external institutions force upon him a role in a community that extends beyond his moral-ethical limits? The tension shifts toward the self-interest pole of behavior; moral-ethical principles are necessarily sublimated. The shift is exaggerated when a person realizes that others in the extended community of arbitrary and basically amoral size will find themselves in positions comparable to his own. How can a person act politically in other than his own narrowly defined self-interest in an arbitrarily sized nation of more than 200 millions? Should we be at all surprised when we observe the increasing usage of the arms and agencies of the national government for the securing of private personal gain?

The generalized public-goods dilemma of politics can be kept within tolerance limits only if there is some proximate correspondence between the external institutional and the internal moral constraints on behavior.[8] This century may be described by developments that drive these two sets of constraints apart. An increase in population alone reduces the constraining influence of moral rules. Moreover population increase has been accompanied by increasing mobility over space, by the replacement of local by national markets, by the urbanization of society, by the shift of power from state-local to national government, and by the increased politicization of society generally. Add to this the observed erosion of the family, the church, and the law—all of which were stabilizing influences that tended to reinforce moral precepts—and we readily understand why *homo economicus* has assumed such a dominant role in modern behavior patterns.[9]

Indirect evidence for the general shift from morally based resolution of conflict and morally based settlement of terms of cooperation to political-legal instruments is provided by the observed rapidly increasing resort to litigation. Modern man seeks not to live with his neighbor; he seeks instead to become an island, even when his natural setting dictates moral community. This movement, in its turn, prompts lawyers to turn to economic theory for new normative instruction.

Despite the flags and the tall ships of 1976, there is relatively little moral-ethical cement in the United States which might bring the internal moral-ethical limits more closely in accord with the external community defined inclusively by the national government. There is no "moral equivalent to war," and, since Viet Nam, we must question whether war itself can serve such a function. Nonetheless, experience suggests that war and the threat thereof may be the only moral force that might sustain the governmental leviathan. Viewed in this light, it is ominous that each president, soon after entering office, shifts his attention away from the divisive issues of domestic politics toward those of foreign affairs. We must beware the shades of George Orwell's *1984,* when external enemies are created, real or imaginary, for the purpose of sustaining domestic moral support for the national government.

While I am not some agrarian utopian calling for a return to the scattered villages on the plains, I shall accept the label of a constitutional utopian who can still see visions of an American social order that would not discredit our Founding Fathers. To achieve such an order, drastic constitutional change is surely required. Effective federalism remains possible, within the technological constraints of the age, and "constitutional revolution" need not require the massive suffering, pestilence, and death associated with revolution on the left or right. Dramatic devolution might succeed in channelling some of the moral-ethical fervor in politics toward constructive rather than destructive purpose.

I become discouraged when I observe so little discussion, even among scholars, of the federal alternative to the enveloping leviathan. Where is the Quebec of the United States? Where is the Scotland? Could a threat of secession now succeed? More importantly, could the emergence of such a threat itself force some devolution of central government power? Who will join me in offering to make a small contribution to the Texas Nationalist Party? Or to the Nantucket Separatists? From small beginnings . . . .

We should be clear about the alternative. The scenario to be played out in the absence of dramatic constitutional reform involyes increasing resort to the power of the national government by those persons and groups who seek private profit and who are responding predictably to the profit opportunities that they observe to be widening. Individually, they cannot be expected to understand that the transfer game is negative sum, and, even with such understanding, they cannot be expected to refrain from investment in rent seeking. Furthermore, as persons and groups initially outside the game come to observe their own losses from political exploitation, they too will enter the lists. As the process moves forward through time, we can predict a continued erosion of trust in politics and politicians. But distrust will not turn things around. "Government failure" against standard efficiency norms may be demonstrated, analytically and empirically, but I see no basis for the faith that such demonstrations will magically produce institutional reform. I come back to constitutional revolution as the only attractive alternative to the scenario that we seem bent to act out. In the decade ahead, we shall approach the bicentenary of the Constitution itself. Can this occasion spark the dialogue that must precede action?

Notes

I am indebted to Roger Congleton, Thomas Ireland, Janet Landa, Robert Tollison, and Richard Wagner for helpful suggestions.

1. Reinhold Niebuhr, *Moral Man and Immoral Society* (New York, 1932), pp. 3, 267.

2. Economists have continued for eight decades to ignore the warnings of Knut Wicksell, *Finanztheoretische Untersuchungen* (Jena, 1896).

3. A possible qualification to this statement is required with reference to the demand-revealing process, summarized by T. Nicolaus Tideman and Gordon Tullock, "A New and Superior Process for Making Social Choice," *Journal of Political Economics,* 84 (December 1976), pp. 1145–160. Even its proponents recognize, however, that this process remains a conceptual ideal rather than an institution capable of practical implementation.

4. See Gordon Tullock, "Public Decisions as Public Goods," *Journal of Political Economics,* 79 (July/August 1971), pp. 913–18.

5. See James M. Buchanan, "Ethical Rules, Expected Values, and Large Numbers," *Ethics,* 74 (October 1965), pp. 1–13.

6. In a tautological sense, all behavior, including that which I label as moral-ethical, can be analyzed in a utility-maximizing model. In this paper, however, "utility maximization" and "self-interest" are defined operationally.

7. In an argument related to that in this paper, Dennis Mueller concentrates on the relationship between the size of community and the ability of a person to imagine himself behind a Rawlsian veil of ignorance. See Dennis Mueller, "Achieving the Just Polity," *American Economics Review Proceedings,* 64 (May 1974), pp. 147–52.

8. Gerald Sirkin refers to the "Victorian compromise" which is, in several respects, similar to the correspondence noted here. See Gerald Sirkin, "Resource X and the Theory of Retrodevelopment," in Robert D. Leiter and Stanley J. Friedlander, eds., *The Economics of Resources* (New York, 1976), pp. 193–208.

9. My diagnosis is restricted to the Western, specifically the American, setting. Perhaps the strongest empirical support for my argument is, however, provided in non-Western collectivized countries through the observed failures to create "new men," via institutional change.

19.

Equal Treatment and Reverse Discrimination

Unnecessary confusion characterizes the discussion of "reverse discrimination" that has attracted the attention of social scientists, philosophers, and lawyers. This discussion has recently taken the form of post-mortem evaluations of the Bakke and Weber decisions of the U.S. Supreme Court. Participants in the discussion, almost without exception, have introduced their own empirical prejudgments into the analysis. These prejudgments reflect wholly admirable ideals, but they may not square with reality as seen by those who make the relevant behavioral choices. Because of the prejudgments, however, analysts have involved themselves in logical dilemmas of their own making.

At the outset of this analysis, I shall present a highly simplified example, in elementary economic terminology, that will serve as the basis for the substantive argument to follow. Then I will demonstrate that, even in the total absence of "discrimination" as usually defined, acceptance of the "equal-treatment" criterion or precept for justice, itself a very limited and highly restricted criterion, is sufficient to provide a possible basis for what is often referred to (erroneously) as "reverse discrimination," given the empirical postulates introduced in the example. After relating my analysis to some, but by no means all, of the discussion in the literature, I will use the analysis to interpret the problems faced by the Supreme Court in the important Bakke and Weber cases. In a general sense, this treatment is intended more as a criticism of the discussion-debate on the issues than as an independent substantive contribution.[1]

I. An Example

Consider a cohort group of N potential entrants into the labor force. This inclusive group of N potential entrants is made up of two equal-sized subgroups or classes, A and B, membership in which is readily identifiable in terms of some unchangeable characteristic: sex, skin color, eye color, height. There is no way that a member of one subgroup, A or B, can shift between classes by modifying his or her own behavior.

All members of the inclusive group, N, seek employment. The economy is assumed to be fully competitive, and no employer or employee has a "taste" for discrimination between members of the two classes, A and B. As an *empirical postulate,* however, assume that the average or mean productivity of the A group of cohorts is less than the average or mean productivity of the B group or class. This difference in the mean productivity between the two classes is known by all members of the society, by all prospective employers, and by all potential employees alike.

Prospective employers do not, however, know anything initially about the *actual* productivity of any single person of either class. This individualized and identifiable productivity can be determined or ascertained only after some demonstration or trial period, during which each person "proves his or her worth." Since the economy is assumed to be fully competitive, once their individualized productivities are known (by assumption to everyone), persons will be able to secure relative wages that correspond to their marginal value contributions. Each and every person will be able, once his or her ability or competence is known, to secure a wage or salary commensurate with his or her net contribution to the value of product.

During the demonstration period, however, persons cannot possibly be paid in accordance with the real values of their contributions since individualized productivities are not known to anyone, employer or employee. Persons will, therefore, be paid during this initial period by some appropriately computed average or mean-value productivity over a whole group. If members of the B group or class are known to have higher average or mean productivities than members of the A group or class, employers in a competitive setting will find it necessary to pay any member of the B group the average or mean productivity for this group alone during the initial demonstration period. Similarly, if employees from the A group are to be hired at all, each of them must accept a wage that is equal only to the mean or average productivity of the group of A employees, which is, by the empirical postulate, less than the average productivity, and hence the initial-period wage, for the B group.

If a single employer should proceed in his hiring policy in total and complete disregard of the classification of prospective employees into the A and B classes, he would presumably offer a standardized wage or salary equal to the mean or average productivity for the whole group of N applicants. In such a competitive setting, however, the single employer following this policy would be unable to hire any employees from the B group; he would be able to hire persons only from the A group, and he would be paying these employees more than they could earn in other situations. His costs would be higher than those for his competitors, and the firm could not long survive. It would face bankruptcy and dissolution in relatively short order. In any plausible description of equilibrium in the competitive economy assumed here, initial- or demonstration-period wages for the B group of workers will remain higher than those for the A group. If, in contrast, there should be some forced standardization of wages over both groups, there would be no workers from the A group hired, or at the least, severe unemployment might characterize the A group of prospective employees.

This simplified example is designed to show that even in an economy that is fully competitive, that works perfectly, and in which there is no preference for or against any prospective employee based on any characteristic other than productivity, the prospective employee from the group or class that is predicted to have the relatively low mean or average productivity suffers a disadvantage in terms of wage or salary prospects, at least to the extent that his or her personal level of productivity is not known during some initial or demonstration period of employment. The phenomenon of initial-period wage differentials, emerging from the operation of efficient market structure as described in the simple example here, is familiar to economists. It has been called *statistical discrimination* by Phelps and Akerlof,[2] but this term seems singularly inappropriate to the phenomena at hand. Prospective employers do not "discriminate" on the basis of the identifiable characteristic as such; this characteristic is used, indeed must be used in the competitive setting as a signal or index for measuring expected value productivity. To introduce the word *discrimination* in this context would suggest that an employer also could be said to "discriminate" against the worker who is known to be less productive by the payment of a relatively lower wage.

II. Equal Treatment for Equals

The example reveals, nonetheless, that the operation of a fully competitive market in the total absence of discrimination, defined in the standard manner, will violate one of the elementary precepts for justice or fairness, namely, equal treatment for equals. In order to achieve the satisfaction of this minimal criterion of justice, some "correction" of the play of market forces may be indicated, even if there may be no efficiency basis for adjudging markets to have failed.

But how are "equals" defined, and how should "equals" be defined in application to the problem here addressed? Although not explicitly introduced in the description of the setting of the example above, I have presumed the existence of some overlap or intersection between individual productivities for members of the A and B classes, once these individual productivities are ascertained. Despite the postulated differences in average or mean productivities for the two classes, individual members of either group may range in productivity over a whole spectrum from very low to very high values. Hence some prospective employees from the A group may turn out to be highly productive, and, conversely, some prospective members from the B group may, when tested, prove to be relatively unproductive. In statistical terms, the range of the two distributions may be assumed to be the same.

A pair of "equals," therefore, is quite simply defined in terms of finally proven or determined value productivity. A member of the A class is defined to be an equal with a member of the B class if, after demonstration, he or she generates the same net value of product. As the example demonstrates, however, a person carrying the A-class characteristic will not be accorded equal treatment with his or her B-class equal in the efficiently operating marketplace. So long as any period exists during which rewards are based on class means or averages rather than on individually measured productivities, some differential in treatment between such equals will be present. The degree, and hence the importance, of this differential in treatment will, of course, depend on the length of the demonstration period.

Once the violation of the equal-treatment-for-equals precept is acknowledged, attention turns to possible correctives that might be introduced. If prospective employers could somehow be informed accurately about individual productivities prior to the determination of any wage or salary scale, no problem need arise. Reasonable attempts toward providing employers with more accurate information, perhaps through the use of test scores, may well be warranted. But it does not seem likely that full satisfaction of the equal-treatment criterion could be attained in this manner.

Additional steps may be indicated, and the obvious candidate for consideration involves some general requirement that *all* prospective employers disregard the information concerning potential employee membership in the A and B classes. If all employers should in some way be denied access to or usage of the information about the observable characteristic, and hence class, of an employee—or all employees—the workings of the fully competitive market (with this constraint) will ensure that initial- or demonstration-period wages are set at the average or mean productivity level for *all* N entrants, rather than at the average productivity levels for the A and B classes of entrants respectively. In this setting, all entrants, whether from the A or B group, will receive identical initial-period wages, and, subsequent to this period, all workers will receive wages based strictly on their individual productivities. Hence, any pair of equals will be treated in precisely equal fashion, defined in this limited example as being the payment of equal wages over their working career.

As indicated earlier, however, such disregard of the readily available and privately valuable classificatory information cannot be undertaken by a single employer. If, however, all employers throw away or fail to use such information, the equal-treatment criterion is met, and with minimal efficiency loss. Prospective employees from the B class (with higher average productivity) will receive somewhat lower wages during the initial or demonstration period than they would receive if the classificatory information should be utilized. But for prospective employees from the A class (with lower average productivity), the relationship is the opposite.

What specific institutional arrangements might generate the results desired? Clearly, a requirement that all entrants, regardless of membership in the A or B class, be paid equal initial-period wages will not work. In such a setting, all employers will continue to utilize the classificatory information as to class by trying to hire only B-class entrants. A-class entrants will be unable to find employment unless they can accept lower wages. Or, in a somewhat more complex but also more realistic scenario, workers from the A class will tend to be hired only in relatively lower-skill categories than their external qualifications would suggest. In order to generate the desired results, which correspond to those where all employers literally disregard all classificatory information about class, employers might be required to hire workers from the two classes in direct proportion to the size of these classes in the total cohort group of entrants, N. That is to say, a *hiring quota,* imposed on each employer, would be one institutional device that would tend to produce the desired results.[3]

In the example, there are equal numbers of potential A- and B-class entrants. A quota arrangement that would require each employer to hire equal numbers from each class would result in initial-period wages for all entrants at the level of productivity for all N entrants. In effect, such a quota system amounts to a requirement for a tie-in purchase of labor inputs. For each B-class employee taken on, the employer must hire one A-class employee. Labor can be hired only in the one-to-one package. Payment therefore cannot exceed the expected average productivity for the two classes taken as one, which is the whole set of entrants.

Note, however, that the analysis here offers no support for *employment* as opposed to hiring quotas. After an initial or demonstration period, wages will be, and must be for efficiency, set at individually determined productivity levels. Different employers will find it advantageous to employ differing mixes of workers as among the differing and separate skill and productivity categories. Firms whose product mix requires the use of relatively large numbers of high-productivity workers would be expected to employ differentially larger numbers of workers from the B class. Employers whose product mix allows the use of relatively large numbers of low-productivity workers will be expected to employ disproportionately large numbers of A-class workers. Given the existence and enforcement of a hiring quota but not an employment quota, it should be predicted that larger numbers of A-class workers will tend to shift to somewhat lower productivity levels than reflected in their initial hiring, with the opposite occurring for B-class workers.

These results stem from the basic empirical postulate that average productivities differ, or are predicted to differ, between the two classes. There is no violation of the equal-treatment-for-equals criterion of justice or fairness reflected in an observed disproportion of employment of the two classes in any skill or productivity category. All equally productive workers are treated equally. Indeed, to introduce employment quotas and to require that all employers employ equal numbers or proportionate numbers from the two classes will violate the equal-treatment criterion. Such a requirement would serve to ensure that some B-class workers will be able to find employment only at skill category levels below those of their "equals," whether from the B class or from the A class. It should be acknowledged that the tendency for any hiring-quota arrangement to be confused with, and hence to lead imperceptibly to, an employment quota represents perhaps a major, and possibly decisive, argument against the inauguration of hiring quotas in the first place.

Elaboration and Criticism

In the operation of the fully competitive market, and with no preference for discrimination, the analysis reveals that the equal-treatment precept is violated. The extension of the analysis shows that the enforcement of appropriately designed and appropriately limited hiring quotas could satisfy the equal-treatment precept. Neither discrimination nor reverse discrimination can be applied in a descriptively meaningful way to these two separate institutional arrangements, the fully competitive market on the one hand and the market as constrained by the suggested hiring-quota arrangement on the other. The failure to distinguish the satisfaction of the equal-treatment precept from the presence or absence of discrimination, forward or reverse, has been a source of logical confusion in the whole discussion.

Economists, generally, have devoted relatively little attention to the set of issues involved here, and their treatment has been marred by a failure to cut through their personal prejudgments about the phenomena to be analyzed. Recall that, in the example developed earlier, the difference in the mean or average productivities of the two classes was stated as an empirical postulate. Once this step was taken, the analysis followed more or less straightforwardly, given the structural setting imposed on the model. Suppose, however, that this empirical postulate is not introduced. Suppose, instead, that the existence of the two readily identifiable classes is postulated, but, by empirical prejudgment, no difference in average or mean productivities is to be allowed for consideration. In this setting, if the market is assumed fully competitive, and if there are no tastes or preferences for discrimination by employers, employees, or customers, there would never be any violation of the equal-treatment-for-equals norm.

Many economists, however, with the empirical prejudgments noted, have observed what seemed to be discriminatory treatment in hiring practices. To explain these as a prelude to proposing correctives, they have searched for market failures on the one hand and for overt preferences for discrimination on the other. They have, in one sense, been led to overlook the simple explanation offered here because they have essentially closed off consideration of the empirical postulate that readily generates the results.[4]

My highly structured and simplified analysis is in no way intended to rule out or to deny the presence of a positive taste for discrimination in situations where labor entrants can be readily classified into distinctly identifiable sets (women/men, black/white, and so on). My purpose is to show that, even in the absence of such taste, the equal-treatment norm is violated unless specific corrective action is taken. And, as later discussion will suggest, confusion between satisfaction or failure to satisfy the equal-treatment precept and the presence or absence of discrimination has a bearing on interpretations of affirmative action proposals and judicial rulings.

The discussion among philosophers has not been so formal as that among economists, and it is perhaps not surprising that the analysis has often been explicitly normative. With relatively few exceptions, philosophers have sought to justify "reverse discrimination" or "preferential treatment" in hiring, admissions, and the like. They have essentially commenced their analysis by postulating the existence or possible existence of preference (governmentally imposed) that is the opposite of the personal preference that is presumed to exist (or to have existed) in the absence of or prior to collective intervention. If participants in these discussions should be required to assume that no positive preference for discrimination would exist in the absence of corrective action, there would be no content in their argument. "Reverse discrimination," even as defined by its most ardent proponents, is justified only to the extent that discrimination would exist in its absence.[5] Even those who have explicitly related equal treatment to the whole set of issues here have failed to recognize that this precept may be violated under the empirical postulate examined earlier and that policy arrangements often referred to erroneously as "reverse discrimination" may be legitimatized on the grounds of this precept alone.

My examination of the legal scholarship bearing on the topics discussed here has not been exhaustive. My sampling strongly suggests, however, that lawyers, like their counterparts in economics and philosophy, have uncritically equated quota arrangements in hiring, selection, and admission policies, with "preferential treatment" of prospective employees or candidates from the class (race, sex) that would have been or was "discriminated against" in the absence of such arrangements. The question posed has been one of justifying preferential treatment, of legitimatizing the use of class-identifiable characteristics. Interesting arguments have been produced invoking such criteria as "overriding social interest," "majority damage-minority benefit," "compensation for prior injustice," and others, any or all of which might well be usefully introduced in a discussion of overtly preferential treatment (for example, the University of California, Davis, medical school admissions procedures).[6]

The legal discussion has overlooked the relevance or even the existence of the way-station positions between discriminatory private preferences on the one hand and reverse-discriminatory state or governmental preference on the other, way-stations that involve the equal-treatment-for-equals precept. The following schema illustrates these positions:

(1)	(2)	(3)	(4)
Preference for members of class predicted to embody high mean productivity	No preference, but hiring selection decisions on basis of identifiable class characteristics	No preference, but hiring selection constrained to prevent use of identifiable class characteristics	Preference for members of class predicted to embody low mean productivity
Violation of equal-treatment precept	Violation of equal-treatment precept	Equal-treatment precept *satisfied*	Violation of equal-treatment precept

The arguments of legal scholars, like those of economists and philosophers, implicitly assume the existence of columns (1) and (4) only; columns (2) and (3) are neglected. The important omission is the failure to recognize that the state described in column (3), which may well involve hiring and selection quotas, might be realized without the necessity to slip over into column (4).

Extension and Application

One feature of our example must be modified if the analysis is to be applicable to the critically important judicial rulings of the 1970s, the

Supreme Court opinions in the Bakke and Weber cases. The setting for these disputed cases did not involve relative wage or hiring treatment of *all* relevant members of a two-class cohort group. Instead, the issues turned on the selection of a subset of the larger group for a restricted and preferred number of openings or positions, as well as the relative treatment of members of the separate classes (races) in the selection process.

The example may be readily modified to fit this situation. Suppose, as before, that a cohort group of N potential candidates for a restricted number of positions, say N/10, are readily identifiable, as before, into the two classes, A and B, and that the average or mean productivity of the latter class is known to be higher than that of the former. The objective is to select the most highly productive N/10 candidates, but nothing is presumed known about individual productivities. How should members of A and B be treated in the selection process if the equal-treatment criterion is to be met?

It seems evident that, given the informational restrictions noted, the selection process could not utilize the information about mean class productivities and still satisfy the equal-treatment norm. In the absence of some effective way of securing information about individuals, only a genuinely randomized selection from the whole set of N potential candidates could be used. This procedure would produce (on average) a less productive set of candidates than a randomized selection limited to the B applicants, but the gain in average productivity involved in the latter procedure could be achieved only at the expense of violating the equal-treatment precept. To satisfy the precept, everyone must be included in the draw.

Suppose, however, that additional information about individual productivity can be obtained by some testing procedure that can be administered at relatively low cost. In such a setting, all N potential candidates can be allowed to take the entrance test. And so long as the test itself is not biased by class, the direct use of the test scores as a means of making the selection for preferred positions violate the equal-treatment precept. This conclusion holds even if the entry test scores are known to be imperfect predictors of individual productivities. But how would class bias in the test itself be assessed in this context? If the mean test scores among members of the A class should be less efficient predictors of ultimate productivities than those for the B class, the test could be said to be biased against members of the A class, or vice versa if the effects were directionally the opposite. Of primary concern for the satisfaction of the equal-treatment norm is the possible arbitrary exclusion, by test scores, of highly productive members of a class rather than the inclusion of some candidates who do not measure up to the ultimately required productivity standards. Inclusion of the latter do not violate equal-treatment norms

directly; a class-biased exclusion of candidates who might ultimately succeed overtly violates such norms. Demonstration of some class bias in a
test could provide some basis for differential weighting of test scores by
class in the final selection of candidates.

The central issues in the Bakke case were of the sort noted here.[7] Bakke
scored higher on the composite test scale than any of the black applicants
who were chosen for the restricted entry into medical school. No argument was advanced to the effect that the tests were either unrelated to
ultimate performance or that the testing procedures were biased by race
in the manner described above. Bakke's argument to the effect that his
rejection was due solely to his race, that he had indeed been denied equal
treatment, and that he was the victim of reverse discrimination seems
unchallengeable.

The issues in the Weber case are much more complex than those in
Bakke.[8] The majority of a reduced-sized Court found against Weber's
claim of unequal treatment. The issue involved the selection, from among
persons already employed, of a restricted number of persons for a preferred program of training. Through a voluntary agreement between Kaiser, the employer, and the union, a quota system for selection had been
set up requiring that equal numbers of white and black applicants be
chosen for the training program. Within each of the two classes, seniority
in plant employment was accepted as the criterion for selection. Weber's
seniority in employment exceeded that of black candidates who were
chosen.

There was no evidence of overt discrimination against black employees
by Kaiser prior to the onset of the quota system. If the empirical postulate
of our example is taken to be descriptive of Kaiser's attitude toward the
mean or average productivities of black and white employees, at least for
some initial period, and, further, if effective union rules on standardization should have prevented differential wages within particular skill categories or classifications, the prediction emerges that black employees
hired for particular skill categories would have been more qualified than
their white employee counterparts. Seniority in employment, however,
commences only upon employment itself and can never reflect the differentials in qualification that may have been present at the time of initial
employment. Hence, it might have been argued, the black worker was not
the "equal" of the white worker with identical seniority, and, hence, the
two seniority listings should have been treated separately and in isolation
from each other.

The majority of the Court did not, however, base its opinion on reasoning of the sort suggested here. Instead, the majority, through the opinion
of Justice William Brennan, chose to deliver an internally contradictory
ruling that gave the appearance of judicial legislation and seemed almost

guaranteed to invoke the scathing dissent expressed by Justice William Rehnquist and endorsed by external critics.[9] Neither the majority nor the minority seemed to have sensed properly the genuine relevance of the equal-treatment criterion and to have understood that the satisfaction of this criterion need not, indeed should not, be classified as "reverse discrimination," just as the failure to satisfy this criterion prior to corrective governmental action need not, indeed should not, be classified as "discrimination," in the ordinary usage of this term.[10]

Notes

1. I have developed some of the analysis here in a more general setting in my two lectures, "Fairness, Hope, and Justice," in *New Directions in Economic Justice,* ed. Roger Skurski (South Bend, Ind.: University of Notre Dame Press, 1983), pp. 53–89.

2. See E. S. Phelps, "The Statistical Theory of Racism and Sexism," *American Economic Review* 62 (September 1972), pp. 659–61; and George Akerlof, "The Economics of Caste and of the Rat Race and Other Woeful Tales," *Quarterly Journal of Economics* 90 (November 1976), pp. 606ff.

3. There may, of course, be other institutional devices that would achieve comparable or even superior results, especially if considered as idealized types. In the presentations of this analysis, economists have suggested the prospects for special contingency contracts, which would allow employees' wages to be adjusted upward or downward ex post facto to account for initial-period absence of productivity information. Such a scheme, if universalized, would of course eliminate the violation of the equal-treatment-for-equals precept in the operation of the fully competitive market. In a practical setting, however, it is difficult to imagine a scheme that adjusts wages downward so as to allow for prior overpayments. My argument should be interpreted primarily as one that offers an analytically defensible basis for hiring quotas, in contrast to the nondefensible bases often advanced, rather than as one that implies that quotas are necessarily the most efficient device, either economically or politically.

4. This procedure is clearly represented by Kenneth J. Arrow in his paper, "Some Mathematical Models of Race in the Labor Market," in *Racial Discrimination in Economic Life,* ed. Anthony Pascal (Lexington: Heath Books, 1972), pp. 187–203, where his discussion commences by assuming the two classes of labor are perfect substitutes in production. As Arrow acknowledges, his model is a generalization and extension of the now classic model developed by Gary Becker in *The Economics of Discrimination* (Chicago: University of Chicago Press, 1957). E. S. Phelps's recognition of the basic analysis is prefaced by reference to "market imperfection" due to scarcity of information. See Phelps, op. cit., p. 659. George Akerlof's analysis is somewhat closer to that presented here, but, once again, he seems to search for market failure implications by postulating that the use of what he calls "indicators" to determine wage levels for classes will, in fact, continue after individual productivities are ascertained. See

Akerlof, op. cit. Michael Spence, like Arrow, postulates that there is no differential in mean productivities between classes or groups and generates his results through the differentials in educational levels. See Michael Spence, *Market Signaling* (Cambridge: Harvard University Press, 1974), p. 32.

An analysis that parallels mine in many respects is contained in Marvin M. Smith, "Toward a General Equilibrium Theory of Racial Wage Discrimination," *Southern Economic Journal* 45 (October, 1978), pp. 458–68. Smith does not, however, draw the policy implications relevant from the basic analysis.

5. For a recent symposium, which contains reference to earlier works, see *Ethics* 90 (October, 1979,): pp. 81–114, with papers by George Sher, Robert L. Simon, and Robert E. Gahringer.

6. For a general overview of the legal perspective, see Laurence H. Tribe, *American Constitutional Law* (Mineola, N.Y.: Foundation Press, 1978), ch. 17. For a clear exposition of several of the issues, see John Hart Ely, "The Constitutionality of Reverse Racial Discrimination," *University of Chicago Law Review* 41, no. 4 (Summer, 1974), pp. 723–41.

7. *Regents of the University of California* v. *Bakke,* 98 S. Ct. 2733 (1978).

8. *United Steelworkers, Etc.* v. *Weber,* 99 S. Ct. 2721 (1979).

9. Sidney Hook, in an introduction to a reprinted circulation of the Rehnquist dissent, goes so far as to state that "the Brennan opinion in the Weber case is the most horrendous decision in U.S. Supreme Court history since the Dred Scott case." *Measure,* University Centers for Rational Alternatives, no. 49 (September/October, 1979) p. 1.

10. The failure to make the distinction between the presence or absence of discrimination, positive or negative, and the satisfaction or failure to satisfy the criterion of equal treatment for equals is exemplified in Carl Cohen's critique of the Weber opinion of the Court. See Carl Cohen, "Justice Debased: The Weber Decision," *Commentary* 68 (September, 1979), pp. 43–53. Cohen's whole argument is marred by the fact that he presumes, without examination, that the quota arrangement for the training program necessarily involves preferential treatment for blacks. Cohen is not, of course, alone in this interpretation. As noted earlier in the brief discussion of philosophers' treatment of these issues, those who support the Court in such rulings as Weber feel obligated to defend preferential as opposed to equal treatment.

John H. Bunzel, in his critique of affirmative action generally, is similarly marred by the failure to distinguish the equal-treatment criterion from the no-discrimination criterion. See John H. Bunzel, "Affirmative Action, Negative Results," *Encounter* 53, no. 5 (November, 1979), pp. 43–51. For my critique of Bunzel's treatment, see "Affirmative-Negative," *Encounter* 55, no. 1 (July 1980), p. 95.

20.

Moral Community, Moral Order, or Moral Anarchy

I. Introduction

In this lecture I shall discuss the "ties that bind" persons with each other in society, and the instruments and attitudes that may break those ties that exist. I am concerned with the ways that persons act and feel toward one another. For this reason, I have inserted the adjective, "moral," before each of the nouns in my title. "Community, Order, or Anarchy," standing alone, would not convey my desired emphasis on personal interaction. To forestall misunderstanding at the outset, however, I should note that there is no explicitly moral content in the lecture, if the word "moral" is interpreted in some normative sense.

My diagnosis of American society is informed by the notion that we are living during a period of erosion of the "social capital" that provides the basic framework for our culture, our economy, and our polity, a framework within which the "free society" in the classically liberal ideal perhaps came closest to realization in all of history. My efforts have been directed at trying to identify and to isolate the failures and breakdowns in institutions that are responsible for this erosion.[1]

My discussion here will be exclusively conducted in terms of the three abstract models or forms of interaction listed in my title: (1) moral community, (2) moral order, and (3) moral anarchy. Any society may be described empirically as embodying some mix among these three forms or elements. A society is held together by some combination of moral community and moral order. Its cohesion is reduced by the extent to which moral anarchy exists among its members. The precise mix among the three forms or elements will, therefore, determine the observed "orderliness" of any society, along with the degree of governmental coercion reflected in the pattern that is observed to exist. The need for governance as well as the difficulty of governing are directly related to the mix among the three elements.

II. Moral Community

I shall commence by defining the three abstract models or forms of interaction. A *moral community* exists among a set of persons to the extent
that individual members of the group identify with a collective unit, a
community, rather than conceive themselves to be independent, isolated
individuals. In one sense, of course, moral community always exists. No
person is totally autonomous, and no one really thinks exclusively of
himself as a solitary unit of consciousness. Each person will, to some
extent, identify with some community (or communities), whether this be
with the nuclear family, the extended family, the clan or tribe, a set of
locational, ethnic, racial, or religious cohorts, the trade union, the business firm, the social class, or, finally, with the nation-state. Most persons
will identify simultaneously and with varying degrees of loyalties with
several communities, of varying sizes, types, and sources of valuation.
The set of communities and the value or loyalty weights assigned to the
members of the set will, of course, differ from person to person. I suggest, however, that it is possible to characterize different societies in terms
of the relative importance of *moral community* as an element of social
cohesion among persons within those societies. It is possible to classify
societies as more or less communitarian (collectivistic), as less or more
individualistic.

III. Moral Order

A *moral order* exists when participants in social interaction treat each
other as moral reciprocals, but do so without any sense of shared loyalties
to a group or community. Each person treats other persons with moral
indifference, but at the same time respects their equal freedoms with his
own. Mutual respect, which is an alternative way of stating the relationship here, does not require moral community in any sense of personal
identification with a collectivity or community. Each person thinks about
and acts toward other persons as if they are autonomous individuals,
independently of who they might be in terms of some group or community
classification scheme. In a moral order, it is possible for a person to deal
with other persons who are not members of his own community if both
persons have agreed, explicitly or implicitly, to abide by the behavioral
precepts required for reciprocal trust and confidence.

The emergence of the abstract rules of behavior describing moral order
had the effect of expanding dramatically the range of possible interpersonal dealings. Once rules embodying reciprocal trust came to be established, it was no longer necessary that both parties to a contract identify

themselves with the same moral community of shared values and loyalties. There was no longer any requirement that trading partners claim membership in the same kinship group.[2] Under the rules of a moral order, it is conceptually possible for a genuinely autonomous individual to remain a viable entity, whereas no such existence would be possible in a structure characterized solely by moral community.

I suggest that different societies may be classified in terms of the relative importance of the rules of moral order in describing the observed relationships among the persons within each society. These rules may either supplement the sense of moral community as a source of social cohesion where the latter exists, or these rules may substitute for moral community to the extent of rendering it unnecessary.

IV. Moral Anarchy

Moral anarchy exists in a society (if it can remain a society) when individuals do not consider other persons to be within their moral communities and when they do not accept the minimal requirements for behavior in a moral order. In moral anarchy, each person treats other persons exclusively as means to further his own ends or objectives. He does not consider other persons to be his fellows (brothers) in some community of shared purpose (as would be the case in moral community), or to be deserving of reciprocal mutual respect and trust as autonomous individuals (as would be the case in moral order).

In a real sense, moral anarchy becomes the negation of both moral community and moral order. It is a setting within which persons violate the basic Kantian moral precept that human beings are to be treated only as ends, not as means. It is perhaps more difficult to conceptualize moral anarchy as a general model of human interaction than the two alternative models already discussed. Moral anarchy seems somehow less descriptive of the behavior that we observe around us. For my purposes, however, I want to employ the model in the same way as the others. I suggest that it is possible to classify different societies in terms of the relative significance of moral anarchy in describing the attitudes and behavior of their members, one to another.

V. Implications for Social Stability and
Governability: Moral Anarchy

I shall now employ the three basic models or elements of interaction in order to discuss problems of social viability and, indirectly, problems of governability in a society. It will be useful to take extreme examples in which one of the three models is primarily descriptive rather than some undefined mix among the three. It will also be useful to change the order of discussion from that which was used in defining the three elements. I shall first take up moral anarchy, then moral order, and, finally, moral community.

Consider first, then, a setting in which many persons behave as moral anarchists. In this setting, life for the individual is "poore, nasty, brutish, and short," to employ the colorful language of Thomas Hobbes. Men who neither feel a sense of community with others, nor respect others as individuals in their own right, must be ruled. Individuals will sacrifice their liberties to the coercive sovereign government that can effectively insure order and personal security. But those persons who act on behalf of the sovereign government may themselves also be moral anarchists. There would seem to be no reason to anticipate that persons who secure powers of governance would be less likely to behave as moral anarchists than their fellows; indeed, the opposite conclusion seems the more plausible here. Social stability is purchased by individuals at the price of a coercive state regime. Repressive government may emerge as a necessary condition in a society with many moral anarchists.

VI. Implications for Social Stability and Governability: Moral Order

In sharp contrast with the setting discussed above, now consider a setting where many persons adhere to the precepts and behavioral rules of a moral order. Each individual treats other persons as deserving of mutual respect and tolerance, even though there exists no necessary sense of belonging to a community or collectivity of shared values and loyalties. In this setting, individuals may be secure in their persons and property, social stability may exist, and the needs for governance may be minimized. Correspondingly, the liberties of individuals are maximized.

In the extreme case where, literally, all persons behave in accordance with the rules of moral order, there would be no need for government at all. "Orderly anarchy" would be produced by the universalized adherence to rules of mutual respect among persons. In a more plausibly realistic setting, where most, but not necessarily all, persons are expected to follow the precepts of moral order, government as such may be restricted to a minimal, night-watchman, or protective-state role.[3] The government need only protect personal and property rights and enforce contracts among persons. In more general terms, the government may be limited to enforcing the laws. It need not do more. In one sense, there is no need for "governing" as such.

VII. Implications for Social Stability and Governability: Moral Community

I have relegated moral community to third position here because this model is much the more difficult of the three to discuss in terms of the implications for overall social stability and for the needs for governance. The difficulties arise because of the many possible moral communities that may exist within a single society simultaneously, communities that may carry with them quite differing implications for the viability of social order. At one limit, if all persons should identify with the community that is coincident in membership with the inclusive political unit, the nation-state, the implications are relatively straightforward. In such a setting as this, all persons act as if they share the same objectives, as members of the national collectivity, including those persons who act on behalf of the government. Vis-à-vis other nations, this model of society might be a source of nationalistic adventure. Or to put the same point in a different perspective, when the national unit is threatened by external enemies, the sense of national community is more likely to emerge as a real force. Since all persons tend to share the same objectives, governance becomes easy. Persons "obey" the sovereign because they feel themselves to be part of the larger unit; conversely, the sovereign also behaves as persons would have it behave. Persons ruled or rulers do not behave toward each other as separate interacting individuals. They do not really consider themselves to be autonomous units.

At the other limit, there may exist no sense of moral community, no shared values, over the whole membership of the inclusive political unit, the nation-state, while at the same time, all or substantially all persons may express and act upon loyalties to collective units, subnationally classified. Persons may identify with specific communities (ethnic, racial, religious, regional, occupational, employment, class, etc.) while sensing no identification with or loyalty to the national unit. This sort of society will have some of the characteristics of that which contains only moral anarchists, discussed above. The difference here is that the relevant entities are themselves collectives rather than individuals. Persons may, in this society, exhibit sharply divergent behavior patterns as between treatment of members of the relevant community and persons who do not qualify for membership. Social conflict will tend to emerge between the relevant communities or between persons who are members of differing

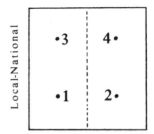

Individualism-Communitarianism
Figure 20-1

communities. Because of the prevalence of such conflicts, there will be a
need for governance, and possibly by a coercive sovereign. Without such
force, the Hobbesian war of each against all may apply to the separate
collectivities rather than to individuals.

In effect, moral community as a concept can satisfactorily be discussed
only in two-dimensional terms. The first dimension involves the general
individualism-communitarianism spectrum, discussed initially. The second dimension involves what we may call the nationalized-localized spectrum, described in the two examples immediately above. A simple, two-
dimensional diagram (Fig. 20-1) will be helpful here.

A society located at point 1 of the diagram is largely individualistic,
with little sense of moral community but with what there is limited to
localized groupings (perhaps family or firm ties). A society located at
point 2 would be, in contrast, largely communitarian, but also with the
loyalties of persons largely limited to localized collectivities, and with
little or no sense of national community. A society at point 3 would remain
largely individualistic, like that at point 1, but in this society there does
exist some sense of national community. At point 4, the society is largely
communitarian, but also, the personal loyalties are largely concentrated
on the national collectivity; there is little sense of localized community.

If we restrict analysis to the more basic concept, moral community,
without reference to the national-local dimension, we can classify societies along the left-right dimension only. Any society classified to fall on
the right side of the matrix would exhibit moral community as a relatively
predominant characteristic.

VIII. Moral Community, Moral Order, and the
       Range and Scope for Governmental Action

In this section, I shall compare the two forces for potential social cohesion, moral community and moral order, in terms of the specific implications for the range and scope for governmental actions. I shall largely

ignore the considerations raised in Section VII concerning the existence of moral communities of subnational memberships. I shall restrict discussion to the sense of moral community that exists among all members of a polity. As noted, in such a setting persons share the same national objectives and need not be "directed," as such, by the state. In a moral order, as noted above, persons further their own objectives within a legal framework that requires no active interference by government.

As we part from the idealizations of these two models, however, and as we allow for a potential threat of moral anarchy in each case, important differences emerge. The necessary conditions required for the maintenance of tolerably effective social stability are considerably more constrained in moral order than in moral community. The difference to be emphasized here lies in that between the individualized basis of any effective moral order and the nonindividualistic or collectivist basis of any effective moral community. In the former, individuals are bound together in adherence to a set of abstract rules or laws which are fundamentally impersonal, and which are grounded in the generalized recognition that all persons are cooperating moral equals. The moral requirements placed on persons in such an order are minimal. The individual need not feel himself to be part of some inclusive collectivity. He need not exhibit feelings of benevolence or altruism toward any other persons, whether these be his neighbors or strangers. On the other hand, if he is expected to abide by the minimal behavioral precepts for such an order, to refrain from lapsing into the role of moral anarchist, he must think that the framework rules of the legal-political order are themselves "fair" in the sense that all persons are effectively required to play by the same rules.

In an effective moral order, a government that discriminates among persons in its treatment, that violates elementary precepts for fairness in dealing with separate individuals, will immediately face resentment and must ultimately expect rebellion. This predicted reaction follows from the very autonomy of individuals; each person remains a person and, as such, can claim entitlement to uniform treatment by those who administer the law. There exists no overriding "community interest" within which individual interests are subsumed.

This setting may be contrasted with one properly described as moral community coincident in membership with the national political unit. Here government may discriminate among persons without necessarily generating negative feedbacks in citizen discontent, provided only that the discrimination is justified, explained, or legitimized in terms of the wider interest of the inclusive national community, an interest that exists by definition of the community, as such, and which is, also by definition, shared by everyone. Since the individual person in such a setting thinks of himself as a member of this community rather than as an individual, he will more readily acquiesce in what would seem overtly unfair treatment under a moral order. In the setting best described as moral community, therefore, the whole set of issues involving "justice" or "fairness" in governmental dealings with separate persons does not arise with nearly the same degree of intensity as it would in a moral order. It follows that government in a society described by national moral community will possess a wider range of options in taking actions than would government operating within a comparable moral order.

The range and scope for governmental action is more limited in a society that locates its source of social cohesion largely in moral order rather than moral community. At the same time, however, such a society (one based on moral order) can allow for greater flexibility and change in the attitudes and behavior of its individual members. As noted, in an effective moral order individuals need not share common purposes; they need only respect each other as individuals. From this it follows that individual attitudes and behavior may be widely varying, and may accordingly change within wide limits, still within the minimal requirement for productive interpersonal interchanges. In a very meaningful sense, individuals are free to select their own private purposes in this setting, a freedom that is necessarily absent in moral community.

The range and scope for governmental action is more extensive in a society that locates its sources of social cohesion in moral community rather than in adherence to the rules of moral order. On the other hand, the society largely held together by moral community is necessarily more vulnerable to shifts in the attitudes and the behavior patterns that might reflect individual departures from the shared purposes of the community. Persons are tied, one to another, by their common identification with the collective, with their shared sense of nationhood, race, class, or ideology. The loss of this identification may involve an unavoidable plunge into moral anarchy. Persons are not free to "do their own thing," within limits, as they might be in a society organized on the principles of moral order, principles that are mutually acknowledged to generate general benefits to all adherents.

IX. The United States in the 1980s

To this point, my discussion has been confined to a generalized analysis of the three abstract models or forms of social interaction: moral community, moral order, and moral anarchy. Any historically observed society will embody elements of each one of these models. Nonetheless, the mix may vary significantly among separate societies, and these differences may be important. In the next two sections, I shall apply the analysis to real-world societies. In this section, I shall discuss the United States in the 1980s in terms of the three models of interaction. In Section X, I shall briefly discuss modern Japan for purposes of comparison and contrast with the United States.

In the United States of the 1980s there is little moral community that extends to the limits of the inclusive national unit, the nation-state, as such, and which embodies the central instrument of the polity, the federal government in all of its arms and agencies. There is relatively little sense of shared purpose among the 225 million of persons in the nation. Individuals tend, instead, to relate to and to identify with communities larger than themselves and their immediate families, but these communities tend to be of subnational sizes of membership, both geographically and numerically. The central government, therefore, is unable to call upon or to exploit a strong sense of genuine "national interest" or "national purpose," although, of course, such an "interest" might be called into being in the face of a demonstrated and well-understood external threat. Further, and importantly, those persons who themselves serve as "governors" possess little sense of "national interest," and they are not seen to possess such interest by those who are "governed." Those persons in positions of political power, like their cohorts who are outside governmental office, identify with various subnational groupings if, indeed, they adhere to moral community at all in any relevant way.

The United States, as a single society, does not depend primarily or critically on the presence of national moral community among its citizens. By historical tradition, the society has been made viable because its citizens have adhered behaviorally to the precepts of a moral order. There has existed a tradition of respect for adherence to the rule of law, for general rules, for promise keeping, for honesty in trading even of the most complex types. Voluntary adherence to the rules and regulations laid down by government remains widespread, including the voluntary payment of income taxes. With relatively few exceptions, government has not needed to become repressive.

For several decades, however, our moral order has been in the process of erosion. Larger and larger numbers of persons seem to become moral anarchists; they seem to be losing a sense of mutual respect one for another along with any feeling of obligation to abide by generalizable rules and codes of conduct. To the extent that such erosion continues and/ or accelerates, the internal social stability of the United States must deteriorate. If confronted with this apparent breakdown in the internal cohesion of the social structure, more and more persons who are not themselves moral anarchists will turn to the arms and agencies of government for more direct protection than seems to be currently provided. The problem is explicitly exemplified in observed increases in criminal activity, which must, after some time lag, result in an increase in governmental coercion on all persons, the lawful and the unlawful alike. The voluntary limits on behavior that have worked in the past, but which now seem to fail, must be replaced by governmentally imposed restrictions. Government necessarily will move toward repression in the society as moral anarchy becomes more and more descriptive of the relationships among persons.

Government itself is partially responsible for the erosion of the traditional moral order in America. As the national government sought to take on a more comprehensive role in this century, and a role that is necessarily coincident with the presence or presumed presence of some "national interest," it has been unable to find moral support in the communitarian sense discussed above. Those who have promoted the extension of government's role under the folly that some national interest exists have, perhaps unwittingly, aided in the breakdown of effective moral order. As laws and regulations have multiplied, competing group interests have been promoted. And persons selected for governmental office have exploited their positions to advance their own private interests under the guise of nonexistent "national purpose." Observing this, citizens have become more disillusioned with governmental processes, and are more and more attracted to assume roles as moral anarchists. Confronted with a government that imposes rules that seem to command little or no respect, individuals quite naturally come to question other long-standing rules that have traditionally solicited voluntary adherence. Restoration of moral order, or even a stop to the erosion process, requires a rollback of governmental intrusions into the lives of citizens, while at the same time, the growth in moral anarchy suggests, for the reasons noted above, an expanded governmental role in maintaining social stability.

Somewhat paradoxically, as our traditional moral order loses its ability to insure social stability, the United States becomes increasingly ungovernable even while the share of resources commanded politically continues to increase and as governmental interferences with the lives of ordinary citizens expand.

X. Japan: Comparison and Contrast

I shall now discuss modern Japanese society for purposes of drawing comparisons and contrasts with the United States. I do this not because I claim any expert knowledge of Japan and its people, but because my initial reflections on the subject matter of this lecture were prompted by an assignment to examine the "governability" of the Japanese.

There is widespread agreement, both among modern Japanese them-selves and among external observers, that there is a relatively strong sense of identification of persons with moral communities beyond themselves, or, in terms of my three models, that Japan is clearly less individualistic and more communitarian than the United States. Disputes may arise con-cerning the relative importance of national and localized moral commu-nities in modern Japan. To a degree, of course, the communitarian sense is limited to subnational groups, and notably to the employing firms. But nonetheless, for many reasons, it remains evident that there does also exist a relevant national moral community. The Japanese, as Japanese, share a set of values that affects their behavior as individuals. There is genuine meaning in the term "Japan, Incorporated."

As I have noted, this relationship between the individual and his fellow citizens in the inclusive national community allows the Japanese govern-ment greater freedom in the formulation and administration of laws and regulations than would be the case in a society more critically dependent on moral order. However, and also for the reasons discussed above, the continuing stability of the society may be dependent on the maintenance of the shared loyalties that now exist. From this it seems to follow that Japan may possibly be more vulnerable to shifts in attitudes and behavior patterns on the part of individuals and groups who somehow lose their identification with the nation. If such identification should be lost, such individuals may lapse directly into roles of moral anarchists.

If this scenario should unfold, there might exist no apparent means through which Japan could recapture its sense of national moral commu-nity short of possible international adventure. If my diagnosis is at all suggestive here, the question that emerges is whether or not a nation like Japan, faced with a possible erosion in its shared sense of moral commu-nity, could adopt essentially Western notions of moral order before moral anarchy assumes predominant importance and generates a breakdown in social structure. Can the Japanese citizen, circa the year 2000 or 2050, who may have lost his identity with the nation as a community, as an entity that commands his loyalty and respect, can he come to understand, appreciate, and live by the behavioral precepts of moral order, precepts that require him to grant fellow citizens mutual respect as moral equiva-lents and which give him criteria for evaluating governmental rules in some personal and noncommunitarian way? Can Japanese governments, in their own right, keep within the limits of power that will allow a functioning moral order to evolve, and further, can Japanese governments hold this stance as Western nations themselves are observed to sink fur-ther into the collectively dominated moral anarchy that now seems their fate?

XI. Prospects for Constructive Reform

In his recent writings, F. A. Hayek has stressed that modern man's behavioral instincts are those that characterize what I have here called moral community and which evolved over the ages in essentially tribal settings. He suggests that Western man very slowly evolved patterns of adherence to abstract rules that he does not understand, the rules of moral order, and which really run counter to his instinctual proclivities.[4] Hayek's response to the first question posed for the Japanese society above would, presumably, be negative. The behavioral rules of effective moral order cannot be "laid on"; cultural evolution cannot be directed. I am somewhat less evolutionist and more constructivist than Professor Hayek, but my concern here is not primarily with what the Japanese society may face in future decades. My concern is with the prospects for constructive reform in the social order of the United States, and I should stress that reform need not depend exclusively on changes in rules for behavior.

I have suggested that those who have promoted the extension of Western national governments have done so in their failure to recognize that the moral order, described by voluntary adherence to abstract rules of behavior, carries implications for the reach of governance. Accordingly, these governments have been allowed to grow far beyond the limits that might sustain and reinforce effective moral order, while at the same time, they have failed to generate effective moral community as a replacement force that might, in turn, legitimate such extended governance. Indeed, the moral anarchists among us have used the instruments of governance to subvert both moral community and moral order as necessary to advance their own ends.

Even in the 1980s, however, relatively few Americans are moral anarchists; most Americans continue to treat their fellows with mutual respect and abide by the rules of moral order. Most Americans also maintain a limited sense of moral community, a sense that could be maximally exploited with appropriate devolution and decentralization of governmental authority. Constructive reform is possible, provided that the institutions of social order are so modified as to make them consistent with the *empirical realities* of modern man as he is, rather than man as the naive reformers of decades past have hoped he might become.

Institutional and constitutional reforms are not equivalent to behavioral reforms, and they need not depend critically on changing "man's nature." In economists' terminology, institutional-constitutional change operates upon the constraints within which persons maximize their own utilities; such change does not require that there be major shifts in the utility functions themselves.

Notes

1. For earlier works that provide some indication of the development of the ideas presented in this lecture, see James M. Buchanan, *The Limits of Liberty* (Chicago: University of Chicago Press, 1975); "Markets, States, and the Extent of Morals," *American Economic Review,* 68 (May, 1978), pp. 364–68; "The Limits of Moral Community," *Ethics and Animals,* eds. Harlan Miller and W. Williams (Clifton, N.J.: Humana, 1983); "A Governable Country," *Japan Speaks 1981,* (Osaka, Japan: Suntory Foundation, 1981), vol. 3, pp. 1–12.

2. F. A. Hayek, particularly in his most recent writings, has stressed the emergence of these abstract rules of behavior through some process of cultural evolution: rules that man does not and cannot understand, and which run counter to those instinctual bases of behavior which find their sources in the primitive sense of moral community. See F. A. Hayek, *Law, Legislation, and Liberty,* vol. 3, *The Political Order of a Free People* (Chicago: University of Chicago Press, 1979), especially "Epilogue," pp. 153–76.

3. The term "minimal state" is used by Robert Nozick in *Anarchy, State, and Utopia* (New York: Basic Books, 1974). I used the term "protective state" in *The Limits of Liberty,* op. cit. The nineteenth-century writers often used the term, "night-watchman state."

4. See Hayek, op. cit.

21.

The Constitution of Economic Policy

I. Introduction

> The science of public finance should always keep . . . political conditions
> clearly in mind. Instead of expecting guidance from a doctrine of taxation
> that is based on the political philosophy of bygone ages, it should instead
> endeavor to unlock the mysteries of the spirit of progress and development.[1]

On this of all occasions I should be remiss if I failed to acknowledge
the influence of that great Swede, Knut Wicksell, on my own work, an
influence without which I should not be at this podium. Many of my
contributions, and especially those in political economy and fiscal theory,
might be described as varied reiterations, elaborations, and extensions of
Wicksellian themes; this lecture is no exception.

One of the most exciting intellectual moments of my career was my
1948 discovery of Knut Wicksell's unknown and untranslated dissertation,
Finanztheoretische Untersuchungen, buried in the dusty stacks of Chicago's old Harper Library. Only the immediate postdissertation leisure of
an academic novice allowed for the browsing that produced my own
dramatic example of learning by serendipity. Wicksell's new principle of
justice in taxation gave me a tremendous surge of self-confidence. Wicksell, who was an established figure in the history of economic ideas,
challenged the orthodoxy of public finance theory along lines that were
congenial with my own developing stream of critical consciousness. From
that moment in Chicago, I took on the determination to make Wicksell's
contribution known to a wider audience, and I commenced immediately a
translation effort that took some time, and considerable help from Eliza-
beth Henderson, before final publication.[2]

Stripped to its essentials, Wicksell's message was clear, elementary, and
self-evident. Economists should cease proffering policy advice as if they
were employed by a benevolent despot, and they should look to the structure within which political decisions are made. Armed with Wicksell, I,
too, could dare to challenge the still-dominant orthodoxy in public finance
and welfare economics. In a preliminary paper, I called upon my fellow

economists to postulate some model of the state, of politics, before proceeding to analyze the effects of alternative policy measures. I urged
economists to look at the "constitution of economic policy," to examine
the rules, the constraints within which political agents act. Like Wicksell,
my purpose was ultimately normative rather than antiseptically scientific.
I sought to make economic sense out of the relationship between the
individual and the state before proceeding to advance policy nostrums.

Wicksell deserves the designation as the most important precursor of
modern public-choice theory because we find, in his 1896 dissertation,
all three of the constitutive elements that provide the foundations of this
theory: methodological individualism, *homo economicus*, and politics-as-
exchange. I shall discuss these elements of analytical structure in the
sections that follow. In Section V, I integrate these elements in a theory of
economic policy. This theory is consistent with, builds upon, and systematically extends the traditionally accepted principles of Western liberal
societies. The implied approach to institutional-constitutional reform continues, however, to be stubbornly resisted almost a century after Wicksell's seminal efforts. The central theme of the individual's relation to the
state, is, of course, an issue that is the central subject matter of political
philosophy. Any effort by economists to shed light on this relationship
must be placed within this more comprehensive realm of discourse.

II. Methodological Individualism

> If utility is zero for each individual member of the community, the total
> utility for the community cannot be other than zero.[3]

The economist rarely examines the presuppositions of the models with
which he works. The economist simply commences with individuals as
evaluating, choosing, and acting units. This starting point for analysis
necessarily draws attention to examination of the choice or decision environment for the individuals who must make selections from among the
alternatives. Regardless of the possible complexity of the processes or
institutional structures from which outcomes emerge, the economist
focuses on individual choices. In application to market or private-sector
interactions, this procedure is seldom challenged. Individuals, as buyers
and sellers of ordinary (legally tradable) goods and services are presumed
able to choose in accordance with their own preferences, whatever these
may be, and the economist does not feel himself obliged to inquire deeply
into the content of these preferences (the arguments in individuals' utility
functions). Individuals themselves are the sources of evaluation, and the
economist's task is to offer an explanation-understanding of the process

through which these unexamined preferences are ultimately translated into a complex outcome pattern.

The eighteenth century discovery that, in an institutional framework that facilitates voluntary exchanges among individuals, this process generates results that might be evaluated positively, produced "economics," as an independent academic discipline or science. The relationship between the positively valued results of market processes and the institutional characteristics of these processes themselves emerged as a source of ambiguity when "the market" came to be interpreted functionally, as if something called "the economy" existed for the purpose of value maximization. Efficiency in the allocation of resources came to be defined independently of the processes through which individual choices are exercised.

Given this subtle shift toward a teleological interpretation of the economic process, it is not surprising that politics, or governmental process, was similarly interpreted. Furthermore, a teleological interpretation of politics had been, for centuries, the dominating thrust of political theory and political philosophy. The interpretations of "the economy" and "the polity" seemed, therefore, to be mutually compatible in the absence of inquiry into the fundamental difference in the point of evaluation. There was a failure to recognize that individuals who choose and act in the market generate outcomes that, under the specified constraints, can be judged to be value-maximizing for participating individuals, *without* the necessity of introducing an external evaluative criterion. The nature of the process itself insures that individual values are maximized. This "value maximization" perspective cannot be extended from the market to politics since the latter does not directly embody the incentive-compatible structure of the former. There is no political counterpart to Adam Smith's invisible hand. It is not, therefore, surprising that the attempt by Wicksell and other continental European scholars to extend economic theory to the operation of the public sector remained undeveloped for so many years.

An economic theory that remains essentially individualistic need not have become trapped in such a methodological straitjacket. If the maximization exercise is restricted to explanation-understanding of the individual who makes choices, and without extension to the economy as an aggregation, there is no difficulty at all in analyzing individual choice behavior under differing institutional settings and in predicting how these varying settings will influence the outcomes of the interaction processes. The individual who chooses between apples and oranges remains the same person who chooses between the levers marked "Candidate A" and "Candidate B" in the polling booth. Clearly, the differing institutional structures may, themselves, affect choice behavior. Much of modern public choice theory explains these relationships. But my point here is the more basic one to the effect that the choice behavior of the individual is equally subject to the application of analysis in all choice environments. Comparative analysis should allow for predictions of possible differences in the characteristics of the results that emerge from market and political structures of interaction. These predictions, as well as the analysis from which they are generated, are totally devoid of normative content.

III. *Homo Economicus*

> . . . neither the executive nor the legislative body, and even less the deciding majority in the latter, are in reality . . . what the ruling theory tells us they should be. They are not pure organs of the community with no thought other than to promote the common weal.
>   . . . members of the representative body are, in the overwhelming majority of cases, precisely as interested in the general welfare as are their constituents, neither more nor less.[4]

This analysis can yield a limited set of potentially falsifiable hypotheses without prior specification of the arguments in individual utility functions. If, however, predictions are sought concerning the effects of shifts in constraints on choice behavior, some identification and signing of these arguments must be made. With this step, more extensive falsifiable propositions may be advanced. For example, if both apples and oranges are positively valued "goods," then, if the price of apples falls relative to that of oranges, more apples will be purchased relative to oranges; if income is a positively valued "good," and, then, if the marginal rate of tax on income source A increases relative to that on income source B, more effort at earning income will be shifted to source B; if charitable giving is a positively valued "good," then, if charitable gifts are made tax-deductible, more giving will be predicted to occur; if pecuniary rents are positively valued, then, if a political agent's discretionary power to distribute rents increases, individuals hoping to secure these rents will invest more resources in attempts to influence the agent's decisions. Note that the identification and signing of the arguments in the utility functions takes us a considerable way toward operationalization without prior specification of the relative weights of the separate arguments. There is no need to assign net wealth or net income a dominating motivational influence on behavior in order to produce a fully operational economic theory of choice behavior, in market or political interaction.

In any extension of the model of individual rational behavior to politics, this difference between the identification and signing of arguments on the one hand and the weighting of these arguments on the other deserves further attention. Many critics of the "economic theory of politics" base their criticisms on the presumption that such theory necessarily embodies the hypothesis of net wealth maximization, an hypothesis that they observe to be falsified in many situations. Overly zealous users of this theory may have sometimes offered grounds for such misinterpretation on the part of critics. The minimal critical assumption for the explanatory power of the economic theory of politics is only that identifiable economic self-interest (e.g., net wealth, income, social position) is a positively valued "good" to the individual who chooses. This assumption does not place economic interest in a dominating position and it surely does not imply imputing evil or malicious motives to political actors; in this respect the theory remains on all fours with the motivational structure of the standard economic theory of market behavior. The differences in the predicted results stemming from market and political interaction stem from differences in the structures of these two institutional settings rather than from any switch in the motives of persons as they move between institutional roles.

IV. Politics As Exchange

It would seem to be a blatant injustice if someone should be forced to contribute toward the costs of some activity which does not further his interests or may even be diametrically opposed to them.[5]

Individuals choose, and as they do so, identifiable economic interest is one of the "goods" that they value positively, whether behavior takes place in markets or in politics. But markets are institutions of *exchange*; persons enter markets to exchange one thing for another. They do not enter markets to further some supraexchange or supraindividualistic result. Markets are not motivationally functional; there is no conscious sense on the part of individual choosers that some preferred aggregate outcome, some overall "allocation" or "distribution," will emerge from the process.

The extension of this exchange conceptualization to politics counters the classical prejudice that persons participate in politics through some common search for the good, the true, and the beautiful, with these ideals being defined independently of the values of the participants as these might or might not be expressed by behavior. Politics, in this vision of political philosophy, is instrumental to the furtherance of these larger goals.

Wicksell, who is followed in this respect by modern public-choice theorists, would have none of this. The relevant difference between markets and politics does not lie in the kinds of values/interests that persons pursue, but in the conditions under which they pursue their various interests. Politics is a structure of complex exchange among individuals, a structure within which persons seek to secure collectively their own privately defined objectives that cannot be efficiently secured through simple market exchanges. In the absence of individual interest, there is no interest. In the market, individuals exchange apples for oranges; in politics, individuals exchange agreed-on shares in contributions toward the costs of that which is commonly desired, from the services of the local fire station to that of the judge.

This ultimately voluntary basis for political agreement also counters the emphasis on politics as power that characterizes much modern analysis. The observed presence of coercive elements in the activity of the state seems difficult to reconcile with the model of voluntary exchange among individuals. We may, however, ask: Coercion to what purpose? Why must individuals subject themselves to the coercion inherent in collective action? The answer is evident. Individuals acquiesce in the coercion of the state, of politics, only if the ultimate constitutional "exchange" furthers their interests. Without some model of exchange, no coercion of the individual by the state is consistent with the individualistic value norm upon which a liberal social order is grounded.

V. The Constitution of Economic Policy

> . . . whether the benefits of the proposed activity to the individual citizens would be greater than its cost to them, no one can judge this better than the individuals themselves.[6]

The exchange conceptualization of politics is important in the derivation of a normative theory of economic policy. Improvement in the workings of politics is measured in terms of the satisfaction of that which is desired by individuals, whatever this may be, rather than in terms of moving closer to some externally defined, supraindividualistic ideal. That which is desired by individuals may, of course, be common for many persons, and, indeed, the difference between market exchange and political exchange lies in the sharing of objectives in the latter. The idealized agreement on the objectives of politics does not, however, allow for any supersession of individual evaluation. Agreement itself emerges, again conceptually, from the revealed choice behavior of individuals. Commonly shared agreement must be carefully distinguished from any external definition or description of that "good" upon which persons "should agree."

The restrictive implications for a normative theory of economic policy are severe. There is no criterion through which policy may be directly evaluated. An indirect evaluation may be based on some measure of the degree to which the political process facilitates the translation of expressed individual preferences into observed political outcomes. The focus of evaluative attention becomes the process itself, as contrasted with end-state or outcome patterns. "Improvement" must, therefore, be sought in reforms in process, in institutional change that will allow the operation of politics to mirror more accurately that set of results that are preferred by those who participate. One way of stating the difference between the Wicksellian approach and that which is still orthodoxy in normative economics is to say that the *constitution* of policy rather than policy itself becomes the relevant object for reform. A simple game analogy illustrates the difference here. The Wicksellian approach concentrates on reform in the rules, which may be in the potential interest of *all* players, as opposed to improvement in strategies of play for particular players within defined or existing rules.

In the standard theory of choice in markets, there is little or no concern with the constitution of the choice environment. We simply presume that the individual is able to implement his preferences; if he wants to purchase an orange, we presume that he can do so. There is no institutional barrier between the revealed expression of preference and direct satisfaction. Breakdown or failure in the market emerges, not in the translation of individual preferences into outcomes, but in the possible presentation of some choosers with alternatives that do not correspond to those faced by others in the exchange nexus. "Efficiency" in market interaction is insured if the participants are faced with the same choice options.

In political exchange, there is no decentralized process that allows "efficiency" to be evaluated deontologically, akin to the evaluation of a market. Individuals cannot, by the nature of the goods that are collectively "purchased" in politics, adjust their own behavior to common terms of trade. The political analogue to decentralized trading among individuals must be that feature common over all exchanges, which is *agreement* among the individuals who participate. The unanimity rule for collective choice is the political analogue to freedom of exchange of partitionable goods in markets.

It is possible, therefore, to evaluate politics independently of results only by ascertaining the degree of correspondence between the rules of reaching decisions and the unique rule that would guarantee "efficiency," that of unanimity or agreement among all participants. If, then, "efficiency" is acknowledged to be the desired criterion, again as interpreted here, normative improvement in process is measured by movement toward the unanimity requirement. It is perhaps useful to note, at this point, that Wicksell's own characterization of his proposals in terms of "justice" rather than "efficiency" suggests the precise correspondence of these two norms in the context of voluntary exchange.

Politics as observed remains, of course, far from the idealized collective-cooperative exchange that the unanimity rule would implement. The political equivalent to transactions cost makes the pursuit of idealized "efficiency" seem even more out of the bounds of reason than the analogous pursuit in markets. But barriers to realization of the ideal do not imply rejection of the benchmark definition of the ideal itself. Instead, such barriers are themselves incorporated into a generalized "calculus of consent."

Wicksell himself did not go beyond advocacy of reform in legislative decision structures. He proposed a required linking of spending and financing decisions, and he proposed that a quasi-unanimity rule be introduced for noncommitted outlays. Wicksell did not consciously extend his analysis to constitutional choice, to the choice of the rules within which ordinary politics is to be allowed to operate. His suggested reforms were, of course, constitutional, since they were aimed to improve the process of decision making. But his evaluative criterion was restricted to the matching of individual preferences with political outcomes in particularized decisions, rather than over any sequence.

The apparent restrictiveness of the Wicksellian constraint, and especially as compared with the extended activity observed in ordinary politics, was perhaps partially responsible for the continued failure of political economists to recognize his seminal extension of the efficiency norm to the political sector. Such restrictiveness is very substantially reduced, and, in the limit, may be altogether eliminated, when the unanimity criterion is shifted one stage upward, to the level of potential agreement on constitutional rules within which ordinary politics is to be allowed to operate. In this framework, an individual may rationally prefer a rule that will, on particular occasions, operate to produce results that are opposed to his own interests. The individual will do so if he predicts that, on balance over the whole sequence of "plays," his own interests will be more effectively served than by the more restrictive application of the Wicksellian requirement in-period. The in-period Wicksellian criterion remains valid as a measure of the particularized efficiency of the single decision examined. But the in-period violation of the criterion does not imply the inefficiency of the rule so long as the latter is itself selected by a constitutional rule of unanimity.[7]

As noted, the shift of the Wicksellian criterion to the constitutional stage of choice among rules also serves to facilitate agreement, and, in the limiting case, may remove altogether potential conflicts among separate individual and group interests. To the extent that the individual reckons that a constitutional rule will remain applicable over a long sequence of periods, with many in-period choices to be made, he is necessarily placed behind a partial "veil of uncertainty" concerning the effects of any rule on his own predicted interests. Choice among rules will, therefore, tend to be based on generalizable criteria of fairness, making agreement more likely to occur than when separable interests are more easily identifiable.

The political economist who operates from within the Wicksellian research program, as modified, and who seeks to offer normative advice must, of necessity, concentrate on the process or structure within which political decisions are observed to be made. Existing constitutions, or structures of rules, are the subject of critical scrutiny. The conjectural question becomes: Could these rules have emerged from agreement by participants in an authentic constitutional convention? Even here, the normative advice that is possible must be severely circumscribed. There is no external set of norms that provides a basis for criticism. But the political economist may, cautiously, suggest changes in procedures, in rules, that may come to command general assent. Any suggested change must be offered only in the provisional sense, and, importantly, it must be accompanied by a responsible recognition of political reality. Those rules and rules changes worthy of consideration are those that are predicted to be workable within the politics inhabited by ordinary men and women, and not those that are appropriate only for idealized, omniscient, and benevolent beings. Policy options must remain within the realm of the feasible, and the interests of political agents must be recognized as constraints on the possible.

VI. Constitutionalism and Contractarianism

The ultimate goal . . . is equality before the law, greatest possible liberty, and the economic well-being and peaceful cooperation of all people.[8]

As the basic Wicksellian construction is shifted to the choice among rules or constitutions, and as a veil of uncertainty is utilized to facilitate the potential bridging of the difference between identifiable and general interest, the research program in political economy merges into that of contractarian political philosophy, both in its classical and modern variations. In particular, my own approach has affinities with the familiar construction of John Rawls, who utilizes the veil of ignorance along with the fairness criterion to derive principles of justice that emerge from a conceptual contractual agreement at a stage prior to the selection of a political constitution.[9]

Because of his failure to shift his own analytical construction to the level of constitutional choice, Wicksell was confined to evaluation of the political process in generating current allocative decisions. He was unable, as he quite explicitly acknowledged, to evaluate political action involving either prior commitments of the state, for example, the financing of interest on public debt, or fiscally implemented transfers of incomes and wealth among persons and groups. Distributional questions remain outside the Wicksellian evaluative exercise, and because they do so, we locate another source of the long-continued and curious neglect of the fundamental analytical contribution. With the shift to the constitutional stage of politics, however, this constraint is at least partially removed. Behind a sufficiently thick veil of uncertainty and/or ignorance, contractual agreement on rules that allow for some in-period fiscal transfers seems clearly to be possible. The precise features of a constitutionally approved transfer structure cannot, of course, be derived independently because of the restriction of evaluative judgment to the process of constitutional agreement. In this respect, the application is fully analogous to Wicksell's unwillingness to lay down specific norms for tax sharing independently of the process of agreement. *Any* distribution of tax shares generating revenues sufficient to finance the relevant spending project passes Wicksell's test, provided only that it meets with general agreement. Analogously, *any* set of arrangements for implementing fiscal transfers, in-period, meets the constitutional state Wicksellian test, provided only that it commands general agreement.

This basic indeterminacy is disturbing to political economists or philosophers who seek to be able to offer substantive advice, over and beyond the procedural limits suggested. The constructivist urge to assume a role as social engineer, to suggest policy reforms that "should" or "should not" be made, independently of any revelation of individuals' preferences through the political process, has simply proved too strong for many to resist. The scientific integrity dictated by consistent reliance on individualistic values has not been a mark of modern political economy.

The difficulty of maintaining such integrity is accentuated by the failure to distinguish explanatory and justificatory argument, a failure that has described the position of almost all critics of social contract theories of political order. We do not, of course, observe the process of reaching agreement on constitutional rules, and the origins of the rules that are in existence at any particular time and in any particular polity cannot satisfactorily be explained by the contractarian model. The purpose of the contractarian exercise is not explanatory in this sense. It is, by contrast, justificatory in that it offers a basis for normative evaluation. Could the observed rules that constrain the activity of ordinary politics have emerged from agreement in constitutional contract? To the extent that this question can be affirmatively answered we have established a legitimating linkage between the individual and the state. To the extent that the question prompts a negative response, we have a basis for normative criticism of the existing order, and a criterion for advancing proposals for constitutional reform.[10]

It is at this point, and this point only, that the political economist who seeks to remain within the normative constraints imposed by the individualistic canon may enter the ongoing dialogue on constitutional policy. The deficit-financing regimes in modern Western democratic polities offer the most dramatic example. It is almost impossible to construct a contractual calculus in which representatives of separate generations would agree to allow majorities in a single generation to finance currently enjoyed public consumption through the issue of public debt that insures the imposition of utility losses on later generations of taxpayers. The same conclusion applies to the implicit debt obligations that are reflected in many of the intergenerational transfer programs characteristic of the modern welfare state.

The whole contractarian exercise remains empty if the critical dependence of politically generated results upon the rules that constrain political action is denied. If end states are invariant over shifts in constitutional structure, there is no role for constitutional political economy. On the other hand, if institutions do, indeed, matter, the role is well-defined. Positively, this role involves analysis of the working properties of alternative sets of constraining rules. In a game theoretic analogy, this analysis is the search for solutions of games, as the latter are defined by sets of rules. Normatively, the task for the constitutional political economist is to assist individuals, as citizens who ultimately control their own social order, in their continuing search for those rules of the political game that will best serve their purposes, whatever these might be.

In 1987, the United States celebrates the bicentennial anniversary of the constitutional convention that provided the basic rules for the American political order. This convention was one of the very few historical examples in which political rules were deliberately chosen. The vision of politics that informed the thinking of James Madison was not dissimilar, in its essentials, from that which informed Knut Wicksell's less comprehensive, but more focused, analysis of taxation and spending. Both rejected any organic conception of the state as superior in wisdom to the individuals who are its members. Both sought to bring all available scientific analysis to bear in helping to resolve the continuing question of social order: How can we live together in peace, prosperity, and harmony, while retaining our liberties as autonomous individuals who can, and must, create our own values?

Notes

I am indebted to my colleagues Robert Tollison and Viktor Vanberg for helpful comments.

1. Knut Wicksell, *Finanztheoretische Untersuchungen* (Jena: Gustav Fischer, 1896), p. 87.

2. The major essay, by Knut Wicksell, "A New Principle of Just Taxation," is included in *Classics in the Theory of Public Finance*, eds. R. A. Musgrave and A. T. Peacock (London: Macmillan, 1958), pp. 72–118.

3. Wicksell, *Finanztheoretische Untersuchungen,* op. cit., p. 77.

4. Ibid., pp. 86, 87.

5. Ibid., p. 89.

6. Ibid., p. 79.

7. In my own retrospective interpretation, the shift of the Wicksellian construction to the constitutional stage of choice was the most important contribution in James M. Buchanan and Gordon Tullock, *The Calculus of Consent* (Ann Arbor: University of Michigan Press, 1962).

8. Wicksell, op. cit., p. 88.

9. John Rawls, *A Theory of Justice* (Cambridge: Harvard University Press, 1971).

10. A generalized argument for adopting the constitutionalist- contractarian perspective, in both positive and normative analysis, is developed in James M. Buchanan and Geoffrey Brennan, *The Reason of Rules* (Cambridge: Cambridge University Press, 1985).

Part V.
FISCAL ECONOMICS AS POLITICAL ECONOMY

22.

"La Scienza delle Finanze": The Italian Tradition in Fiscal Theory

I. Introduction

Now that the important early Swedish contributions on monetary and cycle theory have been made available, it may be asserted that the single most important national body of doctrine which remains largely unknown to and unappreciated by English-language economists is the Italian work in fiscal theory. The linguistic barrier has served effectively to prevent the dissemination of the Italian contribution in this area of applied economics, an area which has been an Italian specialty for at least a century. The only book which has been translated is De Viti De Marco, *First Principles of Public Finance*.[1] While this book is perhaps the most outstanding single work, its contribution cannot readily be appreciated by those not familiar with the Italian tradition. This explains the extremely divergent reactions of Henry Simons and F. C. Benham to the book, Simons calling it a "monument to confusion," while Benham was acclaiming it as the best book ever written in public finance.[2]

A whole body of doctrine, extending over a hundred years and including literally hundreds of contributions by scores of scholars, cannot adequately be summarized and critically discussed in a single essay. In spite of this, I shall attempt in this paper to sketch the broad outlines of the Italian tradition, to isolate a few of the important contributions, and to relate these to the present state of fiscal theory.

Procedure

I shall limit my discussion largely to what may properly be called the "classical" Italian tradition in public finance theory. Chronologically, this covers approximately a sixty-year period extending from 1880 to 1940. With the exception of the work of Francesco Ferrara, which is extremely important, although its influence was exerted in an indirect way, I shall not consider precursors of the main figures in Italian thought. I shall not

discuss contemporary works of the post-World War II period except insofar as these may serve to clarify older contributions and controversies.

After a brief survey of the institutional setting of Italian public finance,
I shall first attempt to identify some of the background factors which
appear to have exerted some influence on the main Italian ideas and to
have produced certain general characteristics in Italian thought. There
follows an effort at classifying the Italian works into two broad categories,
a classification which is necessarily somewhat incomplete. The second
half of the paper begins with the discussion of what I consider to be the
important contributions of the Italians. Properly following this, I shall
conclude with a summary comparison of the Italian with the Anglo-Saxon
tradition.

The Institutional Setting

Contrary to the conventional practice in England and the United States,
the study of public finance in Italy is an independent branch of scholarship. It does not comprise a part of the economics curriculum in the
universities; it has a separate curriculum and a separate existence all its
own. Normally it is taught and discussed as the science of finance and
financial law. Political and legal aspects of finance have been considered
integral parts of the discipline, equally important with the economic
aspects.

This status has not been entirely a happy one. The doctrinal independence of public finance has been attacked and defended in a continuing
controversy. One group, represented by the late Benvenuto Griziotti, has
defended the separateness of public finance on the basis of the subject
matter. This position follows the Germanic tradition of *Staatswissen-
schaft*. In this view, finance should be studied in its total setting, which
includes the legal, political, administrative, and economic aspects. These
various disciplines are included insofar as they are relevant to the consideration of problems of financing state services. The approach taken by
this group has something in common with the American institutionalists,
notably with the position of Commons.

The opposing group has tried to emphasize the economic approach to
state fiscal activity. While this attitude admits differentiation in the subject
of study, it holds that the fundamental distinction should be in method.
The importance of the noneconomic aspects of fiscal problems is not
denied; but proponents of this view are willing to allow these to be
considered by noneconomists.

The whole controversy over the independence of finance as a separate
branch of scholarship has contained much that is sterile. The controversy
has, however, served to emphasize certain methodological issues which
have been neglected or glossed over in the English-language tradition.

These will be discussed in some detail at a later point. But perhaps the most important influence of the doctrinal independence itself has been that public finance, as a branch of scholarship, has attracted many of the better scholars. The science of finance has probably been even more widely respected than general economic theory, and the best Italian economists have felt themselves compelled to do some work in the field. With the single exception of Pareto, who was not without major influence, although he was not a direct contributor, all of the outstanding Italian economists have devoted some time to finance theory.

A disadvantage of the doctrinal independence has been that an excessive amount of work has been done in this field relative to others. Although there probably exist external economies to scholarly research in the specific subbranches of economics, surely the Italians have, in many cases, gone beyond the limits of the full exploitation of such economies. But having established chairs in public finance at many institutions, and having a literal "publish or perish" rule for selection and promotion, Italian scholars have been sometimes forced into relatively unproductive work.

II. Background Influences

Ferrara and the Classical Economics

The influence of classical economics upon Italian fiscal thought cannot be separated from that of Francesco Ferrara. The important classical writings were made available to Italian scholars in translation in the 1850s through the famous series, *Biblioteca dell' economista.* Ferrara selected the works to be translated, supervised the translations, and himself wrote lengthy prefaces to the individual selections. In these prefaces, as in his courses of lectures, Ferrara was intensely critical of many aspects of classical thought. On the whole, his criticisms are excellent by modern criteria, and he anticipated many of the neoclassical contributions. He anticipated, and in some respects surpassed, the subjective-value theorists. He was forceful in his emphasis that value theory must be based on individual behavior, his whole construction departing from what he called "the economic action," the author of such action being the individual who feels, thinks, and wants. The classicists were criticized for their attempts to construct an objective theory of value, and Ferrara was perhaps the first economist completely to shed all of the mercantilist trappings in his rejection of economics as the science of wealth. Value was determined by both utility and cost, with exchange value representing a comparison of these two forces. As a single principle, he developed the idea of the cost of reproduction as a measure of value, meaning by this the cost which would have to be incurred *if* the unit in question were to be reproduced. This principle was extended to apply to goods and services which were not physically reproducible by the introduction of the idea that it is the utility produced by the good, not the good itself, which determines value. Ferrara does not appear to have explicitly discussed diminishing marginal utility as such, although its acceptance is clearly present in his work, as Pareto recognized.[3]

The Physiocratic and classical distinction between productive and unproductive labor was all but demolished by Ferrara. In very persuasive fashion, he showed that the particular form of a good is unimportant, and that immaterial goods or services are equally valuable with material goods. He also rejected the Ricardian rent theory on the basis of a surprisingly modern argument. The idea of differential rent is held to be an undesirable and incorrect heritage of the Physiocratic concept of net product. Rent, or net product, is held to accrue to all factors, not to land alone, and rent, as a distributional share, is attributed to the superior productivity of the productive inputs which receive it.

With this general approach to economic theory, Ferrara was able to reach a profoundly different conception of fiscal activity from that reached by the English classical economists or implied in their works. First of all, he recognizes that social or collective action as well as individual action must be based on individual choice. The state is conceived ideally as a natural outgrowth of the division of labor, and the government is considered as a "producer" of such services as justice, defense, etc. In its pure form, the tax is held to be a payment for such state-supplied services which provide positive utility to the individual.[4] The expenditure for these public services may be as productive as that for private goods and services. In this recognition of the tax as a price and of the productivity of public services, the foundation stone for the whole Italian fiscal tradition is laid. The whole of society enjoys the fruits of state services; specific mention is made of schools, port facilities, roads, asylums, and hospitals. It is to the advantage of each citizen to cede a portion of his private goods to the state in exchange for such services.

This broad view of the fiscal process might suggest that Ferrara was less libertarian than the English classicists. Such is, however, not the case. The "economic" conception of fiscal activity was, to Ferrara, an ideal. In the actual state of the world, Ferrara considered that the levy of taxes tended to be oppressive and constituted the "great secret through which tyranny is organized." Although his analysis is not developed in terms of the specific contrast, Ferrara's distinction between the philosophical or "economic" concept of fiscal activity and the historical or "oppressive" concept may also be considered as an early statement of the more refined distinctions which were later to be very important in Italian fiscal thought.[5]

Although recognizing that public services may be productive, Ferrara was intensely critical of the view, which had been expressed by German writers, that merely because tax revenues are transformed into public spending and are returned to the economy, society does not undergo a net loss. He emphasized the necessity for spending the tax proceeds productively, and he constantly referred to the required comparison between utility and cost.[6] The tax is the instrument by which the consumption of one type of good (public) comes to be substituted for another (private). The test of efficiency is always to be found in a comparison of these two consumptions.

Interestingly, Ferrara's influence on the development of Italian fiscal thought appears to have been rather indirect. Until the publication of his lectures in 1934, Italian scholars made little reference to his works. Yet the similarity between the basic conceptual framework developed by Ferrara and the subsequent development in Italy suggests that his ideas were instrumental. The explanation is probably provided in the direct influence which Ferrara exerted on the thinking of the early writers, notably Pantaleoni and, through him, on De Viti De Marco. Thus it came to be that subsequent Italian scholars looked to Pantaleoni and De Viti as the sources of their discipline, only to awaken in the 1930s to find that Ferrara had been the genuine fountainhead of ideas.

Regardless of the means through which they were transmitted, Ferrara's ideas muted the impact of the classical implications at precisely those points where these implications could bear on fiscal theory. In Anglo-Saxon fiscal thought, this sort of influence has been absent. Here is explained, at least in part, several important differences in the two developing bodies of fiscal doctrine.[7] It explains why the Italians have from the beginning recognized the spendings side of the fiscal account as an integral part of fiscal activity, whereas, even today, this has not yet been fully incorporated into the English tradition. As a corollary to this, the greater Anglo-Saxon emphasis on sacrifice theories of taxation is more readily understandable. The concept of net sacrifice as a result of the fiscal process has been almost completely absent from Italian works. The Ferrarian influence also explains why the single tax has had little support in Italy.

The Theory of Utility

While the Ferrarian model was influential in taking some of the rougher edges off classical economics, it was equally important through its positive contribution in preparing the groundwork for a ready acceptance of the subjective-value approach and the theory of marginal utility. And it is only after Ferrara's major work was completed, and also after the subjective-value decade of the 1870s that Italian fiscal theory emerged in its fullest sense. The origins of "classical" Italian theory, represented in the works of Pantaleoni and De Viti De Marco, appeared in 1883 and 1888 respectively. These represent attempts to apply the theory of marginal utility to the activity of the public entity. While this attempt to explain state action in terms of the marginal calculus was but natural to the Italian familiar with Ferrara's works, it was foreign and unnatural to the Englishman or the American imbued with Ricardo's principles, and therefore was never carried out.

Interestingly, Pantaleoni first applied the marginal calculus to the theory of public expenditure rather than the theory of taxation. He tried to construct a theory of public spending analogous to the theory of consumption for the individual, with the decision maker being the average or representative member of the legislative assembly. Public revenues were to be distributed among the various possible employments so as to equalize the marginal yields from equivalent units in the minds of the average legislator.

De Viti was more ambitious. He attempted to show that an "economic" theory of the whole fiscal process could be developed. His fundamental early work, *Il carratere teorico del' economia finanziaria* (1888), was conceived independently of the work of Emil Sax which appeared in Austria one year earlier and it is, in many respects, vastly superior to the Sax effort. The stated purpose of De Viti's monograph is that of extending the principles of theoretical economics to fiscal activity. The extension is accomplished by accepting the state as the subject for study in lieu of the individual. The task of the economist is held to be that of studying the behavior of the state in fulfilling its tasks, not that of determining the ends of state activity. While the motives for state action may be different from those of individual action, the overriding principle remains that of "minimum means," and, on this principle, De Viti tried to erect his theory. Public activity is held to be eminently productive, and it serves to satisfy collective needs. But the production of public services is costly, and there is required a comparison of satisfaction and cost; this comparison is the essence of the financial calculus.

The Theory of General Equilibrium

With the work of Pantaleoni and De Viti De Marco in the 1880s, Italian fiscal theory achieved an independent status. As the tradition developed, however, the emerging Walrasian-Paretian work on general equilibrium was to exert substantial influence. This explanation of the economic process served to reinforce the Ferrarian orientation toward generality in approach and to draw attention away from the study of particular problems. Thus, except for an early work by Pantaleoni, the theory of tax shifting and incidence, which was largely born in the Marshallian tradition of partial equilibrium, is relatively unimportant. The general-equilibrium approach exerted further influence in forcing Italian theorists to recognize both sides of the fiscal account. The influence of general-equilibrium analysis on Italian fiscal thought came through an acceptance by the Italian writers of the Walrasian-Paretian construction and not through any direct contribution on the part of Walras or Pareto. Walras constructed his model in abstraction from the state, and Pareto removed collective action from economics by his claim that completely different principles of choice are applicable.

The Theory of the Ruling Class

The fourth major idea or conception which appears to have affected Italian fiscal theory in a significant way is that of the ruling class. This owes its origin to both Mosca and Pareto. The ruling-class conception of government, which was perhaps born out of the Italian political turmoil, has been formulated in almost complete independence of the Marxist conception, although clearly the two approaches have much in common. The "ruling class" in Italian political thought need not be historically determined by the laws of production; it can be an hereditary class, an intellectual elite, a political party temporarily in power, or the proletariat. It may be permanent or it may be shifting; it may exert its power through autocratic or democratic forms and institutions. This conception is, therefore, broader and more general than the Marxist. The essential characteristic is the denial of the democratic process in the reaching of social or collective decisions. Social decisions are always made by a group smaller than the total citizenry. The Anglo-Saxon idea of universal participation in the processes of social or collective choice, either directly or through representation, does not appear to have dominated Italian thought or even to have been widely accepted.

The ruling-class conception has forced Italian thinkers, even those who do not accept its validity, to devote greater attention to the form of the state. In this respect the conception has proved to be of great value for the development of fiscal theory. It has made Italian fiscal theorists more explicit as regards their political presuppositions. By contrast, in the non-Italian tradition the political assumptions have rarely been stated with the resultant inherent inconsistencies and contradictions. As Wicksell so acutely noted, the implicit assumption has often been that of benevolent despotism.[8]

Scientism

A final influencing factor in Italian fiscal thought has been the insistence that work in this field remain purely "scientific," or, in current methodological terminology, "positivistic." In the Italian context this characteristic of scholarship is synonymous with objectivity or impartiality, and it carries with it no precise operational connotations. The task of the scholar is solely one of observation; only by a rigorous adherence to the role of the detached observer of the social scene can a genuinely experimental science be constructed. This view, expressed most clearly by Pareto in his works on sociology, has been present in most of the Italian fiscal work.

This positivism has been useful in some respects. It has served to eliminate, from the Italian literature, the lengthy normative discussions on fiscal "justice" which have plagued this field of study elsewhere. The net effect of this approach, however, must be judged as negative. No observer of the social scene can remove himself from the observed, and personal and subjective attitudes necessarily color all activity, including the scientific. The Italian scholar, in his attempt to avoid an open admission of this, tended to become enmeshed in excessive generality. And propositions which he presented as explanatory or descriptive turn out, in some cases, to be valid only on the acceptance of his set of values.

By and large, this attempt at positivism has caused Italian fiscal theory to be much further removed from actual policy issues than is the case in either England or the United States. With rare exceptions, the Italians have not been greatly interested in fiscal reforms, or, perhaps better stated, they have tried to conceal what interest they have possessed. This appears to have been unfortunate, because it is precisely from an open and direct interest in reform that many new insights have been, and can be, achieved and new truths attained—truths that will fully stand up to the most severe scientific tests.

Barone and Einaudi, among the important figures, appear to have come closer to escaping this debilitating influence. Both extended the scholar's task beyond that of mere intellectual observation and speculation. But no Italian theorist appears to have approached his task on the basis of an outright and explicitly stated set of personal value judgments. The simple recognition that in the social sciences the observer is necessarily among the observed nowhere shines through.

III. Principal Features

The Basic Dualism

Perhaps the most important single characteristic of Italian fiscal thought is its dualism. From the contrasting models of the "philosophical" and the "oppressive" states of Ferrara, and the first explicit development in the De Viti De Marco models of the "cooperative" and the "monopolistic" states, Italian contributions can be classified on the basis of the nature of the political entity or, more specifically, on the basis of the location of the decision-making power. The first alternative involves the fundamental premise of democratic choice to the effect that *all* members of the social group participate conceptually in the reaching of collective decisions. This alternative may be called the "cooperative," the "democratic," or the "individualistic," and it stems from the contractual conception of the state itself. As applied to fiscal theory, this approach tends to concentrate on the individual-choice processes and to emphasize the basic similarity between individual behavior in choosing public goods and that in choosing private goods. This has sometimes been labeled the "economic" approach because individual decisions on collective or public goods and services are normally conceived as being ruled by the economizing principles of choice. As Borgatta states, the central hypothesis is simply that "the application of income to the payment of taxes is a particular case of the general law of the allocation of income."[9] The voluntary aspects of fiscal action are stressed, and the tax is considered as a price in the broadest philosophical sense. The general productivity of public services is a central feature. Although he develops his theoretical structure in terms of the two contrasting models, De Viti De Marco is essentially the source of this approach, and his cooperative state model is his standard construct.

His central idea is that in the cooperative state the producers and the consumers of public services are identical. Therefore, it is erroneous to conceive the tax as other than a form of price, a "season ticket." Although he recognizes the inherent struggle among individuals concerning the distribution of the common burden, this is viewed as a problem of political choice making. The essence of the fiscal action per se is the marginal equivalence between the two sides of the account, which must hold for the totality if not for the specific individual member of the group. De Viti does not attempt to develop a purely "individualistic" theory in the sense of Wicksell and Lindahl, nor does he appear to have been impressed by the work of Sax and his Italian followers.

Einaudi is the most distinguished follower of De Viti De Marco in this cooperative or democratic tradition, which has not been the dominant one in terms of number of adherents. Fasiani, clearly the most important figure to emerge in the interwar period, followed De Viti De Marco in the sense that he developed his theory in terms of the contrasting models of the cooperative and the monopolistic state. However, while De Viti De Marco's major stress was placed on the cooperative model, Fasiani's was placed in the monopolistic model.

The alternative model of state activity owes its continuing importance to Pareto and stands directly opposed to the "democratic" model. Ferrara and De Viti conceived society as moving progressively from the tyrannical or monopolistic state toward the democratic and cooperative state.

Pareto was successful in shifting completely this evolutionary emphasis. As of any given period of time, a specific group exerts political power and the individual members of the whole group may be classified into two broad categories, the governing and the governed. Fiscal activity is to be explained solely in terms of the behavior of the ruling group. The important figures in this tradition are Puviani, Pareto, Murray, Borgatta, Barone, Fasiani, and Cosciani.

Within this group a further classification may be made. Certain theorists, especially Borgatta, the most direct follower of Pareto, reject any attempt to use economic analysis in the explanation of fiscal activity. To Pareto and to Borgatta state decisions are made by a different sort of calculus, and there is no such thing as a "science of finance" analogous to economic science. The explanation of fiscal activity should be sought instead in the murky science of sociology. This Paretian emphasis led Borgatta to search for a sociopolitical theory of the fiscal process without much success.[10] This sociopolitical approach, which is still accepted by some writers in Italy, leads to the vagueness and indeterminacy which surround such concepts as "countervailing power" which have recently been advanced in other connections in the United States.

Another more important group has tried to construct an economic theory of fiscal activity of the ruling class. This group includes Puviani, Barone (for whom the political assumption is relatively unimportant), Fasiani, and Cosciani. This approach has tended to stress the coercive aspects of fiscal choices, and excellent criticisms of the individualistic approach have been advanced. The individual "versus" the state has been the center of the discussion, and the efforts of the state to conceal its activity through the creation of fiscal illusions has been an important part of the analysis. On the other side, the reactions of individuals, singly or in groups, to the fiscal power of the collectivity (the ruling class) have been emphasized.

Both of the above-mentioned variants of the ruling-class conception remain "individualistic" in terms of decision making. The idea of any *über-individual* or organic decision maker is explicitly denied. The characteristic feature is that decisions are made by a limited group of individuals, which the system of relationships called "the state" has placed in power, perhaps only temporarily. Little influence is attributed to the actual form of the state or the actual process of choice, and in this respect the vision is closely akin to that of the Marxist.

The genuinely organic conception, in the explicit sense in which the interests of the individual are presumably incorporated in the general social will as embodied in the state, was almost wholly absent from the Italian fiscal literature before the 1930s. During this decade it appeared in the work of Masci, P. Ricca-Salerno, and others influenced surely by the dominant Fascist ideology.

Generality

In many respects, "la scienza delle finanze" resembles philosophy more than it does Marshallian economics. The goal of Italian fiscal theorists has been that of providing generalized or philosophical explanations of the fiscal process. Research has been concerned with the "nature of things" rather than with finding operational propositions in the modern scientific sense. Italian scholars have been interested, by and large, in constructing complete, integrated systems, and the criterion for success has been logical consistency rather than usefulness for making predictions, actual or conceptual.

To many of the modern-day Italian specialists, this traditional approach appears sterile, and there is now a tendency to admire and to emulate the Anglo-Saxon problem-solving approach. At the forefront of this reaction was Fubini, who, writing in the 1930s, sharply criticized the overly philosophic emphasis, which he attributed to the excessive influence of Ferrara. He contrasted this with the Ricardian-Marshallian tradition, which he held to be superior.

In contrast to this understandable and natural reaction on the part of modern-day Italian scholars, the philosophical emphasis has a great deal of value for the Anglo-Saxon scholar who has been trained in the Ricardian-Marshallian tradition and who has been substantially influenced, albeit unconsciously in some cases, by pragmatic-institutionalist ideas.

IV. Specific Contributions

General Methodology

Because of the influencing factors and the central characteristics noted, Italian fiscal theory is strongest in precisely those areas where Anglo-Saxon theory is weakest, and vice versa. If the Italians, on occasion, seem to have overlooked the fundamental purpose of fiscal economics, problem solving, the English-language scholars have also failed to recognize that the analysis, and thus the solutions of particular problems, is conditioned by the methodological framework. And it is because the Italians have concentrated on general principles, on internally consistent systems, that their work can be of immense value.

From the outset and with a few notable exceptions, Italian fiscal theory has been developed in general-equilibrium terms. For the Italian, fiscal theory is concerned with the activity of the state, and not primarily with that of the individual as he is affected by the fisc. This is true equally for the "economic" and "noneconomic" approaches. The theory is rarely individualistic in the sense that the individual or private economy is the central subject of the analysis.

The general-equilibrium aspects are more inclusive than a mere superimposition of taxes and expenditures onto a Walrasian model. The Italian model includes the state, and the more important feature has been the tying together of the two sides of the state fiscal account, taxation and expenditure, and the general recognition of the limited usefulness of any one-sided analysis.[11] It is but natural that this feature should stem from the so-called "economic" approach (De Viti De Marco, Einaudi). But somewhat surprisingly it is also accepted by those who specifically reject the economic aspects of fiscal choice (notably Borgatta).[12]

Pantaleoni held that insofar as the tax exceeds that which the individual would freely sacrifice for the public service, the results of taxation were identical to those of brigandage or plunder. De Viti and Einaudi, through the development of their productivity theory of state expenditure, showed that the Pantaleoni view of a tax could be applied only to an individual or group. For the whole community the estimated net benefits must be at least equal to the costs, or the public service would never be performed under the assumption of any sort of rational choice making for the collectivity.

Perhaps some credence may be given to the claims of the semanticists here, for it seems that by an extremely fortunate choice of words, Einaudi did much to overthrow the brigandage conception of the tax. He labeled the assumption which neglects the effects of the expenditure that of the *imposta grandine*. Literally translated, *grandine* means hailstorm. The tax must be considered as something which destroys economic resources or otherwise removes them from the economy once and for all, without further repercussions or effects. By thus laying bare the implications of fiscal analysis limited to the tax side alone, Einaudi was instrumental in forcing Italian theorists to devote specific attention to this aspect of fiscal methodology.

The analysis of the spendings side corollary with that of the tax side was systematically incorporated into the treatment of De Viti De Marco. In his criticism of the traditional doctrine which neglected the effects of spending, De Viti perhaps went too far. For just as the traditional doctrine had unconsciously employed assumptions applicable, if at all, only to partial-equilibrium problems, De Viti conceived the fiscal process only in its most general framework. Here the tax can best be considered as a "price," but he failed to recognize the tremendous difficulties involved in any complete integration of the tax and expenditure sides, and his specific analyses are often oversimplified. De Viti failed to recognize the usefulness of the *imposta grandine* assumption in analyses aimed only at partial-equilibrium results.

It remained for Fasiani and Cosciani to complete the Italian methodological contribution.[13] Fasiani attempted to identify those cases in which the *imposta grandine* assumption could be legitimately employed, correctly stating that the real test was the fruitfulness in allowing accurate predictions to be made, not the correspondence of the assumption to apparent reality.

The most important and relevant of these cases were (1) when the purpose is that of deliberately isolating partial effects with the incompleteness fully acknowledged; and (2) when the tax is small and the proceeds are spread over many items of expenditure as opposed to the concentrated effects of the tax. The second case is, of course, the traditionally assumed setting for partial-equilibrium tax analysis, and many useful results have been obtained from this model. However, this model or framework has also been used to reach general-equilibrium conclusions and this has been the source of much error and confusion. One of the most familiar examples of this is, of course, the so-called "excess burden" analysis which compares the effects of an income tax and an excise tax. Another is the analysis which attempts to trace the influence of general excise taxes on product prices. Only in the postwar period have economists come to recognize the extreme limitations which must be placed on partial-equilibrium analysis if it is to be useful and to attempt to place their analyses in a more general setting. Precisely because of this welcome shift in perspective, the Italian contribution should only now come to exert its proper influence in fiscal theory. If general equilibrium or general welfare conclusions are sought, Fasiani's second case no longer is an appropriate one, for in "macroeconomic" or "income" terms the summed effect of the use of the tax yield in many different expenditure categories will be dimensionally equal to the concentrated effect of the tax levy. Therefore, the expenditure side must be reintroduced. There remains only the first case, that in which no conclusions can be reached at all, except on an acknowledged preliminary basis, conclusions which are, perhaps, better not even published if the ultimate purpose is that of influencing policy decisions in any desirable way. If fiscal theory is to be of any real usefulness in solving problems of political economy, the Italian conception of the fiscal process must perforce be employed.[14]

Public Services as Productive Factors

Many of the more specific contributions which Italian fiscal theory contains are derivative from the general methodological approach. One of these is the recognition of the general productivity of public expenditure, a contribution which has been developed by those who adopt the "economic" conception of fiscal activity, notably by De Viti De Marco and

Einaudi. The essential idea was present in Ferrara but it remained for De Viti to develop it and to use it as a basis for a principle of taxation.

The De Viti vision of public services goes beyond the mere acknowledgment of the usefulness of such services in a general and unspecified sort of way. Many students accept this view, but still conceive public services as *consumption* services, similar in many respects to bread and buttermilk. While such services may or may not be essential for existence, it is difficult to impute to them a share in the income-creating or productive processes of the economy. De Viti looked at public services differently; to him these were productive services, that is, inputs in the whole productive operation of the economic mechanism. Public services are instrumental to the production of final goods and are on an equal basis with labor and capital. Therefore, it becomes conceptually possible to impute to such services an appropriate distributive share.

If the productive contribution of such services is specific to particular types of activity, these services will be priced in the ordinary manner. It is only when the contribution is not differential among the separate activities that the fiscal problem in a real sense arises. The existence of the tax rather than the price indicates that the contribution of the services so financed is general for all income-producing activity. Therefore, the properly imputed share owing to the publicly supplied input is equal for each unit of income produced. As he put it, each unit of real income is born with a tax claim against it. From this it follows that if some units of income should escape this tax claim, other units must necessarily be charged with more than their properly imputed share of government cost.

This argument is more subtle than it at first appears, and it represents perhaps the most complete attempt to develop a purely economic theory of public activity. Its validity depends, however, on the acceptance of either one of two specific assumptions. Either all public services that affect different lines of activity differently must be assumed to be financed by direct pricing arrangements, or, alternatively, the differential effects exerted on each line of activity must be assumed to be mutually canceling when all public services are considered. Neither of these assumptions seems to be empirically supportable. If either one of them should prove to be realistic, however, the De Viti approach might prove acceptable. It could then with some legitimacy be argued that the ideal tax system is one that subtracts an equal share from each unit of income produced, that is, a purely proportional income tax.

Going beyond the distribution of the tax payment, a means is also provided for the determination of the aggregate amount of public activity. The necessary condition is provided in the equality between the marginal productivity of the public services and the marginal productivity of the resources in private employments. Conceptually, the test for this condition is a simple one. Would real income of the community increase, decrease, or remain unchanged by an incrementally small variation in the amount of government activity? Or, to state the criterion more correctly, would the present value of the community's future income stream be increased, decreased, or remain unchanged by an incrementally small change in the amount of government? It should be noted that the evaluation of real income here need not involve any assigning of values to the public services. This problem is eliminated by the device of assuming that these are purely instrumental and that their value shows up in final goods and services.

The grand design of De Viti was thus to apply the marginal-productivity theory of distribution to the fiscal problem. This theory is, however, an explanation of the workings of the private market economy, given the appropriate institutional framework. Resources will tend to be paid in accordance with their marginal productivity. But the extension of this sort of analysis to the fiscal problem introduces another dimension. There is nothing inherent in the workings of the collective choice-making process to cause the marginal-productivity criteria to be met. This is the great failure of the De Viti model. If, in fact, individuals could respond voluntarily in their purchases of public services, some such theory might provide an explanation. Separate individuals might freely choose the margin between the public and the private employment of resources. But what De Viti failed to see is that, despite the objectivity with which real income might conceptually be measured, this is not the appropriate criterion upon which private individuals will choose. Given any assumed value scale, real income for the community may conceptually be measured. But it is the distribution of such income among individuals which is relevant for individual choices. The criterion of social real income can be made objectively meaningful only if the decision-making power is located in some particular individual, group, or class who chooses to accept this criterion. Once this is admitted, the productivity conception loses much of its appeal and merit.[15]

De Viti's theory can only be rescued if it is changed into a normative one. It must be presumed to define a goal toward which collective action should strive. This involves the acceptance of certain value judgments concerning social welfare. It must state that the only correct evaluation of real income is that provided by the currently existing value scale established. Thus the De Viti attempt to apply the marginal-productivity theory of distribution to the fiscal problem goes beyond the mere acceptance of marginal-productivity payments as the ethically justified system of distribution for the private economy. It proposes to extend this norm to the public economy as well.

If the De Viti analysis is considered as explanatory, it is open to objections on analytical grounds; if it is considered as normative it need not be accepted on ethical grounds. In spite of this, the approach is highly useful because of the insights it offers. First of all, it indicates that if specific public services are really in the nature of productive inputs and do affect certain lines of production differentially, the allocation of economic resources will tend to be affected adversely unless such public services are directly priced. The direction as well as the degree of resource distortion will vary in each case, depending upon, among other things, the elasticity of demand for the final product in question. Only within the last few years has this point come to be widely recognized; only recently has it been made clear that if we do not "price" highway services properly we shall get too many resources devoted to automotive transportation; if we do not "price" the services of firemen we shall get too little investment in fire protection devices, etc.

The De Viti conception also offers interesting insights on the whole idea of the neutral fiscal system. In the English-American tradition, strongly influenced by Pigou, the neutral tax system is supposed to require a set of lump-sum taxes. Any other system will have positive announcement effects. It is obvious that this line of thought stems directly from an undue concentration on the tax side to the neglect of the expenditure side. The De Viti approach indicates that the neutral tax structure is dependent upon the distribution of expenditures which is assumed, and that neutrality can be defined only in terms of both sides of the fiscal account.

Einaudi's conception of public activity closely follows that of De Viti. He suggests that the "optimal" tax, defined as that which leads to the maximum production of real income for the community, is that which bears on each particle of real income equally.[16] His treatment is superior to that of De Viti, however, in that his analysis per se does not depend upon his conception of the fiscal process. He explicitly states his principle of equality as a normative statement for the distribution of taxation. Each particle of real income, defined in the flow sense, *should* be equally taxed. His conclusions follow from this premise. Einaudi is almost alone among the Italians in adopting this methodological procedure.

Critique of Sacrifice Theories

As the discussion of the previous section indicates, the Italian approach can perhaps contribute more in a negative or critical sense than it can in any positive way. We find the Italians assuming the front ranks among the critics of the sacrifice "theories" of taxation, normative "theories" or "principles" which have dominated the Anglo-Saxon tradition, and which remain influential enough to justify whole works being written to dispel them.[17] No important Italian theorist has advanced propositions of the Mill, Edgeworth, Cohen-Stuart, Pigou type, which state that the best tax system is achieved when individual sacrifices are equal or equiproportional or when aggregate sacrifice is minimized. The Italian contribution has been rather in excellent critiques of these propositions, for the Italians follow the developments in the English-language publications quite closely. Notable critics are Barone and Einaudi, both of whom wrote on this subject as early as 1912.

Barone, always a clear thinker, was at his best when he demolished all versions of the sacrifice principle.[18] He applied essentially the same reasoning to all versions. The principle was invalid for two reasons. First, the utility of income for Tizio is not comparable with that of Caio. Second, even neglecting the problem of interpersonal comparability, a general pattern of tax distribution could be indicated only if the utility functions for the individuals were found to be of specific forms. By modification of the shapes of these functions, a progressive, proportional, or regressive tax system could be justified. As for the Edgeworth principle of minimum aggregate sacrifice, Barone acknowledged its superiority over the others in its being neat and precise both in its premises and in its conclusions. He showed, however, that this principle also required the comparability of utilities among individuals. But he went further and asked the question: Does the principle really minimize aggregate *social* sacrifice? Redistributive measures may be applied, without apparent harm to the social structure, in the short run, but the results may well be different if longer run considerations are taken into account. Finally Barone concluded: "This doctrine of minimum sacrifice represents one of the major aberrations which may be reached by the arbitrary calculus of pleasure and pain."[19]

Barone concluded further that all theories of taxation based in any way on the marginal utility of income to the individual are inadequate and purely arbitrary. A system of taxation should be clear and predictable, and it should not be made to depend on the particular psyche of the individual, which cannot possibly be examined in any objective way.

The Barone critique is substantially complete, and today, some forty-five years after it was written, it remains superior to all but a handful of contributions in the Anglo-Saxon literature.

Einaudi developed a critical argument on much the same grounds in his course of lectures in 1910–1911, which were not published.[20] Starting with a simplified arithmetical model which shows how the assumption of a diminishing marginal utility of income could lead to an argument for progressive taxation, Einaudi then asks: Is it possible to sum utilities over separate individuals? He answers by stating that the sacrifices are individualized sensations which each person is able to measure and compare, but that it is impossible to add the sensations of Tizio and Caio. The minimum sacrifice principle is, therefore, of no significance.

Italian fiscal thought has never been plagued with the heritage of utilitarianism which has so influenced the development of fiscal theory in England and America. The minimum sacrifice principle, and its more ambiguous cousin, the ability-to-pay principle, is still a part of our fiscal doctrine. Perhaps the latter principle owes its popularity to its very ambiguity; it can be used to criticize, or alternatively to support, almost an infinite number of distributions of the tax load.

Tax Capitalization

One contribution that is peculiarly attributable to Luigi Einaudi and which also stems directly from the productivity conception of public activity is contained in the analysis of tax capitalization. Einaudi was successful in overthrowing the so-called "classical" views. This was accomplished in a series of essays written between 1912 and 1934.[21] The "classical" or orthodox view held that whereas a partial tax was subject to capitalization, a general tax was not due to the effects of the general tax upon the rate of interest. Italian representatives of this theory were Gobbi and Ricci.[22] This view was discussed in America some forty years ago by T. S. Adams and E. R. A. Seligman, and it has recently been advanced again in a series of articles by J. A. Stockfisch.[23]

Einaudi correctly showed that the orthodox view on tax capitalization depended upon the acceptance of the *imposta grandine* assumption concerning the other side of the fiscal account. He showed that, if the government's use of the tax proceeds is taken into account, the effects of the rate of interest may be different in different situations, depending on the relative efficiency of government's use of the revenues.

The dominant theory stated that if the tax covered an important field of resource return—that is, if the tax was of the type usually referred to as "general"—it must exert some effect on the rate of yield on capital resources. If completely general, the tax will reduce the rate of yield on all earning assets. This would appear to affect capital values; but when it is recalled that capital values are determined by both the yield and the rate of interest, the simple conclusion does not follow. For, accepting a productivity theory of interest-rate determination, the capitalization rate is reduced pari passu with the yield. Therefore, capital values remain unchanged.

Einaudi did not accept this theory, and he showed that it contained the standard fiscal fallacy of neglecting the effects of the expenditure of the tax revenues. Presumably the government plans to use its tax revenues. If so, then the effects upon the rate of interest cannot be determined a priori. Einaudi said that if the funds were used as advantageously by the state as they would have been if left in private hands, the real income of the community will not change, and the rate of interest will tend to remain unchanged. Thus, the general tax will tend to be capitalized. Capital values will be reduced.

On the other hand, if the state uses the funds more advantageously than they would have been used in private employments, a premise of the economic theory of state activity, real income of the community would be increased. Additional savings would be forthcoming, and probably the rate of interest would diminish. As a third possibility, the state may use the proceeds of the tax in some manner less efficient than would be the case if the funds were left in private employments. In this case, the community's real income would be diminished. Savings would be reduced, and presumably the rate of interest would be increased. Thus, if the *grandine* assumption is fully accepted, said Einaudi, the conclusions drawn from the orthodox theory are wrong. Griziotti, in an important early article, substantially supported and reinforced the Einaudi thesis.[24]

The details of the Einaudi-Griziotti argument need not be accepted to recognize the value of this contribution, which reduces to an application of the Italian methodological position to the particular problem of tax capitalization. The error in the orthodox position on tax capitalization regarding the impossibility of capitalizing a general tax stems from the failure to extend the analysis to a genuinely general-equilibrium framework. The effects of a generally imposed tax on resource yields is fully acknowledged; and the effect of the level of resource yields on interest-rate determination is also accepted. But the analysis stops one step short of the necessary generality. It must also include the effect of the expenditure of the proceeds on the rate of yield. In its most basic sense, Einaudi is stating that there can be no truly general tax. All income-producing sources cannot be simultaneously hit because government is also an income-producing source. The fiscal process is essentially a two-sided, balance sheet sort of affair.

The Double Taxation of Savings

As mentioned above, Einaudi was one of the few Italian writers who explicitly stated a value premise at the start of his analysis. This was that each particle of income *should* be taxed equally. A significant portion of his work has been devoted to showing that the tax on personal income levied *in the ordinary way* does not meet this criterion. This argument involved an elaboration of the J. S. Mill-Irving Fisher thesis that the inclusion of income saved in the tax base involves double taxation. Therefore, Einaudi concludes, equity requires the exemption of income saved.[25]

A considerable portion of the Einaudi argument is simply arithmetic. He shows, clearly and precisely, that the present value of a specific amount of income devoted to saving (capital formation) becomes less than the present value of an equivalent amount of income devoted to current consumption if the income from the capital created is also to be taxed. The only way in which the present values of such equivalent units of current income can be equated is by the exemption of savings from current taxation. This is the only means by which savings can be prevented from being taxed twice, once originally as income and secondly on its yield.[26]

The close relation between this argument and the Einaudi argument on tax capitalization discussed above should be mentioned. If, in fact, the classical argument on the capitalization of a general tax were acceptable, there would be no double taxation of savings. For, if taxation did not serve to reduce capital values, there would be no difference in the present values of like amounts of income devoted to savings and to consumption.

Although Einaudi has not been without his supporters, notably Fasiani, the double taxation of savings thesis has not been widely accepted in Italy. The primary influence seems to have been that of De Viti De Marco who employed his own version of the productivity of state services to overthrow the Einaudi argument, much to the surprise of Einaudi. In its most general sense the totality of public services is considered by De Viti as a factor entering into the production of all economic goods and services, that is, all real income. Therefore, each portion of income has a tax claim against it. Recognizing this, it is erroneous to impute the whole of a future income stream to a current private investment of capital. The capital is productive due to the aid of the state environment; therefore, a portion of future income is to be attributed to public productive services. It follows that all units of current income must be fully taxed in order to compensate the state for its contribution; but it also follows that all units of future income must also be taxed. In other words, De Viti said that equality in present values is not the proper criterion for tax equity. He said that incomes of each period must be considered separately for tax purposes. Einaudi argued that capital and income are simply different dimensions of the same magnitudes. De Viti implied that this would be true only in an economy without the state. If the state is introduced, capital and income are not merely different in a dimensional sense; income carries with it a tax claim.

Thus taxing income as earned and then the yield on that portion saved does not involve double taxation at all, but is, on the contrary, necessary in order to achieve objective equality in the treatment of all income units.

In this rather ingenious way, De Viti was able to overcome the force of the tautological exactness of the Einaudi position. Although consistently holding an *ertrag* concept of income, he arrived at conclusions similar in many respects to those produced by the use of the *einkommen* concept.[27]

The Italian Contribution to Debt Theory

The theory of public debt has been a central issue in Italian fiscal theory, and the contributions of Italian scholars are sufficiently unique, both in approach and analysis, to warrant a special discussion.[28] The issue, in effect the debate, has been drawn almost exclusively in terms of the basic Ricardian proposition concerning the fundamental equivalence between extraordinary taxes and public loans.

The Ricardian thesis was elaborated and extended by De Viti De Marco.[29] Ricardo argued that the fully rational individual should be indifferent as between paying an extraordinary tax of $2,000 once and for all and paying an annual tax of $100 in perpetuity, assuming an interest rate of 5 percent. He extended this analysis to apply to all individuals, and concluded that if the government borrows $2,000 and commits taxpayers to finance interest payments of $100 annually, the individual living in a future income period would find himself in an identical position with that which he would have enjoyed had the government chosen to impose the extraordinary tax of $2,000. The individual will fully capitalize the future tax payments when the debt is created, and he will write down the capital value of the income-earning assets which he owns by the present value of these future tax payments.

The limited life span of the individual does not affect the analysis. If an individual pays the once-and-for-all extraordinary tax, his heirs will receive capital assets reduced in value by this amount. If, on the other hand, the debt is created, his heirs will receive capital assets yielding a higher gross income. But when the interest charge is deducted, the net income stream is identical with that received in the tax situation.

The analysis would, at first glance, appear to apply only for those individuals possessing patrimony or capital. Its extension to individuals, members of professional or laboring groups, who own no income-earning assets, is not initially evident. But Ricardo, and De Viti, anticipated this and made this extension. The individual who possesses no capital assets which he can sell to raise funds to meet his extraordinary tax obligation must of necessity borrow privately, thereby obligating himself to meet future interest charges on a private debt. In this case, provided only that the interest rates on the public and the private debts are the same, the individual owes an equivalent interest charge in each future period. The effect of the government's replacing the extraordinary tax with the public loan is nothing more than the replacement of a whole set of private loan arrangements with the public loan.[30]

It is at this point that Ricardo as well as De Viti De Marco became confused. Accepting the restrictive assumptions necessary for the analysis to be valid, how does this analysis affect the question as to whether the burden of the debt is shifted forward in time? Both Ricardo and De Viti suggested that the full burden of the debt must rest on individuals living at the time of debt creation.

But how may the "burden" of the debt be defined? In one sense we may define it as the sacrifice of goods and services which could have been consumed if the public expenditure which the debt financed had not been undertaken. It is clear that burden in this sense must rest on individuals living in future generations. They are the individuals who must sacrifice a portion of their income for debt service which they otherwise could have consumed. And the fact that bondholders receive the interest payments on internal debt does not modify this conclusion. If, however, the burden of the debt is defined in this manner, how can individuals living in future time periods be in equivalent positions in the two situations, with the debt and with the extraordinary tax? The answer can only be that individuals living in future time periods *must also bear the real burden of the extraordinary tax under the narrowly restrictive Ricardian-De Vitian assumptions.* It is true that, under these assumptions, the effects of the loan and the extraordinary tax are equivalent, but the correct inference is that the real burden of both is passed on to future time periods, not that this burden is borne in both cases by the individuals living during the initial period.

This rather paradoxical conclusion may be readily seen when the nature of the extraordinary tax required to make the Ricardian proposition hold is examined. Both Ricardo and De Viti assumed that such a tax would either be drawn wholly from privately held capital assets, that is to say, that individuals would sell off capital holdings sufficiently to finance the tax obligation, or they would create private debts (incur capital liabilities) to the full amount of the individual share of the tax. In other words, the extraordinary tax was to be a capital levy *in fact,* regardless of the form which the fiscal authority chooses. If the full amount of the tax is financed from capital, then it becomes clear that the current generation does not suffer any real income reduction. The current generation essentially "draws on capital" in the form of the public project undertaken.

The failure to grasp this point appears to have been fundamental, but the reason for this is not difficult to find. The individuals who are coercively forced to give up resources, whether these are drawn from consumption or investment uses, are normally considered to "bear" the costs of the project financed. Taxes, of any sort, are held to impose a sacrifice on individuals during the period when the tax obligations must be met. This becomes a reasonable, and correct, inference when it is recognized that the ownership of capital assets itself provides some utility to the individual. This being the case, we can say that regardless of the source of the funds paid out in taxes, the individual undergoes a "sacrifice" of utility. It may also be claimed that, if individuals fully discount future tax obligations, the creation of future interest payments on a debt reduces the present value of an expected utility stream. Thus, both the extraordinary tax and the public debt of like amount must be "paid" by individuals during the time of the original transaction.

Thus, we have reached diametrically opposing conclusions; first we stated that the burden of both the extraordinary tax and the public loan rests, under the Ricardian-De Vitian assumptions, exclusively on individuals living in future time periods. This conclusion holds when we consider burden in terms of sacrificed real goods and services. Secondly, we stated that the burden of both the extraordinary tax and the public loan rests, under the full Ricardian-De Vitian assumptions, on the individuals living during the initial period. This conclusion holds when we try to measure sacrifice or burden in terms of the change in present value of an expected or anticipated utility stream, and when we attribute some positive utility to the holding of income-earning assets.

The confusion of these two concepts becomes especially likely when it is recognized that the actual form of any conceivable tax levy, either extraordinary or normal, must differ from the Ricardian model in the direction which adds to the confusion. The Ricardian model overlooks the essential difference between the coercive levy of taxes and the voluntary subscription to public loans. Any coercive imposition of a tax seems certain to reduce both current consumption spending and investment spending. The assumption that only the latter is affected, that is, only private capital formation is reduced (private liability formation increased), is clearly incorrect. If we make the assumption that an individual attempts at any point in time to attain some marginal equalization between the present value of expected future enjoyments of income and the present value of current enjoyments of income, then any tax imposition will cause him to adjust both types of outlay downward. Some portion of any tax must come from current consumption spending, whatever the form that this tax takes. This being the case, some share of the extraordinary tax comes to rest on individuals living in the initial period, even if we consider only the real aspects and ignore the utility aspects altogether. On the other hand, the public loan operates through voluntary subscription. Individuals are likely to reduce current consumption outlay only insofar as the interest rate encourages an increased rate of saving, a questionable relationship. The major share of funds going into the purchase of government securities does come from private capital formation. The generation of individuals currently living sacrifices nothing in utility and little, if anything, in real goods and services in creating the loan. Therefore, in the real sense, there is a differential effect between the extraordinary tax and the public loan.

This differential effect is further widened when it is recognized that the full Ricardian assumptions do not hold on the utility side either. Individuals do not fully discount future tax payments. If the Ricardian-De Vitian reasoning is accepted for all individuals owning capital assets and receiving sufficient income to allow them to borrow privately, there still may be other large groups of individuals. These comprise the bulk of the lower-income or laboring classes. It is impossible to levy extraordinary taxes on these individuals. The extraordinary tax must be levied on the first two groups. But, if the public debt is created, some portion of the annual interest charges may be placed on the third group. The lower-income classes in future time periods may bear a portion of the burden of the public loan whereas they must, by definition, escape fully the burden of the extraordinary tax. This is the objection which Griziotti raised to the De Viti elaboration of the Ricardian thesis.[31]

De Viti De Marco attempted to refute this objection, but he was not really successful. He tried to show that even the complete exemption of all nonpropertied individuals from the extraordinary tax would not affect his conclusions. Here he introduced a long-run competitive model. He reasoned that such exemption would tend to increase the relative attractiveness of the professional nonpropertied occupations. This would, in turn, cause more people to enter these occupations and to turn away from those activities such as management and administration of property. In the long run, the lot of the nonpropertied classes would tend to be identical with that which they would enjoy even if they were taxed for the service of the public loan. As Griziotti suggested, this represents the stretching of the competitive model a bit too far.

Griziotti went further and argued that, even for individuals owning capital assets, discounting of future tax payments does not take place fully. Individuals do not act as if they live forever, and familial lines are not treated as being continuous. There is nothing sacred about maintaining capital intact, and individuals will not necessarily do so. The equivalence hypothesis requires continued abstinence from consuming capital on the part of those holding capital assets after public debt is created. Whereas the extraordinary tax effectively removes from an individual's possibilities the capital sum (once he has paid the tax he can no longer convert at least that portion of his capital into income), the disposition over this capital remains in his power in the public debt case. He may convert this capital into income at any time, without in any way removing the tax obligation on his heirs which is necessitated by the debt service.

Griziotti's claim that the creation of public debts does involve a shifting of the tax burden forward in time was not successful in overcoming the dominance of the De Viti De Marco elaboration of the Ricardian thesis in Italy. The prestige and apparent logical clarity of the De Vitian argument coupled with the changed conditions were successful in reducing the Griziotti influence. There have been isolated supporters of Griziotti,[32] but the De Viti formulation continues to dominate the Italian scene.

Additional elements of the De Viti De Marco conception of public debt may be mentioned since he anticipated much of the "new orthodoxy," which came to be adopted in the United States only after the Keynesian revolution. To anticipate erroneous ideas is, of course, no great contribution, but De Viti's arguments concerning the problem of debt repayment are surprisingly modern in this respect. Included in his discussion of the public debt is what he called the theory of automatic amortization. De Viti used this to demonstrate that debt should never be repaid. De Viti started from his interpretation of the Ricardian argument that public debt merely serves as a substitute for private debts. He assumes a community of three individuals, only one of whom is a capitalist.[33] Now assume that the state requires a sum of 1,200,000 and levies an extraordinary tax, 400,000 on each individual. Individual 1 being the capitalist, Individuals 2 and 3 will find it necessary to borrow from him in order to meet their tax obligations paying an assumed interest rate of 5 percent. As these individuals save in future periods, they may amortize their debt to the capitalist.

Now assume that the government, instead of levying the tax, borrows the 1,200,000 directly from Individual 1. The annual interest charge will be 60,000, and it is assumed to collect 20,000 from each of the three citizens. As in the first case, as Individuals 2 and 3 save they may utilize this savings to purchase the government securities, which are assumed to be marketable, from Individual 1. Their purchase of government securities in this case is identical in effect to their paying off private debts in the other case. Therefore, as the government securities are widely circulated among the population the real debt is more or less automatically amortized. Individuals in purchasing debt instruments acquire an asset to offset their tax liabilities. The weight of the debt is effectively destroyed; hence debt need never be repaid and there need be no fear that a country cannot bear the burden of public debts, however heavy these might appear to be.

This construction is both ingenious and misleading. Let us consider the private borrowing case carefully. Individuals 2 and 3, as they accumulate savings, increase their net worth, and they must also increase some item on the asset side, let us say, cash. When they accumulate sufficient cash to warrant paying off a portion of the private debt, the transaction is represented on their balance sheets as a drawing down of the cash item and a corresponding drawing down of their liability item. *Net worth does not change with debt repayment.*[34]

The construction is identical with the public loan. As individuals accumulate savings these must take some form, cash, savings accounts, etc. Net worth is increased along with whatever asset item the individual chooses to put his savings into. At one point we assume that the individual accumulates sufficient funds to purchase a debt instrument. In so doing, he reduces his cash item and increases another asset item, government securities. He has, in this particular transaction, merely transformed one asset into another. *His net worth is not modified.* Therefore, the weight of having to pay the annual tax upon the debt instrument is precisely as heavy after as before his acquisition of the security.

De Viti De Marco is correct, in the extremes of his model, in saying that this transaction is equivalent to the repayment of private loans. In this sense the public debt is said to be amortized. But his error lies in inferring from this that public debt should not be repaid in fact. This error is based upon a misunderstanding of private loans. Implicit in the De Viti formulation is the idea that the repayment of private loans is necessarily beneficial to the individual. De Viti assumed that such repayment increases private net worth, and thereby reduces the weight or "pressure" of the loan. He failed to see that the new savings which go into private debt repayment have alternative employments. Whether or not private debt repayment reduces "pressure" on the individual economy, depends solely upon the relative rates of return.

The same is true for public debt. Having demonstrated that the transfer of public debt instruments might be similar in some models to private debt repayment, De Viti inferred that this "amortization" reduces the pressure or weight of the public debt. This is not necessarily true at all. The weight of debt remains as it was before, and the purchase of government securities can modify this only insofar as the relative rates of yield on government securities and other assets place the individual in a more preferred position.

This demonstration that the De Viti argument does not show that public debt should not be repaid cannot be applied in reverse. Saying that De Viti De Marco was wrong in making this extension is not to say that public debt *should be repaid*.

Puviani and the Fiscal Illusion

The contributions discussed so far have for the most part been due to the "economic" branch of Italian fiscal theory represented notably by De Viti De Marco and Einaudi. Several of the particular contributions are derivative from the general methodological approach, which recognizes the productivity of public services. The opposing school of thought has also made useful contributions, and, in some respects, these are more original and unique. Therefore, in some criteria, they should assume first rank. By far the most important of these is the idea of the fiscal illusion. It does not come directly from orthodox Italian fiscal theory, for it has scarcely been noted to a greater degree in Italy than elsewhere. The idea, vaguely expressed in the works of many writers, earlier and later, was crystallized in the work of one man, Amilcare Puviani, who wrote around the turn of the century.[35] In his time, his efforts were largely ignored, and it is only after his "rediscovery" by Fasiani that his ideas have now begun to exert some considerable influence on Italian thought.[36] Almost simultaneously, other continental writers are beginning to incorporate essentially similar ideas into their works on fiscal theory, although apparently independently of the ideas of Puviani.[37]

Puviani was, above all else, a political realist. He looked at the world around him and saw no sign of genuine democratic participation in the process of making collective choices. Such choices appeared to him to be made by the ruling or governing class, and he entertained no illusions about these choices being made in accordance with any vague criteria of general interest. The choices were not even conceived to be rationally made for the benefit of the governing class itself. Decisions as such were usually made on pragmatic grounds, and each was reached on the basis of causing the minimum of social friction.

From this approach Puviani constructed his hypothesis. He stated that the actions of the government could best be explained by the hypothesis that the government always acts to hide the burden of taxes from the public and to magnify the benefits of public expenditures. He was careful to state that governments do not actually do this as a deliberate plan. His hypothesis is, like all such similar ones, advanced as a working model, an *as if* sort of theoretical structure. When the governing group is successful in these attempts, fiscal illusions are created which effectively modify human behavior.

How do the separate parts of the modern fiscal structure fit the Puviani hypothesis? We may look first of all at the revenue or tax side. There is first the effort of governments to secure as much revenue as possible through the use of the public domain, that is, income-producing property owned by the state. Insofar as revenue can be raised from this source, private individuals do not consider themselves to undergo a net burden; the opportunity costs are not individualized, and no checks are imposed on government spending. The second and perhaps most obvious means of creating a fiscal illusion lies in the use of indirect taxes rather than direct taxes. The taxpayer-consumer is not able to isolate the public from the private part of his ordinary purchase price, and in this way the real value of his tax burden appears less than it might actually be. A third and equally evident means is provided in the raising of revenues through inflation of the monetary unit. Here the public clearly is hoodwinked, and it has been through the ages.

The remaining devices which governments use to create fiscal illusions are perhaps somewhat more subtle. Puviani said that the individual was not able properly to balance future income against current income. He will, therefore, consider the annual tax in perpetuity to be of less burden to him than the current capitalized value of that tax stream. Governments fully recognize this and, as a result, public loans are always favored for extraordinary expenditures in preference to extraordinary taxes or capital levies.

Governments also recognize that taxes are more accepted by the taxpaying public if the moment of payment is associated with some pleasurable, and preferably unusual, event. Herein lies the explanation of gift taxation, according to Puviani, and, in fact, all taxes on transfers of wealth. The case of taxation of lottery winnings is clear. Similarly, taxes on nonordinary consumption expenditures which are representative of the fulfillment of lifelong desires are explained on this basis. Examples are taxes on the purchase of fine jewels, objects of art, etc.

A device which always works, and which rings loud bells in application to fiscal structures today, is that of introducing taxes under the guise that they are temporary or expedient and then allowing them to become permanent fixtures of the system. Closely allied to this, of course, is the adage that the old tax is the good tax. This is a principle perfectly in accord with the basic Puviani hypothesis. The governing group will clearly consider the old tax as a good one because people have become accustomed to paying it, and, therefore, its payment does not create as much social disturbance as would a newly imposed tax of like amount.

Still another source of exploitation for the government is provided in the social conflict among classes. By playing off one class against the other, the government can secure the ready acceptance of taxes which would otherwise be difficult. As an example, Puviani states that the wealthy classes can be made to accept heavy taxes if the specter of the upheaval of the lower classes is presented to them. Or, if political and social forces should temporarily place one social class in great disfavor with the rest of the population, the government can take this opportunity to impose excessively heavy taxes upon the oppressed class or group.

Yet another Puviani example which strikes hard to the modern reader is the device of governments' posing the awful and dire consequences of the alternative to a proposed tax. Puviani says that the alternative of the destruction of the social system, the breakdown of international relations, etc., will habitually be posed when a new tax bill is proposed. Modern expenditures for national defense and for foreign aid are clear examples of this sort of attempt on the part of governments, even in nominally democratic societies such as our own.

Both the timing and the form of the tax also can foster fiscal illusions. If collected in small amounts and distributed over time, the tax will always appear to be less burdensome than one which is concentrated in time. Similarly, the collection of a given amount under the guise of many small taxes may well seem to exert less fiscal pressure than the collection of a like amount under one consolidated tax bill.

A final form of fiscal illusion involved in the levy of taxes comes about in the uncertainty concerning the actual incidence of the tax. Governments will try not to levy taxes for which the incidence is known. The aim will rather be to introduce as much uncertainty as is possible, thus keeping the individual in the dark concerning the actual amount of tax which he does pay in real terms.

The examples of fiscal illusions discussed above all appear on the revenue side and act so as to make the taxpayer think that he is paying less than he actually does pay toward the cost of government. The fiscal illusion can be equally important, and is equally used, on the expenditure side. Here the procedure is that of making the taxpayer think that he is getting more from public services than he actually does get. Puviani points out that the taxpayers, through their representatives, have always demanded the right to approve taxes independently and in advance of the demand for the right to make appropriations. And, even where the right of making appropriations has been won from executive authorities, the specialization of modern budgets prevents genuine control from being exercised. This provides the executive authority, the government, with an excellent opportunity to use fiscal illusions in the securing of legislative approval. For this reason, the executive tries to keep the budget as complex as is possible,[38] while fostering the belief among the taxpayers that they are participating effectively in the control of spending.

Although it is not stressed by Puviani, perhaps the most effective means through which the modern executive authority can distort public thinking concerning the efficacy of public expenditure lies in the use of generalized categories which are largely meaningless to the voter-taxpayer. In recent years in this country, almost all types of expenditure have been justified by the catchall category "national defense," and active attempts have been made by the bureaucracy to render this budget category sacrosanct. If this goal could, in fact, be achieved, the fiscal illusion would be complete, and the executive authority would have effectively removed all public constraint. So long as the debate can be kept in terms of Air Force "Wings" without consideration of the makeup of such categories, the illusion will remain. The Puviani approach suggests, of course, that the most productive of all legislative activity in this age of budget specialization is precisely that of the much-ridiculed investigation into the "paper clips for the Navy." Only by the potential threat of detailed examination of budgetary items, can the normal executive power be kept within reasonable bounds.

The importance of the Puviani-Fasiani idea of the fiscal illusion does not lie in any of the particular examples from modern fiscal practice which it does seem to explain. Its importance is rather to be found in the fact that such a large proportion of the modern fiscal system can be explained by a hypothesis which is directly contrary either to the De Viti-Einaudi conception of the public economy or to the classical Anglo-Saxon conception of a fiscal structure based on "ability-to-pay." Puviani asked two simple questions: (1) If a completely rational dictator or class desires to exploit the taxpaying public to the greatest possible degree, what sort of fiscal system will result? (2) To what extent do modern fiscal systems approach this model? As the above discussion indicates, the fit is a surprisingly good one, and certainly the Puviani hypothesis must take its place among the important contributions to fiscal theory. As Fasiani pointed out, this hypothesis does not serve as the single explanation, but neither does any other.

Puviani made no attempt to extend his analysis toward the development of normative principles for fiscal activity. He was merely explaining what happens in the autocratic state. If, however, democratic ideals are accepted, Puviani's analysis points the way toward a set of norms for fiscal activity.[39]

The Coercive Element in Fiscal Choice

It is but natural that those theorists who locate effective decision-making power in a directing class or group should also have emphasized the coercive elements which are involved in the fiscal process. In so doing they have been able to provide both an incisive critique of the "economic" or voluntary theories of collective choice and a substantial contribution in their own right. Important figures in this tradition are Conigliani, Montemartini, Barone, Murray, and Cosciani.

These writers attempt to construct an economic theory of public finance along with those like De Viti and Einaudi and opposed to those like Pareto and Borgatta who deny this as a possibility. But while the economic aspects of fiscal choice are central to this approach, the location of the choice-making power is no longer with the individual, who is both producer and consumer of the public services. The fiscal decisions are made by some directing or ruling class which is, by definition or implication, smaller than the total group. Once this is accepted as a premise, it is evident that fiscal decisions can only be carried out through coercion. It would be unreasonable to expect that individuals who do not participate in the choice process should voluntarily accept and comply with such decisions as may be made.

Montemartini is the apparent source of many of the ideas in this tradition, and his ideas are especially interesting.[40] He viewed the state as an enterprise which produces the service of coercion; the political entrepreneurs purchase this service in order to carry out economic aims. Such political entrepreneurs have available to them three means of meeting any given objective. They may, first of all, achieve it by individual action. Secondly, they may form a voluntary and private association and undertake cooperative action. Thirdly, they may ask that the state do it for them. In choosing among these alternatives, this group will be guided by least-cost criteria. If, by purchasing coercion from the state, the group is able to reduce its own cost, it will choose this means. But Montemartini was clear in his emphasis that the service of coercion itself was costly.

His numerical example is perhaps worth repeating. Suppose that we are considering a society of ten individuals with equal incomes of $10 each. Now suppose that eight of these desire that $56 be spent collectively for the provision of a public water supply. The other two desire that water be provided through individual private efforts. If the eight form a voluntary cooperative association, the cost to each will be $7. But if they can secure the service through a community effort which is financed by a general tax, this cost will be reduced to $5.60. From this example, Montemartini indicated that the lower cost criteria may not always be relevant to the choosing of a collective action over a private one. But the example is not yet complete. The cost of imposing the necessary coercion on the two reluctant individuals has not been taken into account. And if these are fully considered, the public administration of the service may not be selected, even if the actual outlay necessary to finance the service is reduced by public action. Suppose that the public activity can reduce the cost from $56 to $50. If the costs of coercing the two minority members should be greater than $20, the majority of eight would still find it to their advantage to form the private association.

The Montemartini analysis clearly points up one of the major shortcomings of the De Viti-Einaudi analysis if the latter is considered to be explanatory rather than normative. This is the implication that the state's usage of the resources taken away from private employments by taxes must be at least as productive as private uses from which these resources are withdrawn. Unless unanimity is present in the choice (a point which Wicksell clearly perceived and upon which he based his tax theory) there is no assurance that, even in so-called democratic choice processes, the real income of the community will be increased by the allocation of income to public uses.

The essential thesis of several writers in this tradition, notably Conigliani, Murray, and Barone,[41] is that collective choices are by their nature different from individual choices. The basis for this argument is the distinction which was made by both Pantaleoni and Pareto between the problem of maximizing individual welfare and maximizing collective or social welfare. Pantaleoni argued that collective action need not imply coercion so long as it was aimed at the satisfaction of individual utilities. In this case individuals would freely and voluntarily contribute the necessary revenues to finance the public services.[42] In the terminology of modern welfare economics, this would indicate that some collective action could be carried out in accordance with the Paretian criteria for increasing general welfare. Conigliani, Murray, and the others were quick to point out, however, that this sort of action need not involve the state at all. If people will voluntarily contribute to finance state services, anarchism is the ideal social system. They argued that the very need for the state arose only because this was not the typical situation and that coercion was the one essential characteristic of all state action. Pantaleoni admitted the necessity of coercion when the state attempts to maximize in any way collective or social welfare. And he made a distinction between the maximization of individual welfare and the maximization of social welfare even within the choice pattern of the individual. This suggests that each individual acts in accordance with an individualized or personal-utility or preference scale and at the same time with a social preference scale. These may come into conflict at many points, and the individual may deliberately choose to be coerced and to coerce others if the social preference scale is overruling.

Pareto's distinction between the achievement of maximum utility *of* the society and the achievement of the maximum utility *for* the society is similar to that of Pantaleoni.[43] Murray, a close follower of Pareto, extended the Pareto analysis to the problem of fiscal choice. He tried to show that the achievement of any sort of collective or social maximum is impossible without the violation of some of the necessary conditions for the attainment of the individual maxima. State action necessarily implies some attempt in this direction; therefore, coercion is necessary.

Barone's conception of state activity was similar although somewhat more clearly stated. He pointed up the weakness in the voluntary theory of fiscal choice by showing that it is impossible to fix some distribution of the tax burden among individuals and then to say that the amount of public services is chosen voluntarily. The prefixing of the distribution of the tax burden, which is implicit in the work of De Viti and Einaudi, is essentially equivalent to choosing a social welfare function. Once this is chosen and action taken in accordance with it, no pretense of voluntary choice can be maintained. Coercion must be introduced. The individual is not allowed to calculate the utility of public services and make his contributive choice accordingly. Barone sensed fully the necessity of the requirement of a Wicksellian unanimity in order to justify the use of any sort of voluntary theory of fiscal choice. But he denied the possibility of such unanimity being attained; therefore, the theory of finance reduces to the theory of the coercive distribution of the tax burden.

Cosciani is the modern interpreter of this tradition in Italian fiscal theory.[44] He states that the study of finance consists in the examination of the reasons for and the effects of the substitution of coercive collective choices for individual choices. Two sets of individual behavior are involved; first, that of the ruling class in making the decisions, and secondly, that of the taxpaying group in responding to the alternatives put before them. Anglo-Saxon fiscal theory has, of course, almost exclusively been concentrated on the second of these two sets of behavior. In a very real sense, therefore, our theoretical structure is more in keeping with the ruling-class tradition than with the voluntary tradition. The merit of the ruling-class conception appears to be its usefulness in forcing the separate consideration of these two aspects of fiscal action.

Miscellaneous Contributions

Italian theorists have made several other, and more specific, contributions. A few of these may be noted briefly. The first consists in the application of the Paretian indifference curve apparatus to the classical problem of the relative burden of the income tax and the consumption tax. This application was first made by Barone in 1912, utilized again by Borgatta in 1921, and further developed by Fasiani in 1930.[45] It did not appear in English until the celebrated note by M. F. W. Joseph was published in 1939.[46] This "excess burden" analysis has recently been criticized, and correctly so, on the basis of the attempts which have been made to extend the conclusions reached to any general statements relative to the merits of the general income tax and the excise tax. It is interesting to note, however, that this extension was not made by Barone or Fasiani. Both emphasized the partial-equilibrium nature of the conclusions reached and specifically warned that the analysis could not easily be applied to the community as a whole.

A second contribution closely related to the same analysis is that made by Gobbi. He argued that there is no difference in the burden of a consumption tax and an income tax of equal yield.[47] This was based on the alleged invalidity of the Marshallian concept of consumers' surplus. It seems clear that Gobbi was thinking in terms of the community as a whole, and that his rejection of consumers' surplus is based on an early recognition that this is not additive and, therefore, it is of little use in general tax analysis. He stated that the consumer's surplus for all goods must be zero.[48]

A third contribution, made by Pareto and developed to some extent by Borgatta, consists in nothing more than some fragmentary ideas which seem to offer some insights into the process of fiscal choice. Clearly recognizing that all actual choices must be made by individuals, whether in their capacity as taxpayer-voters or as members of some ruling class, Pareto argued that the individual choices which go into the making of collective decisions are necessarily nonlogical. It is therefore erroneous to attribute rationality to such choices and to judge them by any criteria of rational behavior. Nonlogical action is not equivalent to purposefully irrational action. Rather it is action which may be ruled by mixed motives, which has no fixed objective, which involves many uncertainties. The chooser is not able to predict the results of his behavior with any degree of certainty, and even if he could do so, he would have little idea as to what goals he really seeks to maximize. Social man is essentially different from individual man. Out of the complex of actions which are taken, some logical, some nonlogical, it may be possible to discover some uniformities and it is here that a theory of finance must be discovered. It is not surprising that these ideas were not carried much further than this,[49] but any theory of collective choice must take the Paretian conception into account. It suffices to throw out both the voluntaristic approach, which assumes the taxpayer-voter to act similarly to his action in the private economy, and the organismic approach, which attributes some superior rationality to the collective entity.

V. A Comparative Summary

This discussion of the Italian tradition in fiscal theory may be concluded by a brief comparison with the Anglo-Saxon tradition. The latter is directly related to neoclassical economics and is specifically Marshallian in its essentials. Anglo-Saxon fiscal theory has analyzed the effects of particular fiscal measures (almost exclusively tax measures) upon the private economy. The analysis has normally been conceived in a partial-equilibrium framework, although recently the Keynesian influence has served to shift this emphasis somewhat. The usefulness of Anglo-Saxon thought depends upon, and is limited by, this characteristic feature. Fiscal theory has been an adjunct of economic theory, and as such, it has been useful for many purposes, but it has been little else.[50]

It is appropriate to ask whether this is the proper role for finance theory. Surely the function of such theorizing must be that of analyzing and explaining the results of government action, however this action may be motivated. But government is codimensional with the whole economy and includes within its scope all of the individual units of this economy. Government action cannot, therefore, be limited in any genuine sense to any specific subsector. As Del Vecchio wisely remarks, it is impossible properly to conceive fiscal theory in other than general-equilibrium terms. This does not suggest the necessity of using Walrasian-Paretian models for all fiscal problems, but it does imply that the interdependence among variables must be fully recognized. Spillover effects cannot simply be neglected in the faith that these will fade away and become unimportant as is the case in so many areas of applied economics. By their very nature fiscal problems are general welfare problems, not the problems of particular groups of persons, classes, or industries.

The great merit of the Italians is that they have placed fiscal theory in a broad framework in which the necessary interdependence has been fully recognized. By and large, their system is internally consistent. The weaknesses are much the same as those of Walrasian economics. Problem solving has been relatively neglected. We find, for example, little discussion of the incidence of particular taxes or expenditures. But we should not measure contributions in terms of wordage on either side. A great deal of the Anglo-Saxon discussion on incidence has been of little value precisely because the general-equilibrium aspects of the problems have not been taken into account.

Contemporary Italian economists will freely admit that their tradition has suffered from an excess of "system" at the expense of "problem solving." But all good Marshallians must acknowledge just as freely that the latter effort is fruitful only insofar as the "system" or the methodology is sound. While Fubini was correct in holding Marshall up as an idol to the Italian theorists, perhaps a good dose of Ferrara would be equally helpful to modern fiscal Marshallians.

The English-language tradition has almost completely neglected the second major problem of fiscal theory, that of collective choice. This has been introduced only in welfare economics, and this sometimes rarified branch of study has rarely been tied to fiscal theory.[51] The Italian emphasis upon the state or the public entity as the subject of analysis, rather than the private economy, has forced attention to the problem of choice, in reference both to the collective unit and to the individual taxpayer-beneficiary. Much remains to be accomplished here, but students must look to the Italian and other continental sources, notably Wicksell, for any hints and directions; the Anglo-Saxons have defaulted, with the very recent exceptions noted above.

Finally, no reforming spirit has guided the Italians. This has made their arguments seem sterile and devoid of normative content. The normative elements which are present are usually clouded over, perhaps unintentionally, with pseudoscientific pronouncements. This has not been a strong feature of the Italian tradition, but we can lay little claim to superiority here. Unconsciously trapped by our utilitarian heritage, we have accepted and promoted all of the nonsense which is contained in the theories of proportional, equal, and minimum sacrifice, etc. Only a handful of writers, such as Henry Simons, have been able to break through the enveloping fog.

Italian fiscal theory has many deficiencies, and it is certainly not lacking in its own varieties of nonsense. This "science" seems peculiarly addicted to the attraction of "fuzziness," whatever the land of origin. It may perhaps be charged that precious time is wasted in the attempt to sift old and foreign doctrines for good ideas. But if any progress is to be made, fiscal theory must break out of its current straitjacket, and a hybridization may be required to accomplish this. Economists simply cannot neglect a fundamental re-examination of the whole orthodoxy upon which economic policy in this most important subject area has been, and continues to be, made.

Bibliographical Note

The student interested in a short history of the Italian work in fiscal theory should look first at G. Del Vecchio, *Introduzione alla finanza*, 2nd ed. (Padua: 1957). A summary history of doctrine may also be found in L. Gangemi, *Elementi di scienza delle finanze* (Naples: 1948). For a single article summarizing the Italian contribution, Borgatta's introduction to the Italian translation of Wicksell's *Finanztheoretische Untersuchungen* and other essays is recommended (*Nuova Collana di Economisti,* vol. 9, *Finanza* [Turin: 1934]).

The student interested in going to the original source for a surprisingly large proportion of the Italian ideas is directed to the work of Ferrara. Of all the Italians, Pareto included, Ferrara must assume first rank, and in his work may be found germs of later developments, not only in fiscal theory, but in all of economic theory as well. His complete works are only now in the process of being issued, volumes 1, 2, 3, and 4 having been published (Francesco Ferrara, *Opere complete* [Rome: 1955, 1956]). His work in fiscal theory is largely contained in his lectures, which were taken as notes (Ferrara, *Lezioni di economia politica,* 2 vols., [Bologna: 1934]).

Pantaleoni's works in public finance are scattered and they have not been collected in a single volume. Barone's major writings on finance are available in volume 3 of his works (Enrico Barone, *Le opere economiche,* vol. 3, *Principi di economia finanziaria* [Bologna: 1937]). The English translation of De Viti De Marco's *First Principles of Public Finance* is available, but this book does not, in itself, properly convey the Italian contribution. Einaudi's treatise is recommended (Luigi Einaudi, *Principii di scienza della finanza,* 3rd ed. [Turin: 1945]), but his best work has appeared in his essays; the most important collection of his essays is *Saggi sul risparmio e l'imposta* (Turin: 1941).

Almost all of the important work appeared in the professional journals prior to its later publication in book form. Prior to 1920, the *Giornale degli economisti* contained almost all of the important papers. After about 1920, Einaudi's review, *La riforma sociale,* began to attract important contributions.

At the present time, the most important Italian journal in public finance is *Rivista di diritto finanziario e scienza delle finanze,* which was founded by the late Benvenuto Griziotti and which is issued at the University of Pavia.

The most important single work which appeared in Italy in the postwar period has been the second edition of the late Mauro Fasiani's treatise, *Principii di scienza delle finanze,* 2 vols. (Turin: 1951).

Notes

Much of the research upon which this paper is based was conducted while the author held a Fulbright research scholarship in Italy. I am especially indebted to professors Giannino Parravicini and Sergio Steve for their assistance in facilitating this research as well as for their helpful comments on earlier versions of this paper. I also gratefully acknowledge the helpful suggestions made by professors Luigi Einaudi and Gustavo Del Vecchio, both of whom read earlier versions of this paper. Their intimate acquaintance with the whole body of doctrine discussed here has made these suggestions especially valuable. Errors of fact, interpretation, and analysis remain, of course, entirely my own.

1. Antonio De Viti De Marco, *First Principles of Public Finance,* trans. E. P. Marget (London: Jonathan Cape, 1936).

A few additional essays have recently been translated and are included in *Classics in the Theory of Public Finance,* ed. R. A. Musgrave and A. T. Peacock (London: Macmillan, 1958). Essays by Pantaleoni, Barone, Montemartini, and Mazzola are included.

2. H. C. Simons, *Journal of Political Economy,* 45 (1937), pp. 712–17; F. C. Benham, *Economica,* (1934), pp. 364–67.

3. V. Pareto, "Per la veritá," *Giornal degli economisti,* 2 (1895), p. 424. Pareto was an admirer of Ferrara, and traces of much of the Paretian theoretical construction can be found in Ferrara's works.

4. ". . . the tax, in its pure significance, would represent neither a sacrifice nor a violence exercised on the contributor by some superior; it would represent a price . . . for all the great advantages which the state provides for us." *Trattato speciale delle imposte* (1849–1850), contained in *Lezioni di economia politica,* 2 (Bologna: 1934), p. 551.

5. Einaudi has stated that this is the major contribution of Ferrara to fiscal theory. See Luigi Einaudi, "Francesco Ferrara," in *Saggi bibliografici e storici intorno alle dottrine economiche* (Rome: 1953).

6. "The tax itself is neither a good nor an evil. To make an adequate judgment, one needs to compare the sacrifice with the utility which is promised." (Ferrara, *Trattato speciale,* p. 469).

7. Einaudi, in his review of Pigou's *Study in Public Finance,* makes the telling point that if Ferrara's ideas had been accepted outside of Italy, this would have prevented all such efforts as Pigou's attempted distinction between productive and transfer expenditure. Luigi Einaudi, *La riforma sociale,* 39 (1928), p. 164.

8. Knut Wicksell, *Finanztheoretische Untersuchungen* (Jena: Gustav Fischer, 1896). An English translation of the important part of this work has been published in *Classics in the Theory of Public Finance*, op. cit.

See also Pierre Tabatoni, "La rationalité économique des choix financiers dans la théorie contemporaine des finances publiques," *Economie Appliquée*, 8 (1955), p. 158.

An important recent American book develops an approach to collective decision making which has much in common with that propounded by the "ruling class" conception. See Anthony Downs, *The Economic Theory of Democracy* (New York: Harper, 1957).

9. Gino Borgatta, "Prefazione," *Nuova Collana di Economisti*, 9 *Finanza* (Turin: 1934), p. xxxi.

10. Borgatta adopted a different approach when he examined practical problems in fiscal theory. Here he applied economic analysis in the usual sense and neglected his sociology.

11. As Del Vecchio has stated, "The history of the science has proved that theoretically there is no possibility of applying partial theories to the science of finance. Any finance problem, even particular ones, presupposes the whole system of economic relationships." Gustavo Del Vecchio, *Introduzione alla finanza* (Padua: 1954), p. 10.

12. See Gino Borgatta, "Contributi alla teoria della spesa dell imposta," *Studi in memoria di Guglielmo Masci*, 1 (Milan: 1943), pp. 29–46.

13. Mauro Fasiani, "A proposito di un recente volume sull' incidenza delle imposte," *Giornale degli economisti*, 18 (1940), pp. 1–23; "Sulla legittimità dell' ipotesi di un imposta-grandine nello studio della ripercussione dei tributi," *Studi in memoria di Guglielmo Masci* (Milan: 1943), 1, pp. 261–79; Cesare Cosciani, *Principii di scienza delle finanze* (Turin: 1953), pp. 326–31.

14. Any model which incorporates some recognition of offsetting changes, for example in the level of alternative taxes or in the absolute price level, should be classified as equivalent methodologically to the Italian model.

15. This point is made by Papi. See G. U. Papi, *Equilibrio fra attività economia e finanziaria* (Milan: 1942) p. 17.

16. Cf. Luigi Einaudi, "Contributo alla ricerca dell' ottima imposta," *Annali di economia*, 5 (1929).

17. The study by Walter J. Blum and Harry Kalven, Jr., *The Uneasy Case for Progressive Taxation* (Chicago: 1953), is largely devoted to an attack on the sacrifice theories. And, although fiscal theorists might consider the argument as flogging a dead horse, the fact that the book was published and has received favorable reviews in the professional journals is sufficient proof of the point made in the text.

18. Enrico Barone, *Le opere economiche*, vol. 3, *Principii di economia finanziaria* (Bologna: 1937), pp. 149–60. The relevant portions of this work were originally published in *Giornale degli economisti* (1912).

19. Ibid., p. 158.

20. He repeats his argument in Einaudi, "Il cosidetto principio della imposta produttivista," *La riforma sociale* (1933). Reprinted in *Saggi sul risparmio e l'imposta* (Turin: 1941), pp. 286–88.

21. These essays are all reprinted, along with others, in Luigi Einaudi, *Saggi sul risparmio e l'imposta* (Turin: 1941).

22. Cf. U. Gobbi, *Trattato di economia*, 2nd ed., vol. 2 (Milan: 1923), p. 129; U. Ricci, "La taxation de l'épargne," *Revue d'économie politique*, 16 (1927), pp. 878–79.

23. J. A. Stockfisch, "The Capitalization and Investment Aspects of Excise Taxes under Competition," *American Economic Review*, 44 (1954), pp. 287–300; "The Capitalization, Allocation, and Investment Effects of Asset Taxation," *Southern Economic Journal*, 22 (1956), pp. 316–29. See James M. Buchanan, "The Capitalization and Investment Aspects of Excise Taxes under Competition: Comment," *American Economic Review*, 46 (December 1956), pp. 974–77, for an application of Einaudi's argument to the Stockfisch analysis.

24. Benvenuto Griziotti, "Teoria dell' ammortamento delle imposte e sue applicazione," *Giornale degli economisti* (1918), reprinted in *Studi di scienza delle finanze e diritto finanziario* 2 (Milan: 1956), pp. 275–391.

25. Einaudi, *Saggi sul risparmio*, op. cit., and "Contributo alla ricerca dell' ottima imposta," *Annali di economia*, 5 (1929).

26. The Einaudi thesis has been made forcefully by Nicholas Kaldor. See his *An Expenditure Tax* (London: Allen and Unwin, 1955).

27. Cf. Henry Simons, *Personal Income Taxation* (Chicago: University of Chicago Press, 1938).

28. The discussion of this section closely parallels that contained in James M. Buchanan, *Public Principles of Public Debt* (Homewood: Irwin, 1958), ch. 8, appendix.

29. Antonio De Vito De Marco, "La pressione tributaria dell' impostae del prestito," *Giornale degli economisti*, 1 (1893), pp. 38–67, 216–31. Essentially the same analysis is contained in *First Principles*, op. cit., pp. 377–98.

30. The most complete statement of Ricardo's position is to be found in *Principles of Political Economy and Taxation, Works and Correspondence*, 1 (London: Royal Economic Society, 1951), pp. 244–46.

31. Benvenuto Griziotti, "La diversa pressione tributaria del prestito e dell' imposta," *Giornale degli economisti* (1917). Reprinted in *Studi di scienza delle finanze e diritto finanziario*, 2 (Milan: 1956), pp. 193–261.

32. For example, see F. Maffezzoni, "Ancora della diversa pressione tributaria del prestito e dell' imposta," *Rivista di diritto finanziario e scienza delle finanze*, 9 (1950), pp. 341–75.

33. This argument is developed in De Vito De Marco, *First Principles of Public Finance*, op. cit., pp. 390–93.

34. Cf. F. Maffezzoni, "Ancora della diversa pressione tributaria del prestito e dell' imposta," op. cit., p. 348.

35. Puviani's main work is *Teoria della illusione finanziaria* (Palermo: 1903), published in a limited edition and now extremely difficult to locate; I have not been able to consult it directly. I am grateful to the late Benvenuto Griziotti of the University of Pavia for the use of his personal copy of a somewhat older and equally rare Puviani book, *Teoria della illusione nelle entrate pubbliche* (Perugia: 1897).

36. Fasiani has thoroughly discussed and summarized the Puviani contribution in his treatise, and he includes direct quotations of the most important parts. See Mauro Fasiani, *Principii di scienza delle finanze*, 2nd ed., vol. 1 (Turin: 1951), pp. 78–188. I should also mention the work of Vinci, written on the occasion of the fiftieth anniversary of the appearance of Puviani's main volume. See Felice Vinci, *La teoria dell' illusione finanziaria di A. Puviani nel suo cinquantesimo anniversario* (Milan: 1953).

37. Cf. P. L. Reynaud, "La psychologie du contribuable devant l'impôt,"*Revue de Science et Legislation Financiere*, 39 (1947) and 40 (1948).

38. Although this is not the place for an extended discussion, the impact of the Puviani analysis on the very core of modern budgetary theory is evident. Budgetary theory has been formulated on the implicit assumption that some omniscient executive acts genuinely in the "public interest." Once the ruling class conception of the executive is raised or admitted, the whole budgetary conception must, of course, be drastically modified.

39. It is along these lines that I hope to do considerably more work. A whole set of fiscal principles can be developed on the presumption that fiscal choice should result from individual behavior which is as rational as is possible. Therefore, as a normative proposition, all fiscal illusions must be removed. On this basis, important criticism can be made against many elements of the existing fiscal structure.

40. G. Montemartini, "Le base fondamentali di una scienza finanziaria pura," *Giornale degli economisti*, 2 (1900), pp. 555–76.

41. See C. A. Conigliani, "L'indirizzo teorico nella scienza finanziaria," *Giornale degli economisti*, 2 (1894), pp. 105–29; R. A. Murray, "I problemi fondamentali dell' economia finanziaria," *Giornale degli economisti*, 1 (1912), pp. 255–301; E. Barone, *Le opere economiche*, vol. 3, *Principii di economia finanziaria* (Bologna: 1937).

42. M. Pantaleoni, "Cenni sul concetto di massimi edonistici individuali e collettivi," *Giornale degli economisti* (1891), and reprinted in *Scritti varii di economia* (Rome: 1904), pp. 281–340.

43. V. Pareto, "Il massimo di utilità per una collettivita in Sociologia," *Giornale degli economisti*, 1 (1913), pp. 336–341.

44. C. Cosciani, *Principii di scienza della finanze* (Turin: 1953).

45. E. Barone, "Studi di economia finanziaria," *Giornale degli economisti*, 2 (1912), pp. 329–30 in notes; G. Borgatta, "Intorno alla pressione di qualunque imposta a parità di prelievo," *Giornale degli economisti*, 2 (1921), pp. 290–97; M. Fasiani, "Di un particolare aspetto delle imposte sul consumo," *La riforma sociale*, 40 (1930), pp. 1–20.

46. M. F. W. Joseph, "The Excess Burden of Indirect Taxation," *Review of Economic Studies*, 6 (1938–1939), pp. 226–31.

47. U. Gobbi, "Un preteso difetto delle imposte sui consumi," *Giornale degli economisti*, 1 (1904), pp. 296–306.

48. Ibid., p. 301.

49. See G. Borgatta, "Lo studio scientifico dei fenomeni finanziari," *Giornale degli economisti*, 1 (1920), pp. 1–24, 81–116, for a good discussion of this point of view. For Pareto's own statement, see G. Sensini, *Corrispondenza di Vilfredo Pareto* (Padua: 1948), cited in M. Fasiani, "Contributi di Pareto alla scienza delle finanze," *Giornale degli economisti*, (1949), p. 156.

50. This point is made by Earl Rolph, *The Theory of Fiscal Economics* (Berkeley: University of California Press, 1954), p. ix.

51. The recent efforts by Bowen, Musgrave, and Samuelson provide notable exceptions.

23.

Fiscal Institutions and Efficiency
in Collective Outlay

Fiscal institutions have been critically analyzed for their effects on the "efficiency" of the private sector, but almost no attention has been given to the effects of these institutions on the "efficiency" with which resources are allocated to the public sector of the economy. Until quite recently, and with Knut Wicksell as a notable exception, economists have not attempted to analyze political or group decisions with the tools at their command. They have neglected the fact that individuals also "behave" as they participate in collective decision processes and that such behavior can be analyzed in terms of a theory of individual choice.

Limitations of space prevent extensive discussion here of an analytical framework as well as the examination of a number of alternative models. Both the type of questions that should be raised and the type of analysis that may be attempted in answering them may, perhaps, be suggested through concentration on a single example. What effects would a change in the effective progressivity of the federal revenue structure exert on the relative size of the public sector? And would such a change tend to produce more or less efficiency in the allocation of resources to the supply of collective goods and services? For simplicity, the analysis is limited to a reduction in progressivity.

I

Before attempting to answer these questions, it is necessary to ask and to answer a more simple one. How much will a political community choose to devote to the supply of collective goods and services? The outcome will, in general, depend both upon the rules for the making of political decisions and upon the tax institutions that are to be employed to finance the public goods. My approach is based on the presumption that both the political decision rule and the tax institution exist independently of possible budgetary size or composition.

I shall first introduce a world-of-equals model. All persons in the political community are identical in all respects, including the evaluation of the single public good, which, for our purposes, we assume to be purely collective in the Samuelson sense. How much will the group decide to spend on supplying this good collectively? This model is interesting because it is the only one in which neither the political decision rule nor the tax institution exerts an influence on the final outcome, provided only that the tax is a general one that exhibits what has been called horizontal equity. In addition, the outcome will satisfy the necessary conditions for Pareto optimality, second-best considerations aside.

In this model, any general tax will impose the same tax-price per unit of public good on each individual. For example, individual tax liabilities will be identical under capitation taxes, proportional income taxes, progressive income taxes, or expenditure taxes. Each person would choose, were he given the power to decide for the community, that the collectivity finance the same quantity of the public good. Therefore, the delegation of decision-making power to a single person (any person), simple majority voting, or unanimity will produce identical and "optimal" results.

II

A variation on the world-of-equals model allows the analysis to be substantially extended. Assume now that individuals are identical in preferences but that incomes differ. This may be called an "equal preference" model, and in the familiar geometrical analysis it means only that the preference maps for the various members of the political group are equivalent. Individual evaluations of the collective good now differ to the extent that they are affected by incomes.

What particular characteristics of the preference pattern must be present if a system of proportional income taxation is to satisfy the requirements for "full neutrality"? By full neutrality, I refer to that position where all of the necessary marginal conditions for Pareto optimality are satisfied and from which no political decision rule would generate a change. The set of positions satisfying the full neutrality requirement is a subset of those positions that may be classified as Pareto-optimal. In full neutrality the marginal tax-price confronted by each individual is equal to the marginal evaluation that he places on the public good, and the summed tax-prices equal marginal cost. Given these conditions, no individual desires to modify the quantity of the public good that is supplied; all individuals prefer that same quantity. Hence, the political decision rule is immaterial.

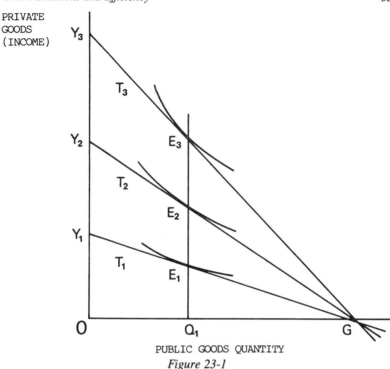

PUBLIC GOODS QUANTITY

Figure 23-1

Fig. 23-1 illustrates the analysis with an indifference curve-budget line configuration. Income (private goods) is measured along the ordinate; units of collective good along the abscissa. The fanlike array of budget lines intersecting on the abscissa in G represents a proportional tax structure. An individual with income Y_1 confronts a budget line shown as T_1 with the tax-price per unit of the public good indicated by the slope of this line, and, similarly, for all other individuals in the group. For simplicity, we assume that the supply price of the public good is constant over quantity, and that, regardless of the tax institution, each individual faces a constant tax-price per unit of the public good.[1]

Assume now that a specific quantity of the public good, say Q_1, is financed by the schedule of tax-prices shown. The preference map configuration that will satisfy full neutrality is obvious; the successive indifference curves must be tangent to the budget lines along the vertical drawn from Q_1 as Fig. 23-1 illustrates. The construction could be modified to fit any postulated tax institution.

A more general statement of the necessary condition is as follows: The income elasticity of demand for the public good divided by the price elasticity of demand must be equal to, and opposed in sign to, the income elasticity of the tax-price schedule.

Income elasticity of demand
$$\frac{\text{for public good}}{\begin{array}{c}\text{Price elasticity of demand}\\\text{for public good}\end{array}} = (-) \begin{array}{l}\text{Income elasticity of}\\\text{tax-price schedule.}\end{array}$$

Full neutrality is present when this condition is met throughout the range of possible incomes. Under proportional income taxation, the income elasticity of the tax-price schedule is unitary. Therefore, the income elasticity of demand must be positive and equal to the price elasticity in absolute value. Suppose, for example, that the income elasticity over the relevant range is positive with a coefficient of 1.5. Clearly, the price elasticity of demand would have to be negative and also with a coefficient of 1.5 in order that the individual at the two income levels (or, in our model, two individuals at the different income levels) prefer the same quantity of the public good.

If income elasticity of demand is positive and exceeds the price elasticity in absolute value, the wholly neutral tax-price structure must be progressive. If income elasticity is positive but less than the price elasticity, the fully neutral structure of tax-prices must be regressive. And, of course, if the income elasticity of demand should be negative, the tax-price confronted by the individual would have to decrease, not increase, as income rises in order for full neutrality to hold.

III

The analysis remains severely limited unless departures from the conditions required for full neutrality can be incorporated into it. Fig. 23-2 allows this extension. On the abscissa is measured income; on the ordinate is measured tax-price and marginal evaluation. A proportional income tax is represented by the line t_1. Three different progressive rate structures are shown; these are t'_1, t_0, and t_2.

For each given level of public good, a marginal evaluation schedule may be derived which relates individual marginal evaluation to the level of income (private goods). Geometrically, this schedule is derived by plotting the slopes of the successive indifference curves as they cut the vertical drawn from the given Q in Fig. 23-1. Let us assume, initially, that full neutrality is present under the proportional income taxation schedule, t_1. In this case, the marginal evaluation schedule, given the quantity of public good Q_1, lies along t_1 and coincides with it. This is noted as v_1 in Fig. 23-2.

Now suppose that a progressive income tax is to be substituted for the proportional tax. Since full neutrality is to be violated, the rule for making

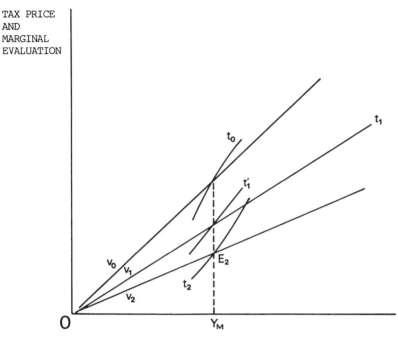

TAX PRICE
AND
MARGINAL
EVALUATION

INCOME AFTER TAX

t_1 - proportional tax
t_1' - symmetrical progressive tax
t_0 - progressive tax, nonsymmetrical, weighted left
t_2 - progressive tax, nonsymmetrical, weighted right
V_0 - marginal evaluation when $Q = Q_0$
V_1 - marginal evaluation when $Q = Q_1$ $Q_2 \rangle Q_1 \rangle Q_0$
V_2 - marginal evaluation when $Q = Q_2$
Y_M - median voter's income

Figure 23-2

political decision now becomes important in determining the outcome. Let us assume, therefore, that collective decisions are to be made under a rule of simple majority voting. It is necessary to distinguish two types of departure from full neutrality, which I shall call here symmetrical and nonsymmetrical. Symmetry is defined with reference to the position of the median voter-taxpayer. Under simple majority voting, with single-peaked preferences, the median voter becomes controlling, and the direction of change in collective outcomes can be predicted on the basis of his behavior.[2] By a symmetrical shift from proportion to progression in rate structure, I refer to a shift that does not modify the tax-price per unit of the public good that confronts the median voter-taxpayer. In other words, symmetrical progression may be introduced by imposing a higher tax-price on the "rich," which is precisely offset by lowering the tax-price to the "poor," without changing the position of the middle man. Since his position is not modified by the change, the median voter will not desire to vote any differently. And, since his vote is decisive in this model, there will be no change in the quantity of the public good that is supplied.

Such a symmetrical change is shown in the progressive rate schedule, t'_1, in Fig. 23-2. The poor will, because of the lowered tax-price, seek more actively to expand public goods supply. The rich, for the opposed reasons, will seek to contract it. But their efforts will be to no avail in the simple majority voting system. The outcome remains unchanged and it remains Pareto-optimal since the excess benefits enjoyed by the poor just offset the excess taxes paid by the rich. No bribery or scheme of compensation could be worked out so as to change the allocative results. In effect, the introduction of symmetrical progression amounts to a shifting from one position to another on the conceptual Pareto income groups.

A nonsymmetrical shift is defined as one that does modify the tax-price to the median voter-taxpayer. Such shifts can be weighted in either of the two directions. A shift from proportion to progression can increase or decrease the tax-price that must be paid by the median voter. If the change is concentrated on reducing the tax-price to the lowest incomes groups, for example, by simply raising the personal exemption while leaving the rate structure above the exemption proportional, the tax-price to the median voter will be increased. If this is the case, which we can call a weighting to the left, the median voter will choose a smaller quantity of the public good, and because his vote is controlling in any majority coalition, the collective result will embody less public spending. One such system is shown as t_0 in Fig. 23-2. If, on the other hand, the change is concentrated on increasing the tax-prices of the highest income groups, for example, by fully taxing realized capital gains, the tax-price confronted by the median voter will be decreased; the curve, t_2, illustrates this case.[3] There will result here a somewhat larger collective outlay on the public good.

In either case, a nonsymmetrical change will modify the final outcome, and the necessary conditions for Pareto optimality will be violated, assuming that they were satisfied before the change.

IV

There is, of course, no way of knowing to what extent the necessary conditions for Pareto optimality are satisfied at any particular point in time. The analysis does enable us to predict, however, the direction of change in total outlay quite independently of the knowledge that we may have concerning individual marginal evaluations. Given the prevailing distribution of personal income, it seems highly probable that, in the neighborhood of the median voter, the federal tax structure takes the general shape shown by t_2 in Fig. 23-1. If this is correct, and if an overall reduction in the progressivity of the system tends to shift the rate structure in the direction of that shown by either t_1, t'_1, or t_0 in the neighborhood of the median, then the tax-price faced by the median voter-taxpayer will be increased. As a result, he will tend to choose a smaller outlay on the public good than under the more progressive structure. In other words, I am suggesting that the predicted reduction in progressivity will itself be nonsymmetrical in a specific direction.

We know that the progression in the federal income tax becomes significant only over income ranges that exceed the income level of the median taxpayer. This fact insures that, in more general terms, political equilibrium is represented by a position similar to E_2 in Fig. 23-2. If, from such a position, the tax-prices imposed on high-income taxpayers are reduced more, in absolute value, than the tax-prices on low-income taxpayers are increased, the tax-price confronted by the median taxpayer must be increased. This remains true despite "tax reductions" that extend over the whole income scale. The relative change in the tax-price at which public goods may be "purchased" through the fiscal process is the determining influence on the behavior of the individual voter. And if this is increased, he will choose to consume fewer public goods than he would have chosen under an unchanged tax structure.

This hypothesis seems intuitively plausible. To an extent, at least, the median or middle-range voters support the current level of public spending for the by-product distributional effects that can only be secured via the fisc. A reduction in progressivity can only decrease these redistributional benefits. And the middle-range voters can be expected to react against the increases in the level of tax-price that they confront. It is considerably more difficult to predict the effects of the reduction of progressivity on overall efficiency in the organization of the public sector than it is upon the direction of change in the size of this sector. To do this, it is necessary to know something about the actual income and price elasticity of demand for public goods. In Fig. 23-2, we have assumed that the income elasticity and the price elasticity are just offsetting over the whole of the income range. (The v-curves are linear as drawn.) This need not, of course, be at all "realistic," and either "progressive" or "regressive" v-curves may be more in accord with the data. If, however, the v-curves in Fig. 23-2 are accepted as reasonable (and there exist certain data in support of this), then the reduction in progressivity, carrying with it some reduction in overall public outlay, will tend to produce greater efficiency. This is because, before the change, the public sector tends to be expanded beyond Pareto-optimal limits. This, again, seems intuitively plausible. Insofar as the distributional by-product is the basis for the spending on public goods, there will tend to be some expansion of the public sector beyond the optimal allocative limits. On the other hand, should the appropriate v-curves exhibit progression, the current rate structure may generate roughly optimal outlay, and any reduction in this outlay would tend to reduce overall efficiency.

I am hopeful that studies currently in progress will reveal something more about the actual shapes of the v-curves and the t-curves. Only when these studies are complete will definitive conclusions concerning the effects on efficiency be possible. As of now, I am prepared only to suggest, without defending my position too strongly, that the reduction in overall outlay which the reduction in progression seems likely to generate will probably increase rather than decrease the efficiency with which the total resources of the economy are divided between the provision of private and public goods.

V

The analysis has been confined to what I have called an equal-preference model. The general appropriateness of this model may, of course, be questioned. Surely, income effects are not the only explanation for differences in individual evaluations of public goods. Tastes differ for public goods as well as for private goods. Some people do not like garlic; others do. Similarly, for foreign aid. These specific differences in tastes, however, are more important in relation to single private goods or single public goods than they are when we come to consider the whole package of private goods, or the whole package of public goods, or, alternatively, a single public good to be taken as representative of the whole package. It seems plausible to suggest that, in this case, income differences do loom relatively large in explaining differences in the evaluations placed on public goods by individuals.

For the model to be relevant at all it is necessary to assume that the public sector includes only goods and services that provide general benefits to the whole of the population. Insofar as discriminatory benefits are provided to particular groups, with remaining groups wholly or largely excluded from enjoying them, the analysis is not applicable. However, in such cases the familiar institutions of taxation are not applicable either. Implicit in the development of the basic institutions of general taxation there seems to have been the idea that income and wealth differences do reflect to an extent differences in willingness as well as differences in ability to pay. If there is, in fact, no relationship between income and wealth levels and the evaluations that individuals place on public goods, almost all of the institutions of general taxation must produce serious distortion in the allocation of economic resources.

Finally, the model of equal preference may be defended as being relevant on quite different grounds. It has been convenient to present the analysis in terms of a single-preference map. When we come to examine empirical data, however, we must, at best, draw on cross-section studies that report on the behavior of a number of individuals. In effect, our empirical limitations force us, whether we like it or not, to talk in terms of some composite or representative preference pattern. This serves, of course, to rescue our whole model from the apparently restrictive limbo that may have seemed its fate. The elasticities to which we have referred in the criterion for full neutrality are derived from data drawn from the behavior of the whole population, not from the behavior of single individuals.

VI

I am prepared to admit that other factors, not accounted for in this analysis, may serve to offset those developed here, and, in so doing, to refute the underlying hypotheses that I have advanced. If, in reducing the overall progressivity of the federal tax structure, the tax-price to the median voter should be increased, as I have suggested, but simultaneously, his tax awareness or tax consciousness should be reduced, the size of the public economy may be expanded and not reduced. This possibility should not be ruled out of account, especially since the reduction in overall progressivity may be accompanied by an increase in the share of indirect taxes (including inflation) in total revenue production. I have also assumed throughout the analysis that the simple models of majority voting retain some relevance for real-world political decision making. This need not be the case, at least in the simple form that the models have assumed here. If, in fact, it should be found that the effective political power of individuals is directly related to income levels, the overall reduction in progressivity may generate an expansion in public outlay from this factor alone. I have also limited the analysis to models of democratic choice. The power of "leaders" in determining the pattern of resource outlay between the public and private sectors has been completely ignored. Insofar as individual citizens do not, ultimately, determine the size of the public sector, the discussion is irrelevant. To analyze the alternative here, we require models of *dirigisme*, not democracy. And this task I leave to those of my disciplinary colleagues who would presume both to advise the despots and to explain their behavior.

Notes

Some of the background work on this paper has been done in connection with a more comprehensive project on fiscal institutions that is supported by the National Committee on Public Finance, under the auspices of the Brookings Institution.

1. For a similar construction in which tax-price is allowed to vary, see R. A. Musgrave, *The Theory of Public Finance* (New York: McGraw-Hill, 1950), p. 122. Note, however, that Musgrave's usage of the construction is different from that of this paper.

2. The basic analysis of single-peaked preferences under majority voting is contained in Duncan Black, *The Theory of Committees and Elections* (Cambridge: Cambridge University Press, 1958).

3. Except under certain elasticity conditions, the income of the median voter, after tax, will be changed by any nonsymmetrical shift in the tax structure. This complication has been ignored in drawing Fig. 23-2 since it does not affect the analysis.

24.

Towards a Tax Constitution for Leviathan

WITH GEOFFREY BRENNAN

I. Introduction

In this paper we analyze *constitutional* choice among tax institutions under a specified set of political assumptions. That is to say, we examine an individual's choice among tax rules and tax instruments when it is known that such institutions, once selected, will remain in being over an indeterminately long sequence of budgetary periods, and in a setting in which the individual is presumed to be unable to predict with precision what his own position will be at any particular moment in this postconstitutional sequence.[1] Our analytical framework differs from that which informs much of the conventional wisdom in normative tax theory as well as from that which has informed much of the Wicksell-inspired, public-choice alternative.

Neoclassical normative tax theory is, in all essential respects, institutionally vacuous.[2] Abstract normative criteria for a "good" tax system are derived in response to the problem posed by the requirement to raise some exogenously determined amount of revenue for governmental use within a single time period. Emphasis is placed on the familiar efficiency and equity characteristics of alternative tax instruments. Within this traditional perspective, the influence of the tax instrument chosen on the amount of revenue demanded or required is neglected or obscured by the "equi-revenue" comparison within which the whole analysis is conducted. In a constitutional setting, by contrast, such possible feedback effects over a sequence by budgetary periods must be explicitly considered: the interdependencies between the form of tax institutions and the revenue demands placed on these institutions cannot be ignored. And, of course, predictions of such relationships will necessarily be embodied in the individual's choice. In this paper, we shall introduce an institutional model within which these interdependencies assume critical importance.

Modern public-choice theorists have already gone some way toward incorporating these effects of tax instruments on public-goods supply into the analysis of constitutional choice.[3] Almost exclusively, however, the public-choice model of constitutional fiscal choice has embodied the assumption, explicitly or implicitly, that postconstitutional or in-period budgetary decisions conform to the public-goods demands of the median voter or his representative in a legislative assembly. Our analysis differs critically from this in that we substitute the model of a revenue-seeking leviathan for the demand-driven and essentially passive government characteristic of early public-choice analysis.

The norms for taxation suggested by the analysis seem to accord more closely with some of the empirically observed attitudes of the taxpaying public than those which emerge from either of the alternative paradigms. Furthermore, the institutional model is in apparent consistency with a large, rapidly growing and uncontrollable public sector. This is in dramatic contrast with the implied setting from which the traditional reform suggestions emerge, a setting that retains residues of the classical economists' assumption of nonproductive public expenditures along with the implicit notion that the governmental share in national product is severely limited. Our model is also sharply at variance with the naively optimistic public-choice perspective which incorporates the productiveness of a possibly large public sector but which does not allow for a supply-side influence on fiscal outcomes.

Our paper is intended to be a contribution to the ongoing discussion of real-world tax reform, rather than an exercise in deriving the logical properties of yet another set of arbitrarily selected assumptions. Indeed, in some sense, the point of departure for our discussion is the observation that tax reform is a quasi-constitutional exercise. Tax institutions are usually intended to be moderately permanent features of the political framework: they set the context within which in-period decisions about public-goods supply are made. Furthermore, the major tax reform process (say of the Carter type in Canada, or the British Royal Commission's) is perhaps more like an attempt at a genuinely "constitutional convention" than any other common aspect of political life (at least in the public finance specialists' experience).

Once this is acknowledged it becomes natural to think of devising tax institutions by appeal to the constitutional calculus of the typical taxpayer-voter rather than by reference to abstract ethical norms. On the other hand, it should be borne in mind that tax reform is *not* the full constitutional arrangement envisaged, for example, in *The Calculus of Consent*[4]: the mandate is necessarily much more restricted. For this reason, although we acknowledge the possibility of nontax institutions which might perform a similar role to the tax rules we discuss and perhaps do so more efficiently, we do not consider such alternatives in this paper.[5] To do so would be to move outside our basic tax-reform orientation.

The central structure of the institutional model is set out in Section II. In Section III, we examine the choice of an individual as he compares a comprehensive and a noncomprehensive tax base as well as alternative rate structures within these. The analysis is extended to many tax bases in Section IV, and to a many-person setting in Section V. Finally, in Section VI, the discussion of the paper is related to commonly held views on tax reform.

II. Government as a Revenue Maximizer Subject to Constitutional Tax Constraints

As Knut Wicksell noted, no persons would approve the imposition of taxes, either at a constitutional or a postconstitutional stage of decision, unless they expect to secure some benefits from the goods and services that they predict will be financed from the revenues collected. Taxes are coercive instruments that allow governments to levy charges upon persons without any corresponding individualized expression of current willingness to pay. Furthermore, in postconstitutional stages of decision, political consent through the action of legislative representatives will not, typically, be extended to more than a simple majority of the citizenry.

What is a reasonable model of postconstitutional fiscal decision making by governments, a model that might be appropriate in informing the constitutional-stage choice among fiscal instruments? Perhaps at one period in history, it may have seemed reasonable to rely on the operation of majority rule in legislatures to hold governmental fiscal activities in bounds. And majority-rule models remain in both the analysis of median-voter behavior and in popular discussion of democracy. Confronted with public sectors of modern scope, and with bureaucracies that demonstrably possess power quite apart from specifically legislated authority, the democratic-limits model of governmental fiscal constraint seems to become increasingly naive. A more acceptable model would seem to be one in which the political-bureaucratic process, as it is predicted to operate postconstitutionally, involves the maximization of revenues within the tax constraints imposed in the fiscal constitution.

This is what might loosely be termed a model of "leviathan." The citizenry has no effective or operational control over government, once established, beyond the constraints that are imposed at the constitutional level; in-period or postconstitutional fiscal decisions are made entirely by the budget-maximizing or revenue-maximizing politician-bureaucrat.[6] The model here is in several respects similar to the "monopoly" or "noncooperative" state theories developed by earlier continental writers, notably some of the Italian fiscal theorists.[7] These monopoly-state conceptions, however, assume that the governmental powers have emerged from some coercive seizure of the state apparatus at some period in history. By contrast, in our model government is voluntarily established by general agreement in a constitutional contract among potential taxpayers-beneficiaries.[8] The problem faced by persons in such a setting involves securing and insuring the benefits of governmentally provided goods and services (including the enforcement of contracts and claims to property titles, without which market trading would hardly be feasible), while avoiding vulnerability to exploitation by the leviathanlike institutions that may be uncontrollable once they are established.

Many different types of constitutionally derived constraints are conceivable, and these need not be mutually exclusive. Here we focus on the subset embodied in the *tax system*. In doing so, however, we assume that there exist some effective constraints on the disposition of tax revenues. Specifically, we assume that the uses of tax revenues must include the financing of at least some goods and services that cannot be provided noncollectively. Without this assumption, as previously noted with reference to Wicksell's statement, a constitutional contract establishing a coercive tax-levying authority could not be assumed to have emerged.

Our stylized constitutional setting is characterized by the further, and familiar, assumption that each person has well-defined predictions about the aggregate level and the distribution of incomes and consumption patterns in all postconstitutional periods, but that he possesses no knowledge about his own future position within the distribution or about the characteristics of his own taste pattern. This general, nonindividualized knowledge is sufficient for him to make some estimate, within broad limits, both of the "efficient" levels of budgetary outlay on public goods, and of the aggregate revenues to be obtained under alternative tax systems. Since the individual remains ignorant concerning his own predicted income or tastes, he cannot identify a cost-share for himself under any particular tax system. He cannot, therefore, predict whether, in-period, he might prefer a larger or a smaller public-goods quantity than that which he predicts to be "efficient" for the whole community. Thus, each individual rationally prefers institutions that will generate the "efficient" quantity, $\overline{G}$, given an independent estimate of the costs of provision. The actual level of outlay on desired public goods and services is given by

(1) $(G) = \alpha R,$

where α is the predicted proportion of tax revenue spent on the desired budgetary component, and R is aggregate tax revenue. Throughout this discussion, the value of α is taken to be exogenous, by which we mean that it is fixed by the operation of constraints other than those incorporated in the tax system.[9] As we have indicated, α is such that

(2) $1 > \alpha > 0$.

Hence, the outlay on desired public goods and services is some direct function of total revenue raised, and the problem that the individual faces at the constitutional stage is to organize tax arrangements so that the revenue raised, when adjusted by α will yield roughly the quantity of public goods and services estimated to be "efficient," at the given estimated net costs—costs that will, of course, be dependent on the value of α. Thus, R will be chosen so that

(3) $\alpha R = \overline{G}$.

The characteristic assumption of our leviathan-type model is that, in each postconstitutional budgetary period, the government will attempt to maximize total revenue collections (and hence total spending), within the constitutionally appointed tax regime—that is,

(4) $R = R^*(b,r)$,

where R^* is the maximum revenue that can be raised from the tax regime, and is a function of b, the tax base, and r, the allowable rate structure. Formally, then, the problem facing the individual is to select b and r, so that

(5) $R^*(b,r) = \dfrac{\overline{G}}{\alpha}$.

What this implies in terms of the desired tax constitution is elaborated in ensuing sections.

III. Tax Base and Tax Rate Constraints in a Simple Model

Initially, we restrict the analysis to a single individual who is assumed to be exercising his constitutional choice between only two potential definitions of the tax base—the one fully "comprehensive," the other falling short of this. We relax these assumptions later, but at this stage the simplification is convenient. It is immaterial for our argument precisely what the noncomprehensive base is, and whether the tax is levied on the "uses" or the "sources" side (that is, whether it is an "income" or an "expenditure" tax). Let us suppose, however, that the noncomprehensive base is money income from labor effort in the market, and that the comprehensive base includes this money income and also the money equivalent of the individual's nonmarket production of valued end products; in other words, the comprehensive base is full income. The question we

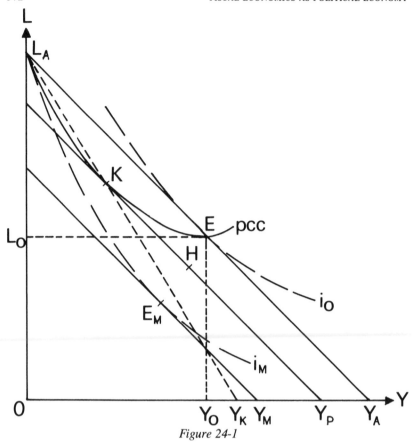

Figure 24-1

examine is whether the person would prefer a tax constitution that embodies the comprehensive base over the one that restricts the base to money income.[10]

The situation is depicted in Fig. 24-1. The indifference curves, labeled with i's, indicate the individual's preferences as between money income-earning activity Y, and, say, leisure activity L. These preferences exhibit the standard properties.[11] The pretax situation is characterized by a relative price between L and Y reflecting the productivity of income-earning activity; the initial equilibrium is at $E(Y_0,L_0)$ on i_0.

Consider now the prospect that the individual would face here if the government should be granted access to the fully comprehensive tax base. In this event, the individual would be exploitable up to the full limits of his potential earning ability, over and above some minimal subsistence. Apart from this minimal limit, all of the "income equivalent," OY_A, is potentially available for governmental use. The government could levy a lump-sum tax that appropriated the individual's *maximum* potential earnings, beyond the subsistence level.[12]

Since it is inconceivable that anyone could ever anticipate an "efficient" public-private sector mix that would require all potential income above subsistence for governmental purposes, it seems clear that a potential taxpayer-beneficiary would *not* select the comprehensive tax base at the constitutional level if he predicts postconstitutional governmental behavior of the type that we have postulated. He will seek to impose constitutional constraints on the fisc, on the ability of the government to tax. He can do so, in our simple case, by allowing the government to levy an income tax only on the ordinary sources of earnings. This constraint, alone, will reduce the potential maximum revenue collections of government drastically—from OY_A to $Y_M Y_A$ in Fig. 24-1. Clearly, if the government imposes a tax on money income the revenue from which exceeds $Y_M Y_A$, then the individual will be better off if he ceases to earn income at all; if he switches to L_A. If limited to the money income base, the government can secure revenues up to this maximum limit, $Y_M Y_A$, only by levying an "ideally" structured *regressive* tax, in which the rate for each level of Y is equal to the slope of i_m. This involves creeping down i_m to the maximum revenue equilibrium at E_m, allowing the taxpayer a minute slice of surplus to ensure only that the position E_m is actually preferred to L_A.

Recognizing this prospect, the taxpayer may wish to impose the further constitutional constraint that the income tax should not be regressive in its rate structure. This would clearly be the case if the money income base, along with the predicted value for α and the revenue-maximizing regressive rate structures, should be predicted to generate outlays on desired public goods and services in excess of the efficient levels of provision. If, for example, the government should be required to stay within a rate structure that is at least *proportional,* it would be effectively confronted with a locus of potential equilibria along the individual's price-consumption curve for varying "prices" of Y, depicted by $L_A KE$ in Fig. 24-1. The revenue-maximizing arrangement in this case occurs at the point where a line drawn parallel to $L_A Y_A$ is tangent to the price-consumption curve, as indicated by K, with the associated revenue-maximizing proportional-rate of tax being, $Y_k Y_A / OY_A$. The precise characteristics of this case, and the analytic resemblance to familiar results in price theory can be isolated by appeal to the corresponding partial equilibrium diagram in Fig. 24-2.[13]

The curve, DD, in Fig. 24-2 indicates the individual's demand for the income-yielding activity; this might be derived from a preference mapping exhibiting the properties depicted in Fig. 24-1. Confronted with the requirement that it must levy a proportional tax, what tax rate will the revenue-maximizing government impose? The question is obviously analogous to that asked of the monopolist who will seek to maximize profits,

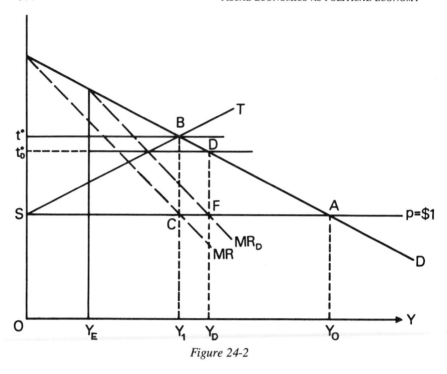

Figure 24-2

with the same answer. We derive a "marginal revenue" curve, *MR* in Fig. 24-2, and the maximum revenue is given where this cuts the horizontal dollar-price line (the marginal cost line), determining a posttax equilibrium at Y_1.

This construction reveals the precise analogy between our model of postconstitutional governmental process and monopoly theory – in an analytic as well as a conceptual sense, our model is appropriately called a "monopoly theory government." The revenue-maximizing tax rate, t^*, can be derived as follows:

$$R = tY_1,$$

$$(6) \quad Y_0 - Y_1 = Y_0 \cdot \eta t, \text{ since } \eta = \frac{-\Delta Y}{Y_0} \bigg/ \frac{\Delta P}{P},$$

where R is government revenue; t is the proportional tax rate and equals $\Delta P/P$

$$(7) \quad \therefore R = tY_0 (1 - \eta t),$$

(8) $\dfrac{\partial R}{\partial t} = Y_0(1 - 2\eta t).$

Setting (8) at zero, we have,

(9) $\quad t^* = \dfrac{1}{2\eta},$

and, substituting t^* in (7), we have,

(10) $\quad R^* = \dfrac{Y_0}{4\eta}.$

Hence, as we might expect, maximum revenue is directly related to the initial size of the taxable base, and inversely related to the value of the elasticity.

As we have indicated, the revenue raised from the given base under a *proportional* tax is less than that which might be raised from the same base under an ideally *regressive* rate structure. We are led to ask what might be the influence of a *progressive* rate structure here. The revenue-maximizing government will have no incentive to shift from the equilibrium proportional rate to any rate structure that embodies progression, since this latter would imply increasing rather than declining marginal rates of tax. The revenue effect can be demonstrated most easily by thinking of the simplest of all progressive rate structures, one that involves only two marginal rates, with the first rate being zero. Consider such a structure, sometimes called a *degressive* one, where income over some initial range to Y_E is wholly exempted from tax. With this additional constraint, the revenue-maximizing proportional rate on remaining units or income falls, and total revenue collections fall correspondingly.

To show this, note that under a degressive structure,[14]

$R = t(Y_1 - Y_E)$

$= tY_0 \left[1 - \eta t - \dfrac{Y_E}{Y_0} \right],$

$\dfrac{\partial R}{\partial t} = Y_0 \left[1 - 2\eta t - \dfrac{Y_E}{Y_0} \right],$

and

$$(11) \quad t_D^* = \left(1 - \frac{Y_E}{Y_0}\right) \frac{1}{2\eta} \text{ which is } < \frac{1}{2\eta},$$

and

$$(12) \quad R_D^* = \frac{(Y_0 - Y_E)^2}{4\eta Y_0} \text{ which is } < \frac{Y_0}{4\eta}.$$

In terms of Fig. 24-2, it is clear not only that the revenue-maximizing degressive structure postulated generates less total revenue than the revenue-maximizing proportional tax, but also that the excess burden is smaller. Under proportionality, the excess burden is measured in Fig. 24-2 by the area ABC. Under the postulated degressive structure, excess burden falls to ADF.

Not all forms of progression yield this result for the change in excess burden. For example, a linear progressive rate schedule (of the form shown by the line ST in Fig. 24-2)[15] will yield the revenue-maximizing *marginal* rate that is equal to the proportional revenue-maximizing rate, with the same posttax equilibrium at Y_1. Note that, in this case, the total revenue obtained under progression is a constant share of that which would be obtained under proportionality where the marginal rate levied at income Y_1 would be applied over the entire income range. Thus, under the rate structure, ST, total revenue raised under progression is one-half that raised under proportionality. But the excess burden in the two cases is identical.

It may be useful to summarize the basic argument of this section. We have observed that the constitutional decision-making calculus of the potential taxpayer-beneficiary, operating under an expectation of a leviathanlike postconstitutional fiscal process, involves his opting for institutional devices that will limit the revenue-raising potential of the tax system. We have explored two ways that might accomplish this. One is by limiting the size of the tax base—increasing the comprehensiveness of the tax base will be, beyond some point, clearly undesirable. The other is by imposing a constitutional requirement that some degree of progressiveness be incorporated in any rate structure. This "defense of progression" is completely different from any to be found in normative tax theory. It stems both from the constitutional perspective within which our whole analysis is developed, and from the unconventional, but highly plausible, assumptions we have made about the predicted workings of the political process. The argument does *not* spring from assumed risk aversion on the part of individuals behind the veil of ignorance, from Rawlsian maximin theorems, or from the more familiar "vertical equity" norms.[16]

IV. Maximum Revenue and Excess Burden

To this point, we have restricted analysis to the simple setting in which the individual chooses between two potential tax bases and among rate structures on these bases. Generally, however, the potential taxpayer at the constitutional stage will have the option of considering many possible base and rate structures, all of which might be estimated to raise roughly the desired level of revenue, G/α, when exploited to the maximum-revenue potential. Retaining the single-person perspective, is there any reason to expect a constitutional preference for any particular method?

Presumably, the potential taxpayer will prefer that arrangement from among the set that will minimize net efficiency loss or excess burden. We may focus initially on the proportional rate case, and assume that the "demand curves" are linear over relevant ranges. In this setting it is interesting to observe that when maximum revenue is obtained from a source, the excess burden is a fixed proportion of revenue raised. For,

$$(13) \quad \begin{aligned} W &= \tfrac{1}{2} t(Y_0 - Y_1) \\ &= \tfrac{1}{2} t(Y_0 \eta t), \end{aligned}$$

where W is the excess burden or efficiency loss generated by the tax. Substituting t^* in (13), we have

$$(14) \quad W = \frac{Y_0}{8\eta} = \tfrac{1}{2} R^*.$$

Consequently, given the assumption of linear "demand schedules," any two bases which yield the same maximum revenue under proportional rate structures will involve identical excess burdens, independently of the size of the base or of the elasticity. Given proportionality, then, the maximum revenue potential becomes the dominant choice criterion—excess burden tends to become irrelevant.

Once we admit progression into the analysis, excess burden may once again assume a role. Suppose, for example, that the choice is to be made between a proportional tax on commodity (or income source) A, and a tax on commodity (or income source) B, that yields identical maximum revenue under a *linear progressive* tax schedule. In this case, the excess burden generated will be larger under the latter, and in the assumption of our geometrical model, will be exactly two times that in the former. This result stems from the fact that, under linear progression, maximum revenue and the corresponding excess burden are identical. Of course, not all forms of progression exhibit this property. Specifically, for the type of degressive structures analyzed in (11) and (12) above, the relation indicated in (14) holds. In this sense, a persuasive case can be made out for degression over other types of progressivity. It is also clear that, with the relevant equal-yield comparison made (that based on maximum potential revenue), a proportional tax and a degressive tax are equivalent on strict efficiency or excess-burden grounds, while either tax is preferable to other forms of a progressive tax.

This result, which indicates that many progressive rate structures generate more excess burden than the equi-yield proportional tax, is not at variance with our conclusion earlier to the effect that a constitutional requirement of progression may be one way of insuring a restriction on the total level of governmental outlay through the limits imposed by the rate structure. We are simply observing here that, compared with equi-income reductions in the tax base, if these possibilities should exist, then progression may be an inefficient means of accomplishing this restriction.

Finally, it may be useful to make a technical comment on the methodology of tax analysis. One feature of the discussion in this section of the paper is our usage of one variety of an "equi-revenue" technique of comparison. These equi-revenue comparisons, however, involve separate base-rate combinations that yield the same *maximum* revenue. It is only within this stringently restricted subset of possible tax arrangements that we have permitted the application of the equal-revenue methodology, and that we have applied excess-burden criteria, appropriately derived from the constitutional perspective. Strictly speaking, even this limited use of the equi-revenue comparison is questionable, because *all* of the separate dimensions of tax selection (maximum revenue yield, excess burden, and such "equity" effects as intrude) are aspects of the same general constitutional choice. It seems clear, however, that given our model of postconstitutional political process, maximum revenue potential will be the predominant issue in the selection of tax institutions.

V. One among Many

So far our discussion has been cast in terms of a single individual's choice calculus. This need not be nearly so restrictive as it might appear, particularly since we have examined choice in a constitutional setting, where the chooser is not expected to know just what his own position will be in postconstitutional periods. Nonetheless, we have neglected the problems that arise when the individual recognizes that, regardless of what his own position will be, he will be one among many taxpayers, with differences among persons in both tax base and in preferences. We may first consider whether or not our earlier results concerning tax-base limitations will hold in this setting. We may look at a simple two-person illustration. In Fig. 24-3, we assume that the two persons, *A* and *B*, will earn an equal

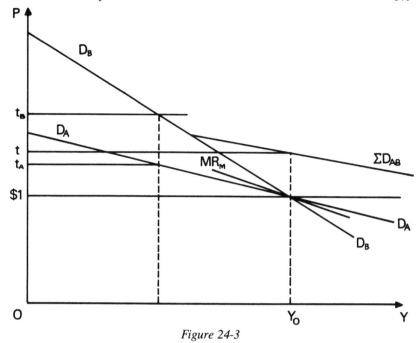

Figure 24-3

amount of money income in the pretax or no-tax equilibrium, Y_0. (Recall that, under our constitutional-stage assumptions the individual will know only that the two persons, A and B, will have the characteristics depicted; he will not know which of the two positions he will, himself, occupy.) The persons are predicted to differ substantially, however, in their response to the imposition of a tax on the limited or money-income base, with leisure (or other valued end products) exempted from tax. The differential responsiveness is indicated by the slopes of the "demand curves" for money income, as shown by D_A and D_B.

The first point to be noted here is that so long as any responsiveness at all is predicted, the argument for the noncomprehensive base developed earlier holds without qualification. Each of the two persons whose preferences are depicted in Fig. 24-3 will be protected against the exploitation potential of government that would be present under full-income as opposed to money-income taxation.

Let us now examine the revenue-maximizing government's predicted tax behavior in this two-person situation. If the government could treat A and B separately and differentially, and if it could levy a proportional tax on each (but not a regressive tax), it would impose a tax rate of t_a on A and the higher rate, t_b, on B. Such differential treatment would clearly allow scope for the extraction of more revenue from the community than would be possible if the government were required to levy the *same* proportional rate on each person. The revenue-maximizing uniform rate, t, is determined in Fig. 24-3 where the "market" marginal revenue curve, MR_m, cuts the dollar price line, with "price" set at the intercept of the vertical drawn from this intersection and the aggregate "demand curve" ΣD. This rate is such that $t_a < t < t_b$. The fact that revenue collections under the revenue-maximizing discriminatory rate structure (t_a, t_b) exceed those under the uniform rate, t, suggests a further means of constitutionally restricting the revenue proclivities of leviathan: by imposing the constraint that tax schedules be *uniform* over persons. Such an argument for *uniformity,* which is related to but different from the more familiar "horizontal equity" norm, has not, to our knowledge, been developed anywhere in normative tax theory.[17]

The construction in Fig. 24-3 can also be used to illustrate a proposition that seems at variance with that reached in models which assume institutional fixity. In the conventional framework, the behavior of individuals within the structure of given tax institutions is analyzed, and any attempt on the part of one person or group to avoid or to reduce tax payments, through recourse to nontaxable sources or uses of income, is interpreted as imposing an *external diseconomy* on less responsive taxpayers.[18] Behavior in reducing tax liability generates costs for others in the community by making higher rates or tax and/or lower rates of public spending necessary than would otherwise be required.

Consider the same issue in our constitutional framework. An individual seeks to limit the revenue-potential of leviathan, while remaining uncertain as to his own position. In this case, he is benefited by the knowledge that at least some taxpayers will be able to reduce tax liability by shifting to nontaxable sources (uses) of income. This may be shown easily in Fig. 24-3. Compare the revenue-maximizing uniform rate, t, with that rate which would be revenue-maximizing if the two taxpayers were predicted to be equally responsive in the manner indicated by D_b. The uniform rate would, of course, rise to t_b, with a higher revenue potential. To the extent, therefore, that a person at the constitutional-choice level can predict that some members of the set of taxpayers will be able to shift to nontaxable sources (uses) in postconstitutional periods, his concern about the exploitative possibilities of leviathan is correspondingly reduced.

Finally, we want to consider whether or not our earlier results concerning the relationship between progression and maximum revenue hold in the many-person setting. It is perhaps intuitively appealing to suggest that the results might not hold, since, if low-income persons should have particularly high elasticities of demand for leisure, it seems as if it might be revenue-maximizing to levy lower rates of tax on their incomes while, at the same time, levying higher rates on incomes above such limits.

Progression offers one means of making this sort of discrimination, while preserving uniformity.

Once more we begin with the simple two-person case, and for simplicity suppose that for any positive tax rate individual B has higher income than individual A. Under the uniform-schedule restriction, will progression always yield less revenue than proportionality? We may answer this question by examining the revenue-maximizing uniform rate schedule in our two-person case. Only if this schedule is progressive, will proportionality raise less revenue than progression. To check this, let us suppose that the tax rate, t_a, is imposed on all incomes over the range from zero to Y_a^1, and rate t_b on all additional income. In this case, total revenue, R, is given by:

(16) $\quad R = 2t_a Y_a^1 + t_b(Y_b^1 - Y_a^1),$

where Y_i^1 is individual i's equilibrium income in the presence of taxation. Now we use the result

(17) $\quad Y_i^1 = Y_i^0(1 - \eta_i t_i) \quad$ for $i = a,b,$

where Y_i^0 is individual i's equilibrium income in the absence of taxation, and η_i is i's elasticity of demand over the range Y_i^0 to Y_i^1, and define γ so that

(18) $\quad \gamma = \dfrac{Y_b^0}{Y_a^0},$

to obtain

(19) $\quad R = Y_a^0[2t_a(1 - \eta_a t_a) + \gamma t_b(1 - \eta_b t_b) - t_b(1 - \eta_a t_a)].$

By maximizing R with respect to t_a and t_b, we determine $\hat{t}_a$ and $\hat{t}_b$ and can examine the ratio

(20) $\quad \dfrac{\hat{t}_a}{\hat{t}_b} = \dfrac{4\gamma\eta_b + \eta_a(\gamma - 1)}{4\eta_a(\gamma - 1) + 2\eta_a}.$

Clearly, the revenue-maximizing rate structure is progressive only if (19) is less than unity in value; or if

(21) $\quad \eta_b < \dfrac{\eta_a(3\gamma - 1)}{4\gamma}.$

Since $\gamma \geq 1,$, we know that

$$(22) \quad \frac{1}{2} \; < \; \frac{3\gamma - 1}{4\gamma} \; < \; \frac{3}{4}.$$

Thus, if there were no particular reason to assume that high-income receivers have lower demand elasticities than low-income receivers, we would expect (20) to be violated. In this case, the conclusion derived in our one-person model would carry over: progression would involve a revenue loss. But, it is also quite clear that (20) may hold; and in the case where η_a is significantly larger than η_b (by no means implausible), then the "right" degree of progression *could* generate more revenue than the revenue-maximizing proportional rate. The "right" degree of progression (from the revenue-maximizing government's perspective) does not, however, seem likely to be large. For example, it can be shown that the maximum revenue derived from linear progression of the type examined above (i.e., a rate schedule of the form $m = \beta \cdot Y^1$) is always less than that generated by the maximum revenue proportional structure.[19]

VI. Tax Limits and Tax Reform

As our analysis has suggested, the tax base and tax rate constraints imposed on governments at the constitutional level should, ideally, be such as to allow for the financing of some roughly efficient bundle of public goods and services. The danger of allowing governments access to revenue-raising instruments that will generate budgets in excess of these requirements is central to our whole model. We should, however, recognize that errors can be made in the opposing direction, that the constitutional tax constraints might, through time, prove to be overly restrictive. In this case, postconstitutional pressures will surely arise for escape through constitutional-style adjustments designed to widen the bases and to allow for more flexible rate structures, to move generally from specificity toward comprehensiveness. Empirically, it will always be difficult to distinguish between genuine constituency demands for a relaxation of such tax constraints, and the ever-present demands of the revenue-seeking politicians-bureaucrats. For the latter group, and their spokesmen, efforts will tend to be directed toward "loophole closing," toward increasing the number of sources that may be taxed. "Tax reform" advocacy on the part of the "bureaucratic establishment" will tend to be centered on "tax base erosion." Indeed one indirect test of the empirical validity of our model of political process lies in the observed lack of reformist concern about relative rates of tax within existing tax-law limits. This offers some evidence to the effect that the revenue limits are indeed being approached.

In the discussion of proposed tax-base changes the attitude of the traditional normative tax theorist and the members of the taxpaying public perhaps differ more sharply than anywhere else. Our analysis is helpful in "explaining" the attitudes of the taxpayers. For example, they are likely to react negatively and emphatically to proposals to move toward taxation on the basis of full income, as, for example, by including the imputed rental values of owned residences in the base for the personal income tax. The normative tax theorist, who advocates such inclusion always from reasoning based on equal-yield comparisons, responds to the taxpayers by arguing that overall rates of tax may be lowered simultaneously with the proposed widening of the base. But the taxpayers may be implicitly, but correctly, rejecting the equal-yield postulate, in their predictions that *any* widening of the tax base must open up further taxing possibilities for a revenue-seeking government.

Illustrations might easily be drawn from recent American fiscal experience. For example, in the early 1960s, a proposal was widely discussed which sought to replace part of the corporation income tax with a broad-based value-added tax. The proposal was quickly rejected, no doubt in part for the reasons suggested: it may have been predicted that, ultimately, the rates of value-added tax would reach heights that would greatly exceed those required to recover revenue forgone under the corporate income tax. In fact, of course, almost any widely advocated tax change tends to be justified in terms of its greater "efficiency" or its greater fairness, springing from the extension of the tax base. And as our analysis indicates, if our perception of postconstitutional political processes bears any relation to reality at all, it is precisely on such grounds that the change should be rejected!

We have, in broad and general terms, examined the basic issue of tax-base comprehensiveness in a constitutional-choice perspective, as opposed to the standard economists' perspective which is limited to single-period alternatives informed by familiar in-period efficiency criteria. We should emphasize, however, that our analysis does not involve a rejection of the efficiency norm, as properly understood. The rational person, who tries to predict his own position as a future taxpayer and as a beneficiary of public goods and services, will try to carry out some efficiencylike calculus in arriving at his choices among fiscal institutions at the constitutional stage, in the prediction that these institutions, once chosen, will remain as quasi-permanent features of the economic-political environment. As our analysis indicates, what is efficient at this level of choice may not be coincident with those institutions that seem to be efficient in the more restricted choice models usually discussed by fiscal theorists.

Our results depend critically on the assumed predictions about the properties of the political process. We have introduced a model of government as a revenue maximizer limited by the tax constraints imposed in the constitution. This model is not to be confused with any one of the following models: the all-powerful government, subject to no constitutional constraints whatever; the benevolent and omniscient government, which provides the ideally efficient in-period quantities of public goods and "prices" these efficiently; the majority-rule democracy that makes fiscal decisions about public-goods supply reflecting the preferences of the median-voter—at least as traditionally conceived.

Each one of these alternative models of government (along with other variants not listed), as well as the one we have introduced in this paper, can be used to "explain" certain features of the institutional reality that we observe. Our claim is limited; the analysis based on the constitutionally constrained but revenue-maximizing government seems congruous with some fiscal institutions in existence that do command deference as "constitutional" elements, while at the same time the analysis seems consistent with many public, as opposed to academic, attitudes toward central issues in tax reform.

To the extent that our analysis does succeed in "explaining" both the institutions in existence and prevailing attitudes toward changes in these institutions, the contribution is positive. We should emphasize, however, that we are not primarily concerned with drawing a contrast between the "what is" of fiscal reality and the "what ought to be" that is contained in the traditional normative discussions of tax reform. Our analysis may well have a higher degree of positive explanatory content than the familiar alternatives. But our discussion is grounded squarely on a normative model of constitutional decision making. Tax-base comprehensiveness is a reform objective that is almost never questioned in the traditional treatments. This paper suggests, first, that tax-base comprehensiveness may be rejected in a normative constitutional-choice calculus under certain political assumptions, and, secondly, that elements of the observed fiscal structure may well reflect this normative framework.

Notes

We are grateful to members of the Public Choice Seminar at Virginia Polytechnic Institute, and in particular our colleague, E. G. West, for helpful comments on an earlier version.

1. In the limit, we may assume that the individual is in some Rawlsian "original position" and behind the "veil of ignorance." [John Rawls, *A Theory of Justice* (Cambridge: Harvard University Press, 1971).] We do not need to impose such

rigid requirements, however, for the constitutional setting to be relevant. Somewhat more plausibly, we may assume only that the individual is highly uncertain about his own future position. Cf. James M. Buchanan and Gordon Tullock, *The Calculus of Consent* (Ann Arbor: University of Michigan Press, 1962).

2. We would include under this rubric the recent "optimal taxation" literature, virtually all of which is explicitly set in this framework. For a useful summary, see David F. Bradford and Harvey S. Rosen, "The Optimal Taxation of Commodities and Income," *American Economic Review,* 66 (May, 1976), pp. 94–101.

3. Notably James M. Buchanan, *Public Finance in Democratic Process* (Chapel Hill: University of North Carolina Press, 1967). The relationship is implicit in Knut Wicksell's whole analytical framework. See Knut Wicksell, *Finanztheoretische Untersuchungen* (Jena: Gustav Fischer, 1896.)

4. James M. Buchanan and Gordon Tullock, *The Calculus of Consent.*

5. One such possibility is that of explicit constitutional limits on the proportion of national product available for public use (or on maximum rates of tax)–the national analogue of the recent tax-limitations proposals in California and Michigan. It is worth noting in passing, that restrictions on maximum rates would tend to cause leviathan to aim at comprehensiveness, which restrictions on revenue as a proportion of GNP would not do. Insofar as comprehensiveness is viewed as desirable in such a context, this might be seen as suggesting a case for rate restrictions rather than revenue restrictions. Because such policy options lie outside the range of those typically available in the standard tax-reform exercise, we do not focus on them in this paper. The ensuing discussion is conducted on the (practically relevant) assumption that such explicit rate and/or revenue constraints are not operative. (Of course, restrictions on nontax means of securing bureaucratic surplus [use of laws, commandeering without compensation, etc.] would be required, both in the case of tax liability and in our discussion, to ensure that the fiscal constraints are operative.)

6. There are evident similarities between our model and that developed by William Niskanen. See his *Bureaucracy and Representative Government* (Chicago: Aldine, 1971).

We should note that the assumption of the revenue-maximizing politician is not inconsistent with the assumption that the politician is constrained by the political process. In the absence of effective constraints on the domain of public spending, or on the government's ability to redistribute private goods among voters, majoritarian democracy may simply involve "maximum" transfers from minority to majority, along with or independently of the provision of genuinely public goods. Our discussion is, however, *phrased* largely in terms of a "monopoly" government in which revenue-maximization arises from the utility maximization of the partially unconstrained politician-bureaucrat rather than from the democratic political process itself.

7. For a summary of the Italian contributions, see James M. Buchanan, *Fiscal Theory and Political Economy* (Chapel Hill: University of North Carolina Press, 1960), especially pp. 24–74.

8. It is perhaps necessary to add the comment that the relevance of our analysis does not critically depend on whether or not governments have been, in fact, established in such a manner. The object of the contractarian exercise is to develop acceptable criteria for normative evaluation.

In this respect, the model resembles that which is familiar to economists in their analysis of the granting of franchises to monopoly enterprises.

9. Interesting questions arise if we allow the revenue yield to vary with α. In particular, there is the possibility of choosing tax institutions so as to constrain the disposition of revenues as well as the aggregate level.

10. The basic conclusions hold equally for the case in which full "neutrality" is precluded, and the choice must be made between the narrower base and the "second-best" alternative, in which different goods are taxed at different rates according to their complement-substitute relationships with leisure (the question of interest in most of the recent "optimal taxation" literature). Our argument is thus equally with "optimal tax" and "comprehensiveness" proponents.

11. By the assumptions of our model, the individual cannot predict his precise preference pattern as between money income-earning and alternative activity in postconstitutional periods. All that is required for our analysis here is that these preferences are predicted to be standard.

12. It should perhaps be emphasized that the "comprehensive" tax is levied on the income side only: the surplus which accrues to the bureaucrat-politician, the excess of revenue collections over public spending (as distinct from the bureaucrat's income, more narrowly conceived), is assumed to lie outside the coverage of the tax system. This assumption can be rationalized in a variety of ways, depending on the particular conception of leviathan that one adopts. In the simple conception of leviathan as the ruling class or monarch, the assumption is tantamount to allowing the king not to pay taxes. In a dominant majority conception, the comprehensive tax may be presumed to fall on all income, but not to fall on the special benefits, transfers, etc., that accrue to the majority coalition as a result of disbursement of the total revenue.

13. The construction in Fig. 24-1 can be used to show how the constitutional-choice setting under our political assumptions transforms the familiar excess-burden argument in favor of the general or comprehensive-base tax. A solution at point K, in the neoclassical argument, is demonstrated to be inferior to that which might be attained with a comprehensive-base or general tax that will yield the *same* revenue, producing an ideal solution at some point like H in Fig. 24-1. This argument presumes, however, that the government, once empowered to levy the general or comprehensive-base tax will, in fact, restrict its attempts to raise revenue to the collections dictated by the equi-yield comparison.

The partial equilibrium version, based on the Marshallian demand curve construction, can be used to illustrate the revenue-maximizing regressive structure, but by virtue of income effects will indicate a different rate structure than that derived from i_m. For similar reasons, the area under the demand curve does not accurately reflect consumer surplus; nor does the standard welfare triangle accurately reflect the welfare loss, or at least will do so only when the income-consumption curve $E_m HE$ in Fig. 24-1 is a horizontal line. In what follows, we set such problems aside as being of no particular relevance to our discussion.

14. A diagrammatic derivation of this result can be indicated by drawing a new MR curve, MR_D, over the range where the nonzero proportional rate is to be applied—as in Fig. 24-2, with the maximum revenue rate being t^*_d.

15. That is, one in which the marginal tax rate, m, is given by $m = \beta Y^1(m)$, where Y^1 is equilibrium income in the presence of tax and β is some constant.

16. The existence of these is not inconsistent with our model. Constitutional preferences for progression as such may exist, and will merely complement the arguments posited here.

17. It is interesting to note that in this model no constitutional rationalization for "horizontal equity" as traditionally conceived emerges. A Rawlsian maximin rule, or generalized risk aversion, might generate a case for reducing the expected variance of the posttax, postexpenditure income distribution in postconstitutional periods, but neither involves a specific, independent desire to tax those with identical pretax incomes identically. By contrast, in the more familiar model of constitutional choice

in which the median voter's preference is decisive at the postconstitutional level, horizontal equity norms may be desired as a means of limiting distortions in public-goods supply. A tax rule which levies burdens only on a small proportion of the population could be expected to generate levels of public-goods supply which are significantly different from the optimum. In our model, however, the median voter is essentially irrelevant and horizontal equity norms are simply subsumed by "vertical equity" ones.

18. For an explicit discussion in such an externality setting, see James M. Buchanan, "Externality in Tax Response," *Southern Economic Journal*, 33 (July, 1966), pp. 35–42.

19. This paper is restricted to an analysis of the opportunities of imposing limits on the revenue-collecting potential of leviathan through constitutional constraints on tax bases and tax rates. This would not, of course, be the only objective of an ideal "fiscal constitution," even if we remain within tax-side questions. To the extent that Rawlsianlike precepts of justice enter into the constitutional calculus, or even the more utilitarian motives of insurance and/or protection, a requirement that general public goods be financed at least partially by the imposition of progressive income taxes may emerge from conceptual agreement among all parties. In this context, our analysis may be viewed as complementary through its implication that progression may, independently, impose its own revenue limits.

25.

The Political Biases of Keynesian Economics

WITH RICHARD E. WAGNER

I. Introduction

Once upon a time it was generally believed that, so long as prevailing institutions constrained monetary excesses, a free-enterprise economy was self-adjusting within broad cyclical limits. Movements away from a fully employed economy would set in motion corrective forces that operated to restore prosperity. One source of disturbance was thought to be the profligacy of government, and it was considered important that governmental proclivities in this respect be constrained. A balanced budget was one of the practical rules that reflected such constraints. The advent of what has been called "Keynesian economics" changed all this. The Keynesian vision was one in which monetary management could not produce a self-correcting economy; more extensive discretionary management which included fiscal policy was required to ensure peak performance. Such discretionary management necessarily required eradication of the principled adherence to balanced budget norms of fiscal conduct. The scope of the Keynesian conversion was wide indeed. It extended all the way from purely academic controversy about Say's Law to real-world practices about whether public expenditures should be limited to the tax revenues raised to finance those expenditures. In this paper we suggest that the explicit Keynesian destruction of the rigid balanced budget rule produced a political bias in the conduct of economic policy in a democratic society, and, moreover, that this bias operates to some extent to make the Keynesian prophecies self-fulfilling.[1]

The acceptance of Keynesian ideas by the politicians and the general voting public is often dated from the onset of the 1960s. The fiscal record of the sixteen years after 1961 tells its own story. Between 1961 and 1976, there was only one year of budget surplus for the federal government. The fifteen years of deficit totalled some $240 billion. Moreover, the annual deficits increased in magnitude over this period. For 1961–68, the cumulative deficit was $60 billion; for 1970–74, it was $67 billion, and for the two-year period, 1975–76, more than $110 billion.

We observe a dramatic increase in the relative size of government over this period, accompanied by inflation unmatched in other than war periods. Total governmental expenditures increased from somewhat less than one-third of national income (from 32.8 percent) in 1960, to a little more than two-fifths (40.4 percent) of national income in 1974. The consumer price index rose by 92.3 percent over this same period, and accelerated more or less in step with the size of the federal deficits.

At a preliminary level of discussion, the effects of Keynesian economic policy on the democratic politics of budgetary choice seem simple and straightforward, whether treated in terms of plausible behavioral hypotheses or of observable political reality. Elected politicians enjoy spending public monies on projects that return benefits to their constituents. They do not enjoy imposing taxes on these same constituents. The pre-Keynesian norm of budget balance served to constrain spending proclivities so as to keep budgets roughly within the revenue limits generated by taxes.[2] The Keynesian destruction of this norm, without an adequate replacement, effectively removed the constraint. Predictably, politicians responded by increasing spending more than tax revenues, by generating budget deficits as a normal course of events. They did not live up to the apparent Keynesian precepts; they did not match the deficits of recession with the surpluses of boom. The simple logic of Keynesian fiscal policy has demonstrably failed in its institutional application to democratic politics.[3] The accumulating record is available for all to see.

At a more fundamental level of discussion, however, many issues arise. Why do politicians behave in the way indicated? Public-choice theory tells us that they do so largely in the expectation that voters will support them. But this merely shifts attention to the behavior of the voters. Why do voters support politicians who behave "irresponsibly" in the fiscal sense? What is there about the acceptance of Keynesian economics that generates the fiscal experience witnessed in the years after 1961? There is a paradox of sorts here. A regime of continuous and mounting deficits, with subsequent inflation, along with a bloated public sector, can scarcely be adjudged beneficial to anyone other than the employees of the federal bureaucracy. Yet why does the working of ordinary democratic process seemingly produce such a regime, and with little hope of basic reform? Where is the institutional breakdown?

In order to examine these questions, we must recognize that neither the economic nor the political setting is that which was presumed to exist by Keynes himself. The underlying economic realities are not those of the 1930s or those that are implicitly assumed as parameters for the application of Keynesian policy norms. Furthermore, the political process within which these norms are to be applied bears little or no resemblance to that which was implicit in Keynes's basic analysis.

We shall first examine the economic *and* the political environment that is presumed for the idealized Keynesian theory of economic policy. Since the economic setting here has been exhaustively discussed, our own treatment can be brief and without detail. Although the discussion can similarly be brief, we find it necessary to emphasize the Keynesian political environment, both because this aspect of Keynesian thought has been almost totally neglected by economists and because of its importance for our central purpose.

We shall then modify the political setting by introducing *democratic* political institutions; we shall examine the applicability of Keynesian policy norms within this setting. In this analysis (which might be called a public-choice approach to Keynesian economics) we distinguish between an economy that is essentially Keynesian and an economy that is distinctly non-Keynesian.

We shall conclude the paper with a brief discussion of the fiscal constitution. In an appendix, we examine critically the Ricardian analytical perspective which, unlike our own, is distinctly non-Keynesian in that it asserts the irrelevance of institutional forms on individual behavior. In contrast, we acknowledge the impact of institutions on behavior, and, indeed, it is this very impact that generates the political biases of Keynesian economics.

II. The Idealized Environment for Keynesian Economic Policy

Lord Keynes claimed that his was a "general theory," and it is surely correct to say that this claim of generality was influential in generating the "Keynesian revolution," especially in the thinking of professional economists. And in the textbooks on Keynesian macroeconomics that emerged after World War II, the generality of the Keynesian message for economic management was stressed. Keynesian management, it was alleged, could prevent or constrain both depression and inflation, and could be employed so as to promote a more stable economy than would be possible under any regime of monetary management.

The Economy in Depression

Soon after 1936, however, critical evaluation of Keynes's basic contribution concentrated on the setting-constrained applicability of the explanatory potential of the theory. The underlying model of the national economy is one of deep depression, and specifically an economy in which policy-induced shifts in aggregate demand can increase real output and employment *without* any effects on price levels. In the elementary diagrams of the early post-Keynesian textbooks, the aggregate supply function was horizontal out to some level of income defined to be that which would generate "full employment." In this setting, the economy is also characterized by an excess of monetary liquidity. Interest rates are at their minimal levels; economic policy which aims at increasing liquidity through increases in the supply of money alone is ineffective.

The policy implication is clear and simple. Effective demand may be increased only by increased spending, and this can be accomplished only if government increases its rate of outlays relative to its rate of revenue withdrawal from the economy. Deficit creation by government offers the only available means of increasing output and employment. The budget deficit may be financed either by money creation or by the issue of public debt instruments. Ideally, money creation is preferable, because of the absence of interest payments. But due to the excessive liquidity in the economy, the sale of bonds will not crowd out any potential private outlays, so that, aside from the minimal interest charges, the issue of debt becomes equivalent to money creation. The means of financing the deficit is unimportant; the critical element is the creation of the deficit and the enhanced rate of total spending in the economy that it facilitates.

The Symmetry of Policy Under Keynesian Political Presuppositions

As noted, Keynes claimed to present a "general theory," and particularly one that contained policy norms applicable to any underlying position of the economy. In this respect, the policy precepts of Keynesian economics were alleged to be wholly symmetrical. Under the existence of depressed conditions, budget deficits were required to restore full employment and prosperity. But when inflation rather than depression seemed to be the danger, budget surpluses were equally advised as the appropriate policy instruments. The time-honored norm of budget balance was, of course, jettisoned, but there was, in the pure logic of Keynesian policy, no one-way departure. The use of the government's budget was a two-edged weapon.

Fiscal policy was equally effective in constraining inflation or depression. Monetary policy, by contrast, was alleged to be asymmetrical. In a depression, monetary policy was deemed to be largely if not wholly ineffective. In an inflationary environment, however, monetary policy could, if desired, be utilized either as a complement to or as a substitute for the restrictive fiscal policy that the creation of budget surpluses represents.

Although particular policy instruments were viewed as asymmetrical, the application of public policy was considered to be fully symmetrical. During depression, the stream of expenditures should be expanded; during inflation, the stream of expenditures should be contracted. In both cases, rational public policy would operate to promote a more prosperous and stable economy.

The Presuppositions of Harvey Road

The idealized economic setting for the symmetrical application of Keynesian theory and policy, sketched out above, is familiar. Much less so is the political-choice setting within which the policy is to be formulated and implemented. Keynes was writing directly for his professional colleagues, the economists. But he was aiming, indirectly, for modification in the policies of national governments. It is essential that we look quite closely at his assumptions about the men who choose for the nation and about the processes through which their decisions are made.

There is relatively little mystery about Keynes's own views. He was an elitist, and he was operating under what his biographer called the "presuppositions of Harvey Road," the presuppositions that governmental policy, and economic policy in particular, was made and should be made by a relatively small group of wise and enlightened men, whether in Whitehall or in Washington.[4] Keynes did not think about the application of his policy norms in what we would, in America, call a democratic setting. The small group of enlightened men who made economic policy would tend to act in accordance with the "public interest," even when this might run afoul of constituency pressures.

In the combined economic and political environment suggested, there could be little or no question raised about the application of the Keynesian policy instruments. In order to secure a stable, prosperous economy, expenditures would be expanded and contracted symmetrically. Budget deficits would be created during periods of sluggish economic activity, and surpluses would be created as the pace of economic activity accelerated. There would be no political pressures operating to render the surpluses fictive and the deficits disproportionately large or ill-timed. The ruling elite would be guided by the presuppositions of Harvey Road; they would not act as competitors in a democratic political environment. Moreover, no bias need be introduced as between public and private sectors because the appropriate dividing line would continue to be determined by the same group of wise men guided by their own vision of the broader public interest of the community as a whole.

III. Generalized Political Implications of Keynesian Economics

The discussion in the preceding section has been necessary both for analytical completeness and as background for our primary purpose. This purpose is to examine the impact of the Keynesian precepts for economic policy in a political decision structure that is different in kind from that which was envisaged by Keynes himself, and in an economic environment that is demonstrably non-Keynesian. Political decisions in the United States are made by elected politicians, who respond to the desires and demands of voters. There is no center of power where an enlightened few can effectively isolate themselves from continuing constituency pressures. Furthermore, since World War II the national economy has never been appropriately described as being in depression of the sort idealized in the elementary Keynesian models. Throughout the three decades of postwar experience, increases in aggregate demand have always been accompanied by increases in price levels, by inflation. Upward shifts in aggregate demand have also been normally accompanied by increases in real output and employment, although this basic relationship has been increasingly called into question since the mid-1960s.

Keynesian policy is centered on the use of the government's budget as the primary instrument for insuring the maintenance of high employment and output. The implementation of Keynesian policy, therefore, required both the destruction of former principles of balanced public budgets and the replacement of those principles by principles that permitted the imbalance that was necessary for Keynesian budgetary manipulation. But politicians, and the public generally, were not urged, by Keynes or the Keynesians, to introduce deficit spending without a supporting logical argument.

There was more to the "Keynesian revolution" than mere destruction of the balanced budget principle as a permanent feature of the fiscal constitution. This destruction itself was a reasoned result of a modified paradigm of the working of an economy. And, in the larger sense, this was really what "Keynesian" is all about. The allocative bias toward a larger public sector, the monetary bias toward inflation — these biases are aspects of, and to an extent are contained within, a more comprehensive political bias of Keynesian economics, an "interventionist bias," which stems directly from the shift in paradigm.

Specifically Keynesian features emerge when the paradigm is shifted away from that which may be summarized under the expression "Say's Equality."[5] The idea that the spontaneous coordination of economic activities through a system of markets would normally produce overall stability was replaced by a vision of an economy that is inherently unstable. The new Keynesian paradigm, or rather the old Malthusian one, is that of an economy continually hounded by gluts and threatened by secular stagnation.[6] An important element in the Keynesian paradigm is the absence of an equilibrating mechanism which insures that departures from trend levels of real output growth are self-correcting. When exogenous shocks force the economy off its expansion path, no corrective devices are predicted to come into play. Hence government intervention follows, almost as a moral imperative. And there is no argument for allowing for a time period between some initially observed departures and the onset of policy action. With no conception of self-correction inherent in the accepted paradigm of the economy, "fine tuning" becomes the policy ideal.[7]

The notion of an unstable economy whose performance could be improved through the manipulation of public budgets produced a general principle that budgets *need not* be in balance. There would be years of deficit and there would be years of surplus, with these deficits and surpluses being necessary for, as well as indicating the enactment of, macroeconomic management. As we noted in our discussion of the Keynesian political framework, however, the Keynesian budgetary policies would be applied symmetrically. In such a political setting of rule by the Apostles of Harvey Road, it might even be said that Keynesian economics did not destroy the principle of a balanced budget, but only lengthened the time period over which it applied. The Keynesian paradigm, in other words, did not seem to change the fiscal constitution within which economic policy is conducted.

But what happens when we make non-Keynesian assumptions about politics? What if we commence from the assumption that elected politicians respond to constituency desires? When this shift is made in the political setting for analysis, the possibilities that policy precepts may contain political biases cannot be ignored. On this score, it should be noted, Keynes's own biographer seemed prescient, for in continuing his discussion of the presuppositions of Harvey Road he mused:

> If, owing to the needs of planning, the functions of government became very far-reaching and multifarious, would it be possible for the intellectual aristocracy to remain in essential control? Keynes tended till the end to think of the really important decisions being reached by a small group of intelligent people, like the group that fashioned the Bretton Woods plan. But would not a democratic government having a wide multiplicity of duties tend to get out of control and act in a way of which the intelligent would not approve? This is another dilemma—how to reconcile the functioning of a planning and interfering democracy with the requirement that in the last resort the best considered judgment should prevail. It may be that the presuppositions of Harvey Road were so much of a second nature to Keynes that he did not give this dilemma the full consideration which it deserves.[8]

IV. Unbalanced Budgets and Democratic Politics

In a democracy, political competition is not unlike market competition. Politicians compete among themselves for the support of the electorate, and they do so by offering policies and programs which they feel will get them elected or reelected. A politician in a democratic society can be viewed as proposing and attempting to enact a combination of expenditure programs and financing schemes that secures him the support of a majority of the electorate.

The variety of avenues for modeling the emergence of budgetary policy in a democratic political system are considerable. A government can provide a single service, or it can provide a combination of services. It can finance its budget by a variety of tax forms, either singly or in combination, and, additionally, it can subject any particular tax to a variety of rate schedules and exemption rules. Furthermore, preferences for public services can differ as among individual citizens, particular features of the political system can vary, and budget imbalance can be permitted.

Changes in any of these particular features will normally change the budgetary outcomes that emerge. Changes in tax institutions, for instance, will normally change the tax shares and tax-prices assigned to different persons. This, in turn, will alter individual responses to particular budgetary patterns. The number of services provided may also matter. With a single service, it is fruitful to conceptualize budgetary outcomes in a plurality electoral system as conforming to the preferences of the median voter. With multiple services, however, the conceptualization is not necessarily so simple, for a trading of votes may take place among persons over issues.

To illustrate, consider the choice of budget size in a democracy operating under a balanced budget constraint. Let a single service be provided, start with a budget of zero, and take account of the gains and losses in terms of constituent support from expansions in the size of the budget. Under the assumption that the public service enters positively into the utility functions of citizens, the expenditure by itself will secure support for the politician. The taxes, however, will reduce the disposable income of citizens, thereby affecting them negatively and reducing support for the politician. In a plurality electoral system, for given preferences and fixed tax institutions, the budget will be expanded so long as a majority would prefer the public service to the private goods they have to sacrifice via taxation.[9]

A full modeling of political competition in a democratic society can become quite complex. Nonetheless, the central notions we have just described are sufficient for our purposes in this paper.[10] What this line of analysis suggests is that the consideration by politicians of the gains and losses in terms of constituent support of alternative taxing and spending programs shapes the budgetary outcomes that emerge within a democratic system of political competition. The size and composition of public budgets in such a system of competitive democracy, in other words, can be viewed as a product of the preferences of a politician's constituents and the constitutional-institutional rules that constrain the political system.

With a balanced budget rule, any proposal for expenditure must be coupled with a proposal for taxation. What would happen if the requirement of budget balance were eliminated? What would be the nature of the pressures of political competition in such a revised, Keynesian constitutional setting? We shall first consider a budget surplus, and then a budget deficit. For each of these cases, we shall also distinguish whether the economic environment is Keynesian or non-Keynesian.

Budget Surpluses and Democratic Politics

The creation of a budget surplus requires an increase in tax collections without a corresponding increase in public spending, or a decrease in the latter without a corresponding decrease in the former. What political pressures result from such budgetary policies? We must distinguish between the direct or immediate and the indirect or secondary pressures. Directly, budget surpluses create no gainers, only losers, regardless of whether the economy is Keynesian or non-Keynesian. In an inflationary setting, of course, the Keynesian and the non-Keynesian policy precepts are identical. In this setting, a policy of budget surplus requires individuals to pay more taxes than before, but without any compensating increase in public output. (Or, to suffer cuts in public outlays, with no reductions in tax burden.)

It could be argued that a sophisticated citizenry should be able to see beyond the direct considerations to the indirect ones. They should understand that a budget surplus was required to prevent inflation, and that this was beneficial. The dissipation of a surplus through public spending or tax cuts, therefore, would not be costless, for it would destroy those benefits that would result from the control of inflation.

Informationally, the requirements for citizens to understand and evaluate the indirect benefits they receive from budget surpluses are stringent. In order for the indirect benefits from budget surpluses to offset fully the absence of direct benefits, it would be necessary for citizens to know fully what is at stake in choosing between politicians who propose to spend the revenues that might otherwise generate a potential budget surplus and politicians who propose to generate the surplus by holding down public outlays. Citizens would have to understand how the surplus would operate in restraining inflationary forces in the aggregate, and they would also have to be able to relate this restraint to a personal level of benefit. That is, it would be necessary for citizens to interpret the aggregate economy in precisely the manner that it is interpreted by the economists (*if only they provided a single interpretation*), as well as to develop a relation between this aggregative pattern and their own personal well-being. The very intensity of controversy among economists over precisely such matters, however, attests to the extreme unreasonableness of such requirements. Therefore, it is likely that the benefits of a budgetary surplus in restraining inflation will to some extent be underestimated by the citizenry.[11]

Even if all citizens were able to reach the same, "correct" interpretation, matters of incentive arise that reinforce the likelihood that a surplus would not be created, or, if created, would be smaller than it would be in a world of full knowledge. Knowledge does not come freely, however, but must be sought after. At the very least, it would be necessary to pursue some line of textbook-type argumentation. This is not a costless activity for the citizen, so the amount of knowledge attained will depend upon the incentives to acquire such knowledge. The costs are apparent, but what are the gains? Most likely, "nothing," and at best, "very little." In politics, unlike in the marketplace, no one person is able to change his personal actions, and through this his personal economic position, in response to changes in knowledge. Rather, personal positions can change only as a majority of citizens decide to act differently, only as the collective-decision process generates different policies. What this consideration suggests is that the gain to any one person of securing knowledge in these matters is practically zero.[12]

Budget surpluses would seem to have weaker survival prospects in a political democracy than in a social order controlled by "wise men." This difference in political viability can also be seen by approaching the matter in the opposite direction. Consider the comparative properties of the creation of a budget surplus and a proposal to utilize the surplus-creating revenue, through tax reduction, through expenditure increases, or through some combination of these. The second of these alternatives would clearly offer direct, immediate, and apparent gains, not losses. Politically, one such proposal would dominate a program of budget surplus creation. The surplus would benefit no one directly, and, would impose direct costs on some if not all of the population; on the other hand, the use of the revenues that might generate the surplus would directly benefit some if not all of the citizens. To the extent that the indirect costs and gains are understood only imperfectly, as they clearly are, actions will tend to be based on the direct costs and gains. Budget surpluses may emerge in a democratic political system, but considerations of information and incentive both operate to suggest that the institutional biases against such surpluses are strong indeed.

Budget Deficits and Democratic Politics

In a democratic society, there are no obstacles to budget deficits in a Keynesian economic setting. Budget deficits make it possible to spend without taxing. Whether the deficit is created through reduced taxes or increased expenditures, and the particular forms of each, will, of course, determine the distribution of gains among citizens. The central point of importance, however, is that, directly, there are only gainers from such deficits, not losers. In the true Keynesian setting, of course, this is as it should be. A political democracy will pose no obstacles to deficit spending in a Keynesian economy.

It is possible, however, for political bias to emerge in the decisions over the appropriate public sector–private sector mix. If the introduction of deficit financing creates signals for taxpayers that public services have become relatively cheaper than before, voters will demand a shift in the composition of real output toward publicly provided services. The "true" opportunity costs of public goods relative to private goods will not, of course, be modified by the use of the budget for purposes of stabilization. To the extent that voters, and their elected legislators, can recognize these "true" cost ratios, no public spending bias need be introduced. It does not, however, seem at all plausible to suggest that voters can dispel the illusion of a relative price change as between public and private goods.[13]

Consider the following highly simplified example. In the full employment equilibrium assumed to have been in existence before an unanticipated shortfall in aggregate demand, the government provided *one* unit of a public good, and financed this with a tax of *$1*. The restoration of full employment requires a monetary-fiscal response of *10 cents*. Suppose now that the response takes the form of reducing tax rates. Taxes fall so that only *90 cents* is collected, while *$1* continues to be spent. The tax-price per unit of public output is only 90 percent of its former levels. At any tax-price elasticity greater than zero, equilibrium in the "market" for the public good can be restored only by some increase in quantity beyond *one unit,* with the precise magnitude of the increase being dependent on the value of the elasticity coefficient. So long as individuals concentrate attention on the value of public goods, defined in the *numéraire*, there will be a clear bias toward expanding the size of the public sector in real terms, despite the presumed absence of any underlying shift in tastes.[14]

The results here require that individuals confront tax-prices that remain invariant over quantities of public goods financed. That is to say, marginal tax-price must equal average tax-price. Institutionally, this requirement is met with most of the familiar tax instruments: proportional and progressive income taxation, sales taxation, property taxation. Tax reductions are normally discussed, and implemented, through reductions in *rates* of tax applied to the defined base. So long as a deficit-facilitated tax cut takes this form, the terms-of-trade between public goods and private goods will seem to shift in favor of the former. The institutionally generated illusion, and the public-goods bias that results from it, can be dispelled if marginal tax-prices are somehow held constant while tax collections are reduced inframarginally. If a deficit-facilitated tax cut could take this latter form, there would be no substitution effect brought into play: individuals would continue to confront the same public-goods–private-goods trade-off, *at the margin*, before and after the fiscal-policy shift.[15]

Deficit finance in a Keynesian economic setting, while possibly altering the public-private mix in the economy because of the generation of false signals, is unlikely to encounter political obstructions. This is quite unlike a policy of surplus finance in the converse inflationary setting. On the contrary, the problem with deficit finance is that once the constitutional requirement of budget balance is removed, there are pressures for budget deficits, even in wholly inappropriate non-Keynesian economic settings. If we assume that the money supply is at all elastic in response, budget deficits must be inflationary in a non-Keynesian setting.[16] As with budget surpluses, the indirect effects of inflation will create losers. The information and incentive effects, however, will operate to soften the strength of these indirect effects. The direct effects, by contrast, will create only gainers, for public spending can be increased without taxation, or taxation can be reduced without reductions in public spending, or some combination of the two.

There are no obstacles to budget deficits, then, in a Keynesian economic setting. But when budget deficits are permitted in a democratic society, pressures for deficits in a non-Keynesian setting are created, pressures that would not exist in a Keynesian political setting. Therefore, the removal of a balanced budget principle or constitutional rule in a political democracy ultimately will generate an asymmetry in the conduct of budgetary policy. The deficits will be created, but to a greater extent than justified by the Keynesian principles; while surpluses may sometimes result, they will result less frequently than required by the Keynesian prescriptions.[17]

When the inappropriateness of the Keynesian political setting is acknowledged, it becomes apparent that the Keynesian paradigm does indeed alter the underlying fiscal constitution. The result has been a tendency toward budget deficits and, consequently, once the workings of democratic political institutions are taken into account, inflation. The Keynesian economic paradigm creates an inflationary bias in a democratic setting: governments respond more vigorously in correcting for unemployment than in correcting for inflation. The one-sided application of Keynesian policy remedies, which emerges from a democratic political setting, may itself create instability in the process. Inflation, it has increasingly been realized, does not generate employment. In fact, inflation attracts resources into employments where they cannot be maintained without further inflation.[18] The inflationary biases of the Keynesian paradigm, therefore, may well be able to convert a non-Keynesian economic environment into a Keynesian one. In this fashion, Keynesian prescriptions applied in a non-Keynesian setting can create a self-fulfilling prophecy. Yet Lord Keynes himself was strongly aware and quite fearful of the long-term destructive consequences of inflation. Keynes, as we have noted, did not envisage a democratic political setting. But Keynesianism changed the fiscal constitution, and did so in a proinflationary manner.

V. The Fiscal Constitution

The arguments of the two preceding sections were designed to demonstrate that the institutions through which fiscal choices are made can, in themselves, exert important influences on these choices, and, further, that the direction of effect can be predicted from a careful analysis of such institutions. If these arguments are accepted, the existence of political biases derivative from the application of Keynesian economic policy rules in democracy cannot readily be denied. This is because it could scarcely be claimed that the abandonment of budget balance represented no change in the basic institutions of fiscal choice. Indeed, the change in institutions was hailed as the instrumental step in the Keynesian policy package.

If our analysis is accepted, therefore, we should not be surprised at the post-1960 fiscal record. Once the last vestiges of the old-time fiscal religion were removed, what was there to constrain the spending proclivities of politicians, and, indirectly, those of voters themselves? And predictions about governmental growth and budgetary imbalance over future years are relatively easy to make, predictions that should disturb almost any observer, regardless of ideological position.

Two means of "improvement" might suggest themselves. We may acknowledge that the fiscal policy precepts derived from Keynesian economics are not applicable in representative democracy. From this, some might go on to suggest that basic choices on macroeconomic policy be taken from the decision-making power of ordinary politicians and placed in the hands of a small group of "experts," "economic technocrats," "planners," who would, presumably, be able to "fine tune" the national economy, in accordance with the true "public interest," and wholly free of political interference. This somewhat naive approach ignores the question concerning the proper incentives for the "experts," along with the demonstrated difficulties in forecasting. Furthermore, the historical record of the Federal Reserve Board, which perhaps comes closest to fitting such an institutional model, should give pause to anyone proposing reform in this direction. Nonetheless, despite such arguments, proposals for "national economic planning" surfaced again in 1975. This direction for change represents an attempt to reproduce for America the basic Keynesian presuppositions for fiscal choice.

There are, of course, strong normative objections to any such removal of decision-making power from the elected representatives of the citizens. If, for these or other reasons, the basic spending and taxing decisions are to be retained by the politicians, the economist who acknowledges the biases of the political process must reconsider his often too-ready acceptance of the Keynesian policy prescriptions. The fiscal policy that is "ideal" for the "ideal" world need not be best for the world of practical politics. This suggests that the economist who seeks to be of assistance must become a "political economist" in a very real sense. He must pay some attention to the political institutions through which any policy advice must be translated into policy actions.

Almost by necessity, the political economist who acknowledges that the biases discussed in this paper exist and are important, but who also works within the basic value precepts of representative democracy, is forced into a consideration of what may be called the "fiscal constitution," the set of constraints within which elected political representatives operate. In this perspective, the acceptance of the Keynesian paradigm, misplaced in its cognitive foundations, has led to the destruction of one important element of this constitution, an element that has not been replaced. And the spending and inflating proclivities that have been unleashed are capable of making the economy appear to conform to the Keynesian paradigm. The sophisticated replacements that have been discussed by economists, budget balance over the cycle, or budget balance at high employment, have not proved to be effective in constraining politicians. In 1976 it seems clear that explicit constitutional action is required to restore some constraint on the proclivities of politicians, and ultimately, of voters toward spending excesses.[19]

Appendix The Irrelevance of Institutional Forms:
Fiscal Choice in the Purely Ricardian World

"Institutions matter." In one sense, this is the central theme of our paper. And, if our arguments in support have been convincing, little more need be added. Nonetheless, a flank has been left unprotected, and we shall, in this appendix, examine critically the arguments that are advanced by modern-day Ricardians, who reject our central proposition, regardless of the political structure. If voters, and their political representatives, are able to see through the "fiscal illusions" that the abandonment of budget-balance creates, they should behave no differently than they would have behaved under the budget-balance constraint. There would in this case be no effects of Keynesian fiscal policy; budgetary manipulation would be of no avail. In this respect, we are with the Keynesians, not the Ricardians. The creation of budget deficits can influence aggregate spending in the economy. To this point we are Keynesian analysts. But it can also influence other decisions; it is this that our paper discusses.

David Ricardo advanced the proposition that tax finance and debt finance are basically equivalent.[20] The imposition of a tax directly reduces the net worth of the taxpayer, but the issue of an equivalent amount of government debt generates an equal reduction because of the capitalization of the future tax liabilities that are required to service and to amortize the debt. Suppose, for example, that the market rate of interest is 10 percent, and that a tax of $100 on a person is replaced by an identical share of public debt issue, with the debt obligation to be met with a payment of $110 in one year. This shift does not affect the taxpayer's net worth. This Ricardian "equivalence theorem," is little more than simple arithmetic in the choice setting of a single person, provided, of course, that the person in question has access to perfectly working capital markets, either as borrower or as lender. Such a person would remain wholly indifferent as to whether the government financed its outlay by tax or by debt since, by assumption, the present value of the fiscal liability, to him, is identical under the two alternatives, and, furthermore by assumption, he is assumed to have full knowledge of this equivalence.

To the extent that shifts among the forms of financing generate or might generate differences in the distribution of fiscal liabilities among persons and groups in the economy, the Ricardian theorem may not apply generally.[21] This difficulty can be forestalled by assuming implicitly that all persons are equal, at least in the relevant respects for this analysis. This allows us to stay within the choice setting for the single citizen.[22]

Under these restrictions, the equivalence theorem can be generalized beyond the straightforward tax-debt comparison. In its most inclusive variant, the theorem would assert that the particular way in which government extracts resources from citizens is irrelevant in influencing either private or public choice. Tax finance may be replaced by debt finance; either may be replaced by money creation; a personal income tax may be replaced by a corporation income tax, a sales tax, or a property tax. So long as the same governmental outlay is financed in each case, and so long as this outlay is shared among individuals in the same way (in this example, equally) there are no effects of institutions on outcomes.[23] The theorem rests on the fundamental presumption that each person has perfect knowledge about how changes in the means of financing government affect his individual net worth. And if the alternatives are presented so as to ensure that the arithmetic value of the fiscal charge is identical under all institutional forms, the precepts of rationality clearly dictate indifference as among these.

We shall criticize the extreme assumptions of this theorem momentarily. The point to be noted here is that, under these strict Ricardian assumptions, the particular form in which public outlays are financed will have no effects on individual behavior, either in the private or the public sector. Voters, and the politicians who represent them, would be fully aware of the real cost of public outlays which would remain invariant regardless of financing methods. Alleged Keynesian biases could not characterize the political choice process in this purely rational, Ricardian world, although the logical bases of the precepts which dictate changes in fiscal institutions are also absent.

At a common level of consideration, the assumptions about information required by the Ricardian model seem to be absurd. Even professional economists are often unable to agree on the consequences of changes in the institutional means of extracting resources from citizens. The continuing and unresolved dispute over the incidence of the corporation income tax is but one illustration. And this inability refers to disagreement over such broad functional categories as consumer prices, factor prices, rents, and profits. Disagreement would be intensified should efforts actually be made to present specific dollar magnitudes for individual citizens. The Ricardianlike proclivity to reduce analysis to mathematical comparison is itself highly deceptive because it conceals the assumption that the tax-payer-arithmetician possesses full knowledge of all the relevant data.[24] But these data often cannot even be estimated without first constructing some hypothesis or model for the working of the economy, and of the way in which a change in the means of financing government works its way through the economic process. In other words, in order to make inferences about his bill for government, the taxpayer must, to be fitted into the Ricardian model, be able to solve some model of the workings of the whole economic system, and be able to relate his personal position to that solution.[25]

It is the *perceptions* of individuals concerning the differential effects of fiscal institutions that are relevant to potential fiscal choice. Empirical evidence abounds to suggest that specialized professional economists are unable to agree on the consequences of many forms of financing budgets. It seems, therefore, reasonable to infer that ordinary citizens do *not* possess full knowledge as to how they may be personally affected by changes in fiscal instruments.[26]

The Ricardian framework is also one that abstracts from distributional differentials among citizens. A shift from, say, income taxation to money creation would affect different citizens differently unless such effects are explicitly ruled out by a world-of-equals assumption. Without some such assumption, the "price" of government would fall for some citizens and rise for others, changes which would, in turn, probably produce differences in the workings of the decision processes which generate budgetary outcomes.

Neither the arithmetical, and hence informational, simplicity nor the world-of-equals character of fiscal activities in the Ricardian model describes modern democratic societies. Different means of financing government convey different signals to different people, and, moreover, persons will vary in their ability to read such signals. Additionally, even if all persons possessed full knowledge, the shifts among financing instruments may not affect all persons equally. Consequently, changes in the institutional means through which government extracts resources, including the replacement of budget balance (which implies tax financing), can alter the resulting public budgetary outcomes.[27]

Notes

1. While this paper was written first, this theme about what might be called the political economy of Keynesian economics is elaborated and refined in our previously published book, James M. Buchanan and Richard E. Wagner, *Democracy in Deficit: The Political Legacy of Lord Keynes* (New York: Academic Press, 1977).

2. During the fourteen-year period, 1947–60, there were seven years of deficit and seven years of surplus. And the total budget was roughly balanced over this period, with the deficits summing to $31.2 billion and the surpluses amounting to $30.2 billion. This summary result becomes even more significant when it is recalled that the Korean War is included in the period covered.

3. Our treatment of the policy implications of "Keynesian economics" is not meant to disparage the strict "economics of Keynes." On this, see Axel Leijonhufvud, *On Keynesian Economics and the Economics of Keynes* (London: Oxford University Press, 1968).

4. "We have seen that he (Keynes) was strongly imbued with what I have called the presuppositions of Harvey Road. One of these presuppositions may perhaps be summarized in the idea that the government of Britain was and would continue to be in the hands of an intellectual aristocracy using the method of persuasion." R. F. Harrod, *The Life of John Maynard Keynes* (London: Macmillan, 1951), pp. 192–93.

5. See Karl Brunner, "Knowledge, Values, and the Choice of Economic Organization," *Kyklos,* 23 (Nov. 3, 1970), pp. 558–80, for an examination of the impact of paradigms (Brunner uses the term, "orientations") which provide the framework for interpreting experiences, upon particular elements of public policy. See W. H. Hutt, *A Rehabilitation of Say's Law* (Athens, Ohio: Ohio University Press, 1974), for an interpretative survey of Say's Equality.

6. For a specific discussion of these two economic cosmologies, see Axel Leijonhufvud, "Effective Demand Failures," *Swedish Journal of Economics*, 75 (March 1973), pp. 31–33.

7. A direct corollary to the view that aggregative shifts are not self-correcting is the notion, even if this is implicit, that such shifts cannot themselves be the results of distorting elements in market structure. Applied to employment, this suggests a tendency to attribute all shifts downward in observed rates of employment to fluctuations in aggregate demand. In such a policy setting, government intervention to correct for increased unemployment that is, in fact, caused by labor market dislocation and structural rigidities, acts to cement the latter into quasi-permanence and to make ultimate correction more difficult.

8. Harrod, *The Life of John Maynard Keynes*, op. cit, p. 193.

9. Anthony Downs, *An Economic Theory of Democracy* (New York: Harper & Row, 1957), pp. 51–74, suggested that the size of the budget in a democracy can be viewed as the outcome of a process in which politicians continue to expand the budget so long as the marginal vote gain from public expenditure exceeds the marginal vote loss from the taxation required to finance the expenditure.

10. For a thorough survey of the literature on the properties of political competition, see William H. Riker and Peter C. Ordeshook, *An Introduction to Positive Political Theory* (Englewood Cliffs, N.J.: Prentice-Hall, 1973).

11. This line of argument is explained in Buchanan and Wagner, *Democracy in Deficit*, pp. 125–44.

12. And even to the extent that citizens do possess such knowledge, democratic budgetary processes may be incapable of acting upon it. The extent to which such action will be forthcoming depends on the nature of budgetary institutions. To the extent that budgetary institutions permit fragmented appropriations, for instance, a prisoner's dilemma will tend to operate to dissipate revenues that might produce a budget surplus, even though citizens understand fully the benefits of surplus creation. Suppose, for instance, that a potential $10 billion budget surplus is prevented from arising through 10 separate spending proposals of $1 billion each, as opposed to a single expenditure proposal of $10 billion. In the first case, although each participant may recognize that he would be better off if none of the spending proposals carry, institutions that allow separate, fragmented budgetary consideration may operate to create a result that is mutually undesirable, akin to the familiar prisoner's dilemma. For an analysis of this, see James M. Buchanan and Gordon Tullock, *The Calculus of Consent* (Ann Arbor: University of Michigan Press, 1962), especially ch. 10.

13. We should note that the preceding discussion of budget surplus would be subject to the reverse relative price change from that discussed here.

14. The model summarized here is essentially equivalent to the one analyzed more fully in James M. Buchanan, "Fiscal Policy and Fiscal Preference," *Public Choice*, 3 (1967), pp.1–10, reprinted in *Theory of Public Choice*, ed. James M. Buchanan and Robert D. Tollison (Ann Arbor: University of Michigan Press, 1972), pp. 76–84.

15. It is difficult to construct permanent institutional arrangements that will meet the marginal tax-price criterion suggested here. Our colleague, T. N. Tideman, has reminded us, however, that, for temporary tax cuts, a pure rebate scheme does accomplish the purpose. Such action does not modify tax rates *ex ante*, and, hence, marginal tax-prices. A pure rebate scheme that is not anticipated offers an allocatively neutral scheme of injecting new currency into an economy during a temporary lapse into a pure Keynesian setting. If, however, the spending shortfall is expected to be permanent, and to require continuing injections, rebates will come to violate allocational neutrality for the familiar reasons.

As soon as persons come to anticipate the *ex post* rebates in making their budgetary decisions *ex ante,* they will act as if marginal tax-prices are reduced. To forestall the public sector spending bias in this permanent setting, some other institutional means of maintaining constancy in marginal tax-prices would have to be invented.

16. See Buchanan and Wagner, *Democracy in Deficit,* pp. 107–24, for an examination from a public-choice perspective of the relation between deficit financing and monetary changes.

17. Grade inflation in colleges and universities offers a useful analogy. An analogue to a balanced budget rule might require a professor to apportion a fixed number of points among his students. A university that desired a 2.5 grade-point average, for instance, would allocate 125 points to a professor who had fifty students. In this setting, a professor, in order to give more points to one student, would have to take away points from another student. With a variable number of points, however, a professor could run a surplus by giving out fewer than 125 points, or he could run a deficit by giving out more than 125 points. Before student evaluations, tight educational budgets, and related matters, the professor was in the position of the elite of Harvey Road. He was immune from political pressures in making choices that resulted in particular grade distributions. Political pressures have intensified in recent years. Budget surpluses (low grade-point averages) have little survival power, and budget deficits (high grade-point averages) are a natural outcome, so long as external constraints are not imposed, for a higher grade to any particular student is essentially costless to the professor, and generally yields benefits to him. Grade inflation and currency inflation, then, seem to have much in common.

18. See Friedrich A. Hayek, *Prices and Production,* 2nd ed. (London: Routledge and Kegan Paul, 1935), for an early though neglected explanation of this theme. It should perhaps be noted that Hayek developed his analysis in terms of an excessive attraction of resources into the production of capital goods. This resulted from monetary expansion, which drove the market rate of interest below the real rate. In these days of massive public spending, however, the story is more complex, for the objects of the increased public spending also generate an excessive attraction of resources.

19. Discussion of particular reforms is not appropriate in this paper. For a brief statement of some of the pertinent constitutional issues that emerge from our perspective, see James M. Buchanan and Richard E. Wagner, "Deficit Spending in Constitutional Perspective," in *Balancing the Budget,* U.S. Congress, Senate, Committee of the Judiciary, Subcommittee on Constitutional Amendments, 94th Congress, 1st Session 1975 (Washington: U.S. Government Printing Office, 1975), pp. 61–64.

20. David Ricardo, *The Principles of Political Economy and Taxation, Works and Correspondence,* vol. 1, ed. P. Sraffa (Cambridge: Cambridge University Press, 1951), pp. 244–49.

21. The prospect that real-world shifts among financing instruments and specifically between tax and debt finance would generate such distributional differences provided the basis for Griziotti's attack on the Ricardian theorem. See B. Griziotti, "La diversa pressione tributaria del prestito e dell' imposta," *Giornale degli economisti* (1917).

22. For a modern attempt to apply the Ricardian theorem, without reference to Ricardo, see Robert J. Barro, "Are Government Bonds Net Wealth?," *Journal of Political Economy,* 82 (November/December, 1974), pp. 1005–18. For a criticism of Barro's analysis, see James M. Buchanan, "Barro on the Ricardian

Equivalence Theorem," *Journal of Political Economy,* 84 (April, 1976), pp. 337–42.

23. This conclusion may seem contrary to the excess-burden analysis in incidence theory and theoretical welfare economics. The assumption that the individual is to be subjected to the same fiscal charge under each institution and that he has full information about this invariance serves to remove the excess-burden setting. The excess-burden of particular taxation arises only because the individual perceives that he can, by modifying his own behavior, affect the total fiscal charge imposed upon him. In this context, the excess-burden framework is inconsistent with the Ricardian.

24. The imposition of "perfect knowledge," while convenient for many economists, generates absurdity in the visions of social order that are implied by such models. On this, see Friedrich A. Hayek, "Economics and Knowledge," *Economica,* 4 (February, 1937), pp. 33–54; and "The Use of Knowledge in Society," *American Economic Review,* 35 (September, 1945), pp. 519–30, both of which are reprinted in his *Individualism and Economic Order* (Chicago: University of Chicago Press, 1948), pp. 33–56 and 77–91, respectively.

25. The same applies, of course, to almost any change in economic policy. This central point is emphasized by Rutledge Vining in his methodological critique of modern political economy. See, for instance, Rutledge Vining, "On the Problem of Recognizing and Diagnosing Faultiness in the Observed Performance of an Economic System," *Journal of Law and Economics,* 5 (October, 1962), pp. 165–84.

26. By saying that behavior depends on perceptions about underlying economic realities rather than on the objective realities themselves, we are implying that errors can be made, and that the probabilities of error may be related to the difficulties of matching perception with reality. In support of our position here, we may cite Frank H. Knight "If we ignore error and values, and stick to objective, physical 'facts,' we are no longer talking about 'economics' . . . Economic behavior is more than mechanical cause and effect. Its indubitable affection by error proves that, and otherwise it should not merit a distinctive name. And subsuming it under positive phenomena would merely deny a large and undeniable realm of reality of the human problem of living and acting." Frank H. Knight, "Introduction" to Carl Menger, *Principles of Economics,* trans. James Dingwall and Bert Hoselitz (Glencoe: The Free Press, 1950), p. 21.

27. For a conceptual and empirical examination of the ability of tax institutions to influence the perceived price of government, thereby modifying budgetary outcomes, see Richard E. Wagner, "Revenue Structure, Fiscal Illusion, and Budgetary Choice," *Public Choice,* 24 (Spring, 1976), pp. 45–61.

26.

Politics, Time, and the Laffer Curve

WITH DWIGHT R. LEE

I. Introduction

Why should a rationally motivated political-decision process generate an inverse relationship between tax rates and tax revenues? Regardless of the objective function of the politician or of the citizen who elects him, there would never seem a logical reason for increasing tax rates beyond maximum revenue limits. In this article, we explain how such a position can emerge and show why, once in such a position, political decision makers may find it difficult to extricate themselves.

To simplify the analysis, we ignore complexities involved in conceptualizing a single rate-revenue relationship in a system that includes many bases and many rates of tax. We assume there is one well-defined base for taxation and that there is a single uniform rate imposed on generation or use of this base.

We postulate that government seeks always to obtain additional tax revenues. This revenue-maximizing assumption, though useful, is not absolutely essential to our result.[1] Neither does this assumption imply that politicians, bureaucrats, or voters expect to secure private-personal gains from increased revenues. They may seek additional tax monies solely for the purpose of financing additional supplies of public goods and services or transfers. Politicians will not, however, maximize the present value of total tax collections in a calculus that incorporates any "reasonable" rate of discount. Governments, as such, have long lives, but political decision makers, as such, have relatively short lives. They possess attenuated rights in the income streams generated by their policies and therefore apply a higher-than-market discount rate to future tax revenues. In particular it is assumed that the political time horizon is shorter than the period of time necessary for complete private sector response to a tax-rate change.

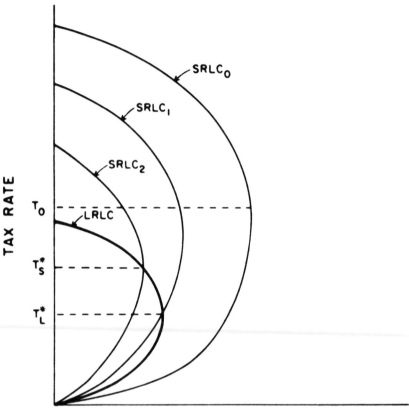

TAX REVENUE

Figure 26-1

II. The Simple Geometry

A simplified construction is depicted in Fig. 26-1. The abscissa measures
total tax revenues; the ordinate measures tax rate. The single heavily
drawn curve, *LRLC,* is the long-run rate-revenue relationship, with "long
run" being defined as the period sufficiently long to allow for full behavioral adjustment to each rate of tax on base. The government with a short
time horizon will not face the long-run Laffer curve, *LRLC.* It will,
instead, face a rate-revenue relationship determined by its own planning
horizon and to the tax rate to which behavioral adjustments have been
made. For simplicity, we assume that full adjustment to any rate change
takes two periods, with the political time horizon extending only over the
first period.

Assuming a zero-tax-rate starting position, the relevant short-run (one-period) rate-revenue relationship is shown as $SRLC_0$ in Fig. 26-1. Note that this is the only short-run Laffer curve that lies wholly outside the long-run curve, indicating that an increase in rates will always increase revenue more in the short run than in the long run. Since from any positive initial rate a rate reduction will always decrease revenues more in the short run than in the long run, the short-run Laffer curve relevant after full adjustment will only lie outside the *LRLC* for rates above the initial rate.

If, facing $SRLC_0$, politicians were completely unconstrained in their choice of tax rates, government would impose tax rate T_0, which would totally eliminate the tax base in the second period. Suppose, however, that political restraints allow a one-period rate increase of only T^*_L, the rate that maximizes revenues on the long-run Laffer curve. Upon full adjustment to this tax rate, government will face the short-run Laffer curve depicted by $SRLC_1$ and revenues can be increased in the short run by further rate increases. Under the assumption that governmental decision makers are interested only in the single period, it is evident that T^*_L is not the political equilibrium rate of tax. Government will move to increase the rate beyond T^*_L.

The political equilibrium rate of tax is shown at T^*_S in Fig. 26-1, where the revenue maximum on a short-run Laffer curve cuts the long-run Laffer curve.[2] Note that at this rate and only at this rate is government maximizing short-run revenue collections at a position consistent with stable rates through time. At equilibrium, those who determine rates have no incentive to change them and those who pay taxes have fully adjusted to the rates in being. The position is, of course, on the down-sloping part of the long-run Laffer curve, but it is also at the maximizing point on the relevant short-run curve. There is no political incentive for rates to be increased or decreased. A reduction in rates reduces revenues in the short run while increasing revenues only in the politically irrelevant long run. The construction allows us to explain the adversary positions in economic policy debates. Those who argue that government would never operate on the down slope of the Laffer curve, and who adduce evidence in support, are implicitly adopting a short-run perspective. Those who argue that rate reductions will stimulate supply-side responses sufficient to generate increases in revenues are implicitly adopting a long-term perspective.

III. Expectations and a Tax Constitution

In Section II, we assumed that taxpayers are passive responders to tax rates, in both the short and long runs. It will be useful to see how the introduction of expectations modifies the analysis. Suppose each taxpayer models government as a short-run revenue maximizer. He will predict convergence to the political equilibrium depicted and immediately adjust behavior as if T^*_s is the equilibrium tax rate. Rather than respond fully to tax rates other than T^*_s, taxpayers will see these rates as temporary and will respond in accordance with the short-run Laffer curve $SRLC_2$. At political equilibrium, both governmental decision makers and taxpayers, as a group, find themselves in a dilemma. Both would be better off if rates could be reduced and revenues increased. But escape from the dilemma may prove difficult. Taxpayers will not respond to a reduction in rates because they predict a return to the equilibrium rate, thereby making full response to any lower-than-equilibrium rate disadvantageous. Government cannot increase tax revenues by moving down the long-run Laffer curve unless it can convince taxpayers that the rate cuts are permanent. But taxpayers will not predict permanence in rates so long as they postulate short-run maximizing behavior by government. The dilemma is not, of course, unique to the rate-revenue relationship.[3]

Even if current politicians should take a longer time perspective, they would have difficulty convincing taxpayers to respond along the long-run Laffer curve. In effect, future policy makers are exerting control over current policy through the expectations created by their probable behavior. Expectations about the behavior of future policy makers create an environment in which rational current policy makers are compelled to behave in the same short-sighted way that their successors are expected to behave. In this expectational setting, there are "mutual gains from trade" to be exploited by governments and by citizens. These gains can be secured only if government can somehow bind itself through some sort of commitment to lower rates below political equilibrium levels (in the short-run model) and to hold these rates down. This establishes a logical analytical basis for the Reagan administration's insistence that multi-year rather than single-year rate reductions be introduced, although it would have seemed more efficient to introduce genuinely constitutional ceilings.

Notes

We are indebted to our colleagues Geoffrey Brennan, Robert Tollison, Nicolaus Tideman, and Gordon Tullock for helpful suggestions on an earlier draft.
1. The revenue-maximizing assumption is weakened in James M. Buchanan and Dwight R. Lee, "The Simple Analytics of the Laffer Curve" (working paper, Center for Study of Public Choice, Virginia Polytechnic Institute, September,

2. Space limits do not allow us to discuss convergence to the political equilibrium position or the stability properties of the position once attained. These aspects of the analysis are examined in Buchanan and Lee, ibid.

3. In many respects the dilemma is analogous to that between the monopolists of money issue and those who hold money balances. For an extended discussion, see Geoffrey Brennan and James M. Buchanan, *The Power to Tax: Analytical Foundations of a Fiscal Constitution* (Cambridge: Cambridge University Press, 1980). The rate-revenue dilemma also resembles the macro policy dilemma motivated by short-run Phillips curve considerations. See Finn E. Kydland and Edward C. Prescott, "Rules Rather than Discretion: The Inconsistency of Optimal Plans," *Journal of Political Economics*, 3 (June, 1977), pp. 473–91.

Economics was composed into type on a Compugraphic digital phototypesetter in ten point Times Roman with two points of spacing between the lines. Times Roman was also selected for display. The book was designed by Jim Billingsley, composed by Type III, Inc., printed offset by Thomson-Shore, Inc., and bound by John H. Dekker & Sons, Inc. The paper on which this book is printed bears acid-free characteristics for an effective life of at least three hundred years.

TEXAS A&M UNIVERSITY PRESS : COLLEGE STATION